# HUNTER'S DIGEST

## 2nd Edition

### Edited by Erwin A. Bauer

DBI Books, Inc. Northfield, Ill.

**HUNTER'S DIGEST STAFF**

*Erwin A. Bauer*
**Editor**

*Peggy Bauer*
**Executive Editor**

*Pamela J. Johnson*
**Production Manager**

*Sheldon L. Factor*
**Associate Publisher**

*Milton P. Klein*
**Publisher**

ISNB 0-695-81314-5                    Library of Congress Catalog Card Number 73-83467

# CONTENTS

# TOP SECRET

## FOR WHITETAIL HUNTERS

by

ERWIN A. BAUER

Photo made from long range of a deer. Does it see the photographer in a tree blind?

**BILL BAUER MIGHT HAVE** been better off staying in bed. At least that's what everyone told him. All of us, except Bill, had venison hanging on the meat pole outside camp. And nobody, except Bill, was getting up before daybreak for one last skinny chance to bag a deer.

The odds were stacked high against my old deer hunting buddy. Even in this northern portion of the state, the chances were less than 50-50 of bagging a deer, either doe or buck, in the whole season. Now only one day remained, and few critters on the face of the earth are as wild and wary as a Minnesota whitetail on the last day of the open season. Still Bill went merrily on his way into the woods before dawn, as he had done every day for the past week. Everyone else remained snoring back in the bed rolls.

What followed was a completely uneventful morning. Bill *would* have been better off in bed. Instead he headed straight for a balsam swamp about a mile from camp and then still-hunted slowly around its perimeter. Now and then he would sit somewhere to watch and listen, but that didn't pay off either. He didn't see any deer and all the tracks he encountered seemed at least a day old.

But it was a pleasant morning. For the first time in a week, the winter sun appeared and by noon it began to melt the soft blanket of snow which covered the ground. By noon the sun felt warm on Bill's back and thawed out his fingers, and that's when things started to break in his favor.

He had been slowly following a deer trail when something overhead happened to catch his eye. It was an old forgotten blind built by a hunter long ago to intercept any deer coming along the trail. Mostly out of curiosity — after finding the rungs on the tree trunk were still strong enough to hold his weight — Bill climbed into the blind and sat down on the wooden box he found there.

*This is a good place to eat my lunch,* he thought.

After that, Bill believes he dozed. He may even have been sound asleep because the next thing he remembered was that a fine whitetail buck was standing less than 100 feet from the blind. It was blissfully unaware that any danger existed nearby.

Bill had a hard time staying calm, and he fought to keep from making any sudden moves or noises. As he raised his .270, the box beneath him creaked and only then the deer looked up in his direction. But then it was too late, Bill put the cross hairs of his scope on the deer and squeezed just as it turned away—an easy shot. Toward the tag end of the afternoon, and just in time to make the last cocktail hour of the hunt, Bill came dragging his buck into camp. He was the happiest man in Minnesota and the deer's rack was easily big enough to win the $25 jackpot.

"I've found the secret for bagging whitetail deer," he beamed. "Just get on top of them."

Tree platform has easy access with ladder steps for climbing in the dark.

Bill had indeed discovered the secret for bagging a trophy whitetail. Probably it's the most certain, deadly, legal method to collect venison anywhere in whitetail country. There is nothing really new about the technique of getting on top—getting above the deer—but too few hunters take advantage of it.

Except possibly for black bears in the East, no big game animal is more elusive than the whitetail. That's doubly true of older males. The sportsman who bags a good buck anywhere in the heavily hunted Midwest or East has really earned it. No matter how skillful a woodsman any hunter may be, the average whitetail is better. Its sight, hearing and sense of smell are vastly more keen than any human being's. And a deer knows the woods in which it lives more intimately than the hunter knows his living room.

But most whitetails (and many other big game animals as well) have one great weakness. It's hard to explain, *but they seldom look up.* Watch a whitetail

Not exactly comfortable is this perch in an oak tree, but it's better than waiting on the ground.

Huge whitetail passes a photographer who sits unnoticed in a tree blind. The cameraman might also have been a hunter.

picking its way along any forest trail, and you will see what I mean. It's constantly alert for what exists all around. The buck tests the wind frequently, turns its ears like radar screens and is always looking ahead. Then, from the instant the first firearm cracks on opening day, a deer becomes *twice* as as alert — *twice* as nervous. But even during the bombardment of an open season, the typical deer seldom looks upward.

Hunting from an overhead blind gives a man a number of important advantages. First, it takes advantage of the deer's weakness. Second, it puts the hunter above the scene with a good view of the area. And finally, it gives him the opportunity to remain completely motionless; nothing betrays a hunter's presence to deer more than his movements.

It's a considerable advantage to be above the scene when hunting any woods, and the higher the better. To prove it, walk out into any timbered area with a friend, stand at the base of a tree and check how well you can see the friend as he walks in widening circles around you until he evaporates into the foliage. Next, climb the tree and have your friend repeat his walking in circles. You'll quickly find that the friend is more easily visible and remains visible from farther away. The same will be true of an approaching deer.

It's difficult to say when or where the first overhead blind was used to hunt deer. But that's of little consequence anyway. What's important is that any sort of overhead device, scaffold or structure might work — as long as it's located in an area which deer are known to frequent.

An old silo might be a good spot, and many a fine trophy has been bagged from the second story of an abandoned farm house. Several falls ago I had the pick of three fat bucks while watching from the window of a crumbling plantation home not far from Maryland's eastern shore. The once-beautiful building was partly overgrown with honeysuckle and was perfectly situated within shotgun range (only shotguns with rifled slugs were legal here) of converging deer trails. The wise deer hunter might look for situations like this wherever he hunts.

(Left and below) A comfortable, permanent tree blind with easy access. Note the hunter also has a thermos of coffee and a small heater for cold mornings.

However, most hunters will have to build their own blinds in trees. Since proper location comes before construction, let's consider that first.

In any given geographical area, whitetails frequent certain spots far more than others and often this behavior is unaccountable. What may seem to be good whitetail habitat, isn't — and vice versa. The only safe solution is to make a reconnaissance, perhaps by driving remote roads, fire trails or lumbering access roads until you determine which places usually contain the most deer. Of course, early and late in the day are the best times to do the driving because deer are most evident then.

It may also be wise to check with veteran hunters in the area, with farmers or even with rural mail carriers to learn about deer concentrations. Once you've found a good area, the next step is to select a specific site for the blind.

The best places to wait are within easy range of heavily used deer trails or crossings. This is doubly true if the trails connect important feeding areas with bedding areas, as beside the edge of a dense swamp or in the heavy vegetation along a river. How close you locate the blind to the trail will depend on how heavy the vegetation is and what type of gun will be used. In a heavily foliaged situation, the blind will have to be nearer to the trail than in more open or park-like woods. It's possible sometimes to clear brush or trees to increase your shooting range. Also, archers and shotgun hunters will want to place their blinds closer to trails than rifle hunters.

The strategically located tree blind is vastly more important to an archer than to any hunter with firearms. A bowman *must* get within close range of his target and no device or technique accomplishes this nearly so well as a good overhead blind.

One example of an extraordinarily successful blind was the one Frank Sanderson and I erected beside the meander of a murky river in eastern Ohio. It was located to take advantage of deer moving from the thick protective cover in the river bottomlands to higher hardwood ridges all around. During the second week of the archery season, Frank bagged a 6-point buck from that blind and later, during the firearms season, two other deer were bagged with shotguns by other hunters using the same stand. This is noteworthy because in

Ohio, only one in 20 gun hunters and less than one in 100 archers is successful in getting venison.

It is true that a few states (notably Wisconsin and Michigan) do not permit building overhead blinds to hunt deer, while a few others impose limitations. In Minnesota, for example, the blind may be no more than 6 feet above the ground. However most important whitetail deer states (such as New York, Maine, Pennsylvania, Texas, Maryland) have no restrictions, although in Pennsylvania it is unlawful to cut or deface trees on state-owned game lands. In any case, the conscientious hunter should be acquainted with local laws before he hunts.

A tree blind can be a simple T-bar or crossbar on which the hunter stands and waits — or it can be an elaborate and comfortable structure in which more than one hunter can play gin rummy to kill time. Perhaps the best deer blind comes somewhere in between.

How elaborate a blind is built may depend mostly on the patience and self-discipline of the hunter. If you can sit or stand for long hours in considerable discomfort, it's a waste of effort to build a large blind.

The ideal situation is to find two, three or four trees growing close enough together to nail floor rafters between them. Then simply nail floorboards or planking across these rafters. A seat can be provided in the same way—by installing another crosspiece between tree trunks—or by using an old wooden box or stool.

Although it really isn't necessary in most cases, you may want to enclose the blind either for camouflage or warmth, with tar paper, burlap or some sort of sheeting. That's well and good, but it always seemed to me that these appear so unnatural that they lose some effectiveness. And a loose strip of burlap flapping in the wind might surely alarm a nervous deer.

The blind should be built so that it doesn't creak or groan under a hunter's weight as he shifts position. Often a covering on the floor (maybe an old throw rug or several burlap bags) can help to muffle sound and even provide some insulation.

It is much more pleasant (and more productive, too) to wait in a blind in warm weather than in low temperatures. In the latter case, a hunter shivers, shifts position and generally is less motionless. However, it's possible to at least partially compensate for cold weather by making the blind more elaborate or by employing a number of curious gadgets to keep warm even on the most bitter days.

Frank Sanderson's brother Homer is one hunter who believes in all the comforts of home in the treetop deer blinds he builds every fall. Unless it is a very balmy day, he would never enter a blind without the following items: a small alcohol tent heater, handwarmers, a Thermos of hot beverage, a good lunch, fur-lined mittens, a rain suit, a folding camp chair or stool and binoculars. Although most deer hunters wouldn't want to lug all of this, they might find that some of the items are very helpful toward greater comfort while perched above the ground.

A hunter can be easily distracted from his main mission while watching from a blind. Once, while bow hunting from a scaffold high in a live oak on Georgia's Blackbeard Island, I watched in complete fascination while a flock of eight wild turkeys strolled and strutted directly beneath me. None ever realized a human was anywhere nearby. It was one of the most exciting, rare spectacles I've ever seen in a lifetime spent outdoors — so exciting, in fact, that I didn't notice the sleek spike buck which seemed to be trailing the turkeys. But drawing my bow spooked the whitetail and it instantly evaporated into the palmettos.

There is no better place than the overhead blind to observe the antics and reactions of deer. It is generally believed that the old buck is the wisest of all whitetails, but 2 years ago I had reason to wonder about it.

The place was Maryland, and it was a drizzly morning near the middle of the open season. After an hour or so of sitting in a tree blind which overlooked a forest glade, things began to happen. All at once and in single file, six whitetails approached the glade, led by a large doe. The last animal in the procession was a fairly good buck. As soon as I saw it, I raised my scope-sighted pump shotgun and figured to shoot as soon as it came closer and into the open.

Now almost without hesitation or delay, the doe bedded down on the edge of the glade and as if that were a command, all the others followed the example. But I was disappointed when the buck bedded in a spot in which it was almost completely hidden from me. I could see only the rack and rump, neither being a big enough target for a rifled slug.

I waited and watched until the suspense was killing, hoping the buck would move. Eventually I began to consider whistling, in hopes the buck would stand up briefly in the open. But the big doe seemed to be reading my mind. In one wild bound it was up and darting swiftly away. The others quickly followed, although in seeming confusion. I never did get a shot at that buck.

Fifteen or 20 minutes later I learned what had spooked the doe, but not the buck. A single hunter came still-hunting through the woods — and he was doing a good silent job of it. But because that big doe was alert, he never even knew there were any deer in the woods. He'd have been better off in a blind.

The following fall, I hunted in Maryland again. This time I went several days before the season to combine some striper fishing in Chesapeake Bay with scouting the deer cover beforehand. It surely paid off.

In this country it isn't unusual at all to see whitetails working the cornfields, browsing on the golden ears fumbled by the fingers of mechanical pickers. Luckily I found one cornfield which deer seemed to prefer bordered on three sides by damp forest and where I had permission to build a blind.

Good whitetail taken from a tree blind. The buck failed to look up to detect danger.

The blind was a pretty good one when you consider that the scrap lumber for it cost me only $1.25. I needed about 1½ hours to nail it together and that left me with a whole day to go fishing and forget about it. That also gave any deer in the vicinity an opportunity to forget about the noise I made while building it. On opening morning I was sitting comfortably in the blind long before day began to break.

As always at the opening, it seemed that daylight would never come. A pair of gray squirrels barked and quarreled directly above me in the crown of the tree and one came within about 10 feet to look me over. There were other sounds in the woods of woodpeckers and shuffling in the leaves. I figured, hopefully, that some of the shuffling must have been caused by deer.

Finally daylight did come and with it was a scene no deer hunter is likely to soon forget. Scattered across the cornfield below me — as singles, pairs and small herds — were 28 deer! Perhaps others were hidden by the mist which hovered over the neatly picked rows.

But my elation didn't last forever because this was a bucks-only season. And if there was a set of antlers in the cornfield, I couldn't spot them in the dim light.

For several moments I debated whether to climb down from the blind and look elsewhere — or to play the waiting game. I had located in deer country, surely enough, but it was *doe* deer country. Somewhere in the distance a shot rang out, followed by another. In another direction I heard a farm dog barking. Some of the does in the cornfield began to wander slowly back toward the woods all around them. Two came directly toward my blind.

"I'll wait it out here," I said to myself.

It was a lucky choice, but still I wasn't entirely prepared for what happened next. I made the mistake of concentrating on the does which soon were standing almost directly under the blind and didn't notice two bucks which had strolled out of the woods about 40 yards to my right. This also was the side on which I was most exposed and any sudden motions would send the bucks into the next township.

Afraid to even bat an eyeball, I noticed that one deer was a forkhorn and the other one was a pretty decent 8-pointer. By turning around only an inch at a time whenever both deer lowered their heads together to nibble on corn, I was finally facing the shooting direction. Next time they lowered their heads I would raise the gun.

It worked perfectly. I rested the 12-gauge pump on the stub of a broken limb, breathed deeply and pulled the trigger. At the shot the small buck bounded away when the larger one staggered and finally collapsed, hit in the shoulder from just above and behind.

In some 50 or more deer hunts spanning about half that many years, this was the shortest time I've ever needed to score on opening day — anywhere. Maybe I'm wrong but I think it's because I knew whitetail deer hunting's top, top secret.

# Challenge of the Rams

## by NAT FRANKLIN

A bighorn ram surveys the Montana landscape all around it.

ANY OUTDOORSMAN WHO knows game animals will agree that the wild sheep is among nature's most magnificent creatures. Few animals have a more majestic appearance in, and adaptation to, their natural habitat, and few are more difficult to approach. In fact, just to get near enough for a photograph or what a hunter would call a good shot is fiendishly difficult, often involving days of strenuous travel.

Even to think of these animals as sheep is somewhat misleading. The true wild sheep of the world have scant resemblance to domestic sheep. The latter are descended from a species native to southern Europe. The others dwell in alpine retreats atop awesome mountain ranges, and while they can be found on three continents—North Africa, Asia, and North America—few people ever get more than a binocular view of them in the wilds.

It is believed that they originated from the lofty plateaus and mountains of central Asia. One species named for Marco Polo lives on the plateaus of Pamir —the "roof of the world"—3 miles above sea level. Another species, the blue sheep, lives in Tibet.

The two species that exist on our continent are the Dall, or white sheep, and the bighorn. For the most part, these and several subspecies range in the most remote parts of the Rocky Mountains, from Canada to Mexico, and in our southwestern desert regions.

Like many wild animals, the wild sheep were not always so scarce or remote. Before the winning of the American West, wild sheep were abundant here and even roamed some lowland areas in considerable numbers. However, expanding civilization and diseases contracted from domestic livestock caused a decline, and forced the survivors to retreat to the highest and

A good Stone sheep bagged in the Cassiars of British Columbia.

loneliest mountain pastures. That is where they must be sought today.

To do so, photographers, hunters, and naturalists find that they must scale the most rugged terrain at inclines and altitudes that strain muscles and lungs to the breaking point. Often the trail will lead along thin icy ridges to reach an isolated slope where the wild sheep graze in seclusion. That's a lot to endure just to get close to a sheep.

Yet it is understandable for anyone who knows the qualities of wild sheep. Consider, for example, the most marvelous and biggest of North America's wild sheep—the Rocky Mountain bighorn.

Mature rams may exceed 300 pounds and are credited with fantastic vision. At the first glimpse of a human being miles away, they seem to evaporate into the vast rocky, snowy landscape. And they do it with ease because they are so well equipped to run and leap over the same terrain which discourages other big animals and challenges even the most expert climber.

The most dramatic time in the life of a bighorn ram occurs in late fall. All summer long the males have lived in bachelor bands, but suddenly the friendship is forgotten as they square off in rivalry for harems of ewes. This bighorn combat during the rut is a violent, yet inspiring, spectacle to watch.

After prancing and studying each other the rams back apart, sometimes as far as 35 to 40 feet. Suddenly, on stiff legs, they launch into a head-on charge at one another. The pile-driver, head-to-head impact can be

Pause during a backpacking expedition for Dall sheep into the Mackenzie Mountains.

Hunting the wild mountain sheep of the world takes a hunter high into the loneliest, loveliest places on earth.

heard as far as a mile away and is repeated over and over again. Even at a great distance the collision has the mighty ringing sound of a heavy hammer striking a great anvil.

Recently, slow-motion pictures were taken that reveal how the shock of the impact ripples through each ram's muscular body, how dust and splinters fly from

(Right) Hunter Frank Sayers packing out a Dall ram, one of the finest trophies in all outdoors.

(Below) Frank Sayers admires a Stone sheep shot, it seems, almost on top of the world.

the heavy horns. Blood drains from the noses and ears, and both contestants reel drunkenly from the furious pounding. It continues until only one is strong enough to walk away with the ewes, and until another challenger comes along. Then the duel is repeated. It is a clear case of survival of the fittest; no wonder such a splendid animal has evolved.

Occasionally, travelers in Alaska, the Canadian Rockies, and in the U.S. Rockies will come upon long-range views of Dall or bighorn sheep, but rarely is it more than a fleeting and distant glimpse. The sheep are wary of man and inclined to seek the natural protection of the most hard-to-reach areas.

As a consequence, the enthusiast who wants to get a really close look to photograph, or study, or hunt the sheep must mount an expedition. This usually means engaging a pack trip outfitter just to travel into sheep country to establish a base camp. This, in fact, is required for hunters, since few areas now allow hunting without a licensed guide.

Once in wild sheep territory, travel is most convenient by horseback and may involve riding for days until sheep are located. Then camp can be set up, the horses unloaded, and the journey continued on foot. This is the exciting and challenging part—the slow and cautious climb up steep cliffs and the traversing of unstable slopes.

The sheep cover this terrain with distressing ease, while their pursuers are likely to curse bitterly at their own lack of agility. As often as not, the rams evaporate from the scene as soon as man appears. But eventually, perseverance is rewarded.

Just being able to view and study the bighorn at close hand is well worth any effort.

Bird explodes suddenly right in front of the gunner near the end of hunting season in Idaho.

# How to Hunt Pheasant Late in the Season

## by BARNEY PETERS

**DURING THE PAST DECADE** or two wildlife biologists have ferreted out some surprising vital statistics on pheasants. More than half of the cocks killed by hunters are bagged on opening day. In some areas figures run as high as 80 percent of the total bag. Why? After opening day—sometimes after the first hour— roosters seem to vanish, to disappear into the landscape. Sportsmen figure the country is "hunted out" and turn to other activities. But the biologists know otherwise; their surveys and live-trapping programs after the season closes usually reveal plenty of male birds, perhaps more than is needed to carry through the winter and to assure good reproduction for the next year.

Pheasants are resourceful, adaptable birds. They've thrived on farmlands in the northern half of the country where other game birds haven't been able to make the grade. They've even prospered because the survivors

of D-Day quickly discard old habits and old haunts. The barnyard dandies of summer and early autumn become the cleverest of game birds simply by moving to places where any hunter knows there couldn't be any.

Here's an example. Farmers are busy plowing just about the time that ringneck seasons end across the land. The furrows they leave, and the unbroken clods of earth, provide perfect cover for hard-pressed cocks. But few hunters relish tramping across muddy, open fields and chances are they wouldn't find birds if they did. There's too much open ground to cover.

But how about the sportsman who scans with binoculars every plowed or crew-cut stubblefield he passes. He's in good position to find game quickly and without much effort. Once a cock is located it's a matter of encirclement, if there are several gunners, or of stalking if the hunter is alone. Generally, the birds hold tight in situations like that.

14

The tag end of the pheasant season is also the time for sowing winter wheat, a process that leaves vast areas of land bare and smooth. What little cover remains—and it's usually sparse—is in fence-rows and drainage ditches. Nowadays every inch is farmed that it's possible to farm. But the point is never to neglect those strips of cover, no matter how thin the vegetation seems. The cover may not be heavy enough to completely hide a rooster, but neither will it be heavy enough for him to run.

Running, incidentally, is a trait that sportsmen must consider no matter when or where they're after pheasants. And it may be more of a problem in the future; some biologists suspect that a curious change is taking place. Each season the birds that flush are those that most often wind up in hunting coats and home freezers. The running birds escape more easily. For this reason some biologists feel a selective strain may be unintentionally developing from birds with the greatest tendency to run.

Kick into brushpiles and rolls of old wire. Watch carefully, when woodlot hunting, for droppings on the ground. If there's plenty of sign, stay right in that woods until you've had some shooting. Otherwise, try elsewhere.

Swamp and marsh hunting is rugged business. But do it properly and you'll have more than a good workout. Plow right into the heaviest cover—but go slowly. Take four or five steps and pause for several seconds. Push through the heaviest grass right to the water's edge for thick bent-over cattails make perfect, warm cover. It will be as difficult for pheasants to run here as it is for you to walk, so take plenty of time—pause frequently. A ringneck will hold fast as long as you seem to be moving past, but stop and he may figure he's been discovered. The pressure is on and there's nothing to do but fly. Then let him have it.

Never pass up a chance to hunt along streams or rivers. Poke into the heaviest brush, into piles of driftwood and undercut banks where they'll often crouch and hide like cottontails. If it's possible, wade out to any islands in the river and tramp through them from one end to the other. Few spots are more perfect sanctuaries for shell-shocked cocks.

Often there's dense cover around farm ponds, potholes and watering tanks. These are hot spots—so always investigate them thoroughly.

After freeze-up, keep hunting around swamps and marshes. Pheasant spend more and more time in such places as the mercury falls. Check on all the clumps of grass and rushes out on the ice. Investigate all the muskrat cabins too. They're natural resting spots for

Eager spaniel is hot on scent of ringneck and hunter is ready for a shot on cold, snowy day.

Pheasants may seem slow on the flush, but once underway they're very fast flyers.

(Left) Idaho pheasant is down and Labrador waits for command from sportsman Lew Martindale.

(Below) Snow flurries fall as pheasant which tried running toward a woodlot is bagged.

Late season pheasant is down and spaniel makes perfect retrieve. Hunter is Dave Duffey, dog editor of *Outdoor Life*.

birds that have been through the mill and perhaps peppered by shot.

If snow falls before the pheasant season ends, make the most of the deadly and fascinating method it provides to collect a limit of cocks. Try trailing. In typical pheasant range, it thaws a little every afternoon and then freezes again at dusk. This makes it possible to pick out fresh tracks at the beginning of a morning hunt. Then it's a matter of following the track, sometimes a mighty long way, until something develops. Eventually the bird runs out of protective cover, squats and flushes when you get too near. There will be disappointments, of course, but few dull moments.

Two hunters, or maybe three, can work at trailing game a little better than a single man. While one pushes along the track, the others make wide swings ahead and around, trying to intercept the birds. It's a fine way to add game to the Christmas or Thanksgiving menu.

The later in the season, perhaps, the more valuable is a good dog. When they're in cornfields and stubble, suitable for running, pheasants often outwit the finest dogs. But it's a different proposition when the cover is thick enough to prevent running or thin enough to make it hazardous. A good, steady pointing dog will eliminate some of the necessity to wade through heavy growth.

He'll be able to cover more countryside, too.

Beagles have become more popular in recent years. The little dogs become extremely valuable where the cocks can run because a hunter can swing around ahead of them to make an interception.

Conscientious sportsmen have often hesitated to shoot pheasants late in the season because they felt too few remained. But that's rarely the case. Some biologists feel we may have been killing our pheasants with kindness by not killing enough cocks. It sounds unreasonable, but it's probably true.

The hens are the important birds as far as good fall hunting is concerned. Shoot one and you've eliminated a large potential for next season. But it's a different matter with cocks. Ringnecks are polygamous and only a few males are needed; in hatcheries and on pheasant farms, only one cock per 10 or 12 hens is retained each winter. And in the wild, extra cocks only compete with valuable hens for what little cover and food exists through the cold and hungry months. Better they should end up roasted.

Pheasant hunting after opening day amounts to this: Look for them in the strangest, most difficult places you can find. Take your time, move slowly and look carefully.

17

## by ADAM WASHINGTON

**BILL RAMP AND I** labored along a rocky spine to a point where we could cover the upper slope of Scapegoat Mountain. The atmosphere at 8,000 feet was rare, so we paused until our breathing was back to normal. Then, from an inner pocket, Bill dug a length of hollow bamboo that resembled a flute and blew a long, shrill blast. "Whoo—eeee-whoo." There was a pause, then a quick "Who—who." For several seconds, the alpine wilderness around us was completely silent. Then clear and sharp, from far below, came an answer. It was a bull elk bugling back a challenge. In all of outdoor America, there's no sound quite like it. The short hairs on the back of my neck bristled and my heart pumped faster.

For 15 minutes, perhaps more, that part of Montana's Bob Marshall Wilderness was still again. It was an uneasy wait. Finally Bill blew on the reed again, and the bull answered. He was mad, and he was coming our way.

For me, the next ½-hour was the longest in history. We scanned the slope below us with binoculars, but if there was an elk anywhere in that broken timber, we couldn't spot him. Twice I checked to see if my .270 was loaded and ready. Otherwise it was completely quiet—until Bill bugled once again. This time there was no interval; the bull answered right back. He not only bugled, but he snorted and whistled. And he was close, almost on top of us it seemed. Five or 10 more minutes passed before we caught sight of him. It was only a glimpse of a gleaming antler tip, but it was less than 100 yards away. Suddenly, the animal stepped into the open, raised his great head and looked in our direction. Then he simply evaporated.

Bill tried calling again, but it was no good. The elk was spooked and had left the country. I began to understand why elk hunting is one of the most unpredictable, rugged and fascinating sports on earth. It had been a

(Right) Grazing in a mountain meadow, this male wapiti looks up suspiciously at first hint of danger. So hunters tread softly.

(Opposite) Among the most exciting spectacles in the outdoors is a duel on a snowy meadow between two large, bull elk.

typical elk hunting experience.

The elk, or wapiti, is considered by many hunters to be America's best game animal. An adult bull is not only tough to kill, but he is one of the most elusive of all game animals, and therefore one of the most challenging trophies. A handsome beast, he sprouts one of the largest and most elegant racks of all hooved animals. And with the possible exception of a ruffed grouse or a canvasback, there is no finer wild meat available in the country. Also, elk are still common enough to be available to hunters in the middle-income bracket. Hunting them is not such an expensive proposition as hunting grizzlies, bighorn sheep or mountain goats.

The elk is part of an interesting chapter in American history. Like buffaloes, they once were plains animals, and their range extended over most of central and northern United States and eastward as far as Pennsylvania. The westward expansion of civilization drove them into the wilderness and mountainous areas where they are concentrated today. During the westward movement, elk meat was much preferred to bison meat. In the early 1800s it sold for 10¢ a pound, an exorbitant price in those days.

Later in the century, when it was discovered that elk tusks contained the only true ivory available in America, the elk received a setback from which it almost did not recover. It is not clear how the fad began, but every male citizen wanted a set of "elk teeth" to be used as a watch fob, a ring setting or a tie pin. When the elk became the symbol of a fraternal organization, the traffic in tusks reached unusual proportions. As recently as half a century ago, a matched pair of tusks brought from $25 to $50. The slaughter of the animals

# HUNTING

was tremendous. Some westerners even gave up ranching to hunt them. The more humane hunters would rope the elk when the winter snows were deep, extract their teeth and turn them loose again. Others simply shot them, removed the tusks and left the carcass to rot. It required legislation forbidding the sale of elk teeth to stop the practice. The law didn't come too soon, for extinction was in the balance.

Nowadays, with intelligent supervision and rigid game laws, elk are doing very well. The elk hunters haven't had it so good for several generations, either, because in certain sections of the West, elk are actually too numerous for their own good. In recent years, there have been instances of mass starvation in winter because there wasn't sufficient food to go around.

The American elk is a member of the worldwide deer family. It is the second largest (the moose is largest) of the species in North America. It was named "elk" by the early settlers because it resembled the elk (the red deer) they knew in Europe. Actually, it more closely resembles an Asiatic wapiti, and it probably should be called the American wapiti.

The elk is a handsome, dark brown deer with a short tail and a well-developed rump patch that is lighter in color than the rest of the body. A full-grown bull may exceed 1,000 pounds; the record shows one healthy bull actually weighed in at 1,032 pounds. However, this is unusual. A typical bull will probably average 700 pounds and a large adult cow might reach 600. Even skinned and quartered, it's no small undertaking to pack an animal of this size out of a remote wilderness region.

Ordinarily, only male elk have antlers. A bull may enter his second autumn (1½ years old) with spike antlers; his third with 4 or 5 points on each side. Thereafter, a bull will probably sport 6-point antlers—and a 6-pointer is known as a royal.

A typical antler is a long, round beam sweeping up and backward. On a mature, healthy bull, the rack can reach massive proportions. The record length for an elk's beam is 64¾ inches; that's more than 5 feet! More than 20 trophies have been measured at better than 60 inches. The record spread distance between antlers came from a bull bagged in Wyoming's Teton Mountains. It measured 74 inches—in other words, the rack was more than 6 feet wide. And these are grown in a single season.

Wapiti are astonishingly quick and agile. Even bulls

# THE MIGHTY WAPITI

(Below and right) Hunting the wapiti takes the sportman high into some of the most scenic and remote corners of the Rockies.

Massive head of antlers make this bull an outstanding trophy.

with tremendous racks can move through heavy timber with incredible speed. In the open, they have been clocked at 30mph, although many a sportsman will swear they move much faster. They can clear average stock fences with ease, and one incident was reported of a bull escaping a 7-foot 6-inch enclosure with little more than a standing start. Even young elk are capable swimmers. Once when a herd of fawns was stocked on an island off the Alaska coast, several of them swam more than a mile to another island.

Wapitis are polygamous. When autumn rolls around, the males begin to feel their oats, and the entire season is spent in collecting a harem and beating off the competition. Although elks will bugle occasionally throughout the year, they do so more in the fall—as a symbol of the rut and possibly as a challenge. It's often their downfall. Many a bull has succumbed to a bamboo or garden hose call made in a home workshop.

An average bull elk is a belligerent customer during the rut. To keep his harem intact, he'll tackle any other male elk who happens by. Seldom observed by men, these battles are brutal, savage spectacles. Homer Sayers and I once watched a pair of them, a royal and a 5-pointer, duel in a meadow along the Madison River in Montana.

These bulls entered the grassy area from opposite sides, and at first each seemed actually unaware of the other. They moved closer together, stopping to graze, and then one of them whistled. It was a soft, high whistle, and evidently it was a challenge, for they lunged together head to head. The rattle of antlers echoed through the forest. This jousting lasted for several minutes, then they backed off and pawed the ground. Finally, one whistled and they began again.

The sporadic dueling continued for about 45 minutes, at a faster and faster pace. In the beginning it hadn't appeared very serious, but the tempo increased until at the end it was a violent affair. They stomped, backed off to tear at the turf, both with hooves and antlers, and lunged forward again. The object seemed to be to drive the antlers into a flank of the opponent, but only once did we see it accomplished. The smaller elk sustained a terrible thrust in the ribs, and it wasn't very long before he lit out for the hills. The winner went back to his grazing.

At all hunting camps you will hear stories of encounters between bulls and hunters. An elk is potentially a formidable and deadly animal, and no doubt some brushes have occurred, but not nearly so often or with such disastrous results as newcomers to the sport are led to believe. Really "hot" bulls, in the peak of the rut, will charge right up to a caller if he is well concealed and the wind does not betray him. They have even surprised hunters by circling and dashing in from behind. But even the most ornery bull will retreat when he finds a human instead of a rival.

A wounded elk is a far more dangerous critter than a "hot" one. Several seasons ago a sportsman dropped a big bull on a steep, shale slope in British Columbia. He walked up close, laid his rifle aside, rolled up his sleeves and prepared to field dress the elk. Instantly, the beast was on its feet and on top of the hunter. Together they rolled down the hill in a flailing mass. Somehow the hunter broke free and escaped. Although he's alive today, he's in no shape ever to hunt anything again.

Another sportsman, in Wyoming's Thorofare Country, hung his rifle on the rack of a fine wapiti he had just shot, preparatory to having his guide photograph the scene. While they were loading the film, the bull jumped up and headed for the heavy timber in high gear, the 30-06 still hanging on his head. The hunter never saw rifle or elk again.

Still another hunter dropped an elk cleanly with a single shot. He walked up, cut the throat to bleed out the animal and proceeded to look for his bullet hole. But there wasn't a mark anywhere on it. A cold sweat came over him when he found the slug had only bounced off the base of one antler, stunning the bull temporarily. It was fortunate that it stayed stunned long enough for the throat-cutting.

Although small bands of elk have been reestablished in Michigan and New Hampshire, the place to hunt them is in the Rockies; in Montana, Idaho, Wyoming, Colorado, British Columbia, Washington, Oregon, and Alberta. Elk hunting is not a sport to be tackled alone, at least for the first time. With a few exceptions, elk live far from beaten tracks and paved highways, so it's no minor task to get in after them. It's even more of a problem to bring one out if you're lucky enough to bag him.

There are many qualified guides and outfitters in all of the western states. With most of them, hunting is a business, and for just a little more than it costs a sportsman to hunt on his own, he can retain an outfitter or packer. Parties of from four to six hunters can enjoy a 10-day hunt, all expenses complete, with a typical Montana packer for around $750 to $1,000 each. The trip might include an opportunity for bears, deer and goats as well.

Here's what a packer furnishes: reliable saddle and pack horses, a guide for each two hunters, a base camp which includes sleeping and cook tents plus all the food cooked by a camp chef. The packer's personnel will take care of wrangling horses, dressing and transporting game out of the backcountry. In other words, it's a complete package deal. A hunter furnishes only his own firearms, ammunition, sleeping bag, camera and personal toilet articles. The odds are excellent that he will get shots at elk, and better than 50-50 that he will return with a trophy.

Most of the packers and guides are expert callers, and to watch them operate is almost worth the trip alone. Late in the season it may be necessary to "still hunt," which means, roughly to travel slowly and carefully through good elk range, keeping an eye peeled for game. Elk are somewhat migratory moving from high country to low in the fall as snows cover up potential browse. Guides are aware of these movements, and they take a hunter at the right altitude at the right time. Alone, a novice can spend an entire hunting trip without ever seeing an elk.

Familiarity with the habits and specific haunts of elk in a particular area has probably accounted for more kills than any other single skill. It's a knowledge that a good guide shares with every one of his customers. One outfitter I know carefully evaluates all of his hunters.

Those who appear to be in the best physical shape or who appear to be good woodsmen are taken still-hunting. The older fellows are placed on advantageous ridges.

There are almost as many opinions on the proper elk rifle as there are elk hunters. Perhaps more of them use the proven and reliable 30-06 than anything else. It delivers a powerful wallop, if a vital spot is hit. So does the .270 which has recently become much more popular along the elk trails. But the truth is that many veterans consider these calibers too light. There's no denying that a bull elk takes a lot of killing; and simply to wound one can lead to a nightmare of trailing through the most dense cover in the West. Elk are so tenacious that a large percentage of wounded animals escape, only to die much later on.

One of the newer calibers well adapted for elk is the .348 Winchester. The Model 70 is light enough to carry without abnormal fatigue, and the slug delivers enough punch to handle the toughest elk. It should have a low power scope attached—say a 3x or 4x. Other good calibers for elk are the .300 and .375 Magnums. These also should be equipped with scopes.

The elk hunter doesn't live who doesn't get "bull fever." It's like malaria—recurring. It attacks you every time an elk strolls within range of your rifle. It hit me several days after the old bull had given Bill Ramp and me the slip on Scapegoat Mountain, when we were in the same vicinity again. Pete Salyers had bagged a fine male the day before, and we were laboring slowly up a murderous slope to dress and retrieve the animal. Bill had a string of pack mules in tow. We had pushed off at dawn, and by mid-morning had reached a bench high up on the mountain. There we stopped to rest. A light snow had been falling, but now it fell more heavily, in large wet flakes. Visibility was cut to almost nothing. While Bill tied the mules temporarily, I made a quick swing around the bench. I knew there was an elk wallow—a small reservoir of water—thereabouts, and I wanted to see if any elk had been active around it.

The snow was rapidly obliterating the scene, but there was evidence that at least four animals had been there recently. The area all around was plowed deep with hoofprints. A heavy crust of ice that had frozen on the wallow was broken. Piles of dung on the ground were still steaming, so I knew the elk had left only minutes before. I also noticed that one set of hoofprints was much larger than the rest; it had been a bull with a harem.

I made a short circle around the scene to pick up the trail, when the old bull bugled. "Whoo—oo-ee-oo . . . who—who." It sounded like he was right on top of me. I had a cold chill. I backed against a twisted pine and froze there. Then I heard Bill answer from behind me. I knew he was hardly 100 yards away, but sounded much farther off than the elk. The butterflies were busy in my stomach. My .270 felt as light as a water pistol, and my

A large bull elk is here being hoisted into an aspen to be skinned, cooled and later butchered.

hands were shaking. Suddenly I had bull fever—without even seeing a bull. Then the elk answered back. It wasn't a bugle this time, but a series of grunts and short, sharp barks. The animal was within slingshot range, but still I couldn't see him, no matter how hard I strained to detect a movement through the screen of snow. Bill bugled again—quickly and softly—and I heard a sound on my left. There, like a ghost in the snow, stood my bull.

I couldn't see the brute distinctly, but it didn't matter. My heart was pounding too hard to raise the rifle anyway. The elk lowered and raised his head, made a wheezing sound and walked slowly in Bill's direction. If he went past me, it wouldn't be safe to shoot. It had to be now. I raised the .270, and the elk stopped broadside. For a moment the bull fever left me. My rifle came up easily, and I was fairly steady when I held the cross hairs on his front shoulder. I squeezed the trigger. The elk seemed to shudder, and then he vanished into the blizzard. It was then that the reaction set in. I was shaking when Bill came running up.

"Did you get him?" he panted.

"I don't see how I could have missed," I said. "But he's gone."

Together we followed his tracks through the snow. Fifty yards away, we found the elk—his rack rammed head-on into a tree and dead as a doornail. There was only one thing left for me to do. I leaned back against another tree and let the bull fever run its course.

I can't wait until I get it again.

# TAKING QUAIL FROM AGRICULTURAL LANDS

by JAMES TALLON

**BY NATURE,** the Gambel's quail is a desert bird, often referred to as the "desert quail." The Arizona Game and Fish Department prints a quail map, and according to it, this 6 ounces of feathered dynamite occupies almost half the southern part of the state, one-third of the western part and a couple of isolated sections—one between Winslow and Holbrook and the other near the New Mexico border at Chambers and Lupton. The bird also calls home large chunks of New Mexico, Utah, California and Mexico; and maybe a few leg it through the southwestern part of Colorado. Some of this quail

The runningest quail of all — the Gambel's of Arizona.

Field of milo hides both doves and quail.

23

A Gambel's quail is great on anyone's table.

land is high desert country, and experts have come to recognize that this species prefers elevations no higher than 5,000 feet above sea level. Through experience, I have found that populations are higher at elevations substantially lower.

Living in Phoenix puts a great deal of excellent Gambel's quail habitat within easy driving range. That metropolis, itself, has been nicknamed "The Queen City of the Desert." The countryside is desert personified, with resplendent stands of saguaro, prickly pear and cholla cactus. This kind of vegetation usually runs hand-in-toe with the landscapes Gambel's quail delight in. Try Black Canyon to the north, the Superstitions to the east, Oracle Junction to the south, the Maricopa Mountains to the west, and you'll often find this bird who prefers footwork to wingwork. All this is desert land, maybe some of it virgin. But the land that has produced some of the best Gambel's quail hunting for me has been manipulated by man—land put to the plow.

I learned about the high use of agricultural acreage by Gambel's quail about a decade ago. By accident. On a blistering hot afternoon in early September, Gene

Mason and I had driven to some farmlands west of Phoenix. Our intentions were to puff a few doves. We found a major irrigation canal, abandoned and overgrown with vegetation. On the north side was a paved farm road, on the south, a grainfield where harvesting machinery was at work. The shrubbery on the shoulders of the canal rose above head-high. It effectively screened us from the sharp eyes of southbound doves anxious to get to fresh, easy picking's the harvester lost. It was perfect for pass-shooting.

Just seconds after we'd taken our stand, a flight of maybe 10 mourners came in, and Gene and I folded a pair. We were not prepared for what came next: At least 2 dozen pairs of wings roared as a fine covey of Gambel's quail beat its way into the skies. The quail had been squatting in the thorn jungle just a few yards away. The birds knew we were there and no doubt thought themselves safe. But the booms of our shotguns shattered their control mechanisms. We watched open-mouthed as the covey went out over the field a few yards, banked to the right and about 100 feet away, settled back into the choked irrigation ditch.

From the birds' viewpoint, it must have seemed an ideal place to set up housekeeping. Later we would learn there was a foot of water in the canal, hidden from us then, so that gave them their moisture needs. Food was within easy—very easy—walking distance and their refuge was more secure than an apartment in a modern metropolis—if they didn't leave it. From a hunter's viewpoint, it was even better. The birds had fallen into this glorious trap, and they could be encouraged to leave it, momentarily. "Why don't we come back in October to see if the raw ingredients for a good Gambel's hunt are still here?" I suggested to Gene.

He bought the idea and a month later we were back on the south bank of the canal with shotguns at the ready. Little had changed. Some of the plants had gone to seed, and their skeletons were armed with spines that seemed even sharper than they had earlier. The first quail we saw were running across open ground in the fallow field toward the canal. Their legs were blurred almost into invisibility. They dived into the thicket. Gene, who has no compunctions about ground-sluicing quail—it's legal in Arizona—says he's after gourmet food and considers a Gambel's airborne and fair game when it gets one foot off the ground. So, when a foursome of birds popped out of the canal and motored before us, Gene touched off a 16-gauge from his pump. The shot raised a cloud of dust behind the birds and set off an explosion of wings—a la our dove hunt—on the right.

The covey broke into two, with a dozen or so birds angling to the left toward the field and the rest heading hell-bent across the paved road to the sparse desert beyond. Despite our surprise, we picked off a cock and a fat hen. It took some lightning thought, which I am not too often capable of. We could not shoot at the right half of the covey because it is against the law in Arizona to trip off lead across a maintained road. That in mind, we automatically swung to the left bunch. Now—to shoot too soon meant the target might fall back into the canal. If it were a clean kill, you might be able to recover it if you wore a suit of armor and had a machete to hack with. If you crippled the bird, you might as well chalk it up as a waste of game meat. Even when over the field, the odds were high for losing a nicked bird. It would, most certainly, swing back for the cover. Thus, a hunter here had no alternative, for good sportsmanship, but to be more exacting, more sure to kill the bird on the wing.

Because of the aforementioned restrictions, the number of practical shots were reduced. I'm guessing now, but I believe we got about seven or eight birds each from the couple of hundred we put up. It was exciting hunting—a real challenge. I loved it and continued to hunt there regularly. Over the years the population seemed to stay about the same, and suffered nil, I suspect, from our hunting forays. Recently I was astounded and shocked to see the canal bulldozed clean of vegetation. The canal was about to be reactivated. The quail were gone. I stood on a bare earth bank as the sun came over the rim of the morning sky, alone, stacked barrels open, feeling limp. Never before have I seen a more graphic example of habitat destruction and what it does to wildlife. But man, in a sense, had created this one and apparently man could taketh away.

We were not, however, dependent upon the abandoned irrigation canal for game.

It is a well-known fact that poor ground cover in even the finest Gambel's quail region means fewer birds. Steve Gallizioli, research chief for the Arizona Game and Fish Department, and an avid quail hunter, once said, "If you can see quail running 75 yards in front, you're not in good cover." In some of Arizona's quaillands, livestock can be blamed for snipping away the vegetation—over-grazing, really—and the subsequent absence of birds. In other places, the land may be naturally barren.

Dense cover, in contrast, can provide top action. How much hunting pressure the birds have been subjected to, of course, determines how close you can get to them. Frequently, though, the coveys go up within easy shooting distances, and you can then walk up the singles, which will hang onto the ground longer.

On some trout streams, particularly the Colorado River in Glen Canyon, I've had the best success when the water was very low. This, I feel, confines the fish to smaller areas and being easier to find are easier to catch. Largely, the same theory can be applied to hunting agricultural lands for quail. A small amount of good cover here, especially in the hotter climes where birds are likely to need shady resting areas, may offer better hunting than large patches of cover in the desert.

All cover, no matter how little, near fields should be investigated. Once, while hunting desert cottontails, I came to the edge of a cultivated area where three fences met. You could have covered the brush growing there with a washtub. I kicked a post and a trio of Gambel's quail—a species of bird quite reluctant to hold—

Gambel's quail racing ahead of hunters near farmland in the Southwest.

Quail-man after Gambel's in farmland. It's exciting walk-up hunting.

erupted from it. On other occasions I have crossed fences interwoven with relatively sparse growth and surrounded with open fields, and had the squeak of a wire telegraph quail half-a-city block away into flight.

For certain, I always scour the fencerows. For this, two shotgunners are better than one. I remember the time when I stood on a low rise and watched a lone hunter working a vegetated fencerow. Quail were running out of the far side and cutting back into the cover again. The hunter was completely unaware of what was going on. Remembering this, my hunting buddies and I get on opposite sides of a fencerow and usually walk swiftly and noisily to put the birds up. Sometimes it is like being in a shooting gallery.

I have had little luck with Gambel's quail holding for a dog. Some of this has appeared in print and I have been criticized for handing out false information. Some hunters swear their dogs will fasten down a Gambel's better than a staple gun. Numerous times I've seen my Brittany spaniel, "Britt," slam on point and a split instant later a bird, or birds, run or flush. Britt is a helluva fine retriever, but not the greatest of pointers. Right now I cannot put the blame on him because I have yet to see *any* gun dog *truly* hold a Gambel's quail. But I enthusiastically hope it is being done—and regularly.

Regardless, I try never to hunt without Britt. Before the irrigation canal was stripped, we hit that hotspot for a few years. He was baffled and frustrated because he couldn't penetrate the laced, birdy interior of the canal; and the hunt being a mutual experience, we looked for cover where we could.

Some of the best Gambel's hunting I have ever run across was at an island of shrubs and brush on a shallow arroyo that lay between two recently harvested grainfields. It was shaped like a sandspit in a river, no more than 10 feet wide and perhaps 150 feet long. The cover was mesquite and catclaw with lower forms of bushes and grasses, sufficient to make quail happy, yet easily worked by a dog. Britt and I sat on the sloping shoulder of a farm road and studied the area for a few minutes. "Old pard," I said, "we'll start at the lower end and make a swing completely around it." Britt grinned like he understood. But before we could get our plan into action, a bay horse with a deliberate pace strode toward our target. The horse waded into it. Limbs and branches popped and cracked. It snipped at the grasses for about 5 or 10 minutes then continued across the second field to some apparent destination.

"Britt," I said, "after the ruckus that guy made, I don't believe there are any birds in there. Seems a few would have spooked. But we'll go take a look anyway."

That was a smart move. As soon as Britt entered the cover, a small covey broke. I got a double. Both birds hit the ground dead, and I figured I was a hotshot today. Britt was coming out of the brush to retrieve the birds when several more flushed. I got another; I had three birds down at once. My gun was a Marlin Model 90, superimposed 12, with a trigger for each barrel. Suddenly still more birds were in the air. The gun got to my shoulder in time, but I triggered the barrel with the spent shell. Before I could switch to the other barrel, the quail curved back into their haven.

The spit must have held 100 birds. They were reluctant to leave it and would repeatedly return after being flushed. The horse didn't have any effect on them, but I was afraid that Britt and I might have them looking for less hectic parts if we applied too much pressure. About that time, 10 or 12 birds changed their tactics and careened for the desert about ¼-mile away. That confirmed my thoughts. My "sensational" skill deteriorated rapidly, and I was lucky to bring down a quail for every three or four shots. Too much shooting. We made one pass around the cover then left. But each year I have found this spot a consistent producer.

Over the past decade I have learned that just about any place where good stands of cover are near cultivated fields—even though they may be fallow at the time—has high Gambel's quail potential. Britt and I, and sometimes hunting friends, have located numerous fine spots to hunt this wonderful game bird in Arizona's agricultural lands. Remarkably, during this time we have seen very few other hunters taking advantage of it.

# 20 Top Tips for Upland Game Hunters

**by LARRY MEULLER**

1. **LOOK FOR GREAT** upland hunting right before a storm when rabbits and birds are hurriedly filling bellies and crops. Once the storm begins, however, the fast shooting is over. Game becomes very hard to find during high winds. They're skittish and flush out far ahead of hunters. When rain starts, most rabbits and birds hold so tight we walk past unaware of their presence. Hunting can be excellent during a light rain, but it usually takes a good dog to find the game.

2. Immense fields of high weeds LOOK as if they'd hold crowds of upland game. They don't. Birds find them too thick and difficult for takeoff and landing. Rabbits feel vulnerable because speed is their protection, and they're terribly slowed in this cover. The exception is pheasants after opening weekend of hunting season. They escape by running into heavy cover. It takes good dogs and/or lots of hunters to rout them out or drive them through to waiting hunters at the end of the field.

3. When hunting rabbits, quail, or pheasants the day after a snowstorm, windstorm, or night of intense cold, walk the frozen beds of small streams. Watch the banks for cottontails or birds hiding in cover where they sought shelter before severe weather moved in. They'll be sitting tight. If hunting in a group, have others walk just outside the stream's fringe of vegetation to bag rabbits or birds that flush from cover.

4. Hunting on snow during a bright, sunny day can be more comfortable—and successful—if sunglasses are worn. Squinting interferes with accurate shotgun pointing. Encountering the sudden glare of a bright, reflecting snowbank can inhibit swing-through as the trigger is pulled or even cause you to lose accurate sight of the game's whereabouts. If sunglasses are forgotten, a good field trick is to rub charcoal under the eyes. To get the charcoal, burn a wooden match thoroughly, let it cool, then crush it in the palm of your hand.

5. Stomping brush, kicking clumps of grass, and wading through heavy cover does two things besides spook game out to the gun. These actions can ruin preferred hiding places and they can leave the gunner off balance or even over his head in weeds and unable to shoot. Some rabbit hunters carry sticks to swat cover and poke clumps of grass. Some quail hunters carry flushing whips commonly used by dog trainers and field trailers. Either can be dropped from the hand as the gun comes up, and neither destroys cover. Both leave the gunner ready when game flushes.

6. Rabbits often sit tight and allow hunters to walk past, especially in cold weather. So do quail, ruffed grouse, and pheasants. But all are conditioned to know what is about to happen when a predator stops and stands dead still, trying to fix the prey's location before pouncing. If we imitate the predator by walking a short distance, then stopping for a minute or so, most nearby game will bolt from cover.

7. Get to know what your game looks like at 30 to 40 yards. This is the best range for shotgunning. The pattern has spread enough to make hitting more certain and the meat less damaged. Foliage and terrain won't always allow a 30- to 40-yard shot, but when it does, it also allows the gunner to calmly make one accurate shot instead of two or three fast misses.

8. Lead shot drifts about 2 feet at 50 yards if there's a 30mph wind. The drift is twice that at 80 yards. Shot

When hunting on very bright days, and even more so over snow, sunglasses are an aid to vision and shooting.

also drops about that much at 80 yards. Now you know why you missed those long shots, or worse yet, only crippled game which escaped. Step off the number of paces to game that was cleanly downed. Learn to pass up shots beyond that range. It will improve your score markedly, help your conscience immensely, and prevent a serious waste of precious wildlife.

9. Cottontails won't run in exact circles of course, but they want to remain in familiar territory. If pushed by beagles, expect them to run along the edge of cover as they return to the general vicinity. Pick a high spot to watch. Hunters have been known to stand on stumps, fallen trees, and even perch on stepladders to get a better view.

(Above) Top tip when grouse hunting is to follow up every flushed bird to the place where it probably landed — for a second try.

(Left) After first few days of season, pheasants are likely to take refuge in heaviest cover in any area.

(Below) Look for rabbits and other upland game to be moving just before the arrival of a storm front.

These hunters, starting out with a pair of bassets, are in for a great day of upland gunning in good game cover.

10. Most cottontailers hunt in groups, advancing in lines to drive and jump the rabbits. Some old squirrel hunter types don't care for this at all. To them, the search is more satisfying than shooting. They sneak along fencerows and edges of fields, concentrating on seeing not the form of a rabbit, but the one thing that doesn't blend with cover— the beady black eye of the rabbit. Some of these solitary hunters carry .22 rifles because their stealth allows them head shots and perfectly clean meat. Others carry shotguns for when the rabbit runs, plus a .22 pistol for when it doesn't.

11. Plan next year's rabbit hunt with a brush pile made of the neighborhood Christmas trees. The best pile size is about 15 feet long, half that wide, and 6 or 8 feet high. If more trees can be collected, additional piles are more effective than a single large one. Ask the farmer for permission, of course, and find out where he'd like it built. He'll appreciate it much more if you'll also offer to cut brush or small trees from along his land or fence rows to add to the pile. An Illinois Natural History Survey report shows a cottontail decline of 87 to 97 percent in areas where clean farming has removed most permanent cover. Nothing brings them back better or faster than brush piles.

12. Pheasants are big, lumbering, easy-to-hit birds. Then why do we miss so many? Because, not only are they large, their long tails make them appear even bigger than they really are. That makes us believe they're closer than they really are. Sometimes we shoot when they're out of range. More often, we simply don't lead them far enough because what we regard as a 30-yard bird may actually be 45 yards away.

13. Because pheasants are so vulnerable while battling the air with stubby wings in noisy takeoffs, many of them place more confidence in their legs—especially after the opening day education. It takes pressure to put these runners into the air. A group of hunters can crowd them by making a drive through heavy cover to standers waiting at the end. But this system is safe only if every hunter can be depended upon not to

When flushed and chased by a beagle, a rabbit probably will run a rough circle to return to the spot. So wait there.

ground swat a bird or shoot before the pheasant is high enough that the shot string will fly well above other hunters' heads. Close working dogs (spaniels, retrievers, even mongrels) are better at raising the birds, and they'll find those pheasants that run again after they're knocked down.

14. A lone pheasant hunter can sometimes get shooting by unhurriedly quartering heavy cover like a springer spaniel. Usually, the birds will move ahead slowly, but will stop at the edge of cover, hesitant to break into the open. If the hunter moves within range of the birds very leisurely so he doesn't spook them, and then stops and waits, one by one the pheasants will get the jitters and fly.

15. Birds dropped in heavy cover often blend with the colors of dead foliage and can't be found. Frequently, when a hunter fails to find the bird immediately, he becomes confused and doubtful about where it fell. To avoid that, watch closely as the bird falls, and get there quickly without taking your eyes from that spot. Upon arrival, drop your hat to mark the spot and begin the search. If the bird isn't found, widen the search in a spiral around your cap. But pay particular attention farther out in the direction you shot. A misjudged fall is almost always at a greater distance than imagined.

16. Quail have changed greatly over the past 40 years. They used to be covey birds that flushed, scattered somewhat, flew a short distance, then hid as singles. Now they fly far, scatter widely, and run in every direction when they land. This makes it increasingly difficult to locate singles. A blast from a hawk call, and two or three more as you approach, may make the birds freeze in position instead of running.

17. An old fox hunter used to yell at his boys, "Get your heads up! You won't see a fox under your feet!" This is at least as important for quail hunters. Even when flushing a covey held by pointing dogs, keep the head up. The time delay and slight disorientation caused by switching the eyes from ground to sky is the cause of lots of misses.

18. Look for quail near thick roosting cover early in the morning, out in the fields feeding at midmorning, back in heavy cover, timber edges, or up brushy draws to rest during midday, and out again to feed during mid-afternoon. If a storm is moving in, anticipate quail still out feeding during midday.

19. Ruffed grouse are our hardest-to-hit upland game birds. They flush unexpectedly in thick woods, and most are behind trees before they're 30 yards away. Many shots will be at 30 feet. So if possible, use a light, fast swinging 20-gauge with an open bore. Swing fast until the barrel covers the bird, then pull the trigger and keep swinging to establish a "lead." Most important, remember that the majority of grouse will be on the rise when gunned at close range. If the gun barrel isn't covering the bird, you'll blow a hole in the air beneath it.

20. In much of America's ruffed grouse habitat, hunters consider themselves fortunate to see one bird per hour. To improve the amount of action, smart hunters never fail to try for a reflush of any bird they miss. They watch the flight carefully and mark where the grouse lands. They can expect the bird to be within 10 to 15 yards of that spot and in cover much like that from which it was originally flushed.

Those are the 20 Top Tips, and here's an extra—the 21st for coming of age as a hunter:

21. Quail are usually flushed in fairly open country. If they're flying to the right or left, swing through, fire, and keep swinging as you pull the trigger. If they're close and haven't leveled out, swing upward and fire when the barrel covers the quail. The same thing applies to an oncoming bird. If they've leveled out going straight away shoot just under the bird, and it will fly into the shot string. Never fire at the covey in general; always pick a single bird as the target.

A hunter can shoot plenty of rabbits on his own, but a good beagle doubles the odds in his favor.

# MULES OF THE IRON JAWS

## by NORMAN STRUNG

Some very large mule deer lurk in the canyons and cedar country of Montana's Iron Jaw area.

**THE IRON JAW MOUNTAINS.** They rise from the dusty plains of southeastern Montana like sawteeth on the edge of the Big Sky. Their appearance is as foreboding as their name; domes and buttes and steep-walled canyons all tangled together in a landscape that God forgot.

The early settlers surely felt the awesome loneliness of the place. Testimony lingers in the names you find on maps of the area—Moon Creek, Pumpkin Creek, Graveyard Creek—and I suspect that the impression is no different to people today. The Iron Jaws amount to one of the least-populated areas in a sparsely-settled state—that's if you're counting human beings.

Big mule deer are another matter though. In terms of trophy-class bucks, the Iron Jaws rate as one of the best areas in Montana. Their topography, and the deer they produce, are much like the famed Missouri Breaks, 150 miles to the north, but unlike the Breaks, the Iron Jaws are virtually unheard of and unhunted.

My introduction to the place came at the hands of Marlin Cooper, a longtime hunting partner and heavy equipment operator from Forsyth, Montana. For several years, Marlin had spun yarns about the Iron Jaws and a family, appropriately named Woods, that lived in

the middle of their majestic isolation. However, we never quite put together the time, the place and an invitation. Then one day we happened to run into Frank Woods in Forsyth. Our conversation turned to the approaching deer season, and in the span of a beer, the elements came together. A month later we drove into the yard of the Wood's ranch, south of Hathaway.

Albert Woods was the patriarch of the clan. His hands were as hard as the rocky ground he stood upon, and his grip just as firm. "Frank tells me you'd like to get a crack at a big buck. Well, we've got 'em. But first, how about some coffee, boys?"

Coffee and conversation—the universal common denominator out West. We were ushered into the low-roofed cabin and seated at a dining table that seemed to stretch into tomorrow. Frank was there, and Albert introduced us to his wife and four other children—Willie, Mike, Matt, and Naomi, the youngest. Then he disappeared into the kitchen and returned with two cups and one of the biggest mule deer racks I've ever seen; 30 inches across and as thick as my wrist at the base.

" 'Course, we don't get one like that every day," he cautioned in his quiet way. "But they're around. You

Studying the Iron Jaw country from a distance through a spotting scope.

saw one bigger than that last year didn't you?'' he asked Frank.

Frank took a sip of the strong, black coffee. "A lot bigger, but he might be dead now. He was gray around the muzzle, but age didn't hurt his brains any. I spooked him out by rolling a rock down a deep canyon, and that mosshorn only ran while the rock was rolling. Just so I couldn't hear his hooves on the shale! I got a shot off at him but missed. I thought I counted 10 points on one side.''

"So what are we waiting for?'' Willie asked.

Mike and Matt nodded in agreement. Even little Naomi stood up to get ready.

"No, you let the men go alone,'' her mother laughed.

"I guess we might as well get with it then,'' Albert agreed. "Everyone seems pretty fired up.''

Our plan was to work as a team. We'd spend the morning scouting for signs of a big animal via 4-wheel-drive pickup and horseback. Once we located some good prospects, we'd come back to the ranch for lunch, decide on the best approach for the biggest deer, then work a drive in the afternoon. It was the usual way that the Woods hunted deer. A family of seven, living 30 miles from the nearest store, without the amenities of indoor plumbing, central heating, phones and electricity, have to work as a team.

"Better take some of this along with you,'' Mrs. Woods said as she passed out chunks of her homemade venison jerky. "I don't know about you and Marlin, but my boys get hungry long before dinner time.''

We split into three parties. Willie, Matt and Mike took the ranch pickup. Frank, Marlin and I took Frank's pickup. Albert saddled his pony and elected to poke around by himself.

Their technique, best described as "divide and roam,'' is standard procedure in the wide-opened West. The idea is to cover a lot of ground exploring until you have some inkling of where the deer are hanging out. Once that ingredient is known, the serious hunting begins.

"We'll be checking out the tumbledown country, where the Jaws first pitch up from the Yellowstone Valley,'' Frank explained, ramrodding his pickup to the top of a steep, rock strewn ridge. "That's where I always find the biggest deer at this time of the year. Dad and the kids are looking over the gentler country where the Jaws flatten out into a high plateau. Big deer get up there late in the season when they're sniffing around does, but I got a hunch they're not there now.''

As we rumbled along the narrow ridge, Frank filled us in on the country that spread out in front of us, including how it got its name.

The original wagon road that wound into the mountains passed by a huge rock formation that seemed to open and close like two iron jaws. The road is no more—it's been sliced and cut deep by erosion, but the name remains.

"How the devil do you find your way around in this country?" I asked. "We've only been out 15 minutes, and I'm lost already."

Frank grinned. "Just something you gotta learn. We run 100 or so wild horses. Keep 'em wild and sell them to rodeos. At roundup, you have to know every rock, every canyon and every waterhole better than them, so you learn early. The whole spread is about 13 square miles. That might sound like quite a chunk to memorize, but little Matt knows the outfit better than all of us. And it really helps around deer season too. You get to thinking like a deer, and know just where they're going to go."

He brought the pickup to an abrupt halt and confronted a 4-inch thick pine, blocking his path. "Huh. That was just a sapling last time I was here." He dropped into compound gear and bowled the tree out by the roots. "Gotta keep your roads open," he laughed.

At the head of the Jaws were spectacular finger-like ridges that reached out high above the surrounding land, then dropped off at breath-taking angles to the valley below. Frank joggled to the end of a finger, and we stepped out.

"You can see forever," Marlin said.

"Not quite forever, but those hills on the horizon are about 70 miles away. And there's never been many people between here and there, either. Bands of Indians used to hide out there, and so did one of the last herds of prairie bighorn sheep. Dad can remember the sheep as a boy. They're extinct now."

Frank shouldered his rifle and scoped the coulees that dropped off on each side of the promontory. "Well, I don't see anything right now, but let's roll 'em out anyway." He picked up a boulder and set it moving. It lumbered along, slowly at first, then bounced higher and higher, spinning wildly as it clacked and careened down the slope.

"There," he pointed across the canyon. "That always gets 'em." He surveyed three deer that were scrambling up the far wall. They stopped and stared at the silhouettes far above them.

"Two does and a buck. Just a 3-point. We'll let him grow up." He rolled out the coulee to his left and came up empty-handed. "Well, no use wasting any more time around here. Better climb back in. We got a dozen more places to check before lunch. Hey! Look here."

Frank pointed to an oval bed under the fan-like branches of a scrub cedar. "This one looks about the

One of author's friends finds his buck dead on a steep rock ledge. He'll have a tough time dragging it out.

size we're after." He stooped to place his forked fingers into the cleft marks pressed in the dust. "Three hundred maybe 350 live weight. Should be carrying a pretty good rack. And still in the cedar. Wait till Dad hears that!"

Frank wasn't exaggerating when he said he knew the country. In 3 hours he picked his way out onto every point that rimmed the Jaws, and spotted deer that Marlin and I would never have seen. But none of those muleys matched his expectations, including one very nice 4-point in a band of does that had me chomping at the bit. That one "lacked the beam," according to Frank.

"It's just a little earlier than we think," argued Albert between helpings of fried chicken and mashed potatoes. "The bucks aren't with the does yet. Oh, the young ones are alright, but not the big fellers."

"That's what we saw too," offered Matt.

Frank nodded. "I guess you're right, Pop. We saw plenty of deer, but 90 percent of them were does in big bunches, and I saw some fresh sign in the cedar."

"Yep," Albert said decisively. "That's the way I figure it. We've got to be looking for magpies in the cedar."

Long shot across canyon and a good Iron Jaw buck is down.

It was a puzzling statement, so I pressed for some more information. When I got my answers, I learned a novel approach to hunting for big bucks.

In the Iron Jaws, and country like it, the latter part of the deer season is undeniably the best for big bucks. Mid-November finds females in season and males in rut, a time when even the biggest and wisest old hat racks do plenty of moving around and lose a good deal of their caution. By rights, we should have hit the first week of that increased activity right on the nose, but summer had lingered on longer than usual that year, and both Frank and Albert theorized the rut had been delayed as a result.

Our mistake had been in paying too much attention to the groups of deer we were seeing, counting on them to hold the bucks. Chances were that the truly big deer were still solitary, and giving us the slip by sneaking off in a different direction while we were glassing the jumped herds.

"Until the rut, finding the fellas takes some doing," explained Albert, "but still they got a weakness and a giveaway. They love to hole up in low stands of cedar, so watch the brush real carefully. And keep an eye peeled for magpies."

"But what does a magpie have to do with it?"

"Don't ask me why," Frank chimed in, "but all of us have noticed that magpies like to hang around big deer. So you look for a bunch of low cedar, and you wait for a bird to fly out. Now when you find cedars and magpies, it won't mean a deer every time, but it sure happens enough to make careful looking worth while."

"And there's lot's of cedar to look at," Mike added, "so we'd better get going right now." He and Matt stood up and headed for the door.

"Not so fast. I need water, and the woodbox is empty," Mrs. Woods cautioned.

"But Mom . . . "

" You can do it while the pie cools."

"Pie?" grinned Matt. "That's different."

An hour later we were driving out on a long ridge that rose high above a brushy swale.

"Man," I groaned to Marlin. "I didn't really need that second piece of pie."

He covered a belch with the back of his hand. "Ditto."

"We'll all get a chance to walk it off," smiled Frank. "The head of each of the coulees that drops into the Jaws is a kind of bowl, and we're going to fan out around the rims while Dad rides up the bottom. He should push something past one of us."

"Sounds good," agreed Marlin. "Where do you want me?"

Frank eased his pickup to a stop and pointed toward a twisted rock outcrop. "Right on top of that hill. You'll get a good overview of this valley and the next one too. Matt and Mike will take a stand on the little divide at the canyon head, and Willie and I will take the hill opposite . . . Hey! Did you see that?"

I followed Frank's point. "No, what?"

"Magpie. He just came barreling out of the cedars near the top of that hill."

"There's something up there!" Marlin caught sight of a flash of white and hit the door of the pickup just as two huge bucks stood up, their head and shoulders poking well out of the scrub.

"Man alive—that's what we're looking for!" Frank and Marlin scrambled for their guns as I watched the

Dragging a buck up and out of the Iron Jaws is no easy matter.

two deer turn their backs and trot over the hill. The weapons were out of their cases just in time to sight in on two white rumps disappearing over the crest.

"They are a good 300 yards off, but I think I saw six and seven points," I muttered, surprised at my tone of voice when in fact, my heart was pounding like a pile-driver.

"Oh, did we mess that one up!" groaned Marlin.

Frank was in a consoling mood. "That's OK, fellas. They had plenty of points, but they were a little short on beam. Tell you one good thing though, two big bucks together like that is a sure sign we're right. If it was rutting time, they wouldn't be quite so friendly. And there's gotta be more around."

"Any chance we could follow them up?" asked Marlin. "That beam thing just doesn't bother me the way it does you."

Frank shook a knowing head. "By the time we worked our way back around the top of the canyon, they'd be a couple of miles away. Besides, Dad's coming up the bottom pretty quick, and we should be in place when he gets here."

"One muley characteristic in open country is that they'll travel a country mile once they're jumped. And the smart, old ones won't even stop and look back, a trait that's practically a muley calling card."

It took us 5 minutes to climb the low hill and Frank placed me first.

"Stand here, next to this piñon pine, and kind of use it like a blind. Muleys aren't real sharp-eyed, so if you don't move, you'll just look like another part of the tree to them. If it doesn't look like you're going to get a big buck, settle for a little one. It falls dark around 4:30 now, and it'll be getting that way soon. Looks like this is the only coulee we'll be able to hunt."

He left me to position Marlin, then find his own spot.

Essentially, Frank and Albert were capitalizing on a dependable trait of muleys, that not even plains animals have overcome: When they're pressed, they invariably want to run uphill. Our posters were arranged in a loose semi-circle, with six sets of eyes capable of seeing every inch of the canyon head, plus a little of the land that lay on either side. If something came through, someone was bound to get a shot. And it didn't take long.

Five does were the first to appear. They ambled up the coulee bottom with only quick glances over their shoulders to even hint at them being worried from below. Then two forkhorns followed, but rather than exposing themselves in the open, they stuck close to the brush, easing along with heads held low, grabbing as much cover as they could find.

The brush patch they were using angled uphill and ended in a pie slice that petered out into open terrain. If they followed it, they'd pass within 40 yards of me. It was a tough decision to make . . . settle for a fat fork-horn, or hope for a trophy rack? My decision was influenced by two homilies and a fact of life.

The homilies were: "A bird in the hand is worth two in the bush;" and "You can't eat horns." The fact of life was that Albert Woods had just ridden into view, and it was doubtful that there were anymore deer in the canyon. I picked the tallest-standing animal and dropped him with a heart shot. Then the air exploded.

Guns boomed out across and above me. The big racks I was looking for had pulled the same stunt as the two forkhorns that tried to sneak past me. But they'd done it on the opposite hillside.

Willie had a deer, Matt had a deer, and Marlin had a deer; four, three, and four respectively. They were all of trophy proportions, even the 3-point, that Frank decided had "better than average beam."

It was dark before the warm glow of gaslights marked our arrival back at the ranch. We loaded our two deer in my pickup and helped Matt and Willie hoist their animals high on the crossbeams of their log barn.

"I feel kind of guilty," I offered, shaking Albert's hand as I stood by the kitchen door. "You and Frank did all the work, and we got the meat."

Albert Woods smiled a smile that was born of genuine hospitality. "That's just the way we wanted it. There's plenty more deer around here for us to get, and we've still got 2 weeks of season left."

I took Mrs. Woods hand and thanked her for the meal. "Anytime. Just make sure you come back and see us again. We enjoyed having you both."

As my pickup rumbled through their yard gate, I felt a lump in my jacket pocket. I reached in and found the jerky I'd been given that morning.

I broke it in half, gave one piece to Marlin, and popped the other in my mouth. It had a delicious smoked-salty flavor, slightly bitter, but you could tell it was the kind of food that would stay with a man for a long time.

# CHALLENGE OF THE BULL ELK

## by
## ERWIN A. BAUER

Daybreak on a wilderness river bank after a light snowfall. It's a good time and place to meet a big bull elk.

**JUST AFTER DAYBREAK** Matt Snow and I found the first fresh tracks. A band of a dozen or so elk had crossed the bare ridge, turned toward Hummingbird Creek, then evaporated into a dense stand of spruce.

"They are not far away," Matt muttered, "but they might as well be in China as in those evergreens."

It was evident that the tracks were very, very fresh because a soft snow which had begun to fall only a few minutes before had not yet obliterated the hoof marks etched in the soft earth. I dropped to one knee for a closer look. One set of tracks was much larger than the rest.

"An old bull almost has to be in that herd," Matt continued. Then almost as if purposely to prove him correct, we heard the shrill fife-like whistle in the timber just below. The bull was so near that we could hear him gasp to regain breath at the end of the whistle.

Of all the magnificent sounds in the outdoors, few match the eerie challenge of a bull elk. I have been lucky enough to hear the roar of an African lion at night and the saw-like cough of a leopard. I've heard timber wolves in full cry, the crazy laugh of northern loons and the haunting wilderness songs of white-throated sparrows. Still, the bugle of an elk never fails to raise the hackles on my neck. Now suddenly, after a week of making footprints over plenty of alpine real estate without seeing an elk, we were practically on top of a whole herd. I could feel the first faint symptoms of buck fever coming on.

"We have two choices," Matt said. "We can try to stalk that bull in the timber, but the chances are poor that we would ever see his antlers. It's just too thick in there. We would probably spook one of the cows, and she would spook the rest."

"Or we can play the waiting game," Matt continued. "If the snowstorm should pass, the animals might drift out into the open again. Our best bet might be to climb a little higher and keep an eye on the timber. We might be able to see the elk emerge and plan our strategy from there."

"Lead the way," I answered.

We needed about 15 minutes to reach a vantage point high on the ridge overlooking Hummingbird Creek. Then we hunkered down against a rock, backs to the wind, and watched the evergreens far below through swirling snow through most of the morning.

At first it was a suspenseful wait, and the scene below us was wildly beautiful. But gradually the cold penetrated deeper and deeper. Trickles of snow water ran down the back of my neck. After a couple of hours, the waiting became torturous and in the long run was all for nothing. We never did see that herd of elk. Sometime during the snowstorm they disappeared to unknown parts and almost 2 inches of snow covered their tracks forever.

"I'm beginning to get the impression," Matt said in camp that evening, "that we're jinxed. Only 3 days are left on this hunt."

Any sportsman who has hunted big game widely around the world would have to include the North American elk, or wapiti, *Cervus canadensis,* among the greatest game animals of all. It is shy, elusive and lives in difficult mountain habitat — in other words, in an environment that is difficult to hunt. One of the largest members of the deer family, *Cervidae,* it is the second largest (next to the moose) of all the deer on this conti-

nent. However, elk are not quite as large as some hunters believe. Bulls range from 550 pounds to 750 maximum and cows from 450 pounds to 600 tops. Claims of bulls weighing 1,000 pounds simply are unreasonable. Maximum weight is reached at about 4 or 5 years.

Elk exist today and furnish some hunting in the following states and Canadian provinces: Montana, Wyoming, Idaho, Alberta, British Columbia, Washington, Oregon, Colorado, Utah, New Mexico, Saskatchewan and Manitoba, with most animals being taken in the first five places named. Very small populations exist in Texas, Michigan, Pennsylvania and Virgina. A fact not commonly known is that a good

(Above) A rare and magnificent sight — two bulls of trophy size together.

(Left) Challenging bull elk means climbing into some of America's toughest real estate of the West.

population of elk has been established on the Afognak and Raspberry islands of Alaska. They were transplanted in 1928 from Washington's Olympic Peninsula and today provide the longest elk hunting season anywhere—either sex from August 1 to December 31. On the Tonki Cape portion of Afognak, a hunter can take two elk.

Before the West was won (or, more accurately, lost) elk were dwellers of the plains and foothills as well as of the high country. But our expanding civilization and competition with domestic livestock for available range has forced the species almost exclusively into the mountain ranges where most live on public (mostly national forest and national park) lands. They do make seasonal migrations, but from low to high elevations and back again with the annual snowfalls, rather than far across the country. During the period when most hunting seasons are open in Canada and the United States, elk — particularly bulls — will be found at the highest elevation at which sufficient browse and grasses are available to sustain them. Most of the year the older bulls live by themselves or in small groups, but beginning in mid-September or so, which is approximately when the annual rut begins, the bulls join the cows and calves. They also become antagonistic toward their summertime bachelor friends.

The rut is the most exciting time of the elk's year; it is

(Right) A splendid old bull elk bugles his challenge to other bulls in his territory. It is one of the most piercing sounds in the wild.

Challenging the challenger with an elk call made of plastic tubing.

also the most exciting time to hunt them. There is much movement and jockeying about among the bulls to establish territories and to acquire harems. This involves intimidation, bluffing, and some actual fighting, and a good deal of bugling. A lovesick bull with reddened eyes, swollen neck and ivory-tipped brown antlers is a splendid sight. I have watched bulls duel with one another, slash at trees and in passion tear up large chunks of earth — and wouldn't trade the experience for anything. Of course, such an impassioned bull may be less cautious than normal and is therefore liable to end up in someone's trophy room.

It is a common misconception that only bull elk bugle and only during the rut. The truth is that both sexes may bugle at any time of the year. But it is during the fall rut when the most resonant, penetrating bugling is heard,

and the bulls are responsible for all of this.

Bugling a challenge has been the death of many good bulls because experienced hunters and guides can take advantage of it. From a great many different materials ranging from old garden hoses to copper tubing, it is possible to manufacture artificial calls which duplicate the bull's whistle. Some individuals become very expert in using these calls.

It is rare that even a good caller can lure a bull which has already acquired a harem. But it has been done. In fact such bulls occasionally have been challenged into very close quarters. Far more often a bull will simply answer a challenge which sounds authentic and thereby reveals his location. That done, it is up to the hunter to make a stalk into shooting range, perhaps calling at intervals to keep in "contact."

However, the most successful callers I've known believe that it is a mistake to call too often. They also *never* call to a bull when they are very close — nearer than 200 yards.

"The closer you call," Mac McKenzie explained to me one day, "the greater the chance that the bull might detect a false note." Mac, who runs pack trips and guides hunting trips in the southern Alberta Rockies, near Banff, is among the best callers I've ever seen in action.

Successfully hunting any big game animal is a matter of knowing something about the species, about its habits, its sign and very often the foods it prefers. Unfortunately for the hunter, elk are the least specialized feeders of all deer and either browse or graze on hundreds of different plants. They have even been observed eating the rotting wood from fallen tree trunks.

But elk do leave a good deal of sign which betrays their presence. Often the hoofprints, large and more blunt than a mule deer's, and smaller and less pointed than moose, are the easiest to spot, especially if there is a blanket of snow in the high country. Mature elk tracks can be somewhat difficult for inexperienced hunters to distinguish from small cattle. The latter tend to be more square in shape.

Elk dung is another telltale sign. In summertime or early fall it resembes cattle dung, but in miniature. Later on, watch the trails and forest openings for inch-long pellets which might be very abundant in good game area.

With experience, an elk hunter also learns to observe browsed places on trees, shrubs and bushes. Bark eaten from an aspen trunk or tree branches broken down when the animals try to reach tender tips above are good signs. (Elk have been observed standing on their hind legs to feed on higher-up browse.) Wallows mudholes and mineral licks around which fresh hoof-

Hidden in an evergreen thicket, a hunter scans the mountainsides for a glimpse of a bull elk.

prints are etched are other good signs.

A hunter has two choices when planning an elk hunt. He can go early in the season when the animals are still in the rut and in the high country — or he can go later when the elk are in larger concentrations and moving toward lower elevations ahead of the snow. The first is normally the most exciting, and it takes the sportsman into magnificent country at a magnificent time of the year. The second may be the most productive, but for me, at least, it lacks the bright fall color, plus much of the spice and adventure of being on top of the world. Either way, a hunter must be prepared for hunting in steep, sometimes rough country. On many trips he must be prepared for snow — and occasionally very deep snow. Sadly, I've had a couple of trips snowed out altogether.

This elk could not resist a call from hunter John Moxley and became his trophy.

A big elk is down. Now follows the chore of field dressing the animal and packing it out of the woods.

Sometimes elk hunting means waiting long hours on a woodland stand to hear the calliope-bugle of a bull.

One good way to proceed is to contact several of the many reliable guides or outfitters who advertise in *Outdoor Life*. But do it as far in advance of the season as possible. Or better still, telephone them and tell them exactly what you would like to do (bag a trophy bull or settle for any kind of elk), when, for how long, and tell them about your previous hunting experience. From that beginning you can work out a hunt to suit your own qualifications.

You could strike out on your own. Many sportsmen with previous big game hunting experience have successfully done so. However, it is wisest, especially on a first elk hunt, to engage an outfitter. Some states and provinces require outfitters for nonresidents. Keep in mind also that it is usually necessary to participate in a drawing to obtain an elk permit or license and this must be done usually well in advance of the season.

Next, get ready for what can become a very rugged experience. It's true enough that grand old bulls have been bagged with very little effort by extremely lucky hunters who scarcely ventured from camp. But this isn't typical. Normally it is necessary to spend many hours in a cold saddle or making footprints across a snowy uneven landscape. Trophy bulls require more time and trouble than smaller animals, but the suspense is worth any effort.

I have covered the subject of getting prepared — getting fit physically — many times before in the outdoor magazines and will not go into detail here again. But the main point is to do enough strenuous exercise beforehand to get legs and lungs in shape. Try to do some horseback riding, too. Be certain your hunting boots are perfectly broken-in and comfortable, even after hiking all day. Those are the main or critical points.

Don't neglect your rifle. More good ones are on the market nowadays than there is room to list here. My own favorite is the 7mm Remington Magnum with a 3X-9X variable scope. An elk is very tenacious of life, and I do not think that anything less than a .270 is really adequate from a conservation standpoint.

However, no matter what the caliber or model of the firearm, it must be perfectly sighted-in to hit where it's aimed. And the hunter must be entirely familiar with handling and shooting it accurately. That fact cannot be emphasized enough. There is no point in making vast preparations, in spending time and often a good deal of money, only to miss a golden opportunity at a large bull when it suddenly is presented.

An elk hunter's clothing should be warm in case of cold weather, but comfortable enough to go afield on Indian summer days. A good warm sleeping bag is essential and so is a foam mattress. It's folly to go far without a durable foul-weather suit, and if it is to be a pack trip, make certain the outfitter will have a rifle and saddle scabbard for your use.

Elk hunting is a great sport for a splendid game animal. Make the most of it if, or whenever, you have the opportunity.

# There's a Woman in Camp

by KATHLEEN FARMER

(Opposite) Having a woman in camp is common nowadays and likely to be more so in the future. And why not?

**POCK-MARKED WITH MUD,** the drab, green 4-wheel-drive bounced, swerved, and slid through wheel-deep greasy pits. Instead of the parallel ruts of a jeep trail, the road amounted to an endless series of brown puddles connected by defiant rocks and stubborn roots. The bronco vehicle seemed to make more headway vertically, toward the center of the earth, than horizontally toward elk camp.

The four grown men shoulder-to-shoulder inside the pickup's cab were hooting and hollering like kids on the Topsy-Turvy Roller Coaster Ride at the amusement park. Passing around a fifth of Johnny Walker, they were toasting to the upcoming adventure of the elk hunt. Even though most of the "brown loudmouth" dribbled down their chins onto their shirts, they felt warm and tense with anticipation. The wild ride over the crazy road foreshadowed an even wilder and crazier hunt. Shivering with delight, they were like teenagers again, sitting on the edge of a bench, waiting to be sent into their first varsity football game.

The country was exactly as they had pictured. Mountainous, rugged, covered with stretching pines. The faithful pickup skidded up what appeared to be a stream bed with the current churning against the lug tires. The vehicle turned right, nearly ran into a 100-year-old Douglas fir, and jerked to a stop. Fred hit his head on the dashboard laughing at the untethered antics of this cowboy, wrestling a truck the way he would an unbroken horse.

"The best way to drive a 4-wheel-drive is to pretend it ain't yours," the guide advised.

"Oh, is this your rig?"

"Nope." They howled at the cleverness of this fellow who would get them their first elk. Even though his young blonde head was inches below theirs, they looked up to him, wishing they could live their lives over again and be just like him. Slowly, they looked through the windshield, not wanting this moment to end. A woman, dressed in jeans and red-and-black checked wool shirt, stepped from a tan 8x10 canvas tent, supported by crisscrossed narrow pine poles.

"Is that a woman?"

"Sure looks like one."

"What's she doing here? A woman in camp is bad luck."

"Maybe she's the cook."

"Where's her husband?" Their lighthearted joviality spent, they felt betrayed by this cocky guide.

"Don't know a thing about her 'cept she has no husband with her—not even a boyfriend. The rest you'll have to ask Sam. He's the outfitter, you know."

"I thought they'd be off limits here. What kind of hunt will it be with a woman along?"

The guide shook his head sympathetically and lifted his Stetson as if the answer might be hidden there. When none was found, he scratched his tonic-doused hair, opened the door, and acted busy. "What kind of hunt *will* it be?" he muttered.

Would a woman want to invade the traditionally all-male domain of the hunting or fishing camp? Yes, the woman who hunts or fishes would. Because prime fishing and hunting can be found on guided trips, an outdoorswoman would naturally be attracted to them. The possibility that she might be a lone woman in camp does not worry her until she arrives.

Once this cast of characters on a mountain hunt would have been all male. But look closer at the one on the left. She's the author.

43

When writing the outfitter about specifics, the outdoorswoman should clearly state that she will not be accompanied by her husband and should request a private tent or cabin unless another woodswoman will be in camp to share the sleeping facilities.

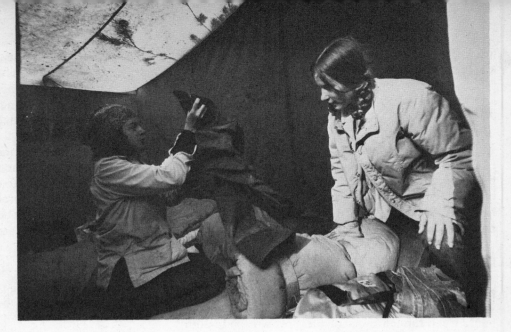

Camp etiquette for a woman surrounded by men can be difficult and full of trial and error for everyone concerned. No one knows what is expected. As a result, the woman is usually ignored until she makes her presence felt. Then, she is teased.

Both men and women seem to feel more comfortable when the lone woman assumes camp chores, such as, cooking and dishwashing. But this role inevitably leads to the sportswoman's substituting work for hunting or fishing. Frustration and resentment grow with the seeming inconsideration of her male companions. She then is forced into the position of standing up for her right to hunt or fish and insisting that the camp cook (who often feigns ignorance) do his job. Even though she starts out being a "nice guy" and serves the men in the manner that they expect, she ends up being disagreeable. The men decide secretly and authoritatively that "camp is no place for a woman. Too rough for 'em."

On the other hand, an outdoorswoman can structure the camp experience to be enjoyable and successful for everyone—even the skeptics. But she must make her position clear from the beginning. When writing the outfitter about specifics, such as, price, accommodations, services, and equipment, she should describe

Expect to be waited on. You paid a great deal of money for this trip.
Your only job is to concentrate on hunting, fishing or photography.

herself as an experienced outdoorswoman who prefers to hunt or fish alone. She should clearly state that her husband will not accompany her (whether she has a husband or not, it is easier to let the outfitter think she is married). She should request a private tent or cabin unless there will be another woodswoman with whom she can share a bunk room. Offhandedly, she should mention other outdoor trips she has enjoyed. In addition, she should ask about weather conditions and the type of fishing or hunting that is generally most effective. But she should always bring raingear, long underwear, a warm jacket, insect repellent, a sleeping bag and foam pad, and extras of socks, jeans, shirts, bandannas. All equipment and clothes should be packed in duffel bags—the largest about 2 feet in length—for easy storing and transporting in panniers.

Within a hunting or fishing camp, democracy does not work. Hunters and fishers depend on the outfitter or

Any woman heading for a hunting camp should be prepared for it. One important thing is that her rifle should be accurately sighted in.

cook happen to be alone in the cook tent before he has begun breakfast, he will undoubtedly and meekly remark, "My pancakes are like bricks but I bet you make them as light and fluffy as clouds." Male camp cooks are notorious sweet talkers and can usually charm the unsuspecting woman into taking over his duties.

*Rule 2:* When walking into the cook tent, always carry a piece of equipment that can be used as an educated excuse. In hunting camps, strap a pair of binoculars securely around your neck. In a rustic fishing lodge, never be without your fishing rod. Then, if you foresee the cook (or sometimes the guide) going into his, "I bet you can cook ten times better than me" routine, casually interrupt with, "I was on my way to glass the slopes for game" or "I want to try this specially tied dry fly while the fish are still ravenous." However, a camera—preferably one with a flash—is the best means of gently nudging the cook into working

guide to lead or direct them to likely spots. The guide decides when he and his sportsmen will leave camp—in big game hunting camps, the guide routinely wakes the hunter and starts a fire in the tent's wood-burning stove. In strange, vast country, the outdoorsperson is dependent on the guide for direction as well as judgment about where to ford a swollen stream or about taking a shortcut cross-country without a trail. It is the rare guide who asks his hunters or fishers their opinion or preference. Instead, the "client" is expected to follow the guide whenever and wherever he goes. Regimentation is usually less in fishing camps and greater in big game hunting ones. A camp is no place to take into account individual differences, likes, or pet peeves. Perhaps this is the reason a woman in camp is expected to play the role of dishwasher and cook. But there are reliable ways to overcome this prejudice.

*Rule 1:* Never be first in the cook tent. If you and the

without his exerting pressure on you to be his assistant. At crucial moments, instead of replying to his humble and persistent entreaty, ask him to beat the batter again so you can shoot a picture of him in action. He will eventually labor with gusto on the chance you might be watching and waiting for a colorful photo of camp life.

*Rule 3:* Never volunteer. A pack animal—either a horse or mule—carries the camp supplies in panniers. These basket-like containers hang on either side of the animal and are hooked onto a pack saddle and tied together and to the animal by a sophisticated series of rope loops ending in a diamond hitch. Leading a pack animal is difficult. Sometimes they rub against trees and the entire pack falls off. Other times they want to jump across a stream instead of walking through it, and the flour and sugar land at the bottom of the current, wet and unretrievable. Guides can skillfully hint that if you volunteer to lead a pack animal, for instance, you will be "one of the boys" and "part of the outfit." Don't be fooled. Volunteering for any type of work that will cut into your hunting or fishing time or that will tire you out enough to lessen your hunting and fishing activities should be out of the question. You are not a "hand." On the contrary, you have paid a sizable chunk of money to hunt or fish and that is what you should do. Saying "no" will actually increase the outfitter's respect for you. He will find he cannot manipulate you as he can most others.

*Rule 4:* Expect to be waited on. Most outdoorspeople pride themselves in being self-sufficient. But in a hunting or fishing camp, the wrangler herds and saddles the horses; the cook prepares and cleans up after meals; and the guide sets up tents and sees that his clients are comfortable. Sit back and relax. Resist the temptation to prove how efficient, useful, and knowledgeable you are in the backwoods. Concentrate on fishing, hunting, or photography. You have worked hard enough on your own camps. Now it is time to rest, soak in the wilderness, and enjoy yourself.

Women often experience an uncomfortable feeling akin to guilt when sitting on a log, watching men perform the chores that women have traditionally done. This more than any other attitude may wear down an outdoorswoman's determination to be treated as an equal and not to be assigned menial tasks. One way to

Before mounting your horse, check the cinch for snugness. This could save an embarrassing spill on the trail.

overcome this feeling of responsibility for the well-being of the camp is to talk to the cook or guide or wrangler while he works. They know their work so well, they could complete their jobs while asleep (and some do). Conversation is a welcome relief from the humdrum chores. And they would appreciate your interest much more than your trying to take over their camp.

*Rule 5:* Expect to be tested by outfitter, guide, and colleagues. Interpersonal relationships of men are riddled with competition and constant testing of each other's strength, knowledge, and ability. Even though the testing may be subtle while watching a football game on TV or more obvious on the golf course, it comprises most of the conversation at camp. Past hunting or fishing experiences, homemade pet theories of the feeding behavior of cutthroat trout or big bull elk, and proven success at hunting or fishing while in camp determine whether an outdoorsperson passes the test. Otherwise, he or she will be perpetually stuck in that hellish bog of "dude."

Know a good story or two to spin around the campfire. Even though hunters and fishers like to hear about the big one hanging in the living room, they especially relish the ones that got away. That means the listeners can try their hands at capturing them. Some outdoorswomen are defensive about their outdoors expertise. But the best way to demonstrate your ability is through action, not through endless stories emphasizing how remarkable you are. Being yourself, down-to-earth, and honest is the most effective and fun way of passing the test. Remember that all "dudes" have to go through an initiation period in camp. The fact that you are a woman will not alter this. However, the way you handle the test can endear you to the rest of the gang and help them decide that having a woman in camp is the only way.

Be knowledgeable about your subject matter, yet be open-minded enough to listen and derive worth from another's opinions. Do not talk out of your hat or quote books. The "boys" will figure your knowledge is "book learning" rather than from the school of hard knocks.

The first test a lone woman will have to pass is whether she will shriek and cower at the sound of a cuss word. By dropping an occasional "damn" or "hell" into your stories, the men may be put to ease and not be tongue-tied over having to "clean up" their language. Although cussing a blue streak is going overboard, it is wise to let your audience know you can handle "rough language." From their frame of reference, that means you can handle roughing it outdoors as well. Undoubtedly, mention will be made about, "I don't know any stories clean enough to tell in mixed company," or "Damn—'scuse me, M'am." The best response is a beguiling smile.

*Rule 6:* Do not flirt, act helpless, nor complain. Traditionally, flirting, acting helpless, and complaining about weather, saddle sores, or a fly in the soup have been the "feminine" way of acting. And these three, more than any others, are the reasons why women have been excluded from camps in the past. Many women are in the habit of getting their way and manipulating men by flirting and acting helpless. In a camp, these modes of behavior are self-defeating. The outcome is not as predictable as it is within a civilized context. You could be laughed out of camp. Or at least given the slowest, dumbest, orneriest horse that leaves you 1-mile behind everyone else. In short, you will have the most miserable time of your life and will probably not understand the ill-disguised hostility of your colleagues. You will have acted just as they expected and will be told in no uncertain terms you don't belong in a camp.

*Rule 7:* Be honest and open about normal biological functions. Announce, "I'm going to visit that big old pine over there." Everyone will understand and will wait for you while respecting your privacy and straightforwardness. Outhouses are usually primitive, consisting of a hole dug in the earth, surrounded by a canvas or polyurethane tarp. The nicer ones have a roof made of roughly nailed boards. The ones with seats can be frosted early in the morning. Be sure you are not the first one there in the morning. The one who "defrosts" the seat is usually the butt of jokes throughout the rest of the day. A red bandanna, tied to a tree limb outside the outhouse entrance, is a good "flag" indicating occupancy.

*Rule 8:* Underestimate your horsewomanship capabilities. A hunting or fishing camp revolves around the horse or mule. Because the outfitter and guide are usually part horse themselves, their practical jokes often center around horses. The hunter who brags about his ability with horse-handling can find himself, arms wrapped around the horse's neck, being bucked up a mountainside, much to the delight of the guide.

If your horse knowledge is meager, do not expect assistance from the guide. To him, riding a horse is like climbing stairs—second nature. Carefully watch the guide handle his horse and try to imitate him. The reins are the steering wheel as well as the brake. To cure a horse of moving forward when you try to mount, lead him in front of a tree. On a steep slope, turn the horse around so you mount him on the uphill side. Never mount a horse on its right side nor put on a rain poncho while riding. That's enough to spook any horse.

*Rule 9:* Expect practical jokes and think of a few yourself. Believe it or not, a week or 10 days worth of constant hunting or fishing can become monotonous, and the outfitter and guide have an entire summer or autumn of the same. The only relief is the practical joke. To have one played on you means they think you are an OK person. To play a joke on them will admit you into the inner circle of the outfit.

Check your sleeping bag for toads and your boots for snakes. Before mounting, be certain the saddle is cinched snugly. Examine the reins—sometimes one breaks for no apparent reason while your horse is trotting down the trail. Look into your coffee cup and stir before drinking. Peek underneath the bread of the sandwich to see what kind it is. Bring your rifle or rod into the tent with you at night. Clean face and teeth and apply makeup in the privacy of your own tent and then forget about primping the rest of the day. Refuse a plug of chewing tobacco. It produces lightheaded dizziness and giddiness that is both embarrassing and frightening while riding a horse. Bring your own insect repellent and do not use the homemade varieties that are passed around camp. Wait for your host to take a drink from a strange looking bottle before you gulp any.

As an outdoorswoman, you have an advantage over the average woman. You speak the same language as those with whom you will share camp. Be able to laugh at yourself. Be confident you can deal with whatever arises. See to it that you hunt and fish with all your heart and soul. Then, you will find camp a memorable experience that you will chuckle about years later. Be flexible, open-minded, and expect to smile. You will convert the all-male camp revelers. Next time, they will want to hunt or fish with a woman just like you.

No longer is every woman in camp simply the camp cook.

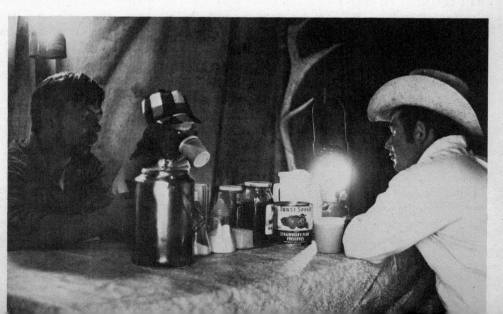

A hunter waits beside a woodland pool late on a snowy afternoon. He knows that soon the ducks will begin to drop in.

# Timber Ducks

## by KEN BOURBON

**ACCORDING TO MANY** sportsmen, the glory years of duck hunting are over. Too many marshes and potholes are being drained. In general, wetlands are vanishing everywhere. The great shooting of the past is finished forever.

But you couldn't prove it by what Lew Baker and I found recently during an annual waterfowling expedition to western Kentucky one fall.

We had made a couple of float trips down the Ohio River, beginning near the Shawneetown, Illinois, bridge as we had often done in the past. But they didn't pan out. In fact we didn't flush as many birds as we had during the lean years.

"Maybe the main flights haven't come this far south yet," Lew said.

We also tried a number of bottomland marshes and

oxbow ponds which had produced mallards on previous trips. Although we did find action, the shooting was nothing to write home about, and the general scarcity of ducks remained a mystery. Then one evening we happened to drop into a crossroads all-night diner for dinner. Among the other patrons were a couple of hunters, unmistakable in mud-spattered hip boots and with duck calls hanging from their necks.

"You fellows finding any birds?" Lew asked.

"Sure," one man answered, "and almost all of 'em back in the timber."

"Thanks a million," Lew said and he meant it.

That was all the tip we needed. Long before daybreak the next morning we were hurrying southward along a wet highway into Hickman County where we turned off toward the Mississippi bottoms and immediately plung-

48

An ice-free pool on a woodland river is a good place to toss out a few decoys at daybreak and to wait.

ed into a pea-soup fog. Slowing down. Lew had trouble finding the cutoff road he wanted, and it was nearly daylight when he at last parked the station wagon beside a rusty old iron bridge which spanned a small and murky stream.

"We're in luck," Lew said as he checked the water. "The level is up and Ole Brinker's woods should be flooded."

From the bridge it is not an easy hike to the woods in the half light. Briars tripped us up. The cover was heavy along both banks and blackberry bushes clutched at my camouflage jacket. Less than 100 yards from our starting point a covey of quail exploded almost from underfoot, and the next sound I heard was the thump- thumping of my heart. A few hundred yards beyond that we could see the first skeletons of oaks, sweet gums and hickories projecting faintly and grotesquely up through the fog. Most were now bare of foliage. Suddenly Lew stopped and held one gloved finger over his lips.

"Listen," he whispered.

Softly at first and then much louder we could hear the gabbling of many ducks in the trees up ahead. Then right away it was drowned out by the same thump-thumping of the heart.

Now we moved very slowly, and the fog was a factor in our favor. It muffled the sound as well as the sight of us, and I hoped we might walk within shooting range of the birds. We were getting closer and closer, hunched close to the ground. But that's when the unexpected happened again. From a puddle we hadn't seen, less than 15 yards away, four wood ducks flushed and scrambled to get out of the tight quarters. Two double guns came up automatically.

I swung on the closest bird and knew I missed the instant I pulled the trigger because I didn't follow through. The second shot only ventilated the fog. Lew's markmanship was just as bad. But what a chain reaction the shooting started!

It's hard to say how many ducks had been concentrated in Brinker's woods, but the shooting put every last one in the air with a roar of wings and quacking. Some hurried completely away. A few circled above in bewilderment. Below them Lew and I stood also in bewildered shock at the spectacle, forgetting to load the guns. A few minutes later, all was quiet once more.

"Well," Lew laughed, "we really blew that one."

"It's not the first time," I answered, "and won't be the last. So let's get settled back in the woods in case any of those birds come back."

"And I'm betting they will," Lew said.

Nowhere in the woods, which covered about 40 acres was the water more than a foot deep, and more often it was only a few inches. A majority of the trees were oaks, and what had attracted the ducks was a bumper crop of acorns as well as a measure of shelter. Lew hunkered down beside an old deadfall, and I found a hiding place between the dark trunks of two oaks which were growing only a short distance apart. What followed was shooting as good as any waterfowler has a right to expect nowadays. A single wood duck buzzed in low just over the treetops and then with wings set, started to settle just to my right. I missed that one, too, with both barrels. But it didn't matter because moments later the action continued. Four mallards dropped in, and I bagged a hen to break the ice. I heard Lew shooting from behind me. Only 10 or 15 minutes after that we had our limits of mixed mallards, woodies and teal.

A valuable lesson is in this incident for most waterfowlers. Ordinarily we think of duck hunting as an open water sport—a blind on a windswept marsh, large spreads of decoys, a dog racing out to retrieve downed ducks, scarlet sunrises and sunsets, punters poling skiffs out to comfortable blinds, Franklin stoves and cozy clubhouses for after-the-hunt drinks. But other types of duck hunting exist as well and one which too many sportsmen overlook is gunning in the flooded woods.

Except for the woodies, or summer ducks, which even nest in hollow trees, not one of our common ducks can be considered a woodland species. And none really spend much, if any, time in the timber expect during autumn when certain nuts and fruits ripen and fall to the ground or, in this case, water. Then it is a different matter. Many species utilize the woodland cafeterias, nearly all of which are in the tier of southern states.

A federal survey 10 years ago listed between 45 and 50 million acres of wet woodlands. Included are forests flooded only periodically, swamp forests, damp hardwood bottomlands and stream borders. Of course this acreage is much smaller today because of destructive channelization and "watershed management" programs of the U.S. Soil Conservation Service and U.S. Army Corps of Engineers. Some of the most disastrous results (both to ducks and duck hunters) of this drainage have been in the Obion River bottoms of Tennessee and in the White River bottomlands of Arkansas. Both regions have long been famous for their hunting in flooded timber, but this splendid sport is being drained away at great cost and for no good reason at all.

But enough of this type of habitat still exists to concern waterfowlers. Although ducks—particulary mallards, blacks and woodies—will eat a great variety of forest foods at times, including every type of acorn, the pin-oak acorn is the most adaptable to wet situations and a pin-oak forest provides the ideal place to find concentrations of ducks during a good part of the hunting season in sections of the southeast.

Mallards like to linger in flooded timber, and it is a splendid place to hunt them, especially late in the season.

There are a good many ways to hunt the flooded pin-oak forests. The simplest is just to wade out through the shallow water accompanied by a good retriever. This jump-shooting method is much more productive in the early part of the season when hunting pressure has not yet made the birds too wary. Toward the tag end of the open season, few ducks can be bagged this way.

It is far better to pick a spot in the woods and wait there for incoming birds. It may be worthwhile to build a blind either at water level or a platform in a tree. But it may also be possible to take advantage of the timber and to blend well enough into the background. Camouflage clothing or netting or burlap are useful for this purpose.

In some areas the hunters do not use decoys, either because they are unnecessary or are too heavy and troublesome to lug long distances over soggy ground. But it has been my experience that they greatly improve the chances of success. Many times I have seen mallards plunge readily into a small spread of blocks, but otherwise circle warily at treetop elevation before dropping down to feed.

Some experienced waterfowlers may disagree, but it also seems to me that calling is more effective in a woodland hunt than when shooting from a blind on an open marsh. It certainly is true that some of America's best duck callers have long been products of hunting in the Stuttgart, Arkansas, area where the best of it is woodland shooting.

A good retrieving dog is worth its weight in gold when hunting the timber.

Because it is a great deal more like upland gunning than marsh or blind hunting, a different type of gun is preferable. Nationwide, the duck hunter's favorite is the 12-gauge pump gun with either a full- or modified-choke barrel. But a woodland shooter might be wise to consider a 12-gauge double, either side-by-side or superposed, with the same short barrels (one improved, one modified) he would use for ruffed grouse. On many occasions the shooting may be much more like grouse hunting in the thickets than traditional duck hunting.

Some of the best shooting I can recall in a career spent outdoors has been woodland waterfowling, and it occurred deeper in the past than I like to admit — at a time over 20 years ago when I was a game warden in a southern Ohio county. This was a hilly hardwood region not even on a minor waterfowl flyway, and duck hunting was not an important sport locally. But squirrel hunting *was* good, and I spent all my spare time in the field looking for them.

One afternoon I found a series of woodland ponds on which I spotted a number of ducks. Woodies, I guessed at first, but on crawling closer saw that they were blacks. At that time the season on wood ducks was closed but was open on blackjacks, so I crawled still closer and bagged two when they flushed. On dressing the birds I found that both had been feeding heavily on white-oak acorns. It didn't seem possible that they could swallow them.

But that rang a bell. During the next couple of weeks, I checked out many other ponds surrounded by oak forests in the country, found ducks on a few and enjoyed more shooting than I ever dreamed was possible in that region. You can take my word that I've never known any better ducks on the table than those acorn-eating blacks.

Of all types of duck hunting, the flooded timber variety may be the least predictable. Unless strictly controlled by artificial damming devices, annual flooding cannot be depended upon and some woodland ponds are likely to dry up during a rainless late summer. Even more unpredictable are pin-oak mast crops. Acorns may be very abundant for several years straight running; then suddenly one autumn there are none. Right now biologists are experimenting with controlled water levels to see if they can somehow achieve a guaranteed mast crop year after year.

From all this it certainly seems obvious that individual hunters — or groups of them — can produce at least a modest amount of shooting for themselves simply by flooding their own forests (which they lease or own outright) every fall. Often this is neither an expensive nor difficult job in flat or bottomland country. A low dike or embankment may be all that is necessary. One way to get more details is to check with the local state waterfowl biologist or with the nearest management agent of the U.S. Fish and Wildlife Service.

A good retrieving dog is more valuable when hunting the timber than many hunters suspect. Last fall in eastern Maryland, Karl Harlow and I noticed that mallards were passing up our spread of decoys on a small marsh and instead were flying high overhead until they reached a woods about ¼-mile away.

"I believe they're dropping right down through the treetops," Karl commented after studying the flights through binoculars.

"In that case," I answered, "let's get over there and wait for them."

Half an hour later Karl and I, plus Karl's black Labrador, Jackson, were slogging out into the flooded timber. Not far from the edge of the trees we found three red freshly fired 12-gauge hulls.

"Somebody has been here just ahead of us," Karl commented.

They had indeed because not far beyond that spot we surprised a greenhead unable to fly, but which Jackson easily retrieved. Its wing was broken. And beyond that the dog retrieved a second mallard. The hunters who preceded us had crippled the two birds which, without dogs, they were unable to retrieve in the standing timber. That should be a lesson to all waterfowlers.

The next few hunting seasons for ducks are calculated to be good ones. But if you're not finding them in familiar haunts, check farther into the flooded woodlands. That could be your ticket to better gunning.

This is a young caribou bull. Old-timers normally carry a white mane on the brisket area.

This is another young caribou bull heading for the George River in northern Quebec.

# BOWHUNTING FOR TROPHY

**MY INDIAN GUIDE, PETE WANISH,** and I had been watching an age-old caribou trail that led from one of Quebec-Labrador's Torngat Mountains down to the George River in northern Quebec. Trails spread out from the mountain top like a giant spider web. Each path was cut deep by centuries of caribou migrations. It was here that we hoped to find a good bull which I would take with bow and arrow.

Dark storm clouds blasted over the mountains and then dumped a torrent of snow and rain on us as we sat beneath a gnarled cedar tree along the riverbank. I was cold, and Pete was shivering. We were almost totally drenched even under protective layers of raingear.

Several small bands of cows, calves and immature bulls filtered through our area. One minute caribou would be crossing to our shore, and then in the next, a group would swim from our side back to the opposite bank. Caribou are funny; they seldom have a clear idea of where they are headed and frequent changes of course are the rule. With a rifle, harvesting an animal would be easy. A bow and arrow hunt is tougher.

The white-maned bulls, the trophy animals, were conspicuous by their absence. We'd watched as many as 500 animals daily, but nothing had the headgear I was looking for. It would be a trophy bull or nothing.

Pete finally tired of glassing the opposite mountain and stood up to stretch his legs. He grunted at me to stay where I was while he moved out to survey the situation on our side of the river. Ten minutes later he ghosted back indicating big bull caribou with sweeping motions of his arms over his head. His black eyes glittered, and he urged me to follow him quickly. I grabbed my Bear compound, left the comfort of the makeshift cedar blind and stepped into the full fury of an autumnal Quebec storm. I hardly noticed.

Thirty feet away Pete was peeling out of his raingear. A sneak was necessary he hissed, and raingear was too noisy in the bush. The wind and rain lashed at my clothing and any portion of my body that wasn't wet when I left the blind, was instantly soaked as my Go Suit came off.

Bow in hand, I followed my guide and paused only briefly to catch a glimpse of caribou antlers moving evenly through a stand of black spruce 75 yards away. They were massive. A forest was on the march through a full gale wind.

Richey (left) glasses with binoculars from a cedar blind while Pete points out crossing caribou.

# CARIBOU
## by DAVID RICHEY

The Indian led the way in a bent-over crouch. We hoped to close to within 30 yards of the animals. I nocked a broadhead but intervening cover was skimpy, and I held little hope of reaching my effective range.

We moved closer trying to take advantage of the meager growth, when I spotted the rear bull looking our way. Three animals were spaced out over a 10-yard area, and once the one bull stopped, the others halted too. We had stopped and knelt behind a clump of willow with nothing between us and them but rocks and dwarf spruce. The vegetation had given out, and we were still too far from the bulls for a shot.

We froze while the three angled out of the bush. They moved away from us in a ground-eating gait that enables them to cover distance rapidly and easily. They paused once at 60 yards, and I could see that one bull was the trophy I'd traveled 2,000 miles to find—a double shovel animal with antlers curving at least 60 inches. I kicked myself for not having taken a shot at 30 yards even through a screen of brush. His were the only set of hardened antlers in the group. The others carried racks still covered with velvet.

The caribou knew something was wrong but couldn't pinpoint the danger until a blast of arctic air circled and betrayed us. The herd bull caught our scent and turned toward the rocky beach along the George River. They were heading for safety on the far shore.

We ran a wind-sprint for the river and arrived just in time to see the three bulls dash down the rocky riverbank right toward us. The boss bull was in the lead and 50 yards away when I saw him. We eased close to the shore and allowed him to come within bow range. My heart was a booming base drum in my chest, and I was sweating in spite of the cold.

The white-maned bull approached to within 20 yards before I came to full draw. I tracked him briefly and made a smooth release. But in the excitement I'd forgotten about the particularly steep downward angle, shot too high, and the broadhead passed just inches over his spine. The animals spun around and crashed down the beach for 300 yards. My last glimpse of that majestic rack came as the animals swam downstream and out of sight forever.

This was my introduction to caribou hunting. I'd had an easy shot at a bull that would have set the Pope and Young scorers on their ear and had blown it. Since that time I've killed four caribou bulls with a bow, all were trophies any bowhunter would be proud to claim, although none were as large as that lost bull.

I live in Buckley, Michigan, and it's a rough 24-hour drive from home to Montreal where you catch a QuebecAir flight to Schefferville, the jumping off place for caribou hunts at Wedge Hills Lodge on the mighty George River. This camp in prime caribou country is a mere 60 miles south of Ungava Bay where saltwater laps at the northern Quebec coastline.

Albert Fortier, owner of the lodge and AirGava Ltd. (the bush plane service that ferries hunters from Schefferville to camp), was on hand to greet me and the other hunters. We moved my cameras and gear into one of the spacious heated cabins, and he told me in halting English about the large number of caribou he'd just seen up the river. Our flight had been through pea-soup fog, but once we had dropped down for the final approach I too had seen at least 500 animals crossing just upstream from the camp. Getting a trophy here will be a piece of cake I decided.

This section of the George River is subject to frequent late-season storms and squalls. It can be raining one minute, snowing the next, and then the temperature can rise to 60 degrees. I've seen it snowing 100 yards downstream while standing in warm sunshine. This part of the world is the breeding grounds for some of America's fiercest storm systems. Caribou are unbothered.

We spent the first 2 days of the hunt climbing rock-studded mountains in search of a big bull. Many times Pete and I had cows, calves and immature bulls pass within 20 feet of us. I could have shot my bull at almost any time but had decided to hold out for a really nice animal. It was during this time I had muffed my shot at

Dave Richey, an ardent bowhunter, and Pete Wanish (right) check out caribou tracks at a crossing on the George River.

things to people, particularly bowhunters. I found that out for myself. They are not the easiest animals to bring down even at close range.

We'd checked out several crossing sites before making our selection for the third day of hunting. In some places the cover was too meager for concealment, and we passed those up. We wanted our blind to be within 30 yards of a crossing, but it had to provide cover adequate to hide any movements I made while coming to full draw. One spot we chose that didn't produce was behind a jumble of rocks near the shore. We were forced to sit in the open and the relentless storms ravaged us with snow, hail and rain. Several lesser bulls crossed within easy range but all were too small and were passed up.

On each of the following days we chose new blind sites, and although we saw a multitude of animals, none was suitable. I began to wonder if this trip was destined to fail.

My last day in camp dawned cold and snowy. Two inches of fresh snow had fallen during the night and more was drifting down from a grey low sky. Pete told me that if the weather broke and the sun came out we would see caribou. He said it so matter of factly that I felt a surge of anticipation. I'd learned enough in several days of hunting with the Indian that I had confidence in his judgment.

Our Zodiac raft loaded, we pushed off for a 6-mile

the trophy bull. It was a miss I'll long remember.

One morning we glassed two massive bulls moving from one mountain to another. We did our best to catch up and cut the animals off but each time they had too much headstart for us and we lost them. It was now apparent that taking a big bull was going to prove more difficult than I had first believed.

The Quebec-Labrador caribou possess characteristics of both the barren ground and woodland caribou. They have the huge antler growth of other barren ground animals and the large body size of the woodland caribou. Quebec biologists place the number of these animals in excess of 50,000 but only 2,500 permits are issued annually. The low number is one reason camp owners, like Fortier, advise early reservations. Only a limited number of hunters are allowed in each camp and the demand for permits far exceeds the supply.

The caribou along the George River feed primarily on lichens and other low growing browse. They migrate and feed at the same time, stopping only momentarily to clip off a bite of food before continuing. Perhaps this is the reason they switch directions so often.

The accepted method for bowhunters to make the caribou connection is to take up a stand at one of the many caribou crossings. Some may feel this is making things too easy and that little "sport" remains. I disagree. The sight of a big bull at close range does strange

Pete Wanish stands in his Zodiac raft and works Dave Richey and his bull caribou downstream to camp.

upstream run. We bounced over ice-covered rocks, shot up through whitewater rapids and arrived at a migration trail we'd located the previous day. I got out here. Deep ruts were etched in the trail from the sharp hooves of countless passing animals. Several caribou had crossed during the night but all were cows and calves according to my guide.

Pete motored the raft downstream about ½-mile and stashed it on the beach. He then worked his way carefully back to the blind where I was adding the final touches with dead cedar boughs. Once it was ready I made a final check to determine that I could indeed come to full draw and shoot if the opportunity presented itself. Satisfied, I sat back to glass for bulls.

The snow squall changed abruptly to a full scale blizzard. Snow needles were driven down through the blind and within minutes we were shivering uncontrollably. Pete toughed it out for 15 minutes before standing and moving about to gather dead twigs and limbs. A fire wouldn't bother animals like caribou, he told me. Caribou, Pete assured me, were often curious about smoke. I was less than confident about this bit of lore.

Blue smoke soon rose from the struggling fire and stung our eyes, but there was no denying the fact that the warmth was very welcome. We continued to glass the far shore and an hour later my binoculars picked up antlers moving through some willows. Pete and I spotted the animals at the same time, my prowess in this

having improved greatly in the last few days.

A big bull ghosted out of the storm-tossed growth and headed for the river. Another bull, somewhat smaller, trotted to the river and both animals began to swim in our direction.

I nocked an arrow, keeping my head low behind the camouflage of the blind. I raised to one knee and watched the bulls swim hard for shore. Pete asked with small signs and his eyes if I could hit the larger bull when he walked ashore. I nodded that I could, but the thought of missing that easy downhill shot the first day nagged at my confidence. I planned to make a better showing with this one.

Both animals hit the beach at the same time and the smaller one stopped to smell our tracks in the sand. The larger bull, the one I'd selected as my trophy, stared intently at the rising blue column of smoke just in front of me. Maybe the Indian had been telling the truth after all. Both animals were within 20 yards, and my palms felt damp but I couldn't get a clear shot at the larger bull.

They pranced around the beach for several minutes, seemingly undecided about what to do next. They seemed curious about the smoke and human tracks but nevertheless not afraid.

My Bear compound was set at 55 pounds, and I'd been holding it at full draw for so long that my arm muscles were beginning to shake from the strain.

After a long hunt Dave Richey finally shot this big bull at short range. It jumped into the river and swam most of the way across before dying. The hunters then dragged it ashore and took this photo.

## Hunt Cost Information

Wedge Hills Lodge, P.O. Box 1950, Schefferville, P.Q. accepts only 50 hunters per season. The cost of a caribou hunt is approximately $1,000 which includes, lodging, food, guide, raft and motor, and transportation to and from camp from Schefferville.

The additional costs include transportation from the hunter's home to Montreal, Quebec City, or Sept-Isle. A plane ticket via QuebecAir to Schefferville from Montreal and return is (at this time) approximately $225. An additional 50 cents per pound is charged for shipping out caribou meat. The airlines charge approximately $100 for transporting whole caribou antlers.

A nonresident caribou hunting license costs $250 and can be purchased in camp or in Schefferville.

Hunters traveling to Wedge Hills Lodge are advised that one evening must be spent in Schefferville on the return from camp. I'd suggest that hunters make reservations at the Hotel Royale.

This Quebec biologist checks out Dave Richey's bull to determine how old the animal is and how strong the herd of 50,000 seems to be. (Photo courtesy of Kay Richey.)

Slowly I relaxed my draw and watched with growing anxiety as both bulls circled our tracks again, always with the smaller animal between me and my target. It appeared they would either head back across the river or move uphill past us. If they chose to move ahead I would certainly get my shot.

They finally arrived at a decision and the smaller bull led the way up the riverbank and past our blind. I came to full draw a second time, took a deep breath and followed the exposed shoulder of the large bull for an instant before making a smooth confident release. Pete, behind me, gasped and then grinned as the arrow buried itself behind the right shoulder. The animal wheeled and headed downhill for the river while the confused smaller caribou crossed within 10 feet of the blind. I nocked a second arrow and shot as the wounded bull entered the shallow edge of the river. A near miss.

The bull bored through the water with the grace of a Sherman tank until it reached swimming depth. Pete was already scrambling down the shore to fetch the raft. I watched the bull swim strongly until it was within 20 feet of the opposite shore. The muscular action of swimming then forced the arrow out of the animal and flung it 4 feet in the air.

But that was the end of the trail for my bull because the extra cutting motion of the exiting broadhead caused additional bleeding. The animal raised its head high out of the water, circled once in the rushing current and died. The force of the stream flow then caught the caribou and began carrying it downstream toward an ½-mile stretch of whitewater.

I was frantic by the time Pete arrived with the raft. We sped down to the drifting caribou, and I grabbed the antlers. This one wasn't going to get away. We towed it to shore just as we heard the roaring of the whitewater right ahead. The velvet-covered antlers later taped 55 inches on each side and a heavy brow tine and spike swept down over his nose. It was a beautiful rack and a most respectable trophy for a bowhunter. This was a last-ditch effort for a caribou bull. I've taken others since, but none have made such a lasting impression. Caribou hunting has got under my skin, and the only relief is another trip. I'm already booking another hunt at Wedge Hills where the forces of nature keep caribou on the move and make bowhunting for caribou a tense and thrilling experience.

# WHEN THE GEESE COME DOWN

## by HANK BRADSHAW

The author with a Greater Canada shot from a blind beside the North Platte River at Lisco, Nebraska. That's ice floating in the river. Waterfowl hunting can be a cold sport.

**SITTING RIGIDLY,** my hands sweating with anticipation, I pressed my face into the dry, brown leaves of our blind on a flooded farm field in Iowa's Missouri River Valley. Overhead, the wings of the geese swished loudly as they flew over, their shrill voices gabbling like old maids to our decoys on the water. My heart sledged against my ribs. I fingered my shotgun in preparation for the jack-in-the-box leap to my feet that I hoped I'd make if the birds came in.

When they disappeared behind me, I could sense their graceful swing, but I dared not turn my head lest they spot the movement. Tensely I waited, searching from the corners of my eyes for the geese to come around. On my left, my two companions also were motionless.

Finally, from the right, the geese emerged. Pumping slowly came 15 grayish-dark Lesser Canadas, their black heads and white chin straps and long, black necks craning as they studied and announced themselves to our decoys. I didn't answer the call; they were too close. Satisfied, they set their wings and glided in, black webbed feet hanging. When they began to flutter down, I bellered, "Take 'em!"

Up, our three guns boomed almost simultaneously, three geese folded wings and dropped to splash in the water. The others, startled, flattened out, broad wingspreads caught the wind like kites. They veered sharply away as I fired again, missing, and then they were out of range. It always amazes me how fast geese, which appear slow, can get away.

We shoved out of the blind, jabbering, so excited we didn't know what we were saying, wading after the downed birds. Geese do that to a hunter. There's a suspense, a thrill, a sense of skillful accomplishment in fooling a wary band of geese that no other form of wildlife affords. When a goose folds, the gates open and

Clark Reed of Guthrie Center, Iowa, shows off two Lesser Canada geese he bagged from a flock of six we decoyed over a flooded field in the Missouri River Valley of Iowa. Maynard Reece, the wildlife artist, and Dick Ranney, Director of Tourism for the Iowa Development Commission, are proud of the geese they also bagged from the flock.

pent-up feelings rush from the hunter to leave him weak with uninhibited emotion, as if headily intoxicated.

The reason is simple. Geese, regardless of variety, are the aristocrats of waterfowl. Inspiring with their clean, trim body lines, elusive by character, a moving part of the scenery as their V's float through the sky, their wild, far-flung cries carrying the image of the lonely arctic tundras from which they fly—these elements build up so much desire in the minds and breasts of hunters that every hard-earned goose becomes a trophy.

Goose hunting success is being shared by more outdoorsmen than ever before, thanks to improved knowledge of where and how to hunt geese, and to the fact that goose numbers are constantly increasing despite the decline of ducks. Previously, geese were more or less bonus birds for duck hunters, with most hunters going through life without enjoying the crowning climax of shooting a goose. But now the goose has supplanted the duck as the magnet that keeps boots on waterfowlers.

If you really want to see hordes of geese using the Missouri River Valley, visit the area in March when the Blues and Lesser Snows crowd the receding snowline north toward arctic nests. Spectators by the thousands trip to watch concentrations of up to ½-million geese feeding in fields or lolling on refuges.

The Valley, a wide, gumbo-soiled, grain-rich plain spreading between sister strips of loess hills, one in Iowa and northern Missouri, one in Nebraska, is the dividing line between the Central flyway west and the

"Firing line" hunters behind a bush near a refuge, hoping a flock goes out or in low enough for a shot. The two Whitefronts on the ground did.

Geese traveling south down the Missouri
River Valley, pushed by a storm in Canada.

Mississippi flyway east. In the fall, farmers, mostly hunters themselves, will usually grant hunting permission to those who appear responsible. Hunters may also register for a four-man blind at Iowa's controlled State Hunting Area of Riverton Wildlife Area or Forney's Lake near Thurman. There is an "open" water area on Riverton, too.

To me, the Missouri River Valley is one of the country's great goose hunting areas. An almost constant filtering of the big birds moves down river from the season opening in late September until it closes in early December. They loaf through Iowa, Nebraska and Missouri, feeding luxuriously on waste corn and soybeans left in fields by mechanical pickers. Severe snow storms up north (covering food) will push hundreds of thousands through at once in a seemingly endless stream, but in the absence of storms, geese fly by the calendar rather than the weather. The best hunting hours are from dawn to shortly after sunrise, and, surprisingly, on warm, sunshiny, lazy afternoons. The peak of the flight comes after mid-October and continues to be excellent until mid-November.

In most other areas of the Midwest, hunting geese has become more or less a "hunting near a refuge" operation. Migrating geese have learned that safety lies on refuges, so they use them as roosting areas and hedge-hop from one to another all the way south. The principal opportunity for hunters comes when the geese fly out of the refuge to feed, or when returning.

Iowa refuges along the Missouri River Valley that beckon geese and lure hunters to fringe areas include De Soto Bend Refuge near Missouri Valley, Forney's Lake and Riverton. At Riverton, for example, the brush around the fields and fence-lines off the area and

behind the refuge blinds, are full of hunters hoping for a chance shot at a flying goose.

In Missouri, refuge stopovers are the rule. Squaw Creek and Swan Lake National, and Fountain Grove State refuges have been long established, with large goose acquaintanceships. The latter two are partially open for controlled hunting. In addition, nearby farmers and lessors rent out pits to day hunters. Some

A goose call, blown by one who understands both it and the geese, is of great assistance on a goose hunt, no matter where.

A flock of Canadas going over our blind near Swan Lake, Missouri, part refuge, part hunting area.

The third method is frowned on by sportsmen. This is known technically as "pass-shooting," but is ignominiously referred to as "sky-busting." These sky-busters, whose numbers have increased hideously since the advent of magnum (long-range) guns and shells, line the edges of refuges and feed fields to try to scratch down a goose from high-flying flocks. But geese quickly learn to spiral up from and down into the refuge or field, crossing fence lines high enough to be beyond range of whatever guns the sky-busters elect to use. But still the shooters blaze away, making the geese so jittery they become difficult to decoy to anything but a field filled with hundreds of feeding geese. When a sky-buster does nick a goose, chances are it will cripple away to die later.

At Devil's Lake, North Dakota, where I have hunted, this rim of gun-strainers around the refuge is jokingly called "the firing liners." However, in a private field, we had "firing liners" of our own a few years ago, near Kerrobert, Saskatchewan. We had dug pits in a field of wheat stubble and swaths, with exclusive permission from the farmer. A contigent of White-fronts had begun to use the field the afternoon before. As

The author in a conservation commission pit-blind on state-owned land around the refuge of Forney's Lake, near Thurman, Iowa. These pit-blinds may be reserved ahead of time by applying to the commission at Forney's Lake. In case of no-shows, a drawing is held the morning of the hunt. This is a pair of blues that swooped down to see why our decoys had stopped in front of our blind.

lessors have organized private hunting clubs. In North Dakota, Devil's Lake State Refuge is a gathering spot. In South Dakota, with exorbitant fees to non-residents, the river itself is a state refuge—geese roost on the big impoundments above the dams.

There are three goose hunting methods widely practiced. The first is the method we were using: selecting a water hole or a feed field on the flyway in a wide, flat area that would be naturally attractive to geese which like to be able to spot danger from afar when they light. Then build a blind or dig a pit (to be refilled), set out decoys, and call flocks that go by.

The second method involves following geese when they leave a refuge, discover with binoculars where they come down to feed, then obtain the farmer's permission to set out a spread of decoys, blind or pit before the geese return (you hope) to feed next morning. Here, too, a seductive call helps if the geese change their minds (usually because of a shift in the wind) and decide to bypass the field.

With either method, geese frequently can be killed with No. 6 shot, maximum loads. It is never necessary to use shot larger than No. 2's. If the geese come in, they'll be within 40 yards. Few cripples result.

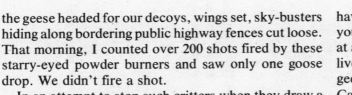

A flock of Canadas going out to feed from a refuge, low enough to give the "firing line" hunter a shot.

the geese headed for our decoys, wings set, sky-busters hiding along bordering public highway fences cut loose. That morning, I counted over 200 shots fired by these starry-eyed powder burners and saw only one goose drop. We didn't fire a shot.

In an attempt to stop such critters when they draw a permit to shoot within refuges that allow hunting, both federal and state authorities have, in many places, restricted the number of shells hunters can take along, and some refuges rule that all shots must be taken when geese are within a specified distance of the blind. Swan Lake, Horicon Marsh in Wisconsin, Horseshoe Lake in Illinois, Oklahoma's Tishimingo, Iowa's Forney's and Riverton and many others allow only a few shells per hunter and have found that more, rather than fewer, geese are taken with much less shooting.

For those who want to get the maximum enjoyment from goose hunting, experts agree that decoy shooting is the ticket. Here are 11 tips that will make geese come easier: (1) Use a lot of decoys, even if many are inexpensive shells or silhouettes; (2) Use the kind of decoys resembling the geese you're hunting. Whitefronts, for example, will avoid lighting near other geese, although sometimes other decoys will attract them within range. When using more than one kind of decoy (Canadas, Whitefronts, Blues and Snows) keep the species separated; (3) If you hunt geese and ducks from the same setout on water, put the goose decoys alone. Only once have I seen geese try to light with duck decoys; (4) If you have learned to call well, call a lot. If not, don't call at all—you'll scare the geese. Practice with records or live geese until you are good; (5) Sound the call of the geese you are trying to inveigle—"Ah—onk" for a Canada, a single high-pitched syllable for a Blue or Snow, a difficult double-noted fluting call for a Whitefront; (6) When geese have committed themselves, have wings set and are coming in, wise callers desist. A single false note will flare the birds; (7) Elect a captain of the blind. Usually a caller, he should be the only one to watch the geese and signal when to shoot. Others look to their shooting area; (8) With geese, more than one caller in a blind helps. Geese are used to the gabble-gabble of a flock. With ducks, usually only a hen or two converse; (9) In a blind, the top of the head and shining face of a hunter are his worst enemies. Move one or show the other and geese are gone; (10) Let geese settle well down over the decoys, refrain from jumping up to shoot at outer range. A goose can flare a long way fast and as soon as you move, he will flare; (11) When you shoot at a goose, swing out ahead of the long neck. Force yourself to pay no attention to the more attractive, large body. When the neck crumples, you've made a killing shot—a shot in the body might only cripple.

Outwitting and bagging a goose is a tremendous thrill, despite their increasing numbers. A feat you'll remember for a lifetime.

# How to Pick a Hunting Pack Trip...

A big game outfitter should know his hunting country well and where the game is located.

# ...and Then Prepare For It

# by ERWIN A. BAUER

**BEFORE DAYBREAK** of a snowy morning in the Montana Rockies one October, Tom Moore wolfed down breakfast in a smoky tent and stumbled out uncertainly into total blackness where his guide and two horses were waiting. Stiff and sore from a 25-mile long ride into camp the day before, it was painful just to climb into a cold saddle. Tender knees, tortured by those long hours in the stirrups, complained as the two rode away, following a thin, still invisible trail toward higher country.

Moore tried to retreat deeper into a down jacket to escape the penetrating cold. He stuffed a cold hand in a pocket and clutched the saddle horn with the other. Despite the multiple discomforts, the hunter suddenly felt exhilarated because this was opening day of an elk season he had anticipated for a long, long time. Moore's uneasiness dissolved into visions of bragging-size antlers dominating his living room back home in Detroit. This was going to be the hunting experience of his lifetime.

But too soon the dream began to fall apart. When his horse lunged to cross a deadfall in the trail, the strain was too great on a rotten cinch strap, and Moore was bucked off onto the ground. After daylight finally came and the damage was repaired, it was soon obvious that the guide was lost. The two spent the rest of the day just trying to navigate in unfamiliar country searching for trails, when they should have been seriously hunting.

And so it went for most of the following week—and the duration of the hunt. The equipment was bad, the guiding was second rate and only two of six hunters who shared that camp had seen male elk. Just one of these had scored. Instead of high adventure in one of America's finest wilderness areas, it turned out to be a dismal trip. All of the hunters in camp pondered whether they would ever bother to go big game hunting again.

Still Tom Moore (which, incidentally, is not his correct name) had a big chance and blew it. Late on an overcast afternoon toward the tag end of the trip, the two had spotted a herd of elk slowly drifting and grazing unalarmed across an open alpine meadow punctuated with small islands of stunted spruce. The animals were almost ½-mile away—too far to squeeze off a shot—but one of the elk (through glasses) was clearly a trophy bull.

"If we can hurry to that next ridge," the guide correctly figured, "we can intercept them, and you will have a 200- to 250-yard shot."

What followed can be blamed only on Tom Moore because the strategy worked perfectly. By the time he finally reached a shooting position, he was puffing and pumping so hard from the exertion that he couldn't begin to hold his rifle steady. His first shot at good range was the only one. An instant later his target had van-ished forever into the nearest dark timber. Tom should have anchored that elk where it once stood.

The preceding incidents are as true as they are tragic. Unfortunately they are fairly typical. A serious and enthusiastic outdoorsman had saved long and diligently to take a big game hunt. His anticipation had been great, and maybe even unrealistic. Something he had envisioned had turned all sour. But the truth is that the bitter experience could have been avoided. Nowhere nowadays is big game hunting an easy bed of roses where trophies are guaranteed—and it certainly shouldn't be. Nor is there any excuse for such a total

Top target of most big game hunts nowadays is a prime bull elk. A head like this is worth a lot of effort and hard preparation.

failure as Tom Moore's.

So exactly where did Tom Moore go wrong? To begin, he did not choose his packer—his outfitter—wisely. And he did not prepare himself to go on a pack trip hunt with any packer. Both can (and did) prove to be very deadly sins.

Let's consider the packers first. Today's packer in

Canada or the American West is a busy, hard-working man with a considerable investment in livestock, tacking and camping equipment. He may be a rancher who only outfits hunters as a seasonal sideline. Or he may be in recreation full-time, taking out fishing trips in the summer. However, which ever category, full- or part-time, does not necessarily establish his credentials. But the investment, plus the short seasons (and hunting seasons tend to grow shorter all the time) explain what often seems to be the extremely high cost. When a sportsman is spending from the $150 minimum up to $300 per day to go hunting, as he will be, he should be doubly certain that the packer he selects is the right one.

Outfitters have their share of unique problems. Although these should not be the concern of a client, it is well that he know about them. The exploding demand for available hunting permits nowadays and the lottery system for drawing (as in Wyoming and elsewhere) make it difficult to plan too far ahead. Sometimes a packer does not know exactly how many hunters he will have until only a few months before opening day. So he has a hard time hiring guides—or at least *qualified* guides who are not only experienced hunters, but who know the hunting country. Too often the elk guide in camp may be the town barber or bartender the rest of the year.

There is another packer problem to consider. On the surface it may appear to be an exciting, even an easy

(Above and right) Packing in the meat and trophies is one of every outfitter's standard services.

way to make a good living in the great outdoors—and this has attracted many men who are not entirely qualified into the business. They do not realize until too late what a tough trade it is. To be perfectly candid, there are many packers hanging on who should not be, and it is too easy to engage one. Their equipment is inadequate, poorly maintained, and their horses may not be in condition for the terrible daily use on rough mountain trails. Failures, turnovers and sell-outs are high. It is well to keep these things in mind.

Of course there are exceptions, but a hunter's best bet is a packer who is not a newcomer to the business and who has been operating in the same area for a long time — the longer the better. The odds are higher that he will be experienced, that he will understand all the problems of packing and such headaches as poor weather and game scarcity, but still likes to hit the trail every fall. There also is no substitute to really knowing the country when you are hunting big game trophies.

When you definitely pick a packer, you will have to put down a substantial deposit at the same time to reserve definite dates. That is another reason to deal only with reliable persons. Initial outfitter contact can be made in more ways than there is room to mention here, but that is less important than what follows anyway. Our first advice is to inquire of several outfitters, not just one, no matter where or which big game you plan to hunt. Then begin a serious inquiry of all.

(Above) End of a successful hunt in Alberta during which three fine bull elk were collected.

(Right)A hunter in good shape and with a good outfitter can figure on bagging outstanding trophies such as this moose.

Hunters must be in tiptop shape and have good equipment to make the most of a big game hunt in western mountains.

Ask exactly how long the packer has been packing in his current area. A couple of years is not enough. Inquire about his guides and his horses. Are his guides relatives, reliable, experienced, or pickups just for a few weeks? Ask for several references (of other hunters) and preferably of some who live near enough to you to be contacted in person or at length by phone. Then check out all of the references and do not pull any punches when you ask them about the quality of their hunts and the service they received. Find out if the horses were good, well treated, if there were always enough to go around. Ask them especially if they know of any dissatisfied sportsmen because it is unlikely any outfitter (in his right mind) will provide names of unhappy clients. You have to locate them, if they exist, on your own. Also check out these unhappy ones, keeping in mind, fairly, that their problems may be their own, rather than the outfitters.

Again with exceptions, the typical, veteran big game outfitter is not a garrulous man, at least not very soon in a new acquaintance. So proceed warily with the person who makes grand promises, who guarantees game, or who otherwise comes on too strong in the beginning. The man you select should be duly licensed by his state or province, if it is required, and he should be a member in good standing of his own state's guide's and outfitter's association. Neither of these assures that the man will be qualified or capable, but they are an added indication.

Almost always the packers who are heavily booked, perhaps well into the future, are the ones who produce. Double check the ones with too many open dates. Keep in mind also that a great reputation isn't everything; it just might be the result of one successful trip with one prominent outdoor writer who has a large audience.

During a long career spent riding and tramping in the Rocky Mountains, I have met my share of packers, have hunted with many and still treasure most of the memories. I have also talked with many, in and out of season, about their relations with hunters and of course about their problems. An overwhelming concensus is that too many non-resident sportsmen arrive in camp totally unprepared mentally, but especially physically, to go big game hunting in the mountains. It is hard to disagree with them.

To hunt elk (which might be considered the most typical of all big game, both in habits and habitat), a hunter must be prepared for high altitude and often

formidable terrain, for long hours of riding, for hiking and climbing, usually on steep non-trails. Weather can range from balmy to bitter in a few minutes. As much as possible he must prepare himself for these things, all of which are trying.

Altitude may be the toughest because there is no way an eastern or midwestern man can acclimate to mile-high and more conditions at near sea level. But he *can* travel to the mountains a few days before his hunt begins to become better accustomed to the thin atmosphere. He can hike forest trails, rent a horse, go fishing, do almost anything for an on-the-spot tune-up.

Admittedly riding at home may not be practical, but

Even after packing in on horseback, a long hike on foot was necessary to bag this black bear in high country.

Most hunters like Howard Copenhaver here are hard-working, conscientious capable men who relish the wilderness hunt.

just a little bit of it on local bridle trails can go far toward toughening up muscles in the legs and the behind. There are riding rental stables around most communities in the United States. But getting the legs in shape by running, hiking, jogging is another matter altogether; it's easy for anyone to do these activities wherever he lives.

For instance how about walking to work for a month or more, instead of riding, before the big trip? Walk up any/all stairs instead of taking elevators. Make it a hard and fast rule. Jogging is terrific and so is swimming. Work out in the nearest sports stadium; daily climb—over and over, always increasing the number of times—from running track to the top of the bleachers. It's handy, and it's free.

The best single thing a large percentage of eastern/southern/midwestern big game hunters can do is to lose weight, lots of it—to trim bodies down as lean as possible. There are more advantages here than can possibly be enumerated, including the main one of just feeling better. The weight watching should begin months before the hunt is scheduled. Assume you are 20 pounds overweight, which is exactly like carrying a 20-pound rucksack on your back—or 30 or more pounds at higher elevations. Get rid of it, and the steepest ridges become remarkably easier to climb. Obviously a mountain horse can also travel farther, faster and be steadier afoot with a light load (rider) than a heavy one.

Good physical conditioning is vital in still other ways which are difficult to define or measure—as in the hunt-er's mental attitude. Much big game habitat in western North America is awesome to say the least. It is a land of narrow trails, sheer canyon walls, sweeping panoramas and windswept plateaus which are likely to intimidate a flatlander, especially if it is his first exposure to such environment. But the better he feels about his physical ability, and his ability to cope, the more confident he will feel when climbing near the top of the continent, and the more he will be able to concentrate on hunting. And certainly the more he will enjoy it.

"Failure," veteran Wyoming elk and mule deer guide Bruce Johnson confided recently, "far more often can be blamed on a hunter's physical condition that on his rifle—whatever it is—and his ability to use it. I've had countless crack shots in camp, clients who could shoot rings around me, but I couldn't get them up among the elk. Like all big game now, the elk are usually high."

Not too many years ago it was much easier than now to bag a really splendid bull elk or sheep or moose or caribou if you had the time and could afford a good outfitter. But that has changed drastically, and increased hunting pressure is a primary reason. This pressure has resulted in "harvesting" much more or most of the annual surplus of big game, especially of the larger, most desirable male animals. So there are not as many trophies to hunt, and the fewer are warier—much warier. You have to hunt harder, farther, longer, often in more formidable country, to score. That can be pure agony or the highest adventure, depending on your physical condition. Training seriously for a month or so before the hunt can more than double the odds in your favor, according to L.D. Frome, a busy and successful outfitter of Afton, Wyoming.

"The record book heads still exist in numbers. But I can look over each new group of hunters," he admitted last fall, "and from their bulging waistlines, pretty much predict which will score and which will not."

On the other hand, many outfitters could themselves benefit from urging their hunters to diet and shape up in the months before open season. Most don't bother. And when hunters finally arrive for the initial ride (often a long one) to base camp, the outfitter might begin with a short basic course in horsemanship. Riding correctly can spare any dude plenty of soreness which might linger through the whole trip. It would also raise the client's level of confidence.

Probably the single best bit of advice to outfitter and sportsman alike, on starting a trip, is to alternate riding with walking. Get off and walk when the riding becomes too uncomfortable, too painful; climb back into the saddle when you get tired of walking—and don't be ashamed to do it. The soreness you save may mean the difference between failure and the greatest hunting trip of your life.

Summed up: Pick your packer carefully and then prepare for him. Carefully.

# Ride the Quiet Waterways to Find Squirrels

## by CHARLES J. FARMER

**OCTOBER ON THE NEW RIVER** near Boone, North Carolina, is so delightfully pleasant that a smooth-bored squirrel hunter tends to experience strong, but erratic impulses of guilt. But, a bushytail stalker really shouldn't feel guilty, you know. Sport is sport. Squirrel hunting is, by most standards, wonderful business with a smattering of rugged outdoors pinched in to keep squirrelers from believing they are in *easy* heaven. There is a slight semblance of work brewed into the conventional, dry land sport and that has its rewards. But I am still hard-pressed to find an inkling of anything that bears the softest hint of labor involved when floating for the chattering tree dwellers.

The mist hangs low over the lazy, fall stream. You and your partner knife through the veil of puff clouds that hatch off the sunrise water. Only the gurgle of the paddles, as they bite into the clear, cold liquid, break the shrouded stillness of the drift through nature.

Eyes scan the trunks and limbs above the rhododendron-frocked banks. Stands of oak and beech

draw fair attention. But the squirrel boys come unglued when they drift up on a patch of hickories. "Hickories," they whisper to each other, knowing full well that neither hunter has to be forewarned. The grays, foxes and a myriad of chicaree reds will be cutting their teeth on green nuts. "Squirrel gold" they call those hickory fruits. The stern man back paddles for more reading time, and the first impulse is to reach and touch the cold steel of the tight-bored thunder stick stowed within handy reach. The bow man slides his paddle under the seat and ever so slowly reaches for the 12-gauge. He stares down each and every hickory as though threatened by the very presence of the shagbark trees. The twitch of a tail, the unnatural "lump" of fuzz resting on a limb, the panicked scurrying of tree trunk racers and ground romping antics of the foxes—the signs that capture eyes and mind.

There it is. The flicker. Mysteriously looming big and bold in a jungle of confusing limbs and leaves. The bead is there without hesitation, and the first rocking "thud" of the morning blisters the misty silence. The autoloader belches again but not because of a first shot miss. Those river hunters seldom embarrass themselves like some of us do. The first gray fell hard and in doing so, spooked another hiding below and originally out of sight. The blue canoe is angled into shore and two, hickory-plump squirrels are dropped in the game bag. "Darn good shooting, Willy," the stern man said in a whisper as his eyes scanned the green nuts hanging

Paradise found! A slow murky stream winds through squirrel country in October. Watch carefully in the foilage overhead.

above in thick clusters. "Thanks . . . let's get going. It's your turn." Clement C. Smith and Willy Washburn Stovall switch canoe positions. That is the custom. Hit or miss, the shooting position in the bow is rotated. What is fair is fair on the river and there's plenty of action to go around.

River floating for squirrels is not new nor is the sport confined in any way to the streams of North Carolina. In fact, there are only a few states in the country that cannot boast of good to excellent floating and shooting. States in the Rocky Mountain west and southwest, for instance, do not have significant numbers of gray or fox squirrels. Some areas lack good squirrel habitat. Others don't have the water, or at least the nice, gentle float streams required for a slow, peaceful drift into squirrel land. Midwestern, southern and eastern states provide the best opportunities by far. And hunters can usually find good squirrel hunting close to home.

Aside from sandwiching two, pleasant sports together—boating and hunting—float shooting has a multitude of advantages. At a time of shrinking habitat, float streams open up thousands of acres for squirrel stalking. Depending on the water navigation laws in each state, hunters have the right to float from one point to another. Many outstanding float streams meander through federal, state and county owned lands. Other streams course through a mixture of public and private lands and hunters can plan their shooting, put-in and take-out points, along public access areas. Perhaps the most important advantage of floating is the ability of gaining access into areas that might otherwise be blocked by private lands and roads—or no roads at all. Because those areas are restricted, hunting pressure is usually kept to a minimum and top quality shooting results. I have not found it difficult, on the other hand, to obtain permission from private landowners to hunt river bottom stretches by canoe. Where farmers sometimes balk at granting permission to dry land hunters, floaters seem to receive special consideration. That is why it is a good idea, when there is any doubt concerning land ownership or access, to obtain permission first.

The slow, silent water stalk by canoe, rubber boat or john boat is a positive advantage and a method that puts squirrels in the bag. Alert to the sounds and techniques of foot hunters, grays and foxes are among the wariest of game animals. However, an approach by water, even through areas that are heavily hunted, usually fools them. Squirrels seem to react to boats as though they were merely logs floating downstream. On numerous occasions, I have drifted to within 20 yards of bushytails resting or cutting nuts on tree limbs. They showed no fear and that was their downfall. Some squirrels have even given me enough time to center them in the cross hairs of a scoped .22. What may seem at first to be tough, tricky shooting with a rifle, is actually quite practical and effective. Despite the remoteness of an area, the same squirrels would react quite

(Left and below) Author goes ashore to hunt more thoroughly a likely forest of oak and hickory. The collapsible stool can be carried in a game pocket.

differently to foot hunters. I can count on one hand the number of times I have caught squirrels resting or feeding while stalking on land. Ordinarily it took a patient wait of 30 minutes or so before squirrels showed themselves. Even at that, they were still wary. Floating, however, seems to produce more *still* shots than the running variety. Squirrels are caught off guard. And because the floater is sitting still when reading the likely haunts along the banks, he is more apt to spot squirrels before they spot him. Generally speaking, float hunting shots are easier and closer than those of the foot hunter.

## Techniques

Squirrel floating is best accomplished by two hunters who have had experience in handling small boats in currents ranging from mild to moderate. Slow streams set the best pace, and hunters should choose their float stretches accordingly. The trees along a fast stretch of river may hold an abundance of squirrels, but spotting and shooting in heavy current is difficult and sometimes dangerous.

The slower the stream, the better the floating technique works. That means, the man in the rear maneuvers the boat into good shooting position for the bow man. Side and back strokes are made slowly and smoothly to avoid any unnecessary rocking of the boat and spooking

Suddenly around a bend you come across a squirrel — your quarry — high in a treetop. But few will be this easy to spot.

(Above and right) Hunter drifts silently, watching and listening. When he bags a squirrel he beaches the canoe to retrieve it.

game. In gentle currents the boat can be held steady enough, even by novice boaters, to allow for clean shots with either shotgun or rifle. The shotgun has an advantage in bouncy, moderate current where snap shots are necessary. A .22 rifle, on the other hand, is ideal on flat, gentle stretches and does not spook downstream game to the extent a shotgun does. Depending on a hunter's tastes and shooting ability, a full-choked scattergun and a .22 make an ideal combination for river squirrels. Safety, of course, is paramount. Shells and bullets are never held in the chamber until game is spotted. Good gun handling techniques closely follow those used in a duck blind's tight quarters.

When hunters stalk and shoot from a boat, they are employing, I believe, the most successful squirrel hunting technique. Remaining in the boat, becoming "part of the river" are the main reasons why bank squirrels are caught off guard.

There are a couple of slight variations of the "in-boat" technique that also work well under certain conditions. The addition of a lightweight, rubber or plastic-coated (to reduce noise) canoe anchor makes it possible to anchor the boat mid-stream at a particularly good-looking spot. For instance, there is a chance that no squirrels were spotted in advance of a fine looking grove of hickories. Yet you know there has to be squirrel activity there. Anchor slightly downstream from the trees and wait, motionless for about 5 minutes. Chances are good you will spot squirrel activity when animals let down their guard after the "danger" has passed downstream. A drag anchor, (a canvas horse feed bucket

works well) towed behind the boat, does not stop you completely, but is effective for more reading time at good spots. You can also use a drag to slow your speed in moderate current.

Another option, when you do not feel like floating through likely habitat without giving it a closer inspection, is to bank the boat slowly and quietly near shore without getting out. Sit quietly for 10 minutes or so and watch for activity.

The reason for the success of floating is eliminating the danger sounds produced even by the most careful foot stalk. However, when the urge hits to stretch your legs, use that time to your advantage. After floating through a good spot, bank the boat downstream. Stalk carefully upstream along the bank or take a stand with a good vantage. Your dry land break may turn up some shy bushytails.

Remember that grays prefer bottomlands that are densely timbered. They spend most of their time in the trees, while fox squirrels, larger than their gray cousins, prefer the edges of wooded areas near farm lots, grain and corn fields. Fox squirrels tend to feed more on the ground than gray squirrels. Recognizing the sounds of gray and fox squirrels is important for determining their presence. Because of the quiet boat approach to likely dens, the floater has another advantage in the sound department. Barks, grinding teeth and the thump of nuts hitting the ground often give away squirrels that can't be seen first. When there are no sounds coming from the squirrel trees, floaters and foot hunters alike will sometimes take two, 50-cent pieces and "chatter" them together to draw comment from the woods.

## Squirrel Boats

The canoe is my favorite. Quiet and easy to maneuver on gentle streams, it is "log-like" in appearance and deadly effective as a squirrel hunting weapon. Whether construction is aluminum, fiberglass, plastic or canvas-wood, the canoe is top choice for squirrel streams. Because of its weight and design, the canoe can be launched and taken out with a minimum of effort. In the event of land or diversion dam portages, the canoe shines. If there be a disadvantage, it is that of stability. Canoes can be easily tipped when not handled properly or when negotiating tricky water. Novices should definitely acquaint themselves with practical canoe operation before harnessing the boat to hunting methods.

Rubber inflatable boats can absorb river running mistakes without the serious consequence characterized by novice canoe handling. They make good shooting platforms and are very stable. With more surface drag, rubber boats float slower and this can be an advantage on streams of moderate current. However, on sluggish streams, inflatables barely move. This means that some heavy paddling or rowing is usually in order. In the event of even the slightest head wind, negotiating the river can end up as work. Inflatables shine in moderate or fast current, but become somewhat frustrating crafts on super gentle squirrel streams.

Aluminum or fiberglass john boats, of 12 to 16 feet in length, often make a worthy compromise between canoe and rubber boat. They are stable river craft, although not as stable as inflatables. John boats provide a low silhouette for that "part of the river" appearance so important in this brand of hunting. They are heavier than canoes, making launching and portaging more difficult. The aluminum boats, especially, are noisier than canoes and rubber boats. A lot of this problem can be solved though with floor carpeting and fiberglass oarlock inserts.

## Special Gear

Since squirrel floaters may be a respectable distance from the nearest road, good planning is an essential ingredient for enjoyment. Streams are characteristically low during fall squirrel seasons. Rarely have I completed a float in autumn when low water did not force some getting out of the boat to walk through low spots or push off sand and gravel bars. For this reason, hip waders or knee length rubber boots are necessary.

Waders can be folded down when not in use so they can be kicked off in case of a hasty exit from the boat. Some hunters I know try to get away with rubber bottomed pacs for low water jams. Most often they end up with wet feet and pants.

Rain gear is a must even though the day may begin bright and cloudless. Nothing is more uncomfortable than sitting in a boat during an autumn squall when soaked to the bone. A baseball cap or wide-brimmed hat keeps rain off the face.

I'm a firm believer in packing along plenty of food and hot or cold beverages for a day on the stream. There is something about a float trip, squirrel hunt and crisp, autumn weather that keeps minds thinking about food. A small, chest-type cooler or insulated vinyl or canvas food bag keeps sandwiches and perishables fresh. You might even want to pack along the makings of a midday shore lunch. Hotdogs or hamburgers, with a can of beans and celery or carrot sticks can bolster body and spirit for the rest of the day. The on-shore pause makes for a refreshing break.

When it comes to good eating, the squirrels in your game bag will definitely provide that. Field dress your game as soon after shooting as possible. Wash them clean with river water and store in plastic sacks. You can skin squirrels on the spot (which is easier when they are freshly killed) or wait until you get home.

There are several excellent ways to prepare squirrels. My favorite is to skin, wash and cut up (into frying pieces) from two to four grays or foxes. Salt and pepper the pieces and brown them in hot, olive oil (about ¼-inch deep) in the bottom of a pressure cooker. Season that oil with a dash or two of oregano and garlic powder to taste. Remove the pieces and drain on paper towel. Pour off the oil. Add the squirrel pieces to the cooker once again. Add approximately 1½ cups water (some pressure cookers may vary); two chopped onions; two chicken bouillon cubes; and moderately dust squirrel with salt, pepper, oregano and poultry seasoning. Cover and cook at 15 pounds of pressure for about 20 minutes after control (round top piece) jiggles. Serve steaming hot over a bed of blended domestic and wild rice. Corn bread makes a wonderful companion starch, and fresh stream watercress (harvested right from squirrel land if you are fortunate) adds a final jewel to the regal feast before you. A mild bouquet of Chablis, served chilled, is a worthy toast to the jaunty squirrel and the feast he provided. It does not take long, once the taste buds have been treated, to relive the river day again and make plans for another soon.

There's a good feeling you get with a good stream and a quiet, responsive boat under you. A feeling, really, like no other because you are knifing into squirrel country in the finest tradition. Like an early trapper, I think. That's a nice state of mind in this day. The grays chatter in the green hickories, and the paddles gurgle. Mist rises, and you are a full-blooded squirrel hunter.

# So You Want to Hunt

# Ruffed Grouse? by ED HUTCHINS

**THE ROAR OF WINGS**—possibly anticipated by your bird dog—someone shouting "there he goes," and perhaps a hasty shot at a blur of brown if it comes into view, is a sequence of events that probably characterizes the meeting of man and ruffed grouse in the autumn woods. The wildness of the ruffed grouse had a special appeal to Aldo Leopold who wrote in *A Sand County Almanac,* "There are two kinds of people: those who can live without wild things and those who cannot." Of the grouse woods in autumn, Leopold said, "I sometimes think that the other months were constituted mainly as a fitting interlude between Octobers, and I suspect that dogs, and perhaps grouse, share the same view."

Carrying a shotgun and following a bird dog are certainly not prerequisite to enjoyment of the ruffed grouse, but few persons other than dedicated grouse hunters are willing to walk all day in rough and perhaps hilly country just for a glimpse or perhaps a fleeting shot at this "king of upland gamebirds." Two main factors become obvious in successful grouse hunting—finding the birds and being able to hit them with some degree of regularity. The finest shotgun handler, unable to find birds, will take no more grouse than the man who can locate birds but cannot hit them.

The ruffed grouse is essentially a bird of the second-growth timber and even more specifically a bird of the edges of second growth. These are the areas that will have brushy cover providing concealment and food of sufficient quantity and variety to support grouse throughout much of the year. However, finding grouse and collecting them are often two entirely different matters. Even with the leaf fall as much as 50 percent complete, the hunter is frequently unable to see more than one out of three grouse well enough to get off a reasonably effective shot. Another factor that works to the advantage of grouse is the near impossibility of approaching them quietly when the floor of the woods is covered with dry leaves.

Grouse are creatures of habit and frequently can be found near the same place at the same time each day, barring some drastic change in natural conditions. Strangely enough, although the grouse population is certain to be larger in the fall than in winter, hunter success seems to improve in the colder months. The exception to this is where snow depths become excessive or the snow heavily crusted. A light, soft snow oftentimes permits grouse to be tracked to a place of concealment where they will likely flush within gun range. Also, snow tends to brighten the woods, thus helping the hunter to quickly get on target if the bird is in range, or at least to follow the bird's flight for a distance sufficient to provide a good chance for a reflush.

The ability to reflush a bird the second and third time is a factor of greatest importance to the grouse hunter, particularly in an area where few birds are found. Thus

The ruffed grouse is one of the most wide-ranging of all American grouse. Generally found in deciduous habitats, particularly of second-growth types, the ruffed grouse occupies a relatively large number of life areas with which its racial variation (about 12 subspecies recognized) seems to be rather well correlated. (Map courtesy of Aldrich, "Geographic Orientation of Grouse," *Journal of Wildlife Management,* 1963)

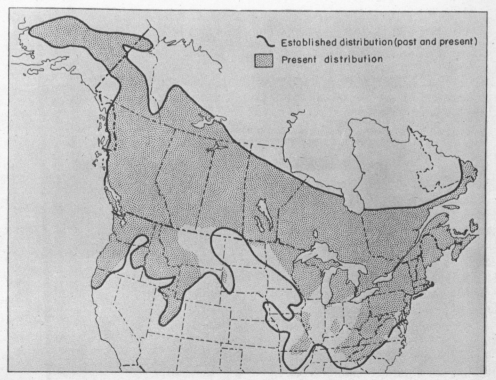

Established distribution (past and present)
Present distribution

In young-of-the-year grouse the two outermost primaries are sharp pointed. In adult birds, the tips of these two primaries will be more rounded. Some practice is required to reliably detect this difference, but it has been successfully applied by experienced workers with an error of less than 1 percent. Birds cannot be aged past 1 year, nor is this method reliable in late winter. Wing at left is from adult bird, at right is wing of immature bird.

it is important to observe very carefully the direction of flight of a bird that flushes out of range or for some other reason is not killed. Direction often can be successfully determined just from the sound. Although the duration of flight varies with the individual bird and often with the location of satisfactory cover in which to alight, there are a few "rules" that might be of assistance in reflushing. The New York State grouse investigation *The Ruffed Grouse, Life History, Propagation, Management* by Bump, Darrow, Edminster & Crissey, 1947

(Right) The ruffed grouse probably offers more recreational potential than any other upland game bird. This bird, with the wide band of the tail unbroken, is almost certainly a male. Another good identifying feature of the male ruffed grouse is the very distinct arrowhead design on the upper tail coverts. Weight of ruffed grouse ranges from about 20 to 24 ounces.

(recently reprinted by Grouse Tales, 17130 Chatfield, Cleveland, Ohio 44111) a 16-year research effort, revealed that grouse, when flushed, tend to settle down in the same type of cover from which they were originally raised except when it is not extensive or is quite open. Birds that flew to cover unlike that from which they were flushed almost always chose heavier cover types. Nearly 1500 flushes were recorded by the New York researchers, and they found that flight distances of from 150 to 300 feet were the rule, unless the birds had been hunted hard in which case distances up to 500 feet or farther were not infrequently recorded. Flights of ¼-mile were not uncommon when a bird was startled

while feeding in light cover some distance from the woods.

Ruffed grouse occur in a variety of habitats, with the optimum population level ordinarily associated with the interfusion of edges of several different types of cover where the grouse can exist on a year-round basis. There are few regions where this is more perfectly achieved than where vast acreages have been blighted and abandoned as a result of unsuccessful farming, surface mining practices of the past and certain forestry methods.

Grouse hunting expert Nelson Groves, of Lancaster, Ohio, checks out a point by English setters "Moose" and "Sam." Dogs are not essential to grouse hunting, but if they will point reliably much time is saved in locating birds.

Some of the finest grouse hunting occurs solely as a result of the misfortune of those who tried to farm the marginal or submarginal soils of Appalachia. The New York study concluded that the quality of a habitat is roughly proportional to the variety in the composition and arrangement of its component cover types; and the poorer the cover, in this respect, the greater the need for edges. Aldo Leopold, the father of modern wildlife management, pointed out over 40 years ago that the potential density of game of low cruising radius (such as the ruffed grouse) is, within ordinary limits, proportional to the sum of the type of edges. It has been observed that the ruffed grouse thrives on man's disuse and abuse of land, and in much of its range the grouse population responds positively to edges created by utility rights-of-way, unreclaimed strip mine pits and spoil banks, forest clearcuts if not too large, and of course worn out and abandoned farmland is the classic setting for the ruffed grouse.

Most grouse hunters prefer to hunt with one companion—never more than two—and it is hard to beat a good pair of pointing dogs as the "third and fourth hunters." You should choose your hunting companion with care as your life and that of your dog are virtually in his hands several times throughout the hunting season. Good judgment in grouse hunting demands that you pass up all shots even remotely directed toward your hunting companion even though you know that you would not be shooting directly at him. Nor is it an acceptable practice to shoot at a bird rising against a hillside unless the dog or dogs are accounted for and

given the same respect as the other hunter. Never, never walk in over a dog on point with your gun aimed at the level of the dog.

A good grouse dog, although not essential, is clearly an asset in most covers and under most conditions encountered in an average season. Basically, a good dog greatly extends the hunting range in terms of locating birds; a bird dog that will point reliably gives warning that a bird is near or perhaps flushed immediately before the hunter and dog came on the scene. Even an unproductive point is a distinct advantage to the hunter as he is reasonably sure that a grouse is within one flush length of the point. Most grouse hunters use a small bell on the collar of their bird dog to provide at least a general idea of his location. Obviously, a bird dog whose range takes him out of hearing distance of the bell is of little value in the hunt. If you can't hear his bell, you most certainly won't be able to see him in typical grouse cover, nor will you have the slightest notion whether he is pointing or merely flushing birds. A dog that will not point, but will nevertheless locate grouse by showing signs of interest or excitement can be a desirable hunting companion if he always hunts within gun range.

Hunting grouse without a dog requires that the hunter personally hunt more thoroughly, remember more accurately where birds have been found on other days, and follow grouse tracks with great dedication under conditions of fresh snow. An old standard technique when hunting without a dog is to walk 25 or 30 yards, then stop for perhaps ½-minute in a good section of

In addition to your shotgun and a few other items of obvious necessity, it is well to consider a blaze-orange cap, a good compass with set needle, a standard whistle to remind your dog to stay where you can keep track of him, and a bird hunter's knife with entrail hook.

cover, all the time being ready to shoot. For the skilled hunter, being without a dog is not too serious a disadvantage. Indeed, he is in a far better situation than if he were accompanied by an untrained dog that flushes most of the birds out of range.

Although the ruffed grouse is a woodland species and has been here certainly since the Pleistocene, it was probably not extremely abundant in the almost impenetrable climax forest that originally covered much of eastern North America. It has been said that of all of man's tools, the ax has brought about the most significant change in the status of the grouse. The first white settlers began to clear the forest almost immediately and the openings created by their extensive logging operations, plus the widespread brushy reversion of woodlots that followed, resulted in a vast improvement of grouse habitat over much of its range. Where the homesteaders cleared relatively fertile flatland their work proved permanent, but those who chose to clear the unglaciated, sterile hill country of Appalachia created much of today's prime grouse habitat by their failure at farming and the subsequent abandonment of the land.

Under certain (and rare) conditions, grouse attain phenomenal population densities. Ralph T. King, in the Journal of Forestry, 1937, reported a grouse to every 1.8 acres in the fall (55.5 per 100 acres). W. Rowan, professor of zoology at the University of Alberta, wrote of a party of four hunters who in the fall of 1941 killed more than 2,000 grouse in 1 week while operating from a single camp some 70 miles northwest of Edmonton, Alberta. But the most remarkable grouse story of all

Cuticular outgrowths along the edges of the toes of a grouse assist the bird in walking on the snow. These modified scales begin to grow in the fall and are shed in the spring. Normal length is about 2 millimeters, but they tend to be longer on birds in the more northern parts of the grouse range.

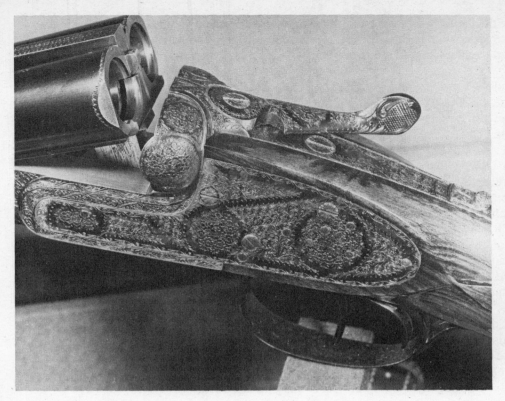

The best gun for the job is ideally the one in which you have the most confidence—not necessarily the most investment. But some guns are better suited for grouse hunting than others. The double gun's tang safety (few repeaters have such safeties) is ideal for the fast shooting required in grouse hunting. Also, there is often some benefit derived from the double gun's choice of two distinct chokes. Under most conditions, barrels not over 26 inches in length and with chokes of cylinder (or improved cylinder) and modified are the best combination. This particular gun, an AYA Model 56, 20-gauge, weighs just 6 pounds.

(Right) You should choose your hunting companion with care as your life and that of your dog are virtually in his hands several times throughout the hunting season.

was that of William B. Mershon in *Recollections of My Fifty Years Hunting and Fishing,* 1923, who told of two hunters in 1891 who flushed 2,000 grouse in 1 day near Hemlock, Michigan. Unfortunately, no estimate of reflushes was given.

The distribution of the ruffed grouse involves a greater area than that of any other non-migratory North American game bird. The 12 recognized subspecies can be divided into two basic color phases obvious to even the most casual observer. Birds with a rufous cast called the "red" phase are found in the southern part of the grouse range, while birds with a predominance of gray, especially on the tail, are found in the north and west and are called "gray" phase. The racial variations in the plumage of the ruffed grouse are extremely well correlated to the various life areas in which the bird is found. The intensity of coloration of the feathers is related to the light intensity and background shades of the environment. The adaptive value of this arrangement is obvious.

The hunter can usually determine the sex of his bird by noting one or more characters of the plumage. However, it must be remembered that a single sex character is not always reliable. Males, for instance, are usually longer and heavier than females but an especially large female is not a lot different from a small male. The ruff feathers on the neck are generally longer and more numerous on males. Birds with an unbroken wide band on the tail are almost always males, while birds with the band broken on the two middle feathers might be either sex.

The color of the tail band and ruff of most ruffed grouse is an iridescent black, but the tail band and/or ruff of about 25 percent of the birds are a brownish-red, the degree of intensity of the color giving rise to such names as "chocolate ruff" and "cherry grouse." A white grouse was taken in Ohio in 1974 by Nelson Groves and me and was presented to the Ohio State University Museum of Zoology as a permanent addition to the study skin collection.

The trend in recent years has been toward lengthening the grouse hunting season. Some states now keep the season open for more than 4 months with no apparent negative impact on the population level of the species. Research in Michigan in the 1960's showed little relationship between the length of the hunting season and the size of the grouse population. Even the most intensive hunting pressure usually fails to take all the grouse from an area. This was demonstrated rather dramatically in New York state a few years ago when two professional hunters cooperating in a research project, tried to shoot out a grouse population on an approximate square-mile area throughout the winter and early spring. The study was run 3 consecutive years. It was found that the hunters became very familiar with the coverts and the birds' individual characteristics by midwinter, but when only a "few" grouse were left they couldn't approach within gunshot of them.

Food shortages for grouse are almost unheard of although there no doubt are instances where distribution of grouse are affected on a local basis by the relative abundance and variety of foods. A grouse food study by Merrill Gilfillan and H. Bezdek in Ohio, reported in the *Journal of Wildlife Management* in 1944, found 77 different food items in the crops and gizzards of 42 adult grouse collected in Ohio between November and March. It is said that adult grouse have been known to use parts of more than 400 different kinds of plants for food.

Today, the need for diverse makeup and interspersion of cover types is widely understood by wildlife managers, and here and there certain plantings and other management techniques are directed at the well-being of the grouse population. But for the most part grouse are the beneficiaries of what might be called "accidental" wildlife management. Some of the best grouse hunting in the Midwest occurs on so-called "pre-law" strip mine areas where little or no reclamation took place following extraction of coal. Even though the mining occurred nearly a half-century ago, the open pit, the spoil bank and even the high walls maintain permanent openings and edges in forest cover that would otherwise no longer serve the needs of

grouse. Unreclaimed strip mines are generally characterized as environmental disasters, and indeed they have probably destroyed more miles of streams than any other source of pollution. However, unreclaimed strip mines at least in the past permanently "dedicated" the land to wildlife purposes. Today, several state and federal programs channel public funds into "rescuing" abandoned strip mine land and returning it to what the sponsors consider useful purposes.

Under the new reclamation programs, at least in the Appalachian region, strip pits, spoil banks and highwalls all are eliminated. Grass cover is established immediately after leveling of the mined area, and within a short time cattle or sheep are in evidence. One of the more recent programs in effect is the Rural Abandoned Mine Program of the USDA's Soil Conservation Service which will pay from 25 to 100 percent of the reclamation cost depending on acreage and proposed use. A recent report from Ohio indicates that this program spent some $3,000 per acre in reclaiming land that probably wasn't worth $800 per acre. Thus, public funds are being used to transform lands that have supported wildlife for many years into lands that will at best support marginal agriculture.

Professor Charles Riley of Kent State University, who is widely recognized as one of the nation's leading experts on strip mine reclamation, says that agriculture on former strip mines should perhaps not be taken too seriously as it is unlikely it will ever be in competition with high-class farmland of which there is no present shortage. Riley predicts that given 20 or 30 years these so-called farmlands, purely on a basis of economics, will revert to forest cover that will support wildlife.

Clear-cutting of hardwood forest lands, correctly considered to be an environmental outrage in many parts of America, can be grouse habitat management of the first order if the areas cut are not over about 50 acres in size. This kind of simple clear-cutting creates extensive edge cover; selective harvesting of timber accomplishes little or nothing for wildlife.

Grouse hunters interested in the long-term future of their sport should study land use patterns in their state. Although hunting generally does not command significant economic impact, the dollars being spent to convert wildlife lands to marginal agricultural use are in many instances dollars from the community at large—including dollars from many persons interested in wildlife. Grouse hunting should generate interest far beyond the mere shooting or killing of a bird that provides sporty shooting and good table fare. The same wildlife covers that support grouse generally contain many other kinds of birds and other animals that can provide both shooting and non-shooting interest. Lastly, the time and effort required per grouse bagged could hardly be justified by someone who fails to appreciate the over-all satisfaction derived from a day in the autumn woods.

## by RUSSELL TINSLEY

THE GRAY FOX AND RED FOX are kinfolks, but the relationship has to be at least cousins twice removed. They possess the same unmistakable shape and are virtually of identical size, but their habits and behavior are totally different.

Consider how each responds to a predator call. The culpable gray often runs in close, throwing caution to the wind. Seldom do you see a wily, suspicious red fox make that mistake. As for smarts, expert caller Murry Burnham compares the red fox to the crafty coyote, which is indeed a compliment.

While their range overlaps in places, the gray fox primarily is an inhabitant of the woodlands, but the peripatetic red fox, one of the original joggers, prefers more open country. The gray has a sweet tooth for baby cottontails; so a high-pitched call which imitates the distress cries of a rabbit will dupe one within gunshot range. Meanwhile, studies have shown that the red eats more meadow mice than anything else, and a call which imitates the pitiful squeaks of a mouse in trouble frequently will bring this fox running.

For bigger predators such as the coyote and bobcat, a lower-pitched call, coarser in tone, to mimic a distressed jackrabbit, might be the ticket. Different strokes for different...well, you should get the idea.

The call itself, however, isn't as important as where and when it is used. A caller who does his homework, learning where different predators roam and something about their everyday habits, is the one most likely to succeed. Calling is much more than randomly wandering into the field and blowing on a call. As with anything, you get more proficient with experience.

Murry Burnham believes it is impossible to blow a properly tuned call the wrong way. In calling contests,

There's no thrill like seeing a predator running toward you.

# Predator Calling Know-How

(Above) A juvenile coyote comes running toward caller crouched in open.

(Below) Predator caller brings a suspicious red fox into close range.

each participant has his own distinctive style, yet each claims that that particular sound produces for him, and that is after all the name of the game.

"Learn where to hunt, how to take advantage of the air currents, and make full use of effective camouflage," Burnham stressed. "I've had people slam the doors of vehicles and talk in loud voices as they walked to where we were to call, and then they were the first to gripe when nothing showed up. A predator is one smart critter; don't sell it short."

Perhaps this is the most common blunder among neophyte callers; they do not have enough respect for their quarry. Keep in mind that a predator is super-sly and wily, an animal that not only has survived among a growing civilization, but one which has thrived and multiplied and expanded its range. This animal possesses a sensitive warning system quick to detect the slightest hint of danger. The caller must short-circuit this radar system if, by blowing on a call, he hopes to lure the critter out of hiding. And this defense system becomes fine-tuned with age. A teenage predator, like its human counterpart, is often more capricious than rational.

A few years ago I was hunting mule deer with bow and arrow in Colorado, not far from Grand Junction in the northwestern part of the state. It was late August, a bright and sunny day. As I was creeping along, I glimpsed a mama coyote with her three almost fully grown offspring trotting along a nearby hillside. I had a dying-rabbit call in the pocket of my camouflage jacket and I fished it out, squatted, and commenced blowing.

The bitch coyote turned and came toward me. As she wheeled around some brush, she caught me in the act of raising my bow and she came unglued, swapping ends in mid-air and taking off in the opposite direction. But the three pups stopped and stared, more curious than frightened. Only when I stood up and began circling, trying to get close for a shot, and let the wind get behind me, carrying my scent to the coyotes, did they spook and run. Moral of the story: Telltale human scent is one danger signal no predator ignores, not even the young and foolish.

Early fall, when the spring-born are large enough to fare for themselves yet still not wise to the facts of life, is a prime time to fox a predator with a call. With the exception of the coyote, however, there isn't much available to be called in the fall, unless you are content simply to take photographs. Most other predators, like the fox and bobcat, are classified as furbearers and can only be called and shot during the open season in the wintertime when pelts are prime.

Come winter and you're talking about a different predator, more mature and wise. You don't dupe one of these by being haphazard and careless. Yet the caller has a few things going for him. Winter is what Murry Burnham calls the "hungry season"; normal food sources are much reduced and a predator is more likely to be prowling about even in the daytime, and while early and late are still the optimum periods, a predator is apt to answer a call most any hour of the day.

Nonetheless, there must be a predator within hearing range of the call if there is any hope of getting it to respond. Offhand this might sound like a rather ridiculous statement. But it is a problem every caller encounters. Maybe there are no predators in the immediate area or, two, the ones present are not cooperative. Successful calling is, at best, a sport of repetition, trying one place and then another until everything falls into place. With experience, the caller will learn to recognize the type of terrain where predators reside and will be able to identify clues such as fresh tracks and droppings along trails and dusty country roads. But this takes time and study; there are no magic shortcuts.

Nothing quite compares to that dramatic sight of a sinister-looking predator running toward you, a moment in time when the roles become reversed and you are the *hunted* rather than the *hunter*. One mistake here and your entire effort will be scuttled. The critter might be rushing to claim what it believes to be a quick and easy meal, but instinct tells it to be cautious. Anything that smacks of a threat will send it fleeing in the opposite direction. And it doesn't take a predator long to make up its mind!

The predator has no obvious weakness. Its senses—smelling, seeing and hearing—are among nature's finest. The fox and coyote depend primarily on their noses for their first line of defense, while the bobcat seems to depend more on its uncanny eyesight. But the caller's

When a bobcat approaches as close as it intends to come, it often squats down.

(Left) Knowing where to call is the important first step toward eventual success.

(Right) Effective camouflage blends the caller into the surroundings.

game plan should attempt to neutralize all three senses. When a predator approaches within sight, remember this is now a swap out, because you, the caller, also are vulnerable, and when the animal comes close, many things can go wrong and something usually does. In most confrontations, the predator emerges as winner.

One way to confuse the animal is to hunt as a team, one person calling, the other shooting. The two might get concealed about 25 yards apart, or perhaps the caller remains on the ground while the shooter gets in the low fork of a tree. The incoming predator homes in on the sound with intense concentration, and often the shooter can raise his rifle, shotgun or bow without being detected, although at times I swear a predator, especially the coyote, has eyes in back of its head.

Calling is best when there is little or no wind, which is one reason to recommend the first light of day, normally a period of calm. If there is any significant air current, the call carries farthest in the direction, downwind, where you don't want it to go. Any predator coming into the wind is going to whiff your scent. Let's face it; there is no effective method for totally eliminating telltale human odor. Commerical scents such as those

In early fall, teenage coyotes like this are much easier to call.

84

(Above) Winston Burnham crouches among prickly pear cactus to do his calling.

(Left) In a few states night calling is legal, and a predator often is more easily fooled in the dark.

made from coyote and bobcat urine, among other ingredients, might confuse a predator briefly if it arrives on the scene and circles downwind, but don't expect them to be infallible. Your best insurance is to have any prevailing breeze at the back of the predator rather than yours, blowing your scent away from the animal's keen nose, but unfortunately it doesn't always work that way. Nope, simply blowing on a call is not taking advantage.

Yet trying to negate the scent factor is only one part of the whole. As Murry Burnham mentioned earlier, the caller should advance into his potential territory with as little noise as possible. Walk softly and use hand signals for communication. When a predator hears something suspicious invading its lair, it becomes edgy, more difficult to fool with a call. Should you get settled and begin calling, for example, and shortly you hear a fox barking in the underbrush, don't be misled into believing the animal is fooled. Just the opposite is true. The fox is suspicious and is announcing the fact; the odds are great that you'll never see it.

Finally, the caller must contend with a predator's superior eyesight. It is intimately familiar with its environment and can quickly perceive what does not belong. The caller should attempt to become as inconspicuous as possible. Use camouflage wisely, the traditional mix of browns and greens in normal woods, and white on snow. Murry Burnham believes the caller can't be too careful. The little things count. Streak your face with grease paint or wear a mesh camo headnet. Back into a bush or push among the leaves of an ever-green to break your outline. Slowly pivot your head as you look; avoid any jerky movement. If hunting alone, try to time any move, such as raising a rifle, when the predator's head is turned or is behind some object. The wise caller will bring his firearm into position, aim and fire in one continuous motion. The predator might be startled for a brief moment—and that will be that.

While a fox or coyote generally will show in a hurry, within 15 minutes or less, a bobcat is more deliberate. Sometimes it takes ½-hour or more for one, sneaking and slinking, to make an appearance. Cat calling demands patience, but it also takes a tremendous amount of willpower to remain quiet and motionless for that length of time. Yet it is a price you must be able to pay.

Predator calling know-how, at least on paper, sounds simple enough. But once in the woods, application doesn't seem so easy. The caller finds himself nagged by self-doubts. Is he calling in the right place? Is he creating the correct sound? What's the wind doing?

This is the learning process every caller must go through. Experience leads to confidence, and self-confidence is the trail to success. When something goes wrong, the caller must analyze the situation and determine where and how he made mistakes. It is often not a matter of what the caller did but what he didn't do.

No, it isn't easy. No one claimed it would be. But pedator calling is fascinating—a sport of suspense—challenging. And success becomes epidemic. Once you call a predator and savor the thrill, you'll want to call another and another. There is no known cure except to go calling every chance you get.

# GRAY SQUIRREL COUNTRY

by ERWIN A. BAUER

A good squirrel hunter waits and watches more than he walks. It is a quiet game to play.

**WHEN DAN BOONE** first crossed over the Appalachian Ridges into Kentucky territory, he found an almost endless "climax" forest. It was an uninterrupted wilderness where the crowns of giant trees were crowded together tight enough to keep sunlight from the ground below. Contrary to what most people believe today, it was not filled with game—not even with forest dwellers like gray squirrels.

Except for the openings and "edges" in the forests caused by fires, disease, and storms, there was little game at all. Actually there are more gray squirrels, more gray squirrel country, and better squirrel hunting today in all of America than there was before it was settled. Perhaps, as we use our land more wisely, there will be even more gray squirrels in the future.

Gray squirrel country now, as always, is beautiful country, and for the hunter to know his way around it is to put more game before his sights. It's a region of mixed hardwoods, with a few evergreens thrown in, that changes to mixed, bright colors in autumn. It's a region of mixed ages in the trees, too, where the woods contain saplings in equal number with mature trees. That means it's almost any timberland in the eastern half of the United States where shafts of sunlight can

Hunter (near lower left) is inconspicuous as he should always be when in gray squirrel country.

filter through to the earth, where the crowns of trees are spread enough to grow heavy crops of mast (animal foods, nuts).

There's also a western phase of the gray squirrel. Its range is a thin north-south strip along the Pacific coast.

When later settlers followed Boone, they began to clear the forest. With each new opening they made more edge and each new edge created more forage for squirrels until finally these animals were abundant enough to be a plague. Where new cornfields bordered the wilderness, farmers often stood vigil all night with torches and drove the squirrels off with clubs. Migrating by the thousands across country, the critters destroyed more than one farm completely. In 1812, finally, the Ohio legislature passed an act which made the killing of squirrels compulsory. Squirrel tails were accepted as payment for taxes.

Community squirrel hunts were organized and the results of some of them seem fantastic today. For example, an article in the Columbus, Ohio, *Gazette* of August 22, 1822, reported that a 1-day community hunt bagged only 19,960 "tax tails" because the weather was unfavorable. One Saturday morning in Bartholomew County, Indiana, folks got to bragging about who was the best rifle shot. They selected squirrels, the most convenient targets, to find out. After a day's shooting, the winner collected 900 squirrels and the runner-up bagged 783. The total kill ran high into five figures.

In those days, people just used the largest words in their vocabularies to indicate the number of squirrels—there were that many. Ernest Thompson Seton once estimated that there were 450 million in a single migration! No locusts or grasshoppers ever left such a path of destruction. But when one year's mast crop failed, there would be mass starvation and a few years were necessary to build up another peak.

In time, farms were expanded and the amount of forest edge was reduced rather than increased. There was more hunting, too, for fun as well as food. The number of gray squirrels diminished to the stable, steady population we know today. The game is no longer a nuisance, but it's abundant enough to be the most popular game animal in many sections of the land. In more than one community, in fact, a man is known by his skill with a squirrel rifle.

Specifically, gray squirrel country contains more woods than farmlands. Fox squirrel country, on the other hand, is mostly farmland, and over wide areas the fox squirrel and the gray squirrel overlap. For grays it can be swampland as is much the best of it in the deep south. It can be hilly—rugged and steep as is much of it in New England, the mid-South, and the East. Or it can be river bottomland as it is so often in the Midwest. But all of these are better according to the number of different trees present. The first rule for selecting a good squirrel woods is to find one with many species of trees with a good mixture of saplings and mature trees.

A good way to invade gray squirrel country is by camping.

Mixed species are necessary for forage the year around. A solid white oak woods, for instance, would be fine for grays in mid-autumn and during years when the acorn crop is good. But what of other times?

A typical southern Ohio woods, for example, contains white oak, hickory, a few maples, beech, probably sour gum and around the edges a few black walnuts. In spring, the buds of the maple, plus fruits, berries such as bittersweet, and insects are eaten. In summer the fruit of sour gum ripens first, and in order after that, squirrels will 'cut' on hickory, pignuts if they're available, beech, acorns, and walnuts. Elsewhere, pecans and butternuts would fit into the schedule. A woods then, should contain a year-round menu.

During the height of fall color, it's possible to evaluate a forest for squirrel hunting from a distance—from the car while touring back roads, in fact. Simply count the colors, the more you can see, the more different kinds of trees. Here are some important leaf colors to remember: red oak—dark red; white oak—orange brown or rusty; beech—clear, light yellow; red maple—scarlet or bright orange; hickory—rusty brown or yellow mixed with brown; silver maple—yellow; sugar maple—yellow orange; butternut and walnut—yellow but leaves fall early; poplar—yellow or almost golden in sunlight.

Squirrels need dens and the more of these in a forest, the greater the capacity for squirrels. It's good to look for 'wolf' trees, the old-timers that have spread wide and crowded out others all around. Trees killed by lightning eventually become dens and so do others that have hollow places because of fires. In summer particularly, squirrels build and use leaf nests. If a woods contains plenty of these, it's a good sign. They're easiest to see in winter when the foliage is gone and more than one wise hunter prospects at this time of year—counting nests, locating dens, and checking to see if enough kinds of trees are present.

Where I hunt the season opens in August or September and on the first day I'm invariably waiting in the same spot, where hazelnuts grow thick. Find a patch of these shrubs and you've found a place that squirrels will also find—almost no matter where it is—the moment the nuts are ripe. It's necessary to get there early, though, for grays go for them like freeloaders for free beer.

Even though grays are the squirrels of woodlands rather than the farmlands, edge is essential. At least the squirrels usually frequent the edges rather than the centers of deep woods. Look for them there. A long, thin tract of forest or a woods that borders a river, is an ideal place. Chances in an ungrazed woods are much better than in a grazed woods. Livestock reduces the amount of ground cover, and consumes saplings which would otherwise grow nuts and berries for squirrels. A 'clean' forest floor also exposes squirrels to natural predators that wouldn't have a chance in normal cover.

Gray squirrel country is also turkey, ruffed grouse, whitetail deer, even pileated woodpecker country. If you find these other critters present, it's a good sign because they depend, at least in part, on the same requirements. Turkeys, grouse and deer are partial to beechnuts and acorns. Pileated woodpeckers need dead or dying trees to drill, as do gray squirrels for dens. One old-timer I knew even considered the presence of honey bees in a woods significant because they frequent woodlots with hollow trees.

Once you know your squirrel country well, concentrate on hunting during the early and late hours each day. Skip windy days if possible, and try to be in the woods on dull, damp days, perhaps after a warm rain the night before. Move as quietly and as stealthily as you can.

The best squirrel hunting advice I ever had came from an old-timer. Badly handicapped by rheumatism, he more than held his own with younger and more agile hunters. "Hunt grays with ears and eyes," he said, "instead of your feet." He followed his own advice by first evaluating the country and then sitting on a comfortable stump in the middle of it.

In gray squirrel woods anywhere it's good business to stop often—to sit motionless as much of the time as you move around. Select a comfortable spot so that you can remain quiet for a long, period of time. And above all avoid sudden movements. When you do change position, do it slowly.

Once I saw a squirrel in a white oak just above the

place another hunter was stationed. Neither could see the other, until the man made a sudden swipe at an insect. The squirrel disappeared immediately—still unseen.

The best arm for a squirrel hunter is a .22 rifle—any .22 that fits the shooter well—with a 3x or 4x scope. To use open sights is to do it the hard way. There's no need for the Varminters or any heavier calibers because they only ruin the finest wild meat available. Some of these can even be extremely dangerous in hilly country because it's impossible to see what's on the other side of a screen of foliage. Use the .22 Long Rifle cartridge as it is much more accurate than either the long or short cartridge.

The shotgun-versus-rifle-for-squirrels argument has raged ever since men have hunted the critters. A common conclusion is that the shotgun isn't sporting, but of course that's not true. Late in the season or in heavily hunted areas, a wary gray is more than a match for an average scattergunner. It can be a more elusive target than other game on which shotguns are commonly used. There are also times and places when a shotgun is certainly the safest firearm to use in woods.

No matter what the gun, though, it's hard to beat hunting in gray squirrel country. It's leisurely, relaxing, and contemplative. It's America's favorite "waiting" game.

Pitch a tent nearby a good, mixed hardwood forest and then be up before daylight.

# Rx for Spring Fever:

# a Bear Hunt in Canada

## by RUSS ALLEN

**IN LATE SPRINGTIME,** twilight seems to last forever in the northern Ontario bush. And if you're sitting in a bear blind, the time passes in very slow motion.

A mosquito whined around my ear, and I slapped at it. That's wrong, all wrong. Such sudden movement can alarm any bruin in the vicinity and send him racing away into the deepening shadows. The mosquito whined again and overhead a white-throated sparrow sang the lonely notes which you can hear on any June evening across Canada.

I fidgeted because the canoe-birch platform on which I squatted was hard and rough. I was thirsty. The mosquito returned again and this time was once too often. I squashed him.

Now the sun dipped below the trees and at the same time I felt a cold chill. A single sliver of golden light illuminated one patch of ground below me—and into that patch of light stepped a bear, as if projected onto a screen.

It was a bear, but it moved as quietly as a house cat on a soft carpet. For a split second the bruin turned, looked at the base of the tree in which I sat and in that instant his black coat glistened. The picture was gone. I strained to see or hear the bear in the bush, but the only sound was the soft rush of the Floodwood River.

All of this had happened so suddenly and without warning that I hadn't even raised the .30-06 which lay across my lap. Ordinarily I'm alert to such opportunities. But this time I sat hypnotized—caught with my reflexes down.

For 10—15—20 minutes by my watch, I fought off a mild case of buck fever while I hoped the bear would come back again. When it was too dark to see anything but the white trunks of the birch trees, I climbed down from the stand and saw the beam of John Moxley's

◄ (Opposite) Even a large black bear can walk as softly through a forest as a small house cat.

flashlight over by the river. Half an hour of paddling later we beached the canoe at Little Abitibi Lodge and soon after that I had a bourbon and water in my hands. So did the dozen or so other sportsmen who had been catching walleyes all day or blind-watching for bears as I had been.

Sitting in that bear blind wasn't really included in any of my plans. Springtime is for fishing, and this was a spring fishing trip. I wanted to catch up on my walleye and northern pike fishing during this holiday with John Moxley in the Little Abitibi region. But before I left home in Ohio, Pete Hughes had casually mentioned that "bear hunting should be good here as is usual the first week in June." Pete owns and operates Little Abitibi Lodge, where we planned to stay, so we included rifles in our duffel as an afterthought. I had little intention of using mine.

Bears and bear hunting were completely forgotten, in fact, until Pete met us in Chochrane, where all Ontario roads leading northward end. From there he airlifted us by float plane to his lodge on Little Abitibi Lake. We were just preparing to land when Pete banked the small plane sharply and pointed to the ground below. On a thin sand beach where the Floodwood River emptied into the lake was a black bear.

For an instant as Pete zoomed low for a better look, the bear stood erect on its hind legs and stared at us. Then it bounded away into the bush. "That bear," Pete shouted over the roar of the engine, "is a big one. I've seen its paw prints, and they're as big as pie plates." But after that it was forgotten.

A sportsman might travel completely across North America and never find walleye fishing much better than we found it around Abitibi. Everything was "right." The walleyes were abundant, fat and in some places hooking them was as difficult as casting a yellow jig into deep enough water. In other places, the pike fishing was almost that good. From Little Abitibi Lake we drifted downstream to Williston, Pierre, Montreuil and Harris Lakes with fast action all the way. By prospecting around a gravel bar near the outlet of Montreuil Lake we located a small area where 1½- to 2-pound walleye seemed to be packed as tightly as sardines in a tin. After an hour or so of catching and releasing them, we moved on to prospect elsewhere.

"In a way," John said, "the fishing is almost too good."

One day we outboarded up the Floodwood River to the first fast water above Little Abitibi Lake. Several other fishermen were already casting the pool below, and we simply joined them. Here also the walleyes were as willing as they were numerous and after a while we beached the boat to boil a pot of tea on shore. That's when I noticed a paw print of a bear as fresh as today in the wet sand. We gave the print the usual, careful look.

Only this was no ordinary paw print. As Pete said, it was frisbee-sized. Suddenly I remembered my rifle, and I had the fever. Then and there John and I decided to go bear hunting.

"I was hoping you would try the bears," Pete said that evening. "I'll check some baits I've already set and rebuild a few blinds right away."

Although it may seem unseasonal, spring bear hunts are as traditional as fishing in Ontario. Nowadays with bear populations probably on the increase, more and more of them have successful endings. Often outfitters like Pete Hughes can make the difference.

Pete knows Ontario bush bears about as well as anybody. He was practically raised with them. His father, Len, known widely as "The Bull Moose of the Northwood," was among the pioneer outfitters of the province and for more than a generation he operated both spring and fall hunts. Of course that's where Pete served his apprenticeship, first as a young guide and eventually as an outfitter whose "territory" extends all the way northward to Fort Albany on James Bay. Fishing is his main business and his first consideration, but still his spring bear hunts today are highly successful.

Most Ontario spring hunts are organized in essentially the same manner. Black bears, no matter where they're found are among the most shy and cunning big game critters. All across North America very few are bagged except by accident (mostly by lucky deer hunters), by running them with dogs or over bait. Bears live in heavy woods or semi-woods and this factor, coupled with the animal's own intelligence, combine to make them mighty elusive.

"But every black bear has a weakness," Pete

explained. "and it's concentrated in his stomach. Bears are always hungry and that's doubly true in springtime just after they emerge from winter's hibernation. Then natural foods are scarce. That's when they're suckers for any well-placed bait."

Right after bears come out of hibernation, most outfitters who cater to hunters begin a careful reconnaissance of their areas, looking for bear sign and fresh bear "highways." The latter aren't too hard to spot in the new vegetation and soft earth. Wherever good bear sign is located, the outfitter will put out a bait and build a blind overlooking it.

Ontario outfitters use a wide variety of baits. Household or camp garbage is the most available, and it's good enough. In areas where there is commercial fishing, it's possible to pick up fresh entrails in large quantities. This also is effective. Spring is also the time when black suckers spawn in small creeks and an hour or two spent spearing will obtain enough to provide several good baits. Twice during my own hunt I spent the midday period spearing suckers to replenish baits which had already been established.

Still other ingredients are deadly as baits, but they're also more expensive. Sweet anise is one of these, and the technique is to saturate a rotten stump with the liquid. Any of the strong fish oils will do just as well. On warm days with low atmospheric pressure the scent evidently spreads widely, and it attracts bears from far away.

The type of blind depends mostly on the outfitter's ingenuity, or on what materials are available and how much comfort the hunter requires. Nearly all are built in trees and as high as practical because black bears (like deer and many other animals) have a tendency to look everywhere but up. A clever bear guide will also be able to predict the directions a bear will approach the bait and the blind will be placed on what is most often the downwind side.

Occasionally it isn't necessary to build a blind at all—as when a natural terrain feature hides the hunter well enough. It's also possible to wait inside the abandoned shacks of old lumber camps and ghost sawmills which bears have become accustomed to visiting for the garbage. A wise operator always keeps plenty of bait around these places.

After the blinds and the baits were in order, John and I spent the mornings and evenings waiting for bears. In between times we fished. Mostly we prospected for large northern pike because the thrill of catching walleyes wholesale had worn off. At dusk of the second day of bear watching the black had appeared for an instant beside my bait. But that was all. It returned, but always after dark. There was nothing to do but sit and wait until he showed up again in daylight.

But the waiting was neither dull nor uninteresting. Instead the opposite was true, what with the big footprints engraved in the sandy soil all around. An old-timer had made those prints. The longer I waited the more suspenseful the waiting became. Every small noise made me more alert and more jittery as well. I recoiled when something as small as a chickadee alighted on a branch nearby or when a red fox came sneaking, half crouched and tail fluffed out, into the bait.

John had plenty of excitement too. After fishing through the afternoon and dressing several walleyes for dinner, he strolled leisurely to his blind. No more than 10 minutes later he heard a noise in the brush near his bait, but for another ½-hour he strained to see what made the noise. He recalls wanting a cigarette, but did not dare to light one. Finally he could distinguish the outline of a bear.

His impulse, he reported later while fishing, was to shoot. The animal was at point blank range and

Hunter waits perched high in tree stand overlooking a bait. Eventually, probably in near darkness, a bear will come.

screened in the brush it looked huge. But something suggested that he wait—the bear was unalarmed and seemed in no hurry to go anywhere—and so he waited.

"I'm glad I did," he said later, "because in brighter light it became a much smaller bear. I doubt if it weighed 100 pounds."

But during his next watch, John didn't wait. It was warm and still and he admits he probably dozed. Next thing he knew a bear was standing just beneath him and this one was no yearling cub.

"I couldn't move as long as the bear stood right below me," he said. "One false move and it would have been gone into thick willows. So I waited until it ambled toward the bait and into the open.

"I held on the animal's shoulder and squeezed. At the report it gave a terrible roar and charged out of sight. Seconds later it roared again. Then that was all. I waited for 30 minutes, climbed down and found the bear, dead as a doormat, about 40 yards away."

While John relaxed, fished for pike and arranged to have his rug shipped home, I spent another day in another blind for a change of pace—and hopefully for a change of luck. But the biggest critter I saw there was a pine squirrel which made as much noise as a small sawmill. If any bears came nearby, the squirrel would surely have warned them. I decided to return to the Floodwood blind. I'd had more action there and besides, I kept thinking about those big pawprints.

"Good idea," John agreed. "That way I can sleep late in the morning while you sit and suffer."

John knew what he was saying. After a while the sitting does become suffering. When nothing happens, you wonder why you suffer—the mosquitoes and the cramped quarters—while your partner is living it up.

It got to be both maddening and frustrating. Every night the big bear, as well as a not-so-big bear came to the bait and either ate or carried away a good portion of it. One day I deposited a canoe-load of black suckers in the baited area. I speared the suckers from a stream infested with mosquitoes while John was catching pike. It was the day he landed a 17½-pounder.

My last day didn't begin too well. If the alarm clock rang, I didn't hear it. In any case I was paddling across the mirror surface of Little Abitibi Lake toward my blind at daybreak. Actually I should have been *in* the blind at daybreak.

I landed the canoe on a miniature sand beach and tied it to a sapling on the bank. Then I walked up to inspect the bait. Maybe I was mistaken, but for the first time the bait seemed untouched overnight. Maybe the bruin also overslept and would be coming in later. But it was really a weak hope. I climbed the ladder to my blind and tried to find a comfortable way to sit. It wasn't long before the mosquitoes found me and bored in savagely.

It's hard to say how long they were boring when things began to happen. I saw the bear far away, but it was only a blur of black, and it was traveling. Next time

I saw it was moments later, still traveling, but much closer. That's the first time I noticed how hard my pulse was pounding. Goose pimples again. Mosquitoes, stay away from my ears. Then the bear was standing on the bait. Big and broadside—and black. When I squeezed the trigger, the bear had a foot-long sucker in its mouth. It slumped right where it was standing.

This wasn't the big Floodwood bruin. Pete reported it still at large weeks later. But it was a bear worth bragging about, especially after seven mornings and evenings on a lonely stand. Now, as all sensible sportsmen should be doing in springtime, I could go fishing again.

Once a spring bear hunt was a somewhat complicated and expensive expedition, but now it's within reach of most sportsmen. A hunter can either drive or fly right into Ontario's best bear country and flying costs little

Portrait of a Canadian black bear.

more than driving. Fast, efficient air service by Trans Canada Air Lines can transport an American sportsman from Cleveland or Chicago or New York in only a matter of hours. John and I had enjoyed a good breakfast in Cleveland and dinner at Little Abitibi.

A good portion of the Ontario's summer resort and fishing camp operators either do or can set up bear hunts and the package costs about $100 per day, usually with a 5-day minimum. Add to this the cost of an Ontario non-resident bear license. A hunter has about a 50-50 chance for success province-wide, but at some camps the odds are much better than that.

Perhaps the best part of any spring bear hunt is the dual opportunity to go fishing in good fishing country at a time when the fishing is the best. Once my bear hide was skinned and salted down, I returned to the walleyes of the Floodwood and gave them the roughest time they've had in many a moon.

MANY YEARS AGO, after tramping all night long through a damp woods, Si Flaugher and I slumped wearily against a deadfall and drank all that remained in a thermos of lukewarm coffee. Soon Si's two red-bones, Blue and Bugle, came in and sprawled in the wet leaves beside us. Bugle tried to bite out a thorn which had lodged in one paw. Blue fell sound asleep. Suddenly I was tired and sore all over. And disappointed.

Back in those days there weren't many raccoons in our part of southern Iowa. But if based on our experience that night, there were none at all because the dogs didn't find a single fresh track. All we actually accomplished was to make too many weary footprints across mighty rugged country. I remember very well how Si summed it up.

"You don't have to be crazy to hunt coons," the old man had concluded, "but it helps."

Well—nowadays the woods are full of coons. We've had a population explosion of the species during the past couple of decades and coon hunting was never any better over most of the country than it is right now. You can find all the action you want. But my old coon-hunting buddy was wrong—all wrong—in his summation, and he would be equally all wrong today.

I submit that you *do* have to be crazy to hunt coons.

Consider one hunt we had near Oskaloosa, Iowa, on a cool night only last fall. Like so many coon expeditions down in that part of the state, this one was organized by Bill Boatman and his first lieutenant, Jim "Butter" Cawley. Also like so many other hunts, the party grew and grew in size until it approached in numbers (and appearance) a band of guerrillas about to overthrow a dictator. Bill invited Ben Moore up from Missouri and that was a good idea because Ben owns some blue-ribbon Grand Night Champion hounds. Ben brought along a friend of his from Chillicothe, also with dog power. Then there was a farmer from over by Osceola, and he brought his son, plus a couple more mean looking dogs. Of course I invited my son, Bob, and Bob took the opportunity to invite a half dozen or so of his classmates at Iowa State University, most of them being on their very first coon hunt. I will not try to list the names and lineages of all the dogs simply because it would take too much space.

# CRAZY ABOUT COONS

## by JOE JACKSON

Old Buglemouth hits a hot trail, and it leads to this tree. "There's a big coon up there," the dog is barking.

And there's the quarry, looking down on a lot of unfriendly hounds.

In case you have never been on a coon hunt, let me describe this motley crew a little further. You could easily tell the experienced ones from the inexperienced. The former mostly wore rubber footgear (hip boots on a couple of them) and carried plenty of illumination. By that I mean they wore miners' headlamps on their caps and carried high-power flashlights in their hands or slung on straps over their shoulders. They also carried canteens of assorted beverages, sheath knives, ropes and leashes. There were two or three .22 pistols in evidence and somebody had a long, curved hunting horn. Nobody was dressed very fancy, quite the opposite, and the only things missing, I mused, were a guitar and bongo drums.

The whole gang assembled at Wildwood Kennels, a canine housing project which Bill Boatman built so he could keep more dogs than any hunter really needs. After washing down several dozen doughnuts with a couple of gallons of sweet cider—you might call it refueling—all hands headed for the woods. Those who owned dogs were practically dragged to the woods by the straining canines.

Actually we never made it to the woods. A faint trail worn by summertime fishermen leads along Paint Creek and past a large bottomland cornfield. At the very edge of the cornfield, one of the hounds bawled and a moment later all were bawling. Next thing I knew, a wild foot race was on—dogs after a corn-eating raccoon and men trying to keep up with coon-chasing dogs.

But that corn must have been vitamin-fortified and the coon very long-winded because soon it led the dogs almost out of hearing. At least all was quiet for several minutes. That suited me just fine because Butter Caw-

Invariably there's a big fight when the hounds catch a coon on the ground — or rather in the water.

95

ley stopped running and all of us had a chance to catch up and rest for a few minutes. But too soon the chase resumed and Butter shouted, "C'mon let's get moving. That's my dog leading the pack."

"No it ain't," another replied, "my Marvin is in first place."

Perhaps I should explain here that there are no ordinary coon dogs. I personally have never met a coonhound owner who did not consider his breed—treeing Walker, Plott, redbone, bluetick, black-and-tan or you name it—as absolutely the best and his dog the best of the breed. A lot of the yakking on any coon hunt concerns the bragging about dogs and on certain occasions, when the competition becomes very keen, it goes beyond bragging. I've seen some fist swinging, too.

For the first time that trip, when the hounds finally picked up the coon's track again on the far side of Paint Creek, it was easy to understand why some outdoorsmen will sacrifice a warm fireside for beating around in the bushes on cold, dark nights. That hound-dog music was something extraordinary to hear. It was an exciting savage symphony carried by the night air. There isn't anything in all the outdoors exactly like a hound-dog chorus in full cry. But it all ended abruptly when the dogs finally pushed the coon up a tree, and we went running pell-mell to the scene across a riffle of Paint Creek. At this point, the inexperienced hunters learned firsthand why the veterans were wearing rubber footgear. Somebody also learned the importance of good illumination when he lost his footing and floundered in a pool of icy water almost waist deep.

"I'll have to keep running the rest of the night," he moaned, "to keep warm."

The scene under the treed coon was pure and unadulterated bedlam. Hounds were barking, bawling and trying to climb up the trunk. It is always a surprise to me

(Above and below) Late evening and these hunters are ready to start the coon hunt. The dogs feel good and the hunters are fresh.

(Above and below) Hounds weren't meant for climbing trees, but they keep trying when a coon is hidden in the top.

to see how well some dogs actually can climb. Above the howling dogs, beams of light were playing back and forth in the treetop as hunters tried to locate the ruby eyes of the target. But the animal was so well hidden that most concluded it had taken refuge in a hollow of the tree. Then Bill spotted it.

"Near the top," he said, "on the right." Then all beams focused that way. The chase ended when somebody shot out the coon with a .22 pistol.

"What a great way to start a hunt," somebody said. A moment later we were flying again.

The rest of the night was pretty much of the same: long chases across cornfields, up steep hills, through bramble patches and honeysuckle, across creeks and through soggy swamps. Even with good lights to lead the way, it isn't exactly like pounding the smooth pavements, and a night of coon hunting means plenty of scratches and bruises along with the complaining muscles. These just can't be avoided. Duck hunters and ice fishermen like to think they are pretty rugged, but they are not in the same big league with the coon hunters. You either relish it or hate it—in other words you're crazy or relatively sane—and a good many sportsmen get hooked on it. Even though they suffer.

There isn't any mistaking the remarkable animal, *Procyon lotor,* the American raccoon, which causes otherwise normal individuals to become nocturnal once the hunting season opens. It's a sturdy, tenacious mammal, robust in form, with the black-face mask of a bandit and from four to six black rings on the tail. It is, in fact, called "ringtail" in some parts of the country.

A generation ago, coons were not really abundant anywhere except in the deep South and with emphasis on coastal lowland areas. But in recent decades they have gradually expanded their range to most of the United States and southern Canada, except the Rocky

Mountains. In much of this new area they have become very numerous—and perhaps even too abundant for their own good and for the good of some other wildlife sharing the same habitat. Of course the growing number of coon hunters are least likely to complain about the raccoon's present prosperity.

Females may breed when less than a year old, and although sexually active, most males (which average larger than females) do not breed until older than 12 months. All raccoons are promiscuous. Most young are born in tree dens, but as more and more coons adapt to nonwoodland environments, many are also born in underground dens, drain tiles, caves, barns and even in city sewer systems. The average litter is four with seven being maximum. When less than 2 months and weighing about 2 pounds, the little ones leave the dens of their own accord. At about 10 weeks, the young begin traveling with the mother who helps them find natural foods and disciplines them, sometimes harshly. A wild coon is very, very old at 7, but pets and zoo captives have been known to live beyond 14 years.

As any old coon hunter knows, an adult coon is intelligent, cunning, curious, a great climber and excellent swimmer. Coons are normally nocturnal, traveling and feeding after dark, except in coastal areas where they must forage whenever the tide is low, either day or night. In the South, coons are active the year-round. But the farther north and the colder the climate, the more they tend to sleep away the winter months in dens, tree hollows or squirrel nests.

Hearing and smell are less keen in raccoons than sense of touch. The species makes a number of natural noises, including growls, snarls, churring and even a quavering call which is owl-like. However, none of these sounds have volume enough to carry very far.

Just as it's characteristic for every coon hunter to brag about his dogs, so does every cooner exaggerate about the size of the raccoon he bags. If some of the claims I've heard were true, it wouldn't be safe to walk unarmed through many woodlands, and the toll in hounds would be great. Anyhow, the largest average coons come from the Midwest—the cornbelt—and the smallest from the Florida Keys where a 6-pounder is a very big one. A typical midwestern adult will run about 10 pounds and anything between 12 and 16 is good enough to brag about. There are a very few 25-pounders and beyond, but most of these weigh less on honest scales than when described by the hunter.

Somehow coon hunting just seems to generate unusual characters and situations. One really addicted cooner I met in Tennessee some years ago used a novel means to transport his hounds from home to woods and back home again. Most are satisfied with kennels or boxes in the bed of a pickup or station wagon, but this hunter bought a huge, secondhand, long wheel-base hearse, complete with black shrouds and angels carved on the doors for the purpose. Inside where the coffin would normally ride, the hunter built individual dog compartments of fragrant cedar and padded them with cedar shavings.

"Ain't nothing too good for my blueticks," he explained, "cause they's the best."

In most ways, coon hunting is entirely unchanged from the first time in history a hunter put his hound on a red-hot track and watched it run. But one innovation is the use of a wooden call, known as a coon squaller, invented and marketed by my friend Bill Boatman. Some hunters claim they can call a coon right down out of a tree—or at least make the animal move and show himself, by squalling. Many swear by it.

"But does it really work?" I asked Bill one day.

"We sell a lot of them," was all he would answer.

Even among coon hunters, Jim Moore is a stand-out, simply because he is so fanatic about the sport. He doesn't miss many nights afield during the open season when, his wife complains, he lives in the woods. By some coincidence, Jim lives in Yellow Springs, Ohio, the site of Antioch College which has a well-deserved reputation as a hippie hall of learning. It is one of those places where, when driving about the campus, it is most difficult to tell the male from the female students.

Well, as usual one night last fall, Jim went out for an evening of sport in a great coon woods not far from the school—unaware that a love-in or something similar was being held in the same place at the same time. Just after dark Jim unleashed his hounds and was pleased when they struck a steaming track very quickly.

The dogs ran a wild race through the woods with Jim close behind them, which ended abruptly beneath a huge old white oak. Then Jim flashed his light upward and did a double-take at what he saw.

"At first I figured I'd treed not one, but two of the biggest coons in the country," Jim reported. "But right away I realized coons don't wear beads and blue jeans. My dogs had treed me a pair of hippies."

"Say man," a voice asked from the tree, "what's with all the dogs making it."

"I'm coon hunting," Jim answered.

"Sounds marve, man," came the voice, "mind if we go along."

"Well no," Jim said. "Come on."

Then and there, perhaps for the first time in coon hunting history, two hippies dropped out of a tree and were on hand an hour later when the dogs treed a genuine raccoon. And all through the evening, more and more of them joined the party, as is usually the case on coon hunts.

"They seemed to enjoy it," Jim told his cronies at the next meeting of the county conservation club, "but one thing still puzzles me. I couldn't tell how many were girls and how many were boys. I had the feeling it didn't make much difference."

As I said, you have to be crazy to hunt coons. There's no doubt about it.

A very versatile dog, Mini would retrieve anything—from ruffed grouse to geese —and love it.

# My Ole Fat Black Dog

## by BOB KRUMM

**NINE YEARS AGO** in August, we lost our dog in a hunting accident. As my wife and I drove back to Jackson, Wyoming, we vowed we'd replace our lost dog as soon as possible.

Once home, a good friend told me of a fellow, Gordon Graham, who might still have a couple of black Labrador retriever pups. I called Gordon immediately. He had one pup left, a runt female. That's just what we wanted. We took one look at the little black critter and were sold. The Grahams had named the runt Mini; we thought the name appropriate and kept it.

That first meeting with Mini seems as if it were yesterday, although it was better than 9 years ago. I thought about it as Mini and I traveled from Jackson to Ocean Lake, Wyoming, last November 19th. That day she pushed through stand after stand of cattails in 10

inches of soft snow. She dug two crippled pheasants out of the dense vegetation and flushed three birds in easy range. I quit with my limit of three pheasants and walked to my vehicle. Mini couldn't climb in. The years of hard work had finally caught up with her. Her joints and muscles were just too stiff for her to jump. I had to lift her in and out when we got home. She couldn't even negotiate the front porch steps. The incident was painful to me. Mini has been my pal and constant companion for 9 years. I realize that our hunting days together now are limited, so if you don't mind, I'd like to relate why my "ole fat black dog," Mini, is so special to me.

There's an old adage that a man has only one good hunting dog in his life. Well, I guess my one good hunting dog is Mini. Since I hunt all the game birds in Wyoming, where I live—sage, ruffed, sharptail and blue grouse, pheasants, chukars, Hungarian partridge, ducks and geese—I need a versatile dog. A dog which can track, flush and retrieve upland game birds as well as retrieve waterfowl. She has done all this and more. She's withstood bitter cold and deep snows, slogged through slimy swamps and panted through hot sagebrush flats. She's even gone along on a spelunking expedition.

Our dog has always been a member of the family. She's been a house dog and has always had a special spot in each room where she could sun herself. I feel strongly that the more a dog is around its master the more it'll do for him. Mini has proved the theory correct.

When the pup was 6 months old, I took her for a walk to a weedy area outside Logan, Utah. It had snowed earlier in the day but 40-degree temperatures had melted off the snow and left the weeds damp. A light breeze hit her and a radical change came over the dog. Her tail started wagging, and she became quite active. Even though Mini was young and had never tracked a bird, it was evident that she was birdy. In the space of 10 minutes Mini had flushed 20 pheasants from the weed patch. She never stopped running in that span of time. She was hooked on birds from that day on, and I was hooked on my flashy little Lab.

Mini's first work experience with upland game birds came when she was 8 months old. We were hunting chukar partridge up Blacksmith Fork Canyon, near Logan, Utah. Mini hit a trail and took off through the rock ledges like a black flash. She jumped a covey of 20 or so birds. I managed to dump one, thank heaven, and she made the first retrieve of her life. It looked as if she'd been doing it for years.

I don't mean to imply that Mini was a "natural." Many dog owners brag of having a dog that hunted and retrieved from day one. I'm always skeptical of those dogs because sometimes the owner hasn't taken the time to train the dog, and the dog hunts and retrieves more through accident than design. A "natural" is as likely to eat his retrieved bird as deliver it to his master.

Many hours were spent with Mini teaching her obedience, running lines and hand signals. Mini took to the lessons quickly and soon 100- to 200-yard retrieves in heavy cover were commonplace.

The hard work started to pay off during her first full hunting season. That fall I was working for the Wyoming Game & Fish Department at the Yellowtail Habitat Unit near Lovell. One day Mini and I were out hunting pheasants. I shot twice that afternoon, missed once, but got three birds.

We had waded to an island in the Shoshone River. No sooner did we get on the Russian olive isle than she came to life. Tail wagging furiously, she charged through the low brush and jumped a pheasant. I managed to track the bird's flight as it twisted through the vegetation. As it flew through a small clearing, I pulled off a quick shot and nailed the bird. It landed in the river, and Mini followed it in with a classy water entry. She swam back with the bird, delivered it to my hand, shook off and hit another trail. She charged into the low-lying trees and brush and jumped a big rooster. He clattered up with a screen of olive branches between him and me. I fired one shot in desperation but didn't touch a feather. Mini ran after the bird and came back in a minute with a live hen pheasant that was unhurt! The season was open for either sex so I put the bird in my bag and continued. Later in a cattail swale, Mini jumped a crippled pheasant, caught it and retrieved it. Two shots and three birds was not a bad average, thanks to Mini.

On yet another day's hunting at Lovell, I cracked a rooster pheasant down in some of the foulest cover imaginable—salt cedar. The ole boy must have come down running. Mini had flushed the pheasant but with the cover so dense she couldn't see the bird land. When Mini bounded out into a small clearing I gave her a line, she disappeared into the tangle of salt cedar and a couple of minutes later reappeared with the live cock bird in her mouth. The bird was looking around and seemed to say, "This isn't in the script: Pheasant gets knocked down in salt cedar, pheasant gets away. It's just not in the script to get caught."

About 15 minutes after that incident, Mini flushed a cock bird from the salt cedar. I was walking along the Bighorn River, and the pheasant was bound he was going to cross it. The bird seemed destined to make it too, after I missed on my first barrel, but the second barrel's full choke load of 6's clobbered him 35 yards out. The rooster smacked down in the Big Horn. Mini came out, and I gave her a line. The river bank was steep and offered no easy entry. She leaped off the 4-foot high bank, hit with quite a splash, and before the column of water had settled she was lined out on the bird and going for it. Mini whined while swimming out and back (she has always done it; she likes birds so much, she can't get to them quickly enough). I grabbed a clump of salt cedar and went over the edge of the bank. When the dog got to shore, I grasped her collar with my free hand and helped her up the bank. Of course, I lost my footing and went in the murky Big Horn up to my knees, but it was a small price to pay to have my dog safely ashore.

On many occasions Mini has shown a canine intelligence you might call bird sense. One day we were hunting with a fellow who owned an Irish setter. The dog locked up on a couple of points and pheasants flushed. Mini watched twice before it dawned on her. She'd circle around and pounce on the pointed birds. She caught two that day. She tried for the third and missed, thank heaven. She did however, manage to pull out some tail feathers from—of all things—a tom turkey as it flapped away. Mini never has been intimidated by the size of the bird: if it's got feathers, she'll retrieve it.

Training is important. Here author encourages Mini to retrieve on command, but it really wasn't necessary. She did it naturally.

Regardless of Mini's determination to retrieve anything with feathers, her diminutive size always has raised hunter's eyebrows. One particular incident comes to mind. It was opening day for goose season at Ft. Collins, Colorado. The guys I was hunting with kept asking me if Mini was big enough to retrieve the large Canada geese that were in the area. At the end of the day my mini Lab had retrieved seven—three of which were cripples. The guys stopped asking foolish questions.

Mini's first retrieve that day involved a swim of more than 200 yards (one way). A heart-shot honker had flown over the reservoir behind our blind and died. I walked Mini over to the point nearest the goose. That bird looked no longer than ¼-inch from where I stood. The ole fat black dog took a line, wavered once but took a hand signal and kept going. I did a lot of praying that time and the good Lord must have heard me. It was the first retrieve of the year for Mini, the water was close to freezing, she was out of shape, and the goose was big (12 pounds or so). A lesser dog would have quit, abandoned the goose and come in. But Mini kept a firm hold on the base of the goose's neck and paddled all the way with it. I'm not ashamed to admit I was crying when Mini finally came ashore.

On another day in another season a Canada goose nearly drowned Mini. On December 28, 1974, A.J. De

Rosa and I sneaked a flock of geese below the Wilson Bridge of the Snake River, Wyoming. The river was more slush than water, it was snowing hard and the 15-degree temperature didn't help matters. As A.J. and I bellied up to a log jam, I could hear Mini starting to whine. She knew birds were in the offing. A.J. and I exchanged nods, jumped up, and drew beads on the alarmed Canadas. Two fell, but they swam to a large island across the main channel of the Snake. Mini had a 35-yard swim to get to the island.

I gave her a line, hollered "back," and the show was on. Mini never hesitated. She plunged into the slushy water and swam for the island.

One crippled goose stood its ground. Mini crawled out onto the island and ran at it. The goose raised its wings and prepared to pummel the dog. But the goose never laid a wing on the dog for she had leaped for the base of the honker's neck and hung on.

Mini turned and headed for the water. Swimming back her vision was obscured by the flopping goose wings. An ice island formed by an uprooted cottonwood tree barred her way. The obstacle surprised her, and it looked like she was going to be swept under the ice island and drown. Most dogs would have tried to swim upstream, but not Mini. She swam downstream and somehow managed to go around the trap. As she neared the shore, I slid out on the ice shelf and grabbed her by the collar with shaking hands and pulled her and the goose onto firm ground.

The other goose retrieve was anticlimactic—a standard swim, track it down and bring it back. I had heard a crunch back on the island, and I knew the goose was dead when Mini entered. There was no messing around this time.

If the second goose incident was anticlimactic, the goldeneye retrieve that Mini made later that day surely wasn't. A.J. and I had eased up over a dike along the main channel of the Snake. A common goldeneye drake was right in front of us. It scrambled for flight, and we both pasted it. It fell, hit the water and dived. When it surfaced, we finished it off, but unfortunately, it had managed to put 40 yards between us.

Mini entered the water and started her winning swim. She shouldered ice flows away and finally reached the duck. By the time she had grabbed it, both she and the duck had been carried downstream quite a distance. As she swam back, her route took her through rocky rapids. One wave completely buried her. She popped to the surface but kept paddling homewards. All that trouble for one goldeneye, which incidentally, she never dropped. That night and for quite a few to come, Mini was fed well-cooked deer meat scraps and allowed to sleep under the cook stove.

Mini has been the type of dog that instills confidence into her owner and master. It seems the more impossible the retrieve appeared, the more likely Mini would make it. I'm sure hunting dog owners know what I'm talking about. The old dog is just plain reliable, and it comes as a surprise when she actually fails. For Mini, the failure is a dead bird that comes crashing down into heavy cattails. Darned little scent is available, and the going is tough. If I mark the spot well, I can keep her in the right area until she finally sticks her nose into enough spots and finds the bird. In 9 years of bird hunting with Mini she has probably accounted for over 1,000 birds and failed to deliver a mere 25. That's pretty good odds and that's why Mini instills confidence and pride.

Today game birds are limited in number. It behooves each sportsman to retrieve every bird he brings down. A good bird dog is invaluable at that time. Besides, what would bird hunting be without a dog? It would be like kissing your sister or eating a caramel with the wrapper on. A dog adds spice to the occasion and makes foggy mornings when the mallards are coming into the decoys as memorable as any in your life. Invariably, the dog has locked in on them before you know they are there. Its whine alerts you. You give a quick feeding chuckle on the call, and the wary ducks come in. You jump up, point the gun at the fat drake which is backpedalling frantically. The over and under recoils,

Is man's best friend a dog, any dog, or just a Labrador retriever?

Author and Lab with a pair of mallards after a difficult retrieve. A millionaire couldn't buy that dog.

the duck crumples, and you swing to the next climbing greenhead. It comes down in a shower of feathers, and the feathers come down as softly as the curtain of fog that descends over the scene. The dog crashes into the black, still water, and its wake disturbs the calm pond surface. Soon both drakes are in hand and the dog is shaking itself off, scanning the skies intently for more ducks.

This kind of memory remains in every duck hunter's mind. Without the dog to share the moment with you, it wouldn't be half as indelible.

For me, that dog is Mini, the dog of my dreams and my memories. She has given me years of enjoyment and not asked for more than a sunny spot to nap in, some food and an occasional pat on the head. When times were rough, she was there. Mini has sat and listened to me pour my heart out when she was the only one who'd listen. She's been the one who would bail me out when I bragged too hard about her. Fellows who would never hunt with a Lab started asking for a pup from Mini after just one outing.

Mini has been a source of pride and joy that time will not take from me. She's the one her veterinarian, Ken Griggs, looks forward to seeing. "She's got personality," he'll say. Mini will take her shots without a fuss and then lick Ken's hand in return. Mini is the one dog Ken does not want to see when I bring her for the last office call. He wants to be out of the office that day.

For now, Mini still hunts with me and keeps her 3-year-old daughter, Maxi, honest. I've cut Mini's outings to half days. Her younger and bigger pup goes all day. Mini's more acute nose and bird sense usually account for her flushing more birds. Maxi's larger size and faster speed usually allows her to accomplish the retrieves. The pair does so well that my hunting buddies have dubbed them the "black bookends," apparently in reference to the way in which Mini and Maxi take care of both ends of a picture book hunting scene.

As I sit at the typewriter, happy memories come to mind—memories that Mini has made. She has managed some incredible retrieves on pheasants and ducks. Once, she brought back two mallards simultaneously— one by the neck, one by the wing tip. She's taken mallards out of muskrat dens, under willows and beneath the water. One snowy weekend at Torrington, Wyoming, she caught five pheasants that were reluctant to fly.

Mini helped me on a ruffed grouse study in Utah and has protected my home from all sorts of "villains" (United Parcel deliverymen, mailmen, policemen, anybody in uniform). She has outsmarted me on all efforts to keep her kenneled or chained. For somehow she manages to get free. She knows the location of every garbage can in town, and she seems to know the dogcatcher's schedule. Even though Mini has her faults, I couldn't bear to part with her. I have been offered $1500 for her by an impressed hunter. But how could I ever sell a member of the family?

# WAIT FOR YOUR BUCK

The waiting game is a lot easier if you have a firm, flat platform with a good view all around.

*by BARNEY PETERS*

**ON OPENING DAY** of Michigan's deer season several years ago, a stranger strolled into a tavern in a small town on the Upper Peninsula. Dressed in shiny new boots and brand new hunting togs, he was obviously a neophyte sportsman.

"Exactly where," he asked no one in particular, "can I bag a big buck in a hurry. I have to be back in Detroit tomorrow."

"Just go outside the village limits," the bartender volunteered, tongue in cheek, "and sit down. They's deer every place around here."

As soon as the stranger left, everyone joined the bartender in a big horse laugh. But they'd hardly finished the next round of drinks when the man returned—with a buck as big as a heifer lashed onto his car fender.

"Just want to thank you guys," he said. "I didn't know deer hunting was so easy!"

The incident which, (according to a news story) is entirely true isn't as ridiculous as it may sound. Although it was intended as a practical joke, the tavern-keeper's advice was about as good as any he could have given to a deer hunter—experienced or a raw beginner. It's as true in Montana, or Missouri, or New Mexico as it is in Michigan, no matter what kind of

(Left and below) Wait for your buck in the right place and you may be dragging the animal out of the woods soon after the season opens.

deer are being hunted. The best, most certain way to bag your own buck this fall is to go out someplace, sit down—and play a waiting game.

Of all the wild critters in American woodlands, I believe deer must be considered among the most shy and wary. As any deer hunter knows, it isn't an easy matter to stalk within rifle range of a good buck. But the odds are much better, perhaps five times better, if you let the deer come to you.

When hunting seasons are open, deer are much more restless than at other times. Mule deer of the West are often traveling from summer to winter range, from high country to lower altitudes. Almost everywhere the rut is either beginning or is in progress. The gigolo bucks especially are wandering about.

But even during all this movement and restlessness, deer are creatures of habit, confining their movements—unless disturbed—to early morning and late afternoon hours. They tend to follow the same patterns, trails, and crossings day after day, week after week, and even year after year. It follows that a wise

The waiting paid off. You now have a fine whitetail buck. The season is a great success.

Wait along a deer stand, in a tree or behind a screen of brush, or along a busy deer trail, and something will come along.

hunter first finds an area which deer are "using," and after that stations himself on a stand nearby. Sounds simple, doesn't it?

Playing the waiting game isn't always as easy as it sounds. It's a skill—or maybe an art—and it requires some preparation. For example, waiting motionless in wintertime can become mighty uncomfortable. But it isn't necessary to suffer either of these inconveniences, and here's how it's done.

After selecting a stand, Lew Baker, a hunting friend, takes a saw, axes, nails, and a roll of baling wire to the site. There he builds his blind in a tree or between several trees. In Minnesota, the law restricts him to a blind only 6 feet off the ground, but elsewhere this regulation doesn't exist. His isn't a slipshod or flimsy structure—it's sturdy and well built. A structure which creaks or groans under a man's weight only serves to alert approaching deer. Another hunter I know goes Lew one step better, he covers the floor of his blind with an old piece of carpet to muffle the scuffling sound of his boots!

Once he is settled on his perch, Lew becomes a sporting goods salesman's dream come true. Besides several layers of down- or dacron-filled clothing and his rifle, he has along the following: a large thermos of hot beverage, foul weather gear, a camera, a tasty lunch, small smokeless heater, and a couple of handwarmers.

Whether it's done from an insulated overhead blind or just by sitting on a fallen tree trunk, the waiting game is the deadliest technique of all for the hunter with a haunch of venison on his mind. Here's why. A man or animal in motion is always easier to see than when standing still. In addition, the man or deer that moves is also making noise, perhaps only a slight noise, but a sound nonetheless. In addition a man who is moving broadcasts his own scent more than when he is sitting in one place. All of this means that the advantage of first discovery belongs to being motionless, no matter whether hunter or hunted.

However, few humans have vision or hearing nearly as good as deer. Therefore, a hunter must use other means to balance the situation back in his favor. Perhaps camouflage is the best of these means. Every experienced hunter has seen deer practically evaporate into their surroundings, and the truth is that a hunter can do the same thing.

There are many ways a hunter can blend into his background while waiting on stand. One way is to remain motionless—and that means *absolutely* motionless. Of course it's difficult to do for long periods, but it's most important. A movement as slight as slapping at a mosquito or winding a watch will certainly spook an approaching deer or one standing unnoticed nearby. If you *have* to move on stand, do so very slowly and deliberately.

Try to take as much advantage as possible of vegetation. It might be cattails, holly bushes, balsam, or prickly pear, it doesn't make any difference. Stay in the shadows rather than in bright sunlight or even in open shade.

In some states, the law requires a deer hunter to wear red or scarlet clothing. But the value of brightly-colored clothing is debatable. If a man remains completely motionless, and is at least partially screened by natural cover, neither deer nor other hunters will spot him very easily. Besides, there's plenty of evidence that all deer (as well as some hunters) are color-blind.

Waiting-game hunters also have their problems. After 2 days of watching, a hunter left his stand just long enough to walk to a spring nearby for a drink of cool water. As luck would have it, at precisely that time a black bear came along, smelled the hunter's lunch, and carried it away with him. Footprints in the soft earth provided the evidence.

Still, the season's tough luck trophy might go to a Colorado sportsman who, after waiting and watching diligently for more than a week in the Rocky Mountains, finally dropped a tremendous mule deer buck. Its head was bigger than anything the man had ever dreamed about.

With trembling hands, the man placed his rifle across the deer's antlers, and stepped back to take a picture of his "kill," but all his picture revealed was the deer's rear end vanishing in the general direction of Wyoming. By some curious circumstance, the deer had been momentarily stunned. When it suddenly revived, it trotted away with the hunter's rifle on its head, never to be seen again.

Some days a man can't win—even if he plays the waiting game and plays it well.

(Left) It isn't an easy matter to stalk within rifle range of a good buck. Your odds are better if you let the buck come to you.

(Below) Waiting on the edge of a Minnesota swamp. Be ready for a fast, running shot.

# Hunting Big Game

Not a big whitetail buck by any means, but still a handsome photo of a winter woodland scene.

To hunt goats with gun or camera, it's necessary to explore some of highest, roughest corners of America.

**ON A GOLDEN MORNING** in mid-September several years ago, I watched a wilderness encounter which too few ever see in the Teton-Bridger National Forest. The arena was a sunlit clearing beside the Thorofare River where a crisp hoar frost still coated the meadow grass. There two huge bull elk challenged and fought for a harem of sleek cows which grazed nearby and seemed to have no interest whatsoever in the outcome.

Here unfolded a primitive, exciting duel as old as the evolution of the species. The beasts bugled, backed away briefly, tore at the frosted turf and then lunged forward, rattling antlers head to head. Steam rose from their wet bodies. Finally one had had enough and hurried away. The victor pranced among the cows which were still unimpressed. But best of all, I captured the confrontation on film, and although the pictures are not as perfect technically as more recent ones, they are among my treasured hunting trophies today.

For the past quarter century I have been a professional hunter especially of big game of the Rocky Mountains. But I do nearly all of my hunting with a camera, color film and a telephoto lens. Not too long ago outdoor photography might have been considered a unique profession. All at once wildlife pictures are beautiful. Nowadays with the expanding new interest both in photography and conservation, it seems that everyone who owns a camera is getting into the act, and it is no wonder. More and more Americans, who relish the outdoors are discovering that wildlife photography is a most fascinating and rewarding way to spend leisure time. Entire vacations can become photo safaris at any time of the year. Fortunately there are unlimited opportunities to film the beautiful animals of our country —occasionally as close to home as the shy deer in our own gardens or pasture—to the remotest national parks. Most of my own photography occurs in the cool

# With a Camera
## by ERWIN A. BAUER

This polar bear photo was made by drifting silently close to the ice floe on which the animal was resting.

This Alaskan wolf was photographed when it came close to our camp on an Alaskan salmon stream.

green forests of the West and for two reasons. First it is my own favorite "natural habitat," and I am more alive and happier in these evergreen woodlands. Second, it is just about the best place of all to find photo targets.

Hunting big game with a camera has a good many advantages over hunting with a gun. For one thing it can be a far greater challenge because a camera hunter must approach much closer to his target. Even with the greatest lenses ever developed, shots at 200 and 300 yards are out of the question.

A cameraman is never burdened with closed seasons, bag limits or other restrictions. I can hunt any time of the year and shoot the most endangered species as well as the most common big game. Hunting in sanctuaries is permitted, even invited, and there are no expensive hunting licenses to buy. Make no mistake about the satisfaction—the rewards—of camera hunting; I am more proud of the photos in my files than of the few

antlers on my wall. And I've had my share of thrills as well as disappointments and anxious moments, shooting some of those pictures.

Big game photography—serious big game photography at least—isn't always without physical discomforts, such as sudden dunkings in cold water or suffering in blazing heat. One dunking years ago can be blamed on an enthusiastic friend who figured that we could film elk and mule deer (and at the same time catch rainbow trout) if we could run through a certain canyon of the Madison River in Montana called the Beartrap. We could do it in rubber rafts and emerge intact at the other end. It seemed like a good idea to me too, until we approached the first rapids. However rapids wasn't the proper word for that funnel. But by then it was too late to turn back, and my lingering impression is that we were violently sucked the complete distance through the Beartrap. Somehow en route, before the camera was doused, I managed to take pictures of the dunking, although not of elk or deer. But what an indelible lesson that was.

However, there may be good in every experience. At least the Beartrap trip taught me a few things about keeping photo equipment dry in similar situations later on. It was an expensive lesson, but very valuable in the long run.

Another lesson was to learn my limits. Far too often in the excitement of the chase, I've found myself in precarious places from which it was difficult to retreat. Time and time again when the targets were mountain goats or bighorn sheep, I climbed to places a human shouldn't really venture without ropes. Maybe I am cured now, but maybe not. Probably it all depends on the size of the next bighorn ram I find.

Thanks to big game photography, I also know what it's like to be lost, or at least disoriented, as I was once deep in Alaska's Wrangell Mountains. On this sheep filming venture, a camp and supplies were to be airdropped at a certain destination in sheep country, but somehow were dropped at the wrong place. Temporar-

ily I was lost trying to find the gear. Completely without shelter, Lew Baker and I managed 3 days of almost continual sleet and drizzle. It seemed inevitable that the only conclusion of the trip would be an insurance claim on waterlogged cameras.

But discomfort can be quickly forgotten when things suddenly break right. One morning, after locating the thin trail which led to our supplies, I felt tremendously exhilarated as I looked at four white Dall rams in my viewfinder. And the sheep stared back at me long enough to get some of the photos I wanted. Then and there, earlier hardships of the expedition evaporated.

Although any kind of photography may appear bewildering at first, the simple truth is that shooting good big game pictures is not that difficult. You do need a certain amount of equipment and some pros carry prodigious amounts of it, but extraordinary wildlife photos have come from cameras which are neither costly nor complicated. Of course filming experience is helpful and so is some knowledge of wildlife behavior. Some hunting experience can be helpful. But even starting from scratch, good big game animal photos are very soon possible.

I believe the best, most convenient camera for wildlife photography is the single lens reflex 35mm. It will handle either color or black/white film. Most of the 35mm cameras on the market today are virtually so foolproof that you simply aim and snap to get a perfect exposure. Which model to buy or use depends more on your budget than on anything else. Often the only difference between expensive and inexpensive models is the small difference in the quality of the lens (which all but experts may not be able to detect) or the feature of being able to interchange lenses.

Because all big game is shy at least to some degree and will not allow humans to approach as close as they would like, one accessory—the telephoto lens—is essential to nearly all wildlife photography. The so-called normal 35mm camera (which has a focal length of 50mm, the distance between lens glass and film inside the camera), which comes with a 50mm lens, produces a picture exactly as the eye sees it. But a telephoto lens with a longer than normal focal length increases the size of the animal's image on film—and therefore makes it seem much closer.

Telephotos for 35mm cameras are now manufactured up to 1000mm (which magnify the subject four or six times) but 200, 300 or 400mm are far more practical for anyone. It is absolutely necessary to hold any telephoto lens perfectly still when filming and to use the fastest possible shutter speed—up to 1/1000 second if the exposure permits it. The explanation for all this is that the longer the telephoto lens, the more it also magnifies any camera motion and so results in fuzzy pictures. Whenever possible, use either a rest (such as the car door or a tree limb) or a tripod for the most sharpness

A very long telephoto lens can bring some trophies closer if the day is bright and the animal motionless.

(Above and below) A telephoto lens is necessary to shoot most big game animals, especially shy walruses as here.

In some parks and sanctuaries it is possible to film animals at very close range, as this mule deer fawn.

A wolf with a deer kill is a seldom seen sight — and rare photo as well.

and detail in the finished picture. Always avoid ugly or unnatural backgrounds such as fences, buildings or wires. Telephoto lenses with small depths of focus will help accomplish this by blurring everything but the subject. But the best way is to adjust your camera angle by correctly approaching the subject to eliminate the unwanted background.

Consider for a moment the types of telephoto lenses now available which are suitable for hunting big game. Most common and usually least expensive are those workhorses of wildlife photography, telephotos in 200, 300 and 400mm focal lengths. You use and focus them exactly as the shorter lenses. But during the past few years, so-called zoom lenses, each with variable focal lengths have become available. For instance one zoom

lenses is fixed at one place—say f8 on a 500mm lens or f11 on a 100mm lens. The correct exposure is obtained by changing shutter speeds. In spite of this handicap, one of my favorite and most frequently used big game lenses today is a 500mm mirror lens mounted on a Nikon F2 with a motor drive.

Many wildlife photographers like to mount their camera and telephoto combinations on a gunstock or something similar for faster shooting. Some commercial stocks are available, but most people prefer to custom-build and design their own. I personally do not like these stocks and regard them as only an added weight to lug around. But there is no denying that excellent big game photos have been made by many of those gunstock fans.

The cougar is another animal rarely encountered, even in those places where it still survives.

lens may offer a range of focal lengths from 70mm to 200mm and another from 100mm to 300mm. The advantage is obvious. With a zoom, a photographer now needs to carry one instead of several lenses. And the optics of most zooms on the market today are remarkably good.

Another recent development constantly being improved is the mirror or reflex telephoto lens. The advantage of these is that they are shorter and lighter, and therefore far more convenient and faster to use than other telephotos of the same focal length. In other words, the tube or actual distance between glass and camera connection of a 500mm mirror lens may be half the length and weight of any other type of 500mm lens. However there are drawbacks. The f-stop of mirror

Although expensive and occasionally temperamental, motor drives can be extremely valuable. Capable of shooting as many as three or four frames per second, they are excellent for sequences and for following animals in motion. But even more, a motor drive permits a cameraman to concentrate on his subject completely, without the bother of advancing the film. For a really serious big game shooter, that one advantage more than justifies the considerable expense of the drive.

Still it is too easy to overemphasize the importance of the equipment. No camera or lens combination is ever any better than the man behind it. Vastly more important than the cost and quality, is to be entirely familiar with the equipment. And familiarity—which means fast, accurate handling and focusing—comes only with

Wildlife is often more confiding in winter and therefore easier to approach, especially on snowshoes or cross-country skis when the snow is deep.

plenty of practice, even if there is no film in the camera.

Practice can begin at home. Take the family pet outdoors and film it in action—running, jumping, retrieving a stick, anything it does. This is good training for staying on target and for more rapid camera handling. Use black and white film at first because it is much less expensive than color. For more advanced practice go shooting at the local zoo, at race horse farms, ranches, rodeos, or even livestock shows. Many modern zoos exhibit wild animals in completely natural surroundings. But no matter where you shoot, your goal should be to shoot automatically—to follow and focus without having to think about it.

Proper carrying containers are almost as important as the camera and lenses. Both the leather camera cases and equipment bags in common use are next to useless for a person spending much time afield searching for big game. I carry my own equipment in an exterior frame backpack with many compartments. Each camera and lens is sealed inside a waterproof, dustproof, ziplock bag. Moisture and dust are genuine bugaboos both to getting good pictures and to smooth operation of equipment. When traveling I carry my gear in sealed aluminum luggage lined with polyurethane to spare shock and rough handling.

Although even freezing temperatures have no real effect on film or equipment (if it is clean and dry), pictures may require slightly greater exposures than the same shots in summertime. But a notable exception would be when it is a marine or snow-covered scene in bright sunlight. If you do not have an exposure meter, consult the exposure data sheet which comes with every roll of film. Do not bring cold cameras suddenly into warm rooms. Condensation will occur, especially inside lenses, and that can cause trouble.

I use two different techniques to photograph wild creatures; I either stalk or play the waiting game. Of course, stalking is done on foot but is unlike hunting with a gun. When a target is spotted I do not try to stay concealed and creep up on the animal unseen. On the contrary, I deliberately stay in sight—where the animal can watch me—and know what I am doing. That way I get as close as possible—slowly, cautiously, never directly toward the subject and never making sudden moves or loud noises. In some parks and sanctuaries where wildlife is used to seeing people, the animals often become very tolerant of humans with cameras. Elsewhere the "stalking" can be done by car; in many of the national parks, animals will allow a vehicle to approach very close, but will bolt the instant a person steps outside.

Let's assume that we have spotted a herd of mule deer when driving through a forested area. First realize that the deer have seen the car as well, even if they did not look up in recognition. Since the animals are fairly distant, our only chance for a photo is to approach nearer. So we begin, staying in full view. We must avoid

Desert bighorns survive in some mountain ranges of our southwestern states. That large ram (right) is the camera trophy of anybody's lifetime.

staring directly at the game. Instead look around and seem disinterested. It is wise to make exposures at regular intervals in the event you never get any closer. Watch for signs of nervousness (which all animals exhibit) such as stomping, drifting away, flicking or flattening ears, snorting, raising a tail—and stop short

Completely surprised, this whitetail fled the instant the shutter snapped.

114

when you see them. One anxious animal can spook the whole herd. If the animal does appear nervous, stop the stalk for awhile and again try to appear disinterested in the target.

Virtually all big game animals are most active very early and very late in the day, which means that these are the best times to be afield. I've found a very early breakfast to be far more important for better wildlife photos than an expensive camera. I use the middle of the day to clean lenses and load film, especially during very hot periods of summer.

The waiting game—sitting in a fixed blind—works best in a baited area in the vicinity of a game trail, a swamp, or a waterhole which wildlife are known to frequent. The blind might actually be your own kitchen from which you film the deer at bait or feeding station just outside. Farther afield, blinds can be anything from a small tent or camouflaged packing crate to a mere screen of natural foliage. Many large animals never expect danger from above and so seldom look up. A tree or platform blind is good for these. Some professional photographers use lightweight, collapsible blinds of aluminum tube framing covered with burlap, weathered canvas or artificial turf material. If left standing long enough, many animals become so used to the structure that they accept it as normal.

Obviously the best places to go filming are those where wildlife is given some protection or to which it is deliberately attracted. A list of these would include all national parks and the surrounding national forests, most national wildlife refuges, many corporation managed forestlands, especially in the Southeast, many state parks and refuges, wintering grounds, municipal or private reserves and sanctuaries.

There is only one conclusion to make. Wherever there is forestland in America, there is also wildlife. And that means happy hunting grounds for all hunters with cameras.

Look for large animals where their food is most abundant, as in willow thickets for winter moose.

It's exciting enough just to see bull elk dueling during the fall rut. But it's even better to capture the scene on film.

Caribou, at times whole herds of them, can be easily seen at Alaska's McKinley National park.

I WASN'T READY for that moment. I never am. The roar of a thousand wing beats erupting like detonated dynamite, the rapid bark of Bill's trusty scattergun, our staunchly pointing dogs suddenly alert for plummeting birds, a blurred field of fire filled with buzzing bombshells, a fleeting target out there in front of my own gun muzzle, a frantic shot—and then another, an explosion of feathers—and then silence. Dead silence while the judge and I took stock.

All of that and a bit more had been crammed into an action-packed couple of seconds. That's the explosive flush of a covey of bobwhite quail, one of the most dramatic moments in all of American hunting. As I said, I am never quite ready for it though I have hunted the bobwhite for over 40 years. But about that "a bit more."

Many quail hunters live for the explosive flush of the covey. I have already elaborated on the reason, but as any experienced bird hunter knows it isn't the covey flush that puts birds in the hunter's game pocket. Hunting the single birds does that. The singles are the scattered birds, the temporary refugees from the covey. To hunt them successfully, the hunter must follow their flight as they scatter from the covey flush. That is the "bit more" action the bird hunter must get into the

pletely neglects this important moment in bird hunting. This is understandable. Marking down dead birds is to be commended, but the veteran hunter relies on his dogs to recover the kill. Actually, a fast-thinking hunter can do both—mark down his dead bird or birds, and then follow the flight of the rest of the covey. This too requires concentration, but it comes with practice.

Rarely will a gang of birds hang together when flushed. Instead they scatter—often widely and to different points of the compass. Some may cross streams and lakes beyond the reach of the hunter and his dogs. Hunters usually work the closest birds first and follow up on the splinter groups if there is time and they can be reached.

The quail, like most ground-nesting birds, spends little time in the air, resorting to sudden, explosive flight only when danger demands it. While it is a strong flier it can not flit about through the woods as does the average songbird. Once aloft it likes to glide on set wings, and it lacks the ability to suddenly alter its course. For this reason it is not unusual for a quail to fly against a building, an automobile or even a tree.

Because of its limited maneuverability, the bobwhite quail seeks an opening in the forest canopy through which to reach its beloved forest floor. The hunter

# Singles Fill the Bag
## by BOB GOOCH

already overcrowded few seconds.

Effective singles hunting begins with the covey find. The hunter gets into the act when he approaches his dogs on a covey point. As he approaches the point, he should attempt to pinpoint the likely escape route the birds will take. Usually they can be expected to streak for the nearest cover—a point of woods, a swamp, a wooded cliff, a fresh cutover, or like cover. The experienced hunter can pick it out quickly.

This determined, the dogs should be approached so that the fleeting birds will be in front of the hunter—not buzzing back overhead, or off to the left or right where part of the hunting party will be blocked from the shooting. This approach is just as important to the usually productive singles shooting that will follow.

Covey shooting requires the utmost in concentration, but the successful singles hunter has to switch his attention immediately to the fleeing birds—and he has just a couple of seconds to do so. He must follow the flight of the birds and establish the general location where they put down. It is seldom possible to fix the exact spot.

The inexperienced hunter will likely become so engrossed in retrieving the downed birds that he com-

should seek the single birds around such openings. Old logging roads, trails, utility right-of-ways and the like attract many flushed birds, and the hunter should work the vicinity of such areas thoroughly. Streams also provide openings in the forest canopy and it is not unusual to find single birds here. Cutovers are natural areas and so are swamps where there is limited overhead cover.

While the bobwhite likes an opening in a forest canopy it also needs cover, and for this reason the modern bobwhite rarely puts down in an open field. The modern hunter does not depend upon such opportunities to fill his limit—anymore than he depends upon the covey shooting.

Some of the very best covey dogs do poorly on the singles. The reason will become obvious. Good covey dogs range widely, move fast and cover a lot of ground, and the feeding coveys lay down a lot of scent for them to work on. It's a real joy to watch a fast covey dog circle a field, pick up a trail and pin down the birds. It is stylish quail hunting, but in many ways mostly reminiscent of a bygone age.

The single bird, on the other hand, is air-washed from its hasty flight. Most of its body odor is temporarily gone by the time it alights. It hits the ground and streaks for the nearest cover leaving precious little scent for the dogs to work on. Alone and scared it huddles with feathers and wings clamped tightly against its body putting out very little scent.

The best singles dog is the opposite of the covey dog. It is more methodical, probably has a stronger nose and is slow and thorough. Good singles dogs are usually also excellent retrievers, good at locating dead birds.

Frequently, the continental breeds such as the German short-haired pointer make better singles dogs than

quail hunter adopts many of the tactics of the grouse hunter. In fact good singles cover and good grouse cover are often the same where the ranges of the two birds overlap. Cutover forests are a fine example.

The modern bobwhite lives by its wits. In the fields the coveys are edgy and jumpy. They explode at the slightest hint of danger, and many flush long before the hunter can get within range. This is one reason so many bird hunters look to the singles for their limits.

Unlike the feeding covey, in the open and exposed, the single bird is naturally isolated and frightened.

These South Carolina hunters could get fair shots at quail seeking openings in the forest canopy.

do the traditional English pointers and setters because of their penchant for working closely and checking out every likely bird cover.

Ideally, the complete quail hunter has both in his kennels. For years I have got by with a pair of dogs, a big-going English setter and a plodding German short-haired pointer. They make a good team, honor each other's points and do their respective jobs. They rarely hunt together, however. The short-hair simply cannot keep up with the setter—and doesn't try to.

Once he switches from covey hunting to singles, the

Huddled under a log or shrub, it is afraid to expose itself. It will hold well for the dogs. A hunter can walk within a few feet of the single bird, and it will not flush, but like the grouse, it cannot stand the suspense created when the hunter stops walking. Apparently fearing it has been spotted, it will often flush wildly.

The singles hunter should be ready to shoot at any moment. He never rests his gun on his shoulder when he is in territory where he marked down the flushed birds.

Because it is so reluctant to flush, the single bird

Appomattox, Virginia, quail hunters Fred and Cecil Wooldridge move in on a covey point. These birds will likely flee to woods in background, and hunters are in the correct position for good shooting and marking down the flight of the birds.

The author with his English pointer (now deceased) and a trio of quail.

offers better bird dog work—if the dog has a sensitive enough nose, and takes the time to pinpoint his game. Unlike the covey the single bird will sit tight for the dog. This too makes the singles hunting more productive and attractive to the experienced hunter.

Flushed birds may huddle in twos and threes as well as alone. They may or may not get up together. The wise hunter is always ready for that late riser.

Every grouse hunter I know will swear the flushed birds quickly put trees or other obstacles between themselves and the hunter. This is probably mostly supposition, but the single bobwhite quail will behave in the same manner. It happens often.

Just recently I followed a flushed covey into a partially cutover pine forest where at least a half dozen birds had alighted. My German short-haired pointer nailed a bird almost immediately. As I moved in on the point, not one, but three birds got up. Frantically I tried for a shot, swinging desperately from one departing bird to another—but always there was a tree to block my shot. Was that a disgusted glance my dog gave me as we moved on? I had not fired a shot.

Work an area thoroughly if you know the birds are there. I have often spent a couple of hours combing such cover and giving my dogs plenty of time to work it out. If you get up one bird, chances are there are a half dozen more in the immediate vicinity. It can be slow hunting—but productive. The singles hunter works for his game, filling his game bag usually one bird at a time.

What I have said so far has been in the light of bird hunting as I know it in the southeastern United States, a vast region of farms, wood lots, forests, swamps and marshes that stretches from the Mississippi River east to the Atlantic, and from southern Ohio and New Jersey south to Florida and the Gulf of Mexico.

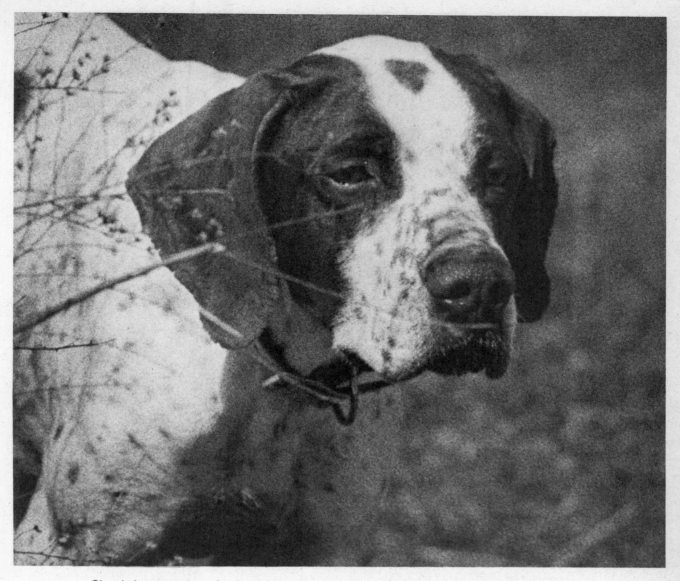
Classic intense pose of pointer frozen on single bobwhite. The dog is total concentration.

The situation is a bit different in the big prairie states of Kansas and Oklahoma where the tree cover is so limited the birds have not learned to use it. I spent a week hunting quail in Kansas last season — in the famous strip-mine region in the southeastern corner of the state where the bobwhite is in the sandy hills north of Platte and in the arid southwest where the bobwhite and scaled quail keep each other company.

The midwestern birds are often flushed from the shelterbelts or hedgerows that divide the endless fields of grain and grass, and the singles are put down in the open, something the eastern bird rarely does. They are easy to follow and flush again — a far cry from eastern singles hunting.

Above all the eastern singles hunter needs a fast gun, one that fits him well and mounts quickly. He often hits the trigger just as the stock touches his shoulder. A bird darting through the woods or a thicket leaves little time to calculate lead, follow through and observe the usual rules of good shotgun handling.

The best singles hunter shoots by instinct. With his eye always on the bird he whips his gun to his shoulder and touches the trigger. It is the modern shotgunner's answer to the flamboyant gunman of the Old West who nailed his man from the hip.

For this fast swinging shooting a light gun is the answer and I am willing to sacrifice firepower if I have to. My 12-gauge Browning gives a wider pattern and a better chance on birds in the open, but when most of my shooting is going to be in the woods, my light Remington 20-gauge automatic comes off of the rack.

I load size 8 light field loads in either gun, though some hunters like size 9 loads for the early season and then switch to 7½'s late in the season when the birds are faster and stronger.

Slashing through the briers, cutovers, laurel thickets

Bird dog stops, freezes on point, to signal: "There's a single quail hiding just ahead, boss."

and swamps also places special demands on the hunter's clothing. The trousers, particularly, take a beating. One of my hunting partners goes through a good pair every season. Brush pants are a must. They protect the legs from briers and thorns but an occasional one will get through the best trousers. For this reason, and because brush trousers against the bare skin are uncomfortable, I normally wear a pair of light sweat pants or the bottom half of long johns beneath my trousers. They add comfort, warmth and additional protection from those briers and thorns.

The shooting jacket is less vital but it too should be made of tough fabric. I wear blaze orange when the deer and quail seasons overlap. I don't want some eager deer hunter to mistake me for an alarmed whitetail slashing through the woods.

Gloves are a necessity not only for warmth, but as protection against the briers and thorns. Even then the bird hunter's hands will bear scratches. They are the mark of a dedicated singles hunter. I like gloves with snug-fitting cuffs that fit beneath the sleeves of my jacket. The shooting finger should be of light fabric so the hunter can retain his sensitive touch. There is seldom time to remove the gloves before shooting.

Light, tough and reasonably waterproof boots ease the many miles of walking, travel over rough terrain and mucking through the swamps. The famous L.L. Bean boot with the rubber bottom and leather top is a good choice. Like the trousers, the boots take a beating, but a good pair will last several seasons.

Singles hunting breeds a special kind of hunter, one who enjoys good reflexes, sharp ears and eyes and is good at instinctive shooting. Because he learns to shoot fast and concentrate on a single, fast-moving target, the good singles shooter is more often than not a mediocre covey shot.

The bobwhite quail flushing alone from a dense hiding place knows every trick of the ruffled grouse — and maybe a few more. As it flashes through the hardwoods or thick pines the hunter gropes for a shot, but his entire load may end up in the branch or trunk of a tree. The fast-disappearing bird does seek openings however, thus giving the hunter his chance. Even in dense cover enough shot will often get through to drop the bird — sometimes only winged. Then a good singles dog is a blessing.

It is rare indeed that the singles hunter will get a second chance at the entire covey. One reason is that the birds usually break up into several splinter groups. Most hunters feel they are lucky when they jump half of a flushed covey.

Hunting the singles is tough. If the hunter is not in good physical condition he soon will be — or give up. With briers and brush tearing at his gloves and trousers, it can be rough hunting in rough cover, but one by one the singles hunter slowly fills his limit. At the end of the day he will be physically dulled, but mentally sharp — and in high spirits.

In the sack that night he will sleep like a bear in mid-winter — and so will his dogs.

120

# Fare for the Table

## by PEGGY BAUER

IT APPEARS THAT bookshelves abound with recipes for big game. And why not? Elk, deer and moose are delicious as a main course. Then too, there is usually so much meat that the cook is free to try dozens of methods of preparation before the freezer empties out.

Small game and birds are quite a different matter, however. Here recipes are few, but with the current boom in the price of pelts, more furred animals are available for the table than has been the case for many years. Birds are a perennial favorite in spite of the fact that their "pelts" are worthless to most hunters.

In this article we will concentrate on these two categories, small fur bearing creatures and feathered game. And to help round out the meal, four surprises at the end.

## Squirrel, Raccoon, Opossum, Muskrat

### Squirrel

More than one student of the American Revolution gives credit for the Colonial victory to squirrels. Any army they argue, with men who can regularly sneak soundlessly through the trees and shoot a squirrel from his perch could surely outshoot any regiment of His Majesty's men, especially when the lobsterbacks march in a straight, tight line wearing bright red coats. It would be hard to argue with this logic.

Now, 200 years later, we no longer fight the British and things have vastly altered in our relations with the Red Man, but the hunting of squirrels continues. And so does their popularity on the table. Squirrels make good eating whether roasted, braised, broiled or stewed. The meat ranges in color from pink to medium red and darkens with the age of the animal. Squirrel meat is velvety, short fibered, firm and lean and has little or no suggestion of gaminess.

Years ago Iowa State College in Ames printed a recipe for squirrel with dumplings which remains our favorite.

### Ozark Special Squirrel With Dumplings

2 squirrels, pan dressed
3 tablespoons fat
2½ to 3 cups water
1-teaspoon salt
⅛-teaspoon pepper
⅓-cup sliced onion
½-cup diced celery
1-cup carrot sticks
2-3 tablespoons flour
Dumpling dough (recipe below), or Bisquick

1. Brown the pieces of squirrel in fat (half butter), cover with water, season and simmer about 1 hour. Add vegetables and water if needed and cook 20 minutes more. Thicken juices with a smooth paste of flour and ¼-cup water.

2. Use Bisquick recipe or prepare dumpling dough using 1-cup flour, 1½ teaspoons baking powder, ½-teaspoon salt, 1-tablespoon fat and ½-cup milk. Drop dough by spoonfuls on stew, cover tightly and steam 12 to 15 minutes; or drop on greased perforated top of steamer and steam over boiling water.

3. Serve at once on heated plates, in heated vegetable dish with dumplings on top, or on heated chop plate with dumplings around stew. Add a tossed green salad or a fruit salad, crusty rolls or corn sticks and tart jelly.

### Fried Squirrel

Another fine recipe to come out of the Midwest is this from Missouri, published by their Conservation Commission.

After the squirrel is dressed and cut up, soak it in salt water till free of blood. Drain and gently squeeze each piece free of water. Roll in flour and fry in a deep skillet filled with enough lard to bubble around each piece of squirrel. Over each piece shake salt, pepper, a little garlic salt or powder and some special game seasoning. Fry on each side to a golden brown. Season each side.

After both sides of squirrel are browned, turn heat low and add at least a glass of water, cover skillet with a tight lid and steam. If it is a young squirrel, by the time the water is gone the squirrel will be very tender and ready to eat. If an older squirrel, add more water and continue steaming until squirrel ''sticks tender'' with a fork. The squirrel will be rather soft and sticky if taken out of the skillet directly after steaming. If it is preferred more crisp, when water is gone take the lid off skillet and fry a few minutes longer on each side.

### Baked Squirrel

For a no hassle method to prepare squirrel try this:

Flour, salt and pepper meat and brown in a skillet. Place in covered baking dish. Cover with 1-cup of ½-milk-and-½-cream, ½-cup chopped celery, ½-cup chopped onions and a small can mushrooms. Bake until tender.

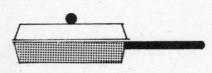

### Raccoons

Coons are found in most of the contiguous 48 states. They are often exasperating neighbors, and coon tales, true and otherwise, are widely exchanged. One such story which we know to be factual and which illustrates the critter's resourcefulness follows.

Our friends Charlie and Kathy Farmer had a pet raccoon which they swore was smarter than they were. Occasionally it had to be taken to the vet, a trip which the animal soon learned to despise. Some instinct warned the raccoon when it was Vet Day and it simply evaporated at the appointed hour. So the Farmers decided on this last trip to outwit their pet. It was and remains, the most grievous mistake they ever made.

The night before the date with the vet the Farmers captured the unsuspecting creature, locked it in its cage and put the cage in the car. Triumphant cheers were heard from the cabin. But by some means still not clear, the animal escaped during the night and to show its displeasure attacked the Chevrolet engine. All hoses were found dismembered and left dangling at grotesque angles; wires were disconnected and frayed, tubing was bent and various fluids oozed and leaked to the ground.

Later the man from the authorized General Motors Service Center slowly lowered the auto hood and put in a call to his superior in Detroit.

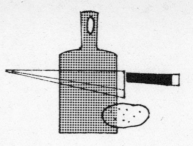

But raccoons do have positive attributes, too. Their pelts are deep and warm and, besides making Davey Crockett and others a warm cap, were quite the rage during the ''20's'' when long coon skin coats were high fashion. Coon makes good eating too, if properly prepared and even where the pelts are not prime the masked ones are hunted just for the meat.

In preparing the critters for the pan it is particularly important that the scent glands in the front arm pits be carefully cut out. Some meat will have to be discarded with them. Also all fat, especially that between the muscles, must be removed. Wipe the meat well, removing any stray hair, and rub the carcass with a tablespoon of soda. Rinse it thoroughly inside and out in several changes of water and drain. With all this careful preparation for the pan, raccoon on the table will be a flavorful treat.

### Roast Coon With Dressing and Milky Gravy

1 dressed young coon (6½-7 lbs.)
2 stalks celery
1½-2 tablespoons salt
¼-teaspoon red pepper
2 medium onions
1 carrot
1-teaspoon black pepper
1-cup water

Place pan-ready coon in deep roasting pan and barely cover with warm water; add onions, celery and carrots; cover and simmer gently ½-hour. Lift coon out. When broth is cool skim off all fat, strain. Mix salt, black and red pepper and rub well into the coon inside and out. Stuff with the following dressing:

*Dressing*
20 slices of day-old bread or 3 quarts soft bread crumbs
1½ teaspoons salt
Pepper, black and red to taste
1 egg
1-cup milk
1-cup finely chopped onion

Tear bread into small pieces. Sprinkle the salt, black and red pepper to taste over the bread. Beat the egg, add the milk, and moisten the bread with it. Mix in the onions, and pack the dressing lightly into the cavity; truss if desired.

Put the coon on its back in a roasting pan with a tight lid, add some broth and roast at 350 degrees until tender (about 2 hours). Remove cover, add a little more broth if needed, and roast uncovered to a rich crusty brown. Drain off liquid and reserve to make gravy. Keep coon covered to remain hot. To make gravy, melt ¼-cup butter in skillet, add 6 tablespoons flour and blend until smooth. Skim the fat off the liquid saved from the roasting coon, stir the liquid gradually into the butter-flour mixture and cook, stirring constantly, until the mixture boils and thickens and then 2 more minutes. Taste and add more seasonings if needed plus enough milk to make 2 cups gravy. Serve boiling hot with coon.

### Chicken-Fried Coon

For an easier meal cut the meat into small pieces and either fry or roast them.

Soak raccoon pieces in milk to cover for 40 minutes. Remove (reserving the milk), roll in well seasoned flour and fry in deep fat. Gravy can be made in the same pan by draining off most of the fat, stirring in flour and seasonings and browning the mixture. Use the reserved milk as liquid.

### Roast Coon With Apples

Place small coon pieces in a covered roaster with quartered apples, onion slices and a handful of raisins. Add a cup of water or broth and roast until tender.

### Coonburgers and Fixin's

Ground raccoon with green tomatoes and eggplant slices makes as tasty a dinner as you have ever eaten.

1-lb. raccoon meat
1-ounce salt pork
½ medium onion
1 stalk celery
½-inch strips green pepper
½-cup bread cubes
¼-cup milk
½-teaspoon salt
⅛-teaspoon pepper
dash cayenne pepper
½-teaspoon thyme
¼-cup fat
½-cup catsup
1-teaspoon Worcestershire sauce

1. Cut meat off bones and grind fine with salt pork and vegetables. Soak bread in milk, add with salt, pepper and thyme to meat and mix well.

2. Shape into 6 cakes and brown in fat, turning to brown well. Pour mixture of ketchup and Worcestershire over top, cover and simmer or bake in a slow oven (325 degrees) for 30 minutes or until done.

3. Serve on slices of fried eggplant or green tomatoes with browned potatoes, Harvard beets, coleslaw, cornbread and blackberry jam or mint jelly.

### Opossum

Opossums are unlikely looking creatures for the table. Not only do they have a peculiar looking body with a face as pointed as the bare tail, but they also have a peculiar taste which some 'possum fanciers like, but others try to hide with highly seasoned dressings or a strong barbeque sauce.

Possums are generally found in wooded stream areas, and they eat insects, carrion, fruit, fish and frogs. It is whispered that some cooks cage the captured animal for a week or so, and feed it, denying it carrion and fishy foods and thereby end up with a better tasting meat.

The opossum differs from other small game animals in that it has large amounts of soft, creamy, granular fat which must be wholly removed before cooking to avoid a very greasy dish. There are two schools of thought on further preparation: One states that the 'possum should

be immersed in very hot water for 1-minute and then have the hair scraped from the skin with a dull knife or hog scraper without cutting the skin. After this the animal is slit from neck to hind legs and entrails removed. Head and tail are discarded and the entire carcass washed inside and out with hot water.

The other school of thought says to skin the animal and then dress it. In either case all agree that 'possum should be soaked overnight in a brine solution (or vinegar) and rinsed with hot water just before cooking.

It appears that there is only one way to serve opossum and that is with sweet potatoes. However there are several ways to prepare this dish. The first method comes from an old woman of Indian and French blood (more Indian than French) now long at her eternal rest.

### "Breed" 'Possum and Sweet Taters

Leave the skin on the opossum, scraping and singeing the hair off and scrub the skin with soap and water. Rinse thoroughly with clear water. The opossum is then drawn and cleaned and parboiled until slightly tender. The drained opossum is then placed in a baking pan into which a cupful of bacon grease was melted.

Sweet potatoes, as many as desired to pile around the opossum, are scrubbed with skins on, and boiled until slightly soft before putting in the pan with the meat. The animal is basted from time to time with the bacon grease, and the whole thing declared done when the meat is nicely brown and easily pierced with a fork and the potatoes soft and pliable.

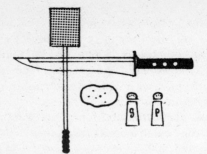

### Roasted 'Possum and Sweet Potatoes

A midwestern dish of possum with sweets is this:

1 opossum (2-2½ lb.)
salt, pepper, sage
apple and raisin stuffing
2 cups stock
¼- to ⅓-cup flour
3 or 4 sweet potatoes
2 tablespoons brown sugar

1. Rub inside of oven-dressed opossum with seasonings, fill with stuffing (see below), truss, season the outside and place on a greased rack in shallow pan, if lean, brush with fat and cover with cloth dipped in melted fat.

2. Roast, uncovered, in slow oven for 1½ to 2 hours, allowing 30 to 35 minutes per pound. Remove cloth the last half hour and place parboiled sweet potatoes (peeled and halved) around opossum; baste all several times with drippings in pan, dusting meat with flour, and potatoes with brown sugar after each basting.

3. Place potatoes around opossum on heated platter, garnish and serve with buttered peas and turnip cubes, french fried green pepper rings, orange and onion salad, steamed brown bread and cranberry relish.

*Apple and Raisin Stuffing*
1-cup chopped onion
¾-cup chopped celery tops
¼-cup chopped parsley
½-cup butter or other fat
6-8 cups soft bread cubes
1-2 cups cubed apples
⅛-teaspoon nutmeg
½-cup raisins
1½ teaspoons salt
⅛-teaspoon pepper
dash cayenne
½- to 1-teaspoon sage
1-teaspoon thyme

Brown vegetables lightly in fat in large heavy frying pan, stirring to cook evenly. Add the apples, raisins (and ½-cup chopped nuts if desired), bread cubes and stir carefully, and cook until well mixed and lightly toasted. Add seasonings, using larger amounts for more highly seasoned stuffing. Toss with two forks to mix well.

### Muskrat

Another small fur bearer, the muskrat carries a name that few want on their menu. "Rat" isn't something considered edible, although the muskrat is no more rat than the squirrel. However, to solve the dilemma other names have been successfully substituted, such as musquash, marsh rabbit or marsh hare.

Muskrat flesh is tender, dark and short fibered and should be soaked overnight in a brine solution. It is better to cut the joints with kitchen shears rather than break them as they part with jagged bone edges. Cut the lean carcass in pieces setting aside the flank and ribs for grinding and using the rest in the following recipe favored by musquash gourmets.

### Musquash Sauerbraten

2 musquash, pan dressed
1-teaspoon salt
⅛-teaspoon pepper
dash ginger
½-cup vinegar
5 tablespoons sugar
5 cups water
1 bay leaf
⅓-cup fat
1 medium onion, sliced
⅓-cup chopped green pepper or parsley
¼-cup chopped celery
¾- to 1-cup raisins
2 tablespoons flour
⅓-cup sour cream

1. Use meaty pieces of older musquash. Rub pieces with mixture of salt, pepper and ginger and place in bowl. Bring vinegar, sugar, water and bay leaf to a boil; pour half of it over the meat and let stand 4 to 8 hours. Remove the meat and drain. Pat dry. Discard used marinade.

2. Brown meat in hot fat; remove pieces to stew pan or Dutch oven. Cook vegetables in drippings in pan about 10 minutes, stirring to brown slightly, and scatter over meat. Add remaining marinade to drippings in pan, bring to boil stirring and pour over meat. Cover tightly and simmer 1½ hours or until meat is very tender, adding small amounts of hot water as needed.

3. Arrange meat on heated platter with small carrots and potatoes.

## Fried Muskrat

An easy way to prepare muskrat is to fry it, and using this recipe the cook is free at the end of the cooking time to attend to the rest of the meal.

Retrieve the pieces of muskrat from the brine, drain, rinse and pat moderately dry. Dip the pieces in flour filled sack and shake well. Then dip into a prepared egg batter (the flour helps the batter to adhere well) and brown quickly in a generous amount of fat. When brown, cover and braise for 45 minutes to an hour or until tender. Make milk gravy in the roasting pan and pour over the meat just before serving. Try it with acorn squash cooked with nutmeg, molasses and butter plus biscuits.

To dress up the humble hare for fancy company try this one:

2 muskrats cut into bite size pieces
salt and pepper to taste
butter or cooking oil
2 tablespoons of tomato sauce
1-cup sour cream (or one can condensed mushroom soup)
paprika and nutmeg
2 medium onions chopped fine
½-pound mushrooms (fresh or canned)

First remove sour cream from refrigerator to warm to room temperature. Then cook onions gently in the butter or butter-oil combination in a Dutch oven and remove from pan. Add a bit more oil and brown muskrat pieces and remove them. Add a dab more butter and lightly brown mushrooms (drained well if canned). Spoon the muskrat pieces and onions back into the roasting pan and mix together. Season liberally with salt, pepper, paprika and nutmeg. Add tomato sauce and a bit of water and simmer for about an hour or more until meat is very tender. Add half the sour cream and stir. Cook for 10 to 15 minutes over *very low* heat (or it will curdle). Stir in remaining sour cream and serve immediately over hot rice on a heated platter.

## Grouse, Goose, Turkey and Pheasant

### Grouse

This is our favorite company platter. The rice cooking method is something every cook should learn and use with any rice recipe.

### Stuffed Grouse on Savory Rice Bed

4 grouse with livers
salt and pepper
4 tablespoons butter
½-cup shallots or green onions
4 large mushrooms, minced (or a small can of mushrooms)
4 slices white bread crumbled
¼-cup chopped parsley
¼-teaspoon each marjoram, tarragon, basil
1¼ cups beef broth
4 slices bacon
4 cups Carolina long grain rice
Optional: 1-cup each chopped onion, mushrooms, pecans; 3 tablespoons snipped parsley and ½-cup butter.

*For the stuffing:* Season the cavities of the cleaned birds with salt and pepper. Chop livers fine and sauté in butter with shallots or onions and the mushrooms. Season to taste with salt and pepper. Add bread, parsley and herbs and mix. Add beef broth just to moisten. Lightly fill the cavities with the stuffing and skewer shut. Rub each bird with 1-tablespoon butter and cover with fat bacon strip. Place in greased roasting pan in 400-degree oven and roast for 40 minutes basting occasionally.

*For the Rice Bed:* For perfect rice the floury coating on each grain must be gotten rid of or it cooks to a sticky film, binding the grains together. The best way to do this is to precook the rice in lots of water.

Measure 4 cups of Carolina long grain rice (more than four people can eat, but it makes a large enough bed for the birds on the platter) and slowly sprinkle it into 8-10 quarts of boiling salted water so the boiling does not stop. Stir to loosen any grains sticking to the bottom. Boil uncovered for about 10 minutes and then bite a grain to ensure that it has no hard center, but is still not fully cooked. Drain and fluff the rice with a fork under hot running water for several minutes. Wrap the bundle of rice in a damp well-rinsed tea towel and place in a colander. Cover and let steam over boiling water for 20 to 30 minutes until the rice is tender. If desired, toss with butter-sautéed mushrooms, onions, chopped pecans and fresh parsley.

*Just before serving:* Gently spoon the rice on a heated platter and arrange the birds on it. Pour fat from the roasting pan and discard, add the remaining beef broth. Boil while scraping to incorporate the bits in the pan and pour over the birds.

## Grouse En Casserole

The people at Wild Turkey Bourbon Distilleries assure us that this recipe for grouse, using their product, will lure the staunchest teetotalers off the wagon. (It is safe, since high heat evaporates all alcohol.)

One 1-lb. grouse, dressed
4 medium potatoes
3 tablespoons butter
2 tablespoons oil
½-lb. small white onions, peeled
salt and pepper
¼-cup Wild Turkey Bourbon
1 beef bouillon cube
½-pound small mushrooms
One 15-oz. can small whole carrots
½-cup dry white wine

Pre-heat oven to 375 degrees Fahrenheit. Peel potatoes and cut each lengthwise into 4 sections. Melt butter and oil in flame-proof casserole over direct heat. Add potatoes and onions and saute until golden. Remove vegetables and set aside. Then brown grouse on all sides in casserole. Sprinkle with salt and pepper. Add wine and bourbon and ignite. When flames subside, add bouillon cube and blend well. Add mushrooms, onions, and potatoes. Cover. Place casserole in 375-degree oven. Bake 1-hour, basting occasionally with juices in casserole. Drain carrots, add to casserole. Bake uncovered until grouse is browned and tender.

## Goose

Somehow nothing seems more Christmasy than wild goose on the table surrounded by red candles and greenery. The following recipe calls for apricots in the dressing, but prunes can be substituted and make a moister dressing which enhances an older, drier bird. Either way, it's delicious.

## Roast Wild Goose With Apricot Dressing

One 6- to 8-pound young wild goose
juice of 1 lemon
salt and freshly ground black pepper to taste
¼-cup butter
¼-cup chopped onion
1-cup chopped tart apple
1-cup chopped dried apricots
3 cups fine, soft bread crumbs
4-6 slices bacon
melted bacon fat

1. Preheat oven to moderate (325 degrees).
2. Sprinkle the goose inside and out with lemon juice, salt and pepper.
3. In a large sauce pan, heat the butter, add the onion and cook until tender. Stir in the apple, apricots, bread crumbs, ½-teaspoon salt and the ⅛-teaspoon of black pepper.

4. Spoon the stuffing lightly into the goose cavity. Close the opening and truss with skewers and string. Cover the breast with bacon slices and cheesecloth soaked in melted bacon fat. Place the goose, breast up, on a rack in an open roasting pan.
5. Roast until tender, 2 to 3 hours, basting frequently with bacon fat and the drippings in the pan. If the age of the goose is uncertain, pour 1-cup water in the pan and cover for the last hour of cooking. Remove the cheesecloth, skewers and string.

## Roast Wild Goose With Currant Sauce

For a bird without stuffing try this one with currant sauce. This is especially nice to save time. The bird goes in the oven right away and while it roasts, you may, if you wish, make a dressing on top of the stove and serve it separately. A rice stuffing with chestnuts is a good choice.

One 12-lb. goose, dressed
2 cups chicken broth
2 large onions
2 tablespoons cornstarch
1-teaspoon pepper
1-teaspoon salt
1-cup currant jelly

Preheat oven to 325 degrees Fahrenheit. Wash and dry goose. Sprinkle with salt and pepper inside and out. Peel onions, chop coarsely and put in the cavity of the bird. Place goose, breast side down on a rack in a roasting pan. Cover bottom with 1-inch to 1½ inches cold water and bake for 4½ hours, adding water as needed. Turn and roast breast side up for another 2 hours allowing about 25 minutes per pound for the total cooking time. Remove onions from cavity, pour off water from pan and roast ½-hour longer to crisp skin.

*For the currant sauce:* Skim all fat from the drippings. Mix cornstarch with some of the broth and then pour into the remaining broth. Add currant jelly and stir constantly to loosen and incorporate the browned crust stuck to the pan. Simmer for 15 minutes. Serve separately in sauce boat.

## Turkey

This was Benjamin Franklin's favorite bird and one proposed to be our national bird only to lose out by a pin feather to the bald eagle. A metallic burnished beauty, strutting and displaying its way across much of our open and lightly wooded country, the wild turkey is as welcome a sight on the table as in the field. This first recipe comes from Sylvia Sebastiani, wife of August Sebastiani, the noted California winemaker. It was first printed in her own cookbook of family recipes called *Mangiamo (Let's Eat!)*, and has a distinctly Italian flavor.

### Sylvia Sebastiani's Roast Turkey and Dressing

One roasting turkey (wild)
dry bread cubes from one loaf of sour French bread
½-cup chopped parsley
½-cup grated Parmesan cheese
1 or 2 teaspoons poultry seasoning
2 teaspoons salt
1-teaspoon pepper
1-teaspoon garlic salt
1½ cups Sebastiani dry white wine
1½ cups melted butter
½-cup butter
2 chopped onions
½-bunch celery, chopped
2 cloves garlic, chopped
1 to 2 cups broth

*Broth:*
turkey neck and giblets
salted water
¼ onion
1 stalk celery

In a large bowl combine bread cubes, parsley, cheese, and seasonings. In melted butter sauté onion and celery, sprinkling with salt, pepper and garlic salt to taste. Add garlic and sauté lightly. Prepare broth by boiling neck and giblets in salted water with onion, celery, and garlic. Let cool. Add cooled broth to onion-celery mixture, then mix well into bread cube mixture.

Rub turkey with olive oil and season generously with salt, pepper, and garlic salt. Stuff with dressing and skewer shut. Place in the center of a large piece of aluminum foil. Pull foil up closely around bird and seal

with a double fold at edges. Put turkey on rack in shallow pan and roast at 450 degrees, 15 to 20 minutes per pound removing or folding back the foil to let the skin brown about 20 minutes before it's done. If the turkey is domestic, omit the foil altogether, roast at 325 degrees and baste with wine and butter occasionally. Turkey is done when the leg joints move freely. Remove from oven and let sit an hour before carving. Keep warm with foil covering plus several tea towels. This allows the juices to soak into the tissues and makes a moist, easy to carve bird.

### Pennsylvania Dutch Wild Turkey in a Pot

An entirely different way in which to handle the wild turkey is in a pot—no stuffing, no browning.

One wild turkey, cut up
2 onions chopped
1 clove garlic, minced
1 bay leaf
2 whole cloves
½-teaspoon mustard seed
2 tablespoons cornstarch
¼-cup sugar
½-cup vinegar
2 teaspoons salt
10 peppercorns

Place turkey in a large pot or Dutch oven with 4 cups water. Add onion, garlic, bay leaf, cloves, mustard seed, salt and peppercorns. Cover and simmer 2 hours. Remove turkey and strain broth. Return broth to pot and add cornstarch, combined with sugar and vinegar. Cook stirring constantly until sauce thickens. Add turkey and simmer 15 minutes or more.

### Pheasant

Many kitchens (including mine) limp along successfully without a microwave oven or a fancy new food processor, but I'd certainly hate to make do without my Redi-Smok. This is a cylindrical electric smoker something like a portable oven. It can be used outdoors or even in an airy garage and cooks or smokes almost anything. Smoked pheasant, either for immediate home consumption or to give as gourmet gifts, is one of the better uses for Bill Carney's Redi-Smok (3827 Colgate, Houston, Texas 77087). Of course you can try this in other smokers, but that's at your own risk.

## Bill Carney's Smoked Pheasant

One pheasant
½-cup pork sausage
½-cup chopped apple
¼-teaspoon garlic salt
½-onion, chopped
½-teaspoon coarse black pepper
1-cup garlic flavored croutons or breadcrumbs
⅓-cup cooking sherry

Wash pheasant and wipe dry. Mix all ingredients and stuff loosely into cavity.

*Sauce to Cover Pheasant*
Melt ¼-cup butter and mix with:
   ¼-teaspoon paprika
   ¼-teaspoon Worcestershire sauce
   ⅛-teaspoon garlic salt
   ⅛-teaspoon black pepper

Blend well as you bring to a boil. Paint outside of bird with sauce. Set pheasant in individual foil saucer (don't wrap). Smoke approximately 3 hours.

## Roast Pheasant Madeira

Here's a more traditional roasting method.

One large pheasant
salt and freshly ground pepper
1 bay leaf
1 clove garlic
few celery leaves
1 slice lemon
4 slices bacon
melted butter
Madeira sauce

1. Preheat oven to moderate (350 degrees).
2. Sprinkle the pheasant inside and out with salt and pepper. Place the bay leaf, garlic, celery leaves and lemon in the cavity. Tie the legs together with string and turn the wings under.
3. Cover the breast with bacon and a piece of cheesecloth soaked in melted butter. Place the pheasant, breast up, on a rack in a baking pan and roast until tender, about 30 minutes per pound, basting frequently with melted butter.
4. Remove the cheesecloth and string. If desired, serve the pheasant on a bed of rice accompanied by Madeira sauce.

*Madeira Sauce*
Remove the pheasant to warm serving platter and add 1-cup consommé to the pan. Stir over moderate heat, scraping loose the browned particles. Blend 2 tablespoons flour with 2 tablespoons butter and stir into the gravy little by little. When the gravy is thickened and smooth, add 2 or 3 tablespoons Madeira wine

and the cooked liver, finely chopped. Pour some sauce over the bird and serve the remainder in a sauce boat.

## Four Surpise Recipes

And lastly we present four surprises—treats that will taste delicious with any of these recipes or any others.

The first is from Alaska. It is from Wein Air Alaska's Brooks' Camp where anglers from all over the world come to catch fish, watch bears, and to sit three times a day at the picnic tables in the dining room and devour the family style meals served up there. Robyn Thorson, the young, apple-cheeked, enthusiastic kitchen boss gave me this recipe for her cranberry bread.

## Brooks' Camp Fresh Cranberry Bread

Combine:
   1-teaspoon soda
   1-cup shortening
Mix well and blend in:
   3 cups sugar (or 1 to 1½ cups honey)
Then beat in (one at a time):
   4 eggs
Alternately add:
   1½ cups orange juice (less if using honey) and the dry ingredients:
   6 cups flour (white)
   2 tablespoons baking powder
   1 scant tablespoon salt

Add dissolved yeast mixture to other ingredients after they have cooked and stir well. Gradually stir in 5 or 6 cups flour until dough is stiff but still soft. Put in greased bowl and cover with damp cloth. Let rise 1-hour in a warm place (not hot) or until doubled in size. Punch down and you are ready to start cooking. Use cast iron skillet. Grease hands with oil or butter for easier handling. Pinch off about 1-inch balls and flatten and stretch to shape as a pancake. Drop in 1½ inches hot vegetable oil (or Crisco) until golden on one side. Turn and brown on other side. Drain on paper towels. Butter and use as bread or serve as dessert with jelly, honey or sugar and cinnamon mixture.

### Mother Bauer's German Style Green Bean Salad

This salad, with its sharp taste, is delicious with game. It also tastes better when made well ahead which is something I admire in any recipe.

1-cup water
½-cup vinegar
½-cup sugar
1-teaspoon pickling spices
1-pound fresh green beans, or 2 boxes frozen whole beans
1 small red onion sliced thin

Bring water, vinegar, sugar and spices to a boil and simmer 10 minutes. Pour over mixture of beans (cooked only to tender-crisp stage) and onions separated into rings. Chill, turning now and then, for 24 hours and serve in the sauce.

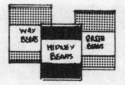

### Broiled Fruits

The final touch to the meal is broiled fruits and it does make a happy ending.

Remove the juice from a 20-oz. can of pineapple chunks and reserve it. Spoon the pineapple into a greased shallow broiler-proof dish. Core and quarter, but do not peel, one red apple. Cut each quarter in three pieces and add to the pineapple. Peel and section two oranges and add them to the dish, too. A handful of raisins is alright, too. Combine ½-cup of the pineapple juice, ¼-cup honey and ¼-cup rum or orange juice. Mix until honey is dissolved (heat, if necessary) and pour over the fruit mixture. Mix gently.

Broil until very hot and slightly carmelized. Top with dollop of sour cream or whipped sweet cream sprinkled with chopped nuts. Nice with a scoop of ice cream, too.

Stir in:
   3 tablespoons grated orange rind
   1½ cups chopped walnuts or pecans
   4½ cups cranberries (coarsely chopped)

Grease and lightly flour four loaf pans. Divide the batter evenly and bake at 350 degrees for 1½ hours or until they test done, and cool on a rack.

### Scones (Indian Bread, Trail Bread, Squaw Bread, Fried Light Bread)

One of the nicest things about going on a pack trip or hunting with Wyoming outfitter L. D. Frome, is enjoying the cooking his kitchen cowgirls turn out. A treat we always look forward to is what in the West are called scones, a very different critter from the comparatively dry tasteless scones in the British Isles. Here's how Patty Hardesty (who rides and wrangles as well as she cooks) makes 'em.

Dissolve:
   1 package active dry yeast
   2 teaspoons sugar in ½-cup lukewarm water (not hot)
Melt:
   3 tablespoons butter over low heat
Add:
   3 tablespoons sugar
   1 scant tablespoon salt
   2 cups water (or milk for a richer batter)

The shoveler duck is one species often overlooked by gunners seeking the other glamour waterfowl.

# ODDBALL DUCKS

## by TOM HARDIN

Baldpates, or American widgeons, are fast flying birds and at times abundant in small marshes.

THE RAW NORTHEAST WIND that whistled across Lake Erie toward our beach blind was ice-cold, and the snow stung our faces. It was painful to face the gale, but no serious duck hunter could afford to turn away. The reason? Fast flights of buffleheads kept trading back and forth to provide some of the finest—and trickiest—pass shooting we'd ever seen. My hunting partner, Homer Sanderson, was trying to light a cigarette when another flock of birds sailed erratically downwind. "Mark right!" I said sharply.

When the firing was over, five empty shells had been added to the scattering around our feet, but our Labrador retriever had only one duck to bring in. "Well I'll be damned," Homer said. As a rule he's an excellent waterfowl shot, and I've had my moments too, but that day we were shooting holes in the storm. Another flight came over a few moments later, veered to look over our decoys and swung parallel to shore. We managed to drop two. It took all morning to limit out at four apiece.

You might wonder why anyone would work so hard in freezing weather, or even bother to hunt buffleheads at all. Well in the first place, this was really fast shooting—at mile-a-minute targets. In the second place, it never dragged; there were continual flights of buffleheads, with a few goldeneyes sprinkled among them. And in the third place, such hunting is sometimes the only waterfowl sport for hunters like me (and maybe most of you) who can't afford to lease a waterfowl marsh or join a conveniently located but expensive shooting club.

I have nothing against the standard ducks—the mallards, blacks, pintails, scaup and canvasbacks—but you can add substantially to your hunting opportunities by not restricting yourself to these species. It's a fact that the smaller, "oddball" ducks are more numerous than the standard varieties in some areas. The canvasback hasn't even been legal recently, although it probably will be again as soon as the species becomes more abundant. Because of the differences in habitat, you may often have access to the oddballs on public land.

Long ago one of my hunting friends dubbed buffleheads "oddball" ducks, and we soon applied the label to many other species that are too often ignored by waterfowlers: baldpate (or widgeon), bluewing and greenwing teal, gadwall (or gray duck), goldeneye (or whistler), ruddy duck and wood duck.

Who knows what the hunter will flush when sneaking a pond along a margin of willows?

It's true that some of these—the woodie, for instance—are hunted fairly heavily in a few areas, but in general they're scorned. There are other worthy though little-hunted waterfowl species, but those I've listed are my favorites and—more important—they're abundant in many areas. Every year regular duck forecasts predict which varieties are likely to be in greatest supply during the upcoming season, which flyways will probably see the finest shooting and what part of the season is best for each species. The hunting methods discussed in this article apply wherever the birds are found.

In recent years, I've done a lot of my oddball hunting in oddball places. One such spot is a lonely strip of gravel beach along Lake Erie; late one season during abnormally cold weather, I noticed that small ducks were very active there. A look through binoculars revealed that they were goldeneyes and buffleheads. Neither species is very popular among hunters in this region, but they're sporty, edible ducks nevertheless. A couple of days later, a friend and I had the time of our lives with them. Even our blind was an oddball affair, a makeshift rig that the traditional duck hunter would scoff at. We found a small derelict scow washed up on shore, and we dragged it to a point that extended pretty far out into the water. We piled dried grasses—cattail and smartweed—around it and sat inside on pieces of driftwood. It wasn't long before we had our limits.

I've mentioned hunting late in the year in cold weather, but some species also give you the chance to begin your waterfowling very early. Bluewing teal and woodies, for example show up in most areas at the opening of the federal season—which lasts from the beginning of October to the beginning of January in most years. Of course, seasons, limits and the abundance of particular species will vary from state to state, but the same generalizations about early or late migrators apply along the main flyways.

My oddball season begins a week before legal opening day in Ohio, where I live. No, I don't poach, but I do reconnoiter. I check all the small creeks and potholes, swamps, bogs and public marshes I can find within about an hour's drive from my home. Most of them are empty, but I find concentrations of wood ducks in enough places so that on opening day it's easy to bag Ohio's limit of two.

Collecting a couple of woodies always gives me great satisfaction, aside from the fun of hunting. First, I believe they're the most delicious of all ducks. Second, the males have a mixed plumage of red, brown, blue, green and white that makes them the most beautiful waterfowl in North America. Many of the feathers are valuable or even essential in tying certain trout flies.

If you live in the eastern half of the United States, you may have heard shooters claim that all the teal have gone south before the season opens. Maybe some have, but during my prospecting for woodies I've found teal in good numbers. The secret is *not* to look for them on the big open waters where many hunters think they can be found, instead, try the small farm ponds, sloughs and nearly dry buttonbrush swamps. The bluewings are very early arrivals; the greenwings come just a little later.

Hunting woodies and teal is not the same type of sport as conventional waterfowling. You spot your targets and then stalk them, trying to get within reasonable range before they flush. It's a good idea to use field glasses or a spotting scope to search along the banks and undercuts of distant waterholes, but even this

In Alaska and scattered parts of the West, Barrow's is one uncommon duck which hunters might meet.

132

Inside his barrel blind inserted in the edge of a marsh, this hunter is ready for any duck that comes along.

doesn't always help because the birds are often hidden by tall grass. If spying doesn't pay off, all you can do is get down on your hands and knees and crawl toward a likely waterhole in the hope that your stalk will be productive. You never know for sure where oddballs will show up.

Two years ago, I went hunting with a friend on a marsh he'd leased, looking for the standard rather than the oddball species. A little after daybreak, I took two robber ducks, or widgeon. Both were difficult shots, and I felt rather proud of myself. "Damn widgeon," my friend grumbled. "Nothing but trash ducks around here any more."

Trash ducks? I'd be happy to hunt widgeon, or baldpates or robber ducks or whatever you may call them, just about every day. I'll concede that they're not quite as wary as the bigger blacks that have been peppered a time or two, but some early flights of blacks aren't very sophisticated, either. In fact, the young ones are often stupid about decoys.

I've had some pleasant surprises from baldpates. One unseasonably warm October afternoon I stalked a pond that often held a few teal. But this time it was empty, so I sat down in the tall grass beside the pond and began to doze. I was awakened by a familiar mellow whistling almost at my feet. Baldpates! I sat up suddenly and that was a mistake. They flushed before I could grab my gun. However, I went back to that pond on another day, and took a couple to make up for my earlier error.

Last year, again hunting with my friend Homer Sanderson, I found baldpates in slightly unnatural surroundings. The water level in Lake Erie was very low, and we discovered a boulder-and-gravel reef a few yards offshore that rose about 6 feet above the surface.

We built a blind of boulders and driftwood and had some excellent action.

Perhaps because of hunting pressure in the marshlands and grain fields along shore, ducks kept pitching into the sheltered side of the reef all day. There were blacks and mallards plus a few scattered pintails, but most of the birds were baldpates. It would be an understatement to call the shooting splendid.

Another way to take the oddball ducks is to float a river. You merely launch a canoe or other shallow draft boat and drift downstream. Ordinarily, the later in the season you do this, the better. The best time of all is when the lakes, ponds and potholes are frozen and the birds are almost *bound* to be on the rivers. Late last season, while floating down the lower Scioto River in southern Ohio, I filled my day's limit of (any) four waterfowl by taking four different oddballs—a goldeneye, a ruddy, a woodie and a gadwall. I was surprised to find the wood duck so far north at that time of year, but these puddleduck species are full of surprises.

There are two schools of thought with regard to floating a river for waterfowl. One school advocates piling the boat high with camouflage material in order to drift into the ducks without alarming them too soon. The other theory is that there's no sense in decorating the craft because the camouflage won't fool the ducks; if they're in a mood to let you get close, they will anyhow.

While I'm a camouflager myself, I have to admit that when there's a strong current you can often approach ducks in a naked boat. Some of them usually stay close to shore, avoiding the current and often taking cover beneath overhanging willows or grass. Others stay in the eddies or backwaters created by deadfalls. In either case, they can't see the boat until you're in range.

Regardless of your hunting method, the value of

reconnaissance can't be overestimated. In areas where no Sunday shooting is permitted, you can use the day for a drive through the country to check on waterfowl movements. You may also find it helpful to question farmers and even rural postmen about where they've noticed ducks feeding.

I own a number of smoothbores, but I generally use either my Browning Superposed over/under or Remington Model 870 pump for oddballs. They're both 12-gauge, and the Browning has modified and improved-cylinder barrels while the Remington has a modified choke. These are good choices for relatively short ranges and small ducks.

At least some of the oddballs are available to almost every American sportsman. At times, they're easier to bag than the standard varieties, and at times they're harder, but they're nearly always worth a try. Below are a few extra hints on gunning for these ducks. Bear in mind that the recommended shot sizes are based on the assumption that you're using a modified choke (or modified and improved in a double) and that your gun is a 12-gauge. Now here are the tips for each species:

A bufflehead is retrieved by a black Lab.

**Baldpate** (also called widgeon or robber): Will decoy readily but are quick to take alarm, so jump shooting is second best. Fast, erratic flyers; generally travel in compact flocks. Most active at daybreak. Often accompany canvasbacks and redheads—which they rob of food. White belly and forewings very conspicuous in the air. Hens are dull gray-brown; drakes have white foreheads, green "spectacles." Use No. 5 or 6 shot.

**Bufflehead:** Arrive late in the South, are most abundant all across the North. Flocks normally small, but group together in bad weather. Fly low to the water, fairly fast, with deceptively rapid wingbeat. Best hunting is along open beaches and shorelines. Birds will circle decoys but seldom pitch into them. Hens and young drakes are dull gray-brown; mature drakes are black and white with black head and white hood above eyes. Use No. 6 or 7½ shot.

**Gadwall** (also called gray duck): Fly in small flocks, usually in a straight line, with rapid wingbeats. Drakes whistle and "kack-kack" softly. Toss-up between jump shooting and using blind and decoys; occasionally taken by floating Midwestern rivers. Hens are grayish-tan; drakes are same but with brighter gray, black band near tail; both have white wing patch visible in flight. Use No. 5 or 6 shot.

**Goldeneye** (also called whistler): Very strong fliers; travel in small flocks. Wings create whistling sound in flight. Exceedingly wary. Large concentrations winter on Great Lakes and along both seacoasts, often settling at the edges of ice sheets. Hunt along rocky shorelines or, late in season, float along open rivers. Hens are dull gray with faint white collars, drakes have black heads, white bellies, white spot below each eye. Use No. 6 or 7½ shot.

**Ruddy duck** (also called butterball): May swim or dive rather than fly when surprised. Will rise from water awkwardly, and they're erratic fliers when underway. Found in both fresh- and saltwater. Blinds and jump shooting are good along coasts, while floating rivers is effective inland. Hens are gray with pale cheek patch; drakes are ruddy (a rust-red color) with large white cheek patch. Use No. 6 or 7½ shot.

**Teal, bluewing:** Fly swiftly in small flocks, low over marshes, dodging and twisting. Jump shooting or floating is best, but decoys work early or very late in day on shallow marshes or potholes. No use hunting late in season. Hens are dull brown; drakes have blue forewing patch, dark heads with white cheek. Use No. 6 or 7½ shot.

**Teal, greenwing:** Often gather in large flocks; twist and circle in flight. Jump shooting or floating is best, but birds decoy easily on stormy days. Hens are gray-brown with green bar on wings; drakes have reddish-brown head, green spectacles, green bar on wings. Use No. 6 or 7½ shot.

**Wood duck:** Fly in fast, fairly direct line, even through timber. Flocks are usually small and tend to set down on wooded streams, ponds and swamps. Jump shooting is best, floating is second. Hens are dull gray with white patch around each eye; drakes are brightly multi-colored with green patches on head. Use No. 6 or 7½ shot.

There you have the rundown, and now here's one last tip: When you go hunting for oddball ducks, take along plenty of ammunition. These species are all rather small, and they have the sort of lively flight habits that separate the shooters from the cussers. For fast shooting, they're hard to beat.

# The Sheep Hunting Syndrome

## by ERWIN A. BAUER

A good stone sheep taken in the British Columbia Cassiars. The left horn broken off reduces the trophy score.

IN THE 20 YEARS SINCE my first mountain sheep hunt, I have never met another sheep hunter who did not consider the sheep the greatest game animal on the face of the earth. Sheep hunting can be an addiction cured only by advancing age. For almost anyone who loves challenge and lofty places, to stalk the first sheep is to be hooked forever.

It is true that some kinds of hunting are more dangerous, and for many, danger is the most important ingredient. Nor are the odds for success in sheep hunting very great; but that only makes the game more worthwhile. In addition, a sheep hunter must suffer. He must scale lung-busting mountains, toil along thin, icy ridges using handholds as much as footholds. He must be soaked with sweat in biting cold, and sometimes he must even ponder why he had opted to go sheep hunting in the first place.

But, once a hunter bags a sheep, he wears the accomplishment as if it were a badge of honor. From that time on, any other kind of hunt is a mere warm-up for the next sheep hunt.

There is an excellent insight into the sheep hunter's philosophy in *Great Arc of the Wild Sheep* which is really a sort of sheep hunter's bible. Author James L. Clark, of the American Museum of Natural History, dedicates his work to "those hardy sportsmen of the world who prefer to meet the challenge of the climb and secure one fine sheep head rather than to hunt at lower levels for easier game." Some sheep hunters believe that there *are* no other game animals.

The true wild sheep of the world populate a series of awesome mountain ranges spanning three continents from the Mediterranean Islands across central Asia to North America. These sheep have the generic name *Ovis*. There are five species of *Ovis* and, depending on which scientific authority, upward to almost 100 subspecies distributed around the globe. About 25 subspecies of *Ovis canadensis,* the bighorn, and *Ovis dalli,* the white (or Dall) sheep, inhabit or once inhabited, North America. Several subspecies including the Audubon sheep are extinct.

For purposes of record keeping and trophy measurement, hunters divide North American sheep into four classifications: bighorn, desert, white and Stone. The desert is a bighorn subspecies and the Stone a subspecies of the white. The aim of every serious sheep hunter is to collect a trophy head of each, a feat known as a Grand Slam. But because of the rarity and inaccessibility of the desert sheep, this goal is not often accomplished and only a few sportsmen can claim four heads in their trophy room. These few consider themselves the royalty of the whole outdoor fraternity, and their pride is easy to understand.

Considerable disagreement exists over the origin of wild sheep in America. Perhaps they arrived by some prehistoric land bridge which once connected Alaska and Siberia. In any case our sheep have an astonishing

Go sheep hunting anywhere the splendid animals exist and you are likely to encounter some of the most severe weather.

similarity to their Siberian cousins. It is believed that any variations between the two are simply a result of adjustment to a particular environment. But there is still the enigma of how and why such a completely non-migratory animal ever traveled so far.

The first European to describe (and perhaps to see) wild sheep in America was Francisco Coronado, the Spanish explorer. During his search for the Seven Cities of Cibola in 1540, he wrote of a "large, curl-horned animal" which was undoubtedly an Arizona desert bighorn. After that there is little record of sheep for almost three centuries until 1800 when one Duncan McGillivray, a Canadian fur trader, shot a bighorn on the Bow River, in Alberta. The 1806 journals of Lewis and Clark noted the "animals of immense agility," bighorns, found at Gates of the Mountains on the Missouri River, Montana.

Before the winning (or losing) of our West, sheep were very abundant. At that time they were not confined only to the highest, loneliest mountain pastures as today. It wasn't until they learned about firearms that they became so super-sophisticated and so difficult to hunt.

One point should be made very clear at this time. Trophy hunting by sportsmen had (and has) nothing whatever to do with the present limited numbers of

Dall sheep horns collected in Alaska's Wrangells. Many hunters believe the Dall is the handsomest wild sheep.

A pair of bighorn's horns like these come once in a lifetime, if ever, so pack them out carefully.

sheep. Blame instead our expanding civilization, the need of available pasture for livestock, and disease contracted from domestic sheep. The fact that as many as 100,000 wild sheep remain on the continent today can be in part credited to sportsmen's conservation agencies which have financed sheep studies and research projects.

The most marvelous of all American sheep is the Rocky Mountain bighorn. Rams may exceed 300 pounds and they have been credited with the equivalent of 8x vision. That may not be an exaggeration. The home of the bighorn is above timberline in most ranges of the Rockies from Colorado northward into Alberta and British Columbia. The smaller desert sheep inhabits isolated arid mountain ranges in Arizona, Nevada, Sonora, Chihuahua and Baja, California. It isn't abundant anywhere. It lives in country very inhospitable to humans. Because of its depleted numbers only a few permits to hunt are issued in any season.

Due to its conspicuous color, the white sheep is the easiest to spot faraway on a mountainside. Except, however, in McKinley National Park where it has long been protected, it is not easy to approach anywhere. The white is the sheep of Alaska, Yukon and the Mackenzie Mountains of Canada's Northwest Territories.

The blue-black Stone is a subspecies of the white and the main chunk of its natural range is in northern British Columbia. An intergrade between the white and Stone which occurs where their ranges overlap has been called the Fannin sheep. Like the Stone and white, Fannin rams reach a maximum weight of about 200 pounds.

Another wild sheep, the Barbary, or aoudad, from North Africa, not of the genis *Ovis,* has been established in the New Mexico mountains and on some Texas ranches. It is multiplying sufficiently to provide limited hunting on a quota basis. But probably most sheep hunters would prefer to see native sheep reestablished rather than an alien introduced.

Hunting success depends on a combination of desire (determination might be a better word), good physical condition, being able financially to afford a sometimes lengthy hunt, and knowing sheep country. There really isn't any substitute for the first three. The high altitude hunting is costly in time, energy and money, but a sheep hunter *could* get by (as most beginners *must* do) by relying on a guide or outfitter to interpret the country.

During most open hunting seasons rams will be segregated into small bachelor bands and very seldom mixed with ewes and lambs. The all-male groups will have one or two old monarchs bigger than the rest, perhaps with just an inch or two longer horns, but this difference separates the once in a lifetime trophy from an average head of horns. Still, not even the most *massive* elk or moose racks can be considered with just the *average* sheep, or so a sheep hunter will assure you.

When you are ram hunting, you constantly are looking upward to high hanging basins, to green glades just below or on the edge of rimrock, usually facing the south. An ideal place is where water seepage from a glacier or snowfield ice combined with sunlight grows enough succulent grasses to keep the animals from wandering far away in search of forage. But do not expect to find many rams on single, postcard-picture peaks from which there would be no escape from danger. Instead look for a conglomeration of peaks connected by ridges and divided by deep canyons, all of it difficult to traverse.

There are never any dull moments mountain sheep hunting. Discomfort, yes. Cold, chills and muscle spasms, of course. But there is never any boredom. A hunter rides or hikes out across naturally spectacular terrain, the view is always spectacularly vast; and he never stops looking. If he does not always spot sheep, he may see a grizzly, caribou, wolves or a wolverine, all animals which sometimes share the same high real estate. Then, eventually, there is the day—and the moment—when a good ram is spotted and the long, upward stalk begins.

There really isn't much use in trying to describe a stalk for sheep. All stalks are different; most are slow,

Sheep hunting means climbing, sometimes until you can't climb any more, to reach where the big rams live.

tedious and even agonizing. You wind up with lungs on fire and legs feeling like worn-out innertubes. And chances are good that when you finally reach the destination, the spot within rifle range of the target, the rams will have evacuated to another mountain far in the distance. So you sit and try to decide whether the situation is worth following up. In a capsule, there is no other hunting to match it.

A sheep hunt is rarely an inexpensive undertaking. Before ever starting out there is the matter of a license, and the minimum non-resident fee anywhere in the United States or Canada is around $100. A year ago, a few Baja California desert sheep permits were going for around $600 a copy.

Next, an outfitter must be engaged and because the trip by pack and saddle horses will be into very remote mountains, this is also expensive. Figure on around $100 per day per person and more than that in most northern sheep country. A sheep hunt shouldn't be scheduled for less than 10 days or 2 weeks and some outfitters are reluctant to go afield for so short a period.

The pack train carries the hunters into sheep country where camp is pitched. Then from camp the hunters ride out looking for sheep. When these are located, hunting continues on foot. For this type of expedition, the hunter needs a certain amount of suitable equipment.

Put a warm sleeping bag and foam mattress at the top of the list; a good night's sleep between hunting days is extremely important. All hunting clothing should be soft, warm and light in weight. Don't forget long underwear, plenty of warm socks and a suit for foul

Not many shots at sheep are made under ideal conditions. You may be trembling with excitement, nearly dead from exhaustion or altitude, or more likely experiencing both of those conditions. Add such factors as wind and running animals and you have all the ingredients for missing. The rifle should have a scope sight of 4x or one of the fine new variables such as 2½x-7x or 3x-9x now available.

I have shot several sheep with a .270 and 7mm Remington Magnum calibers using bullet weights of 150 grains. The combination has been adequate, although

Herd of bighorn rams. One or two are legal size, but no really big male is in this picture.

weather which will not tear or rip easily despite hard use. A couple of extra pairs of gloves can come in handy.

Every experienced mountain hunter has his own preferred footgear. My favorites are mountain hiking boots of good quality with tough vibram soles, such as Danner 6490s. If it is wet, I wear rubber-bottomed pacs. No matter what the shoes, though, they should be well broken in before any hunt anywhere.

Obviously the rifle is of the utmost importance. So is knowing how to shoot it. It makes little sense to travel 1,000 miles for just one shot—and not be prepared to make it count. A flat trajectory is important, both to reach far out (although the average shot will probably be between 150 and 250 yards) if that is necessary, and to compensate for the shooter's error in estimating the range. Also the bullet should be heavy enough to down the animal if the shot does not hit a vital spot.

some hunters may prefer something slightly heavier because grizzlies may be encountered in mountain sheep country. A saddle scabbard is necessary to carry the rifle when riding, and I use a sling when making my own footprints uphill.

Both binoculars and spotting scope are invaluable, and the binocs are never off my neck when hunting. There are new very lightweight models on the market which far surpass any others manufactured to date. A spotting scope can save much unnecessary climbing to get a closer look at rams which may not be big enough for trophies.

There are many ways a sportsman can spend the autumn days upcoming. But nothing, absolutely nothing, matches a mountain hunt for a wild sheep. All the silver loving cups and lettered plaques in all the nation's showcases do not compare with the head of a trophy ram. Take this old sheep hunter's guarantee for that.

# ANTI-HUNTING:

# A Very Wasteful Issue

## by ED KOZICKY and JOHN MADSON

TODAY'S SURGE OF anti-hunting sentiment is nothing new: In one form or another, it has existed in this country for a long time.

Reasons for anti-hunting feelings have varied over the years. Sport hunting was once regarded as the idle pursuit of such ne'er-do-wells as Rip Van Winkle, and the only acceptable sport hunters were the well-to-do. By the early 1930s, with game supplies at a low ebb and modern conservation just getting underway, there was widespread sentiment against hunting, and it was felt that it was only a matter of time before it ceased to exist as a sport. However, the Great Depression gave people other things to think about, and also temporarily changed hunting from a sport to a necessity. It put food on the table.

As the Depression eased, World War II focused attention on matters other than hunting. But then came Korea and Vietnam—long, bloody holding actions that wearied the public of killing and provided new reasons for opposing recreational hunting.

At the same time, the period after World War II saw a shift from a rural to an urban-oriented society. Hunting is basically a rural art, and Americans were growing away from their rural traditions. How many people today have ever helped their fathers butcher hogs, cattle or chickens for family use? As we became more urbanized we abandoned homey skills and the traditions of those skills. To millions of Americans today,

◀ (Opposite) For many Americans, autumn could not possibly be the same without cold daybreaks in a duck marsh.

Hunters have paid for much conservation and wildlife management which has benefited the whitetail deer, as well as many non-game species.

the rural art of hunting is as obsolete as the quilting bee.

Then came the miracle age of electronics. The outdoors could be brought into the living room through a picture tube, and Disney film productions lost little time in doing so. A vast Sunday evening audience was riveted to the Disney version of wildlife. Starting with a proven formula for success—the humanization of wildlife with such cartoon characters as Bambi—the Disney studios went on to depict Mother Nature as a kind old grandma who provides a peaceful and idyllic existence for her charges. Little mention was made of nature's stern realities—of the survival of the fittest, the constant struggle for food and cover, and the rule of fang and claw. Many viewers began to feel that wild animals live in perpetual harmony in enchanted forests, a vision of freedom, peace and beauty that was missing from their own lives. In their new-found love of wildlife—whether real or imagined—they could not bear the thought of those wild creatures being hunted or trapped.

Others, having considered the matter a little deeper, confused conservation with preservation. Since they recognized wildlife conservation as something "good," they felt that killing wildlife must surely be "bad."

They have never quite understood that wildlife conservation and the modern hunter are inseparable, nor that preservation is only a minor element of conservation.

We professional game managers have been partly at fault. During the growing interest in wildlife, we gave the public little or nothing to do to benefit wildlife. We have given them no direct action programs of their own, and the wildlife-loving public has longed for direct personal action. Consider the booming industry in songbird feeders and foods during the past 10 years. But this wasn't enough. Some people, denied a positive role in wildlife conservation, began to champion a negative cause—anti-hunting. It is a natural cause to champion—spectacular, righteous, and certainly inflammatory and easily understood. These same elements were found in the early action taken by sportsmen who attempted to increase game supplies with such obvious approaches as predator control, game farms, and indiscriminate stocking. Real progress wasn't made until emotional guesswork gave way to professional game management, and the real problem emerged; the need for adequate habitat.

Emotion is a prime ingredient in any crusade, but if real progress is to be made, common sense must prevail and lasting solutions must be based on facts, not emotion. Anti-hunters are still in the first stage, with demagogues playing on emotion and prejudice in an effort to gain a following. For example, Cleveland Amory,[1] whose most notable contribution has been advocation of a "Hunt the Hunters Hunt Club"—the main ground rule of which is not to shoot a hunter within the city limits. Can such sick humor lead to reasonable solutions of social problems? Certainly not—it only adds fuel to the emotional fire on both sides. Yet, this self-styled "conservation expert" has found an opportune time to sell books and exploit TV talk shows even though he has no real field experience of any kind, nor any background in resource management. Such a person angers the dedicated hunter, and widens the gulf of misunderstanding between the hunter and the non-hunting nature lover.

It appears to us that the greatest gap between hunter and anti-hunter exists at the lowest levels of outdoor experience, knowledge and perception. The greater the lack of real outdoor knowledge and perception, the greater this gap between hunter and anti-hunter.

The gap narrows as outdoor experience and understanding of nature increases, and the deeply involved hunter and the deeply involved naturalist may merge until they are indistinguishable. As he matures, the ideal sportsman is a balanced blend of hunter, naturalist, and conservationist. He's a man with many polished outdoor skills and abilities, and whose affection and knowledge of nature are matched by his efforts to conserve it. The same can be true of the non-hunting outdoorsman. We know skilled and experienced naturalists who have never hunted, but none of these are vociferous anti-hunters.

Still, such people are likely to wonder why men hunt at all. Many hunters wonder, too.

Some of the best answers have come from the eminent Spanish philosopher, Jose Ortega y Gasset,[2] who was intrigued by hunting as a basic human pursuit that is as profound as it is universal. As a philosopher, he felt that the needs of living men are shaped by a pre-history that is still urgent within them; he believed that essential human nature is inseparable from the hunting and killing of animals, and that from this comes the most advanced aspects of human behavior.

If we really try to understand our urge to hunt animals, we will find issues in favor of it. Among these, Senor Ortega y Gasset believed, is the fact that hunting is one of the pure forms of human happiness. It is a diversion in the most exact sense—a recapitulation of our racial youth, a return to fundamentals that we instinctively feel are free, basic and right. For 99 percent of our racial life we have been hunters, and the little time frame in which we now exist seeks to deny us the freedom in environment that made us what we are. No wonder we would rather hunt pheasants than shuffle papers in the office.

One of the great points in favor of hunting is that it's a classic exercise in freedom. For many men, it is the truest, most personal exercise in freedom that is available today—and we support wildlife populations not just so we will have something to kill, but in order to have a

Scenes such as this of a herd of elk on an autumn morning can be enjoyed by non-hunters in many parks and sanctuaries of America.

As every hunter knows, regulated open seasons in the fall do not endanger any of our native wildlife. But they do provide much wholesome recreation.

would go out of autumn and life would take on a passive tameness.

We are told that man is ethical only when he does not kill, and that we should curb our instincts in the cause of reason and humanity, and stop killing animals. Yet, all of us know that it is the carefully reasoned "humanizing" of our planet that is doing the most deadly damage to wildlife. Genuine hunting, done ethically, is based on giving advantage to the animal in many ways. Humanization of our natural world, on the other hand, tends to ultimately disadvantage everything that is not human. The real hunter, seeking freedom in a return to Nature as it really is, does far less damage to wildlife than the modern man who seeks to bend nature to his own ends.

The moral question of hunting or not hunting is locked in an impasse. The anti-hunter cannot understand how someone can love and kill game at the same time, nor why anyone would enjoy hunting. It is a paradox beyond his comprehension, and the hunter is rarely able to explain his actions in a lucid and rational way. Each extreme involves personal emotions that are difficult to convey to the other. But while the modern sport hunter may be unable to explain his actions to the satisfaction of the anti-hunter, should it really be necessary to do so? The prime consideration should never be whether it is morally "right" or "wrong" to kill animals, but whether or not the act of hunting jeopardizes the existence of the hunted species. And with that consideration, the act of modern sport hunting is not "wrong."

From early history, the hunter concerned himself with welfare of game, and developed certain traditions, laws and ethics that governed the taking of game. It is the hunter who willingly spends money in the form of licenses and special taxes to support game management. It was a hunter who saw the need for biological facts and principles by which to manage game—Aldo Leopold. It was a hunter who promoted ways to finance the biological research needed to manage game—"Ding" Darling.

In his brilliant book *Game Management*,[3] Aldo Leopold wrote:

Hunting for sport is an improvement over hunting for food, in that there has been added to the test of skill an ethical code, which the hunter formulates for himself, and must live up to without the moral support of bystanders. That the code of one hunter is more advanced than that of another is merely proof that the process of sublimation, in this as in other atavisms, is still advancing.

The hope is sometimes expressed that all these instincts will be "outgrown." This attitude seems to overlook the fact that the resulting vacuum will fill up with something, and not necessarily something better. It somehow overlooks the biological basis of human nature—the difference between historical and evolutionary time scales. We can refine our manner of exercising the hunting instinct, but we shall do well to persist as a species at the end of the time it would take to outgrow it.

reason to hunt. As Ortega puts it: "One does not hunt in order to kill; on the contrary, one kills in order to have hunted." Put another way we do not hunt for the joy of killing, but for the joy of living.

Our critics piously tell us that it is not necessary to kill to enjoy wildlife. Of course it isn't. Genuine hunters know that as well as any man—and certainly better than most. We're frequently told that the camera is a greater challenge than the gun, and that wildlife photography is a demanding pursuit that's worth all the study and effort that you can give it. But although wildlife photography is a special end in itself, it is not hunting in the real sense, and can never be. Ortega y Gasset believed that "camera hunting" for wildlife, in its most offensive form, "represents the maximum tradition of affected piety"—and suggested that wildlife photography relates as much to hunting as platonic love relates to the real thing. Each has special values, but neither can be wholly substituted for the other.

There is no real substitute for hunting—even though many of us could have a full life without ever killing another animal, and find plenty to do outdoors without shooting and killing. But without hunting, the salt

America's waterfowl, especially, are managed to preserve that valuable resource forever.

Since modern game management has been established, with hunting based on biological surpluses of wildlife, no game species in North America has been severely depleted by sport hunting, and many species have been brought from scarcity to abundance—antelope, wild turkey, deer, elk, and others. Revenues from sport hunting have also helped preserve wildlife habitat for the benefit of not only game, but for many non-game wildlife species.

The current wave of anti-hunting emotion will eventually spend itself, only to be renewed by future zealots. It's a pity that there is always a faction seeking to force its morality on another. If one doesn't like hunting, then one shouldn't hunt. But attempts to impose personal anti-hunting attitudes on others can only lead to bitter controversy and recrimination in which neither side really wins and wildlife is almost certain to lose. The time and effort spent in this conflict of hunter vs. anti-hunter would be far better spent in furthering positive conservation efforts. Our greatest objection to the anti-hunting movement does not lie in any threat to sport hunting, but in the wasted time and effort that it entails.

Wildlife's greatest problem today is not controlled hunting, but uncontrolled use of the environment. With an expanding world population and our commitments to feed other nations, with our problems of balance of trade and imported energy and trends to monoculture in agriculture and forestry, what of our wildlife resources? The developers, drainers, channelizers, polluters, dam builders, and agri-businessmen are busy, and wildlife gets many promises but few benefits. There is no shortage of problems confronting wildlife. On midwestern and southern flood-plains, hardwood forests are being sacrificed on the altar of $12 soybeans. The Cache River drainage in northeastern Arkansas is a grim example of this—and the main defender of that irreplaceable waterfowl habitat is Dr. Rex Hancock of Stuttgart, who happens to be a duck hunter. The Garrison Diversion Project in North Dakota is another example, as is the South's pine forest monoculture that has been labelled "The Third Forest." All over the United States, quality wildlife habitat is being drained, cut, tamed, stripped, and reshaped to make more money. The need for hunter and non-hunter to work together was never more important—and the chance to do so has never been better.

One of the most common complaints of the virulent anti-hunter is that wildlife conservation is in the grip of hunting interests and that the non-hunter has no voice in wildlife management. And here again, we are wasting our potential.

The environmental 1970s have brought the cream of American youth into colleges and universities to pursue studies in natural resources. They come with a dedication that augurs well for our country's future. The sad fact of life, however, is that most public resource agencies, universities, and private efforts are already well-staffed with resource specialists. What is needed is new money to take advantage of this dedication and academic excellence. The skilled manpower is available, and the time is ripe for important new management programs—particularly programs for non-game wildlife species.

Millions are spent each year for the management of game species, but practically nothing is spent on the "poor relations"—the non-game wildlife. These are no less beautiful nor unique than our game species, nor less worthy of concern. We must broaden wildlife conservation to include all species of wildlife, and not just the favored few. Conservation of non-game wildlife has special meaning because it is everyday wildlife; it includes species that are adaptable to cities and suburbs if given half a chance, and which can be enjoyed by millions who never have the chance to spend time in forest, fields and marshes.

It is not reasonable to expect hunters to support the management of both game and non-game; although they provide millions of dollars for wildlife conservation, it is hardly enough, and our national wildlife is only getting half the attention that it deserves. Non-game wildlife management is an ideal course for non-hunters who are aching to do something but do not choose to support game species that will be hunted.

There's no good reason why action can't be taken. Most game management and research techniques can apply to non-game wildlife, and there is a whole new generation of trained, dedicated wildlifers anxious to find jobs in their chosen work. What is needed, obviously, is enabling legislation and funding. In a Winchester-Western booklet, *A Law for Wildlife*,[4] various ways to fund non-game wildlife programs are discussed.

Instead of wasting our efforts on the propriety of hunting—which is something like the old theological debate over how many angels can stand on the head of a pin—we should be working together with all types of wildlife and joining forces against the despoilers of natural environments. There's no better way of putting this than by paraphrasing one of Aldo Leopold's closing comments in *Game Management*[3]:

There is, in short, a fundamental unity of purpose and method between hunters and anti-hunters. Their common task of teaching the public how to modify economic activities for conservation purposes is of infinitely greater importance, and difficulty, than their current differences of opinion over hunting. Unless and until the common task of wildlife conservation is accomplished, the question of hunting is in the long run irrelevant.

# References

1. Amory, Cleveland. *Man Kind? Our Incredible War on Wildlife*. New York: Harper and Row, 1974.
2. Ortega y Gasset, Jose. *Meditations on Hunting*. New York: Charles Scribner's Sons, 1972.
3. Leopold, Aldo. *Game Management*. New York: Charles Scribner's Sons, 1939.
4. Conservation Dept. *A Law for Wildlife*. Olin, East Alton, Illinois: Winchester-Western Division, 1972.

Hunting has always been a traditional rite of autumn, for fur and food as well as for the exhilaration of being outdoors.

# Ranch Safaris-

Leopards are found on some ranches in all of South Africa but they are hard to hunt because they have been persecuted as killers of calves.

**ACROSS THE PLAIN** three black sables grazed on the green grass just beginning to emerge after a range fire. They were all bachelor bulls. Through my binoculars even I could see that one of them, the one on the left, had a magnificent pair of horns.

"If we can get to that termite hill," said Robin Skinner, pointing to a treed mound about 300 yards away, "you'd be within good shooting distance." The problem was lack of cover. The plain had been burnt bare 2 or 3 weeks before. The stalk would not be easy.

"Let's give it a try," I replied.

We made the first 100 yards or so without too much difficulty. The next hundred wasn't as easy. Our only cover was an odd small tree. Slowly we crawled on our bellies, moving only when the sables grazed or faced away from us. It was a slow and laborious stalk.

I could feel the tension and excitement surging in me. My heart pounded like a drum and a few small butterflies fluttered in the pit of my stomach. As we neared the anthill, even the nape hairs on the back of my neck stood up. I could feel a prickly sensation of goosebumps on my neck. Goosebumps in the midday heat of Africa!

My thoughts went back to the last time I had felt this

way, but that had been long before and far away. I had been a highschool kid then, sitting on a high ridge when I spotted a big whitetail buck slowly meandering my way, browsing as it went. I had never wanted anything more than that buck until now. Right now I wanted that sable. It epitomized a dream come true.

We crawled the last 20 or 30 yards at a fast pace, using the termite hill as cover. Then we slowly inched our way up into the trees that grew on it. The bulls were still peacefully grazing. It had been a perfect stalk. The closest of the three was about 250 yards away.

"Your bull is in the center now. He'll measure a good 46 inches; well in the record book. Take him!" Rob whispered.

I didn't need any urging. The jet black bull was magnificent. His hide shone in the strong African sun as if it were polished and the scimitar-shaped horns rode on his head like two regal plumes. In the face of action the tension from my body disappeared. The bull was broadside now, offering a perfect shot. Bracing myself against one tree I took a rest on a limb of another and took a careful aim. When the scope's cross hairs settled on the bull's chest, I squeezed the trigger. The blast

# African Hunting on a Budget

Greater kudu, one of Africa's top trophies, found throughout southern Africa in good numbers.

Springbok, found in Southwest Africa, are also on some ranches in Botswana and South Africa.

from my old Husqvarna .30-06 seemed far away. I was nearly oblivious to it. With the shot the sable bull jumped forward and went down. It was about as true a one-shot kill as a hunter can make. The other two bulls galloped off into the mopani forest beyond. My knees wavered a little and certainly my hands began to tremble. I could hardly believe that I had just stalked and killed a fine sable bull, an animal that is rated by many as one of Africa's top trophies.

During the remainder of my 10-day safari I bagged a respectable kudu, a waterbuck, a very fine bushbuck, plus half a dozen of the more common plains game species such as zebra, wildebeest, impala, warthog and a couple of the small antelope—the steenbuck and a duiker.

An African safari always was and still is today an outstanding hunting adventure. But no doubt most hunters who want to go on safari are in the same boat as I was. Upon investigating what the trip would cost I knew that my plans would have to remain a dream. A traditional safari out of the pages of Hemingway or Ruark books is an expensive undertaking. The rates today run around $500 and $600 per day. And more.

Yes, you read the figures correctly. And you must book a minimum of a 21-day safari. It you want to hunt such an animal as the black rhino then you must book a 30-day safari.

On top of this, of course, come licenses, concession fees and in some cases trophy export fees. These can easily mount to $5,000. Then there's the air fare, another $1,000 or more from New York. The cost of crating, packing and shipping trophies to your taxidermist runs anywhere from $1,000 to $1,500 depending on how many and which animals you shoot. In addition are incidental expenses such as hotel accommodations before and after the safari, bar bills, souvenirs and of course tips for your professional hunter, gun bearer, skinners, trackers and camp staff. This can come easily to $500 and probably $1,000. When you total up the entire tab most traditional safaris easily come to around $18,000.

But not all African hunting is that expensive. One of the best kept secrets about African big game hunting is that many of the large ranches in such southern African countries as Rhodesia, Botswana, Southwest Africa and South Africa have game. And on some of the

147

Nyala, one of South Africa's top trophies, can be hunted now only in that country.

ranches this game can be hunted, for a fee, of course.

The wildlife on some of the private land is amazingly abundant. Yet it wasn't always. At one time game was considered competitive with cattle for grass so it was not tolerated. Game habitat along with the game was destroyed. But enlightened wildlife management showed that many species of African antelope such as the kudu for example, are browsers that feed on tender twigs and shoots of trees and brush. This made cattle and some wild species compatible.

But the primary reason that game is numerous on many of the large ranches of Botswana, Rhodesia, Southwest Africa and South Africa is that in these countries it belongs to the land owner. And the land owner can dispose of the game as he wishes—including the sale of hunting privileges and even the meat. As a result, game has become a valuable commodity because it generates income. Because game generates income, so even those species of game such as zebra or wildebeest, which are grazers and do compete with cattle for grass are tolerated or even encouraged.

All this paved the way for enlightened wildlife management programs in this part of the world. As a result the population of many species has increased and some of the ranchers have actually formed "safari" companies with complete outfitting services for hunters.

What does a ranch type hunt in Africa cost? First, let me say that the costs are reasonably constant in all four of the southern African countries. But the exact dollars and cents answer depends on just what animals you

want to hunt. Should you choose some of the smaller antelope your costs will be much lower than if you want to hunt sable, kudu or nyala. The trophy fees for these larger animals are much higher than for most modest impala or a warthog.

Also, if you want to hunt the major trophy animals you must usually book a longer hunt. For example, if you want to hunt sable and kudu you will almost certainly have to book a 10-day hunt. If you want a buffalo in your bag, you may have to count on a 14-day stay. But if you will be happy with an impala, warthog and a duiker, you may reserve only a 3-day safari.

The highest cost for this sort of hunt is around $300 per day, but the average is considerably less. Ranches that can offer hunting for such game as buffalo, lion, leopard and so on usually charge more because these game species are in high demand.

Too, there are ranches where you may hunt on your own in Rhodesia and Southwest Africa. You pay only a trophy fee after the animal is bagged in addition to the cost of your own outfit including vehicle, camping gear and food. However, to make such arrangements one has to be on the spot. Advertising in such publications as the *Rhodesia Farmer,* Agriculture House, 113 Moffat St., Salisbury, would very probably produce a ranch or two on which to hunt.

In South Africa there are ranches that offer hunting for a daily fee of about $50. In such cases the ranch supplies a camp, frequently guest cabins, all bedding, cooking utensils, cutlery, the services of a camp ser-

Glassing for game from a hill over-looking a dry river bed.

vant, a cook and a Zulu guide. The hunter must supply his own food and vehicles.

What game is available on these ranch hunts? This again varies from one country to another. Not all game is compatible with ranching. Lions, for example, are not because they prey on cattle. Elephants need such a large space that this alone rules them out. Also they would be destructive of fences. Buffalo and rhino are also destructive of fences, but a few large ranches do have them. Leopards are classed as vermin but since they rarely kill cattle, preferring small antelope, they are not persecuted as are lions. Many of the large ranches do have leopards.

Despite the fact that lions are cattle killers some of the ranches bordering such big national parks as South Africa's Kruger, Rhodesia's Wankie, or Southwest Africa's Etosha Pan offer limited lion hunts. When male lions mature, the boss of the pride—their sire—forces them to leave. These young bachelor males frequently take up residence outside the park boundaries where they become legal game.

In short, almost all indigenous game animals of southern Africa can be hunted on the ranch type hunts. But the trophy fees for the less abundant and highly desired game animals is very high. For example, the trophy fee for a lion in South Africa is about 1500 Rand or about $1,800, while the trophy fee for white rhino is about 2500 to 3000 Rand. If you are looking for an African hunt at a modest cost, you have to forget about bagging a lion or a white rhino.

Eland found on some game ranches in Rhodesia, Botswana South Africa and Southwest Africa. This is Africa's biggest antelope in size and weight.

Ranch hunts and the game that can be bagged vary from country to country. Here's a rundown.

**Rhodesia:** This beautiful and now bleeding country was the cradle of game ranching. It still offers some of the best hunts in southern Africa. Unfortunately the terrorist warfare by leftwing guerrillas has made much of Rhodesia unsafe. There are areas of the country where terrorism is minimal and American and European hunters are still hunting there. But, I frankly wouldn't recommend it.

Game available here includes excellent sable,

perhaps the best in Africa, good greater kudu, eland, waterbuck, wildebeest, smaller antelope such as bushbuck of three different races, common reedbuck, southern impala, plus the very small antelope such as southern bush duiker, Sharpe's grysbok, oribi and the rock dwelling klipspringer.

A few of the ranches also have sassaby, roan antelope, giraffe and buffalo. Leopard, crocodile and even hippo can be hunted in several places as well. Such game as zebra and warthog are common. So are bushpigs, but because of their nocturnal bush-dwelling ways they are seldom seen. Among small predators, jackal are common, but hyena less so.

Ranch type hunts in Rhodesia can cost around $300 per day but it is possible to find some that charge much less. Where buffalo or lion are available charges are higher.

A west German friend recently returned from a Rhodesian hunting trip. He went there cold—no hunt booked—and rented a Volkswagen van on arrival. He then drove out into the ranching country and contacted ranchers—and made his own hunting arrangements. His hunting costs were about $50 a day, plus the rental fee of the van, gasoline and food. The total costs were less than $100 per day. The trophy fees of the animals he bagged were additional.

Hunts as short as 3 days can be arranged but on such short hunts you are restricted to the more common antelope. A hunter is generally allowed one animal per day. Greater kudu and sable cannot generally be taken on hunts of less than 10 days. This is about the amount of time needed for a good general bag of plains game.

Trophy fees vary from ranch to ranch, depending to a degree on the abundance of particular animals but also on their demand. But a good average would be sable around $400, kudu $300, waterbuck $300, zebra $200, wildebeest, bushbuck, reedbuck $100 each, warthog $50 each.

It is still possible for a hunter to make a completely outfitted 10-day plains game hunt in Rhodesia for a price of around $3,500. This includes safari costs and trophy fees for about 10-head of plains game including kudu and sable. Rhodesia also has large safari firms operating on government owned concessions and offering more or less traditional safaris. Their costs may not be as high as those of Zambia, Tanzania or Botswana, but are in the $400 per day range. Information on hunting in Rhodesia can be obtained from Office of Rhodesian Affairs, 2852 McGill Terrace, N.W. Washington D.C. 20008.

**Botswana:** This is a dry relatively sparsely populated country which offers some of the best hunting in Africa, with such renowned safari firms as Safari South and Selby, Kerr and Downey operating there. It offers a variety of game including such species as sitatunga in the northern swamps and gemsbok

A good sable bull bagged in Rhodesia. A few ranches in South Africa also have sable on them.

around the Kalahari desert.

Ranch type hunts are relatively new to Botswana. The ranches are located primarily in the southern portion of the country near the South African border. Excellent greater kudu is the primary trophy here but some ranches have gemsbok. Other game includes wildebeest, springbok, duiker and jackal. Leopard is also available.

Last summer two friends and I hunted on several ranches in Botswana with excellent results. Game was very abundant. Everyone in the group got kudu better than 50 inches.

The only way a hunter can bring firearms into Botswana is by booking a hunt with a safari firm. There is one safari company, Wildlife Management (Botswana) (Pty.) Ltd., P.O. Box 1068, Gabarone, Botswana, that specializes in ranch hunts. Wildlife Management Ltd. has agreements with several ranchers for exclusive hunting rights. The costs on a 2x1—two clients to one guide—hunt run about $180 per day.

The trophy fees are competitive with Rhodesia but on the average slightly lower. Kudu is about $300, gemsbok and zebra $250 each, wildebeest $125, bushbuck $100, impala $60, warthog $40. The trophy fee for leopard is about $900. It is illegal to bring spotted cat products into the U.S., however. It is possible to do a 10-day ranch hunt for plains game in Botswana for a total price of around $3,500. The hunter's bag would include about 10-head including greater kudu and gemsbok.

**Southwest Africa:** Ranch type hunts have been going in Southwest Africa for a decade or longer, thanks to the pioneering firm of Basie Maartens Safaris. Greater kudu and gemsbok are the primary game animals but eland are also available and Cape hartebeest and springbok are common. So are steinbok, bush duiker and ostrich. Hartmann's mountain zebra, known for its unusual markings, can also be hunted on some of the ranches in Southwest Africa.

Ranches in the northern part of Southwest Africa also have blue wildebeest, Burchell's zebra and the Damaraland dik-dik. There are several safari firms that specialize in such hunts. Their names and addresses can be obtained from Director, Nature Conservation and Tourism, Private Bag 13186, Windhoek, Southwest Africa. The costs vary. The safari firms generally charge around $200 or $300 per day. One of these, Basie Maartens, offers a special father and son hunt in which the son can hunt for the cost of a non-hunting companion.

The cost of a 10-day hunting trip in Southwest Africa could easily run around $4,000 or a bit more for a hunt with one of the safari companies. That cost would include trophy fees for a fairly good bag of game, including eland. But a hunter who is willing to hunt on his own could do such a hunt for much less. The problem will be to find a ranch or ranches by mail on which to hunt. But any hunter who goes to Southwest Africa on his own, rents a vehicle and then starts to make inquiries, won't have any trouble finding a place. Many South African hunters find hunting in Southwest Africa cheaper than at home.

The trophy fees in Southwest Africa are generally cheaper than elsewhere. Some ranches ask as little as $200 for kudu or gemsbok and as little as $35 for a springbok. Eland has the highest fee, about $350.

A hunter who is willing to hunt on his own should be able to organize a 10-day hunting trip in Southwest Africa for under $3,000 including trophy fees, but he should budget $3,500 if he wants to include an eland.

**South Africa:** Zululand Safaris has been offering hunts on a few large ranches in Natal for a decade or more, but during the last few years dozens of ranches in South Africa have opened for hunting, with a variety of game available. A few have buffalo and excellent kudu. Gemsbok are occasionally offered. However one of the primary trophies of South Africa has to be the beautiful nyala, one of the spiral-horned antelopes that can no longer be hunted elsewhere.

Other species of antelope that can be bagged only in South Africa include black wildebeest, bontebok, blesbok, southern mountain reedbuck, vaal rhebok plus such small antelope as blue duiker and red duiker. Other plains game includes sable, antelope, roan antelope, Cape hartebeest, common reedbuck, several races of bushbuck, eland, blue wildebeest, Burchell's zebra, warthog, bushpig and small antelope as grysbok, oribi, steinbuck and bush duiker.

Some ranchers charge about $50 per day and sup-

A very fine greater kudu bagged on Talana Farms in Botswana.

ply the services of a cook, camp servant, game scout plus a completely equipped camp. The hunter needs to supply a vehicle and food. But prices can go as high as $300 per day for a fully outfitted ranch hunt, including the services of a professional hunter. There are a number of ranchers who offer outfitted hunts for about $200 per day.

Generally the trophy fees for bontebok and nyala are the highest, up to $500. The trophy fees for the more common game are less, kudu and waterbuck $350 each, zebra and black wildebeest $300 each, mountain reedbuck and vaal rhebuck $90 each, blesbok, common reedbuck and bushbuck $75 each, impala, springbok and warthog $60.

The cost of a South African ranch type hunt is in the small ball park as in the other countries of southern Africa, but it is easier to find a place to hunt. For example, such ranches as Theunis Bester even have a brochure printed about the hunting on their land. Copies of these brochures can be obtained from South African Tourist Corporation, Rockefeller Center, 610 Fifth Avenue, New York, N. Y. 10020. There is little doubt that the era of the traditional safari that Hemingway and Ruark wrote about is coming to an end. But even then such hunting trips were beyond the financial means of most hunters. Happily a ranch type hunt in southern Africa is not.

Any hunter who can afford a big game hunt in Alaska, the Yukon or northern British Columbia can afford a ranch hunt in southern Africa. And he is bound to get more game for his money.

# Squirrel Hunting in a Nutshell
## by ERWIN A. BAUER

**OF ALL THE IMPORTANT** days on a sportsman's calendar, none exactly matches the opening of the squirrel season. For one thing, this is usually the first of *all* game seasons to open. For another, it comes at a golden time of year — in early autumn, when days grow cooler and the forests are flaming with color. But most of all, the day is important because both fox and gray squirrels are splendid game animals. Squirrel hunting is fascinating business in itself. It is also the greatest possible tune-up for other hunting later on.

There are six basic ways to hunt bushytails. There is the waiting game. This calls for spending most of the time sitting down, alert and watching all around. Still-hunting is another method. In this the hunter travels slowly through a woodland, alternately walking and stopping. It is also possible to hunt by boat, by teaming up with another hunter, by using a dog and by calling. Which way is best depends upon the time of year, the terrain, the abundance of mast at any particular time and the condition of the forest — on whether it is wet or dry.

But no matter what the method, to be successful requires that a squirrel hunter bring all his skill as a woodsman into play. It is very similar to hunting whitetailed deer in that an outdoorsman must really match wits with the game.

Perhaps more sportsmen wait out the squirrel than hunt them by any of the other means. This is only natural, since the drier the woods are (and very dry, crisp woods that are noisy because of fallen leaves are often a fact of early fall), the more successful is this technique. When you yourself do not move, you do not make any noise. At the same time it is easier to hear any noise a squirrel might make overhead or in passing.

The secret of playing the waiting game effectively is first to find a good spot to wait, and second to remain as nearly motionless as possible. The first is far easier than the second.

Usually what you find on the forest floor and the types of trees in the forest will tell you where to sit. Look for nut trees — hickory, beech, oak, pignut, pecan — and then look for fresh squirrel cutting beneath them. When you find an area where cuttings are more abundant than anywhere else, you have found a good spot to spend some time.

Every outdoorsman has had the experience of animals approaching very close to him without recognition as long as he remained motionless. But the slightest movement sends the critter scurrying away, and the slightest movement in a quiet squirrel woods will alert all the squirrels within range. To avoid unnecessary movement, be comfortable while sitting. Take along a cushion — or even a folding canvas stool or chair.

Never make sudden moves if you can avoid them. When shifting your position, do so gradually, carefully. You will have to turn your head to thoroughly cover the area all around you, but do this slowly too. If you hear a squirrel — or a strange noise — do not swing abruptly to look in that direction. Always turn slowly.

Any squirrel hunter must learn to "read" the noises he hears in a squirrel woods, since many birds and small mammals make similar sounds. At a distance it is easy to confuse the chatter of a blue jay with the bark of a squirrel, and chipmunks sometimes make comparable sounds when rattling through the leaves on the ground. When you are able to distinguish one sound from another, you will be able to concentrate more in listening for squirrels alone. But sitting isn't every outdoorsman's dish. I guess I'm too curious about what exists in the other side of the woods to sit very long in one place. For me still-hunting is the most fascinating, if not always the most productive.

The best still-hunter is the one who can walk through a woods while advertising his presence the very least. He must walk quietly. He must not crush dry leaves or snap twigs underfoot. Obviously, still-hunting is best in a damp woods — or right after a rain has soaked the forest.

This stop-and-go hunting requires wearing soft, well-broken-in shoes. Sneakers are excellent if there are no copperheads and timber rattlesnakes in the area. Otherwise depend on soft, 10-inch boots. Also wear "soft" clothing (a flannel shirt, for example) which does not make a scraping or raspy sound as it brushes against vegetation. Some of the new camouflage clothing is very good — although in heavily hunted areas where other hunters are likely to be, it's a good idea to wear red or yellow shirts and caps.

Movement is always more noticeable in bright light than in dim light. On sunny days, always keep to the shadows and avoid open sunlight when moving through the woods. You'll greatly increase the odds in your favor.

A skillful squirrel hunter moves softly through any woods, avoiding bright light.

(Opposite page) Often a hunter will only get brief glimpses such as this through fall foilage.

Sometimes two can play the still-hunting game better than one — if it is a large enough forest. The strategy here is to walk parallel courses, perhaps just barely in sight of each other, although that isn't necessary. Teamwork pays off here. One hunter stops and watches while the other moves ahead slowly. If a squirrel is spooked by one hunter, there is a good chance it will flee in the direction of his companion. Often the first hunter has no idea there is a squirrel anywhere around until his companion shoots.

One morning last fall I had a rare opportunity to see how this works. I had been sitting in one place for 15 minutes or so without seeing any sign of squirrels and was planning to move. But my son Bob, who was sitting about 200 feet away, stood up and began walking to

Occasionally a squirrel will reveal itself fully as here on an oak tree trunk.

another position. That's when two grays that had been crouched unseen in a tree directly above me shifted position to keep an eye on Bob. Luckily, I saw them and bagged one.

Sometimes hunting late in the season with a dog can be productive. But unless most of the foilage has fallen, it doesn't pay off. A good squirrel dog (and I have seen many hunting breeds, as well as mongrels, that were great on squirrels) picks up a squirrel's track on the ground and then traces it to a tree. But if the tree is large and leaves remain in the crown, it's wasted effort. You probably will not be able to spot the hidden animal anyway. Some squirrel dogs are silent trailers and some will bark. I am not certain which is better.

The best squirrel dog I ever saw was a rat terrier that was generally silent but would yip-yip softly beneath the squirrel tree. It belonged to my friend Bill Hendershot, then a conservation official. Sometimes it would circle around the trunk while yipping and in that way cause the squirrel to move and betray its hiding place. Incidentally, this terrier also retrieved the fallen squirrels and probably saved cripples that otherwise would have been lost.

There are a number of excellent squirrel calls on the market. At least, they perfectly imitate the chattering or quarreling of a squirrel. But for me at least, calling squirrels has been only occasionally successful.

A hunter's best tactic here is to go into a known squirrel area, sit and then try to locate squirrels by occasional calling. But beforehand he should know exactly how a squirrel barks. Although I have never been able to call a squirrel from far away into range, I have often had one answer me and of course give away its location. That is a big help on days when other tactics do not work.

Other types of calls and noises have been used with success. Years ago in the southern Ohio hill country, I hunted with Jake and Nat Henthorn, tobacco farmers who carried pieces of gravel in their hunting coats. If no squirrels were moving, Jake would grind the pebbles together in the palm of his hand. he claimed this made squirrels hiding nearby very nervous. Maybe it did. Anyhow, he shot more than his share of bushytails from the hardwood hills around his home.

Other hunters I have met used both crow and hawk calls to excite squirrels. It is understandable that either of these sounds might have an alerting effect on all the wildlife in any woods.

What makes a good squirrel woods? Ordinarily it is a woods containing a good mixture of nut- or fruit-bearing hardwood trees — in other words, a year-round supply of food for squirrels. A woods that contains only one kind of tree will not have a high squirrel population — unless it happens to be an abnormal year when the mast crop is heavy in that one area and very light elsewhere.

Sometimes in autumn there is a general scarcity of nuts. That is the time to hunt in forests (or the portions of forests) that border on cornfields. All squirrels readily eat corn — and plenty of it — when other foods are scarce. It is usually easy to detect where squirrels have been visiting a cornfield. Ordinarily they will forage only on the fringes of it and by their weight will bend the stalks down to the ground. They will also carry whole cobs into the forest and sometimes leave a littered trail of bare cobs to help mark their path to a den tree.

No matter how you hunt, always keep looking for sign. Look for broken-down cornstalks, nutshells and cuttings beneath nut trees. large hollow den trees and large leafy nests which squirrels built in the fall are giveaways. An abundance of nests in a woodlot is usually good evidence of many squirrels living there.

The more heavily hunted they are, the more wary

Top tip for squirrel hunters: Look for the elusive animals where their mast (food) is most abundant.

down. After a few minutes, pull hard on the rope and rustle the bush; the squirrel might be startled into shifting to *your* side. Or instead of the rope, toss a stick or stone into the leaves on the far side of your target tree. If that doesn't work, find another squirrel someplace else.

There is one way to hunt squirrels that for me, at least, is more pleasant than all the rest. It is often the most effective as well. I mean by hunting from a small boat or canoe — perhaps drifting downstream on a river that meanders through forest country.

For one thing, you can cover plenty of ground, and the constantly changing scene adds to the adventure. In drier years, squirrels will be close to the waterways rather than away from them. In addition, it is possible to move more quietly and with far greater stealth in a canoe than it is by walking.

The squirrel float trip is an especially good possibility for the sportsman who didn't get his fill of fishing during the summer. He can cast for bass or trout as he drifts downstream — while watching the treetops and keeping a gun across his lap. It's really living.

Rifle or shotgun? That all depends. By choice, the rifle is the one for me. I like the demand for greater concentration and marksmanship. The shotgun, on the other hand, is light, and more productive when squirrels are so few and far between that every shot means a lot.

When a hunter spots a squirrel, it doesn't necessarily follow that he will get a shot at it. The target must be within range. For a shotgun hunter, that means 35 yards or so; to shoot beyond that range means a near-certain loss of a cripple. All squirrels are tough and tenacious, and unless several pellets reach vital areas, they will escape. The shot should be 6s or 7½s.

Some truly excellent rifleman might consistently make kills with a .22 beyond 40 yards, provided they used a good rest. But the wise hunter will wait for his squirrel to wander closer, or he will try to narrow the range by stalking. Whenever possible, use a tree trunk, limb, deadfall or whatever solid is handy for a rest. Then aim for the midpoint of the front shoulder, a place that allows some margin for error. If you are an especially accurate marksman, try to make all your shots head shots. I use Hollow Point bullets. There may be some meat loss with these, but I'd rather have that than a squirrel drilled through a nonvital spot. In that case it will usually die in a hidden part of the tree.

Another consideration often tips the scales these days in favor of the shotgun — its safety. When there are other hunters in a deep woods, where visibility isn't too good, I believe the scattergun is a necessity. I do not want to take even the remotest chance of causing an accident.

Any way you hunt him, the squirrel is the greatest target since the bull's-eye, even if you go afield with bow and arrow or slingshot. And come to think about it, that would be hunting squirrel the hardest way of all.

squirrels become and the less they move about in broad daylight. That means the best times to be in the woods are beginning at daybreak (or before) and during the hour or so before darkness. Probably three-fourths of all squirrels are taken in these periods.

There are a number of tricks well-known to veteran squirrel hunters that are worth repeating here. Say you know for sure that a squirrel is hiding in a certain tree. Even though you walk slowly around it, you still can't spot him. The reason is that the squirrel also keeps circling and staying on the side of the trunk away from you. There are several ways to fool the animal — sometimes. Carry along either a rope or several stones. Tie one end of the rope to a bush or small tree on one side of the target tree and then walk to the opposite side and sit

## by FRANK WOOLNER

**UPLAND SHOOTERS ARE** singularly close-mouthed folk. If anyone who is a complete stranger tells you the precise location of a hot spot for either grouse or woodcock, regard him as one of three things—a liar, a dolt, or a careful friend who believes that you can be trusted to keep a confidence.

The best work a buddy-system, but never vector in the crowds. This secrecy involves such little ploys as the use of motor cars not known to be the property of

(Right) A woodcock hiding in one of those thick, briar-loaded patches.

local aces, plus hiding said cars in remote areas—even if that means trudging over a brushy hill to reach some heavenly corner where woodcock are known to plummet into the popple and alders, or where grouse feed on the wealth of autumn. It can be reasonably cloak-and-dagger, a well planned operation.

Smart gunners spot coverts by prospecting. There are perfectly logical ways to do this, and there are some that have been touted although they are nearly worthless. Let us examine the bad news first, and then proceed to advanced espionage.

One of the problems is season. A trout fisherman, poking along some sparkling little stream in May or early June, may flush a number of grouse and woodcock. That angler may be an upland hunter in October and November and, if he is rather naive, he may conclude that this location is bound to pay off when the first multi-colored leaves spiral down. Maybe, but usually he's wrong. The birds are there in springtime because that is where fodder is concentrated and overhead cover defeats predators. Come fall they'll be elsewhere.

Where woodcock are concerned, a spring singing ground often hosts longbeaks in April or May, but doesn't produce in October. *That's* a courting area and—if surrounding terrain lends itself to nesting and rearing chicks—there will be a certain number of native 'doodles on the perimeters prior to any mass exodus in fall migration. Often transient migrants resolutely decline to descend there, so it's a sort of a one shot deal.

It is useless to assume that grouse and woodcock do not change their habitat as seasons progress: They do, and it is a matter of necessity. Forage changes and cover changes; that which is precisely right in spring and high summer is likely to be worthless in bright autumn.

As a matter of fact, the late autumn to early winter shifting of gears may be most pronounced. Game birds must feed, and they seek cover. In the hot and humid

# THE COVERT

aisles of early fall when red maples are just beginning to flow, summer still fights a rearguard action. Then woodcock and grouse will be found in areas they will shortly scorn. Much of it is due to canopy.

In the beginning, this canopy is thick. Woodcock and grouse can patter along under low screens, and they are happy as clams. The minute that low screen is destroyed by Mother Nature they feel like the naked and the dead, and they get out of there. Now a hunter begins to think about the real upland hells, the tangles of briar, juniper, birch, poplar and sporadic conifers, to study the impact of environment—how it works and how it can be utilized.

This involves cruising and investigation. Topographical maps offer one royal road to success. A man who knows how to read a topo can read the ground ahead. It isn't difficult yet there is a curious reluctance to study map and compass. Everything is there, down to the last bog and ridge. There are old trails, country roads and state highways, the locations of ancient farmhouses proaching a covert and in working its depths. Part of it is dog, and part man-sense, knowing what a bird is likely to do under a given condition—while giving that flyer credit for upsetting all of our supposedly superior intellect. If we are often defeated, that is a good thing too, since sport would pall if victory were guaranteed.

On strange ground there is no foolproof way to figure precise approach. You can surely think of the wind, whatever there is of it, and the slant of sun. These are important because scent (for a dog) is borne on errant breezes, and sunlight can get in a man's eyes when he is swinging on a grouse or woodcock that is towering

(Left) Poor position in early season jungle with lowering sun in the gunner's forefront.

straight into a burning fireball. That's basic, as is the fact that you can't see much in an early season jungle and must therefore defeat said jungle by strategy. The covert approach was old hat long before international agencies provided a different definition.

However, serious upland gunners gravitate toward tracts they know as well as they understand the moods of their families. This is ground often cruised, so familiar that every boulder and scrubby wild apple tree boasts a charisma all its own—bolstered by years of victory and defeat when birds have boiled out of low cover. A first trip may be disaster compounded, made sweet only by the accumulation of knowledge that will ensure success on another day. It is hard to go in cold.

For a moment, let's discuss some of the cabbages and kings so often ignored. Where possible, go in with the sun at your back—or at least quartering from left or right. Upland addicts offer a thousand alibis for missing, and one of the prime tear-jerkers is a bird that "flew right into the sun." No matter what you do, this will happen, yet we have enough trouble without inviting more.

Check the wind. If it's nonexistent or exceedingly gentle, strategy dictates no major adjustments in approach. However, any freshening breeze should be taken into account for three reasons: A dog finds it more difficult to lock into scent when all of those perfumes are being whisked away in front of a tail wind; flushing birds invariably launch into the wind; and most upland flyers are frightened by any suspicious sound borne to them by helpful air currents.

Grouse in hard-hunted coverts are spooky, and they tend to become almost paranoid as gales build. It is then that a shooter mutters about wild flushes—and sometimes ensures them by approaching with the wind at his back. Pats can hear, and often they don't like what they hear. Keep the wind in your face. Remember that, like all natural aviators, birds take off into the wind. You'll have a better chance to take the towering straight-away.

# OPERATION

long gone. Contour lines and symbols spell it out.

A canny customer looks for alder edges and the scattering of poplar, birch and conifer in a damp area for woodcock. He hunts overgrown upland pastures for grouse, places where worm-riddled apples cover the ground and barberries cluster like rubies against forgotten stone walls. There will be change as the Montreal Express begins to blow, and that must be taken into account.

Bird dogs often seem to know good coverts, and I say this fully aware that the statement may be disputed. Certainly, by eyesight, they recall those they have visited before and get to champing their jaws and whining plaintively as the road dips down and—there it is.

Dogs also sense something beyond our comprehension, part sight, perhaps a subtle perfume drifting through an open window. They get excited and, if sitting on the front seat beside you, will annoint the windshield with wet nose smudges.

There are factors to take into account while ap-

Certainly a canny grouse or a little male migrating woodcock (which often flies like a zany jacksnipe instead of towering feebly as most of the literature suggests) may immediately break hard port or starboard, but he'll be up front, every so often coming back in a quick wing-over turn and a low-level pass that rattles all but the most experienced of shooters.

Ruffed grouse *can* be moved by a jump-shooter. In order to cash in, however, that gunner must know his ground and be quick enough to swing coolly and rapidly at the first whirr of wings. Woodcock frequently seem loathe to flush, the primary reason why a jump-shooter harvests so few of them. Gun at port arms, one moves in cautiously, kicking at the dry shards of a departed summer and—nothing happens! Except that the dog's eyes bulge and he may shiver uncontrollably, hypnotized by warm scent.

Just about the time a man harbors dark thoughts about false points, lowers his shotgun and prepares to chastise his dog, that occult little 'doodle spirals out in a wild twitter of wings and—you wind up making alibis while the sweet aroma of burnt powder hangs in still air. Fine dogs cut a white eye back and then go about their business, thoroughly disgusted by human bumbling.

Perhaps it is kindergarten rehashing to discuss the physical act of flushing a game bird, yet this is an art in itself. In youth, prior to working with fine pointers, setters and Britts, I fatuously assumed that odds were stacked against a jump-shooter because every flush was unexpected. Actually, going in over solid point can be a far more nerve-shattering experience than the quick swing where everything happens so fast that you don't have time to get psyched.

A hunter's adrenalin builds to flood tide the moment he sees that wonderful dog poised like a granite statue in woodland shadow and shine. Beginners get jittery, and there is no veteran who does not feel the blood begin to pound in his temples. Under these circumstances it is not too hard to miss.

On grouse, jump-shoot strategy involves stop and go—with emphasis on stopping at planned intervals dictated by location. Briar-torn aces forever scan foreground cover and try to divine hiding places. The better practitioners employ cadence in walking, for a continual, casual sound of progress is less likely to alarm a pat than hesitancy. This doesn't mean uninterrupted hiking, but simply the approach to a probable site of action—after which the calculated halt becomes mandatory.

In grouse cover, one learns to evaluate each possible jackpot location, whether it be a brushpile, a blowdown, a stone wall in a thicket, a tangle of wild grapes or an ancient apple tree challenging surrounding birches. If a pat has been skittering along through the run ahead of man-sound, that biddy is likely to hide in the first available sanctuary.

Gunner-tactics then call for a steady approach to whatever hidey-hole is indicated, to casually arrive at a pre-judged spot and—to halt suddenly. Usually, if a grouse is there, the termination of sound will blow his cool, and he'll come out in a blur of beating wings. You're hopefully flat-footed and ready.

It is abject stupidity to approach a wall or fence and to clamber over it without any halt. One will fare quite as badly in bulldozing through a brushpile or blowdown, to move straight into sere swamp edges, into known loafing or feeding grounds. The great trick is to recognize these possible bonanzas and to plan attack. Pick a spot to halt and go there without any break in stride. Stop, gun at port arms! Wait a few moments, and then take

Heavy foliage yet sunlight over the shoulder is helpful.

Topo map and compass pinpoint possible bonanzas.

another step forward. Halt again. Few grouse can resist the urge to boil into unforgiving air.

Similar tactics often pay off in the follow-up of pats flushed in cover where a shot proves impossible. They don't fly very far and perhaps you can see them vol-plane into a thicket 100 to 200 yards ahead. Granting that some last-minute curve to right or left may occur, and often the bird will run after touchdown, chances are that it will be fairly close to point of contact.

Mark that location carefully, perhaps by a specific tree or some other terrain feature. Then mosey well over to a right or left flank and resume the approach. To go straight in on line of flight is tricky, since that is what the bird instinctively expects, and fears.

Again it is a steady advance, eyes sharpened to pick out a most likely hiding place. Again it is the calculated sudden halt. Almost always a second flush will occur the moment you terminate forward progress and, if you've guessed right, the pat may be a far easier target than it was on first encounter.

Consider another minor serving-up of the walrus' cabbages and kings. Initially, gun-carry in an upland covert. Boasting a mighty careful dog, it is feasible (although still rather chancy) to go in with a shotgun tucked under your arm or slung over a shoulder until the

moment of solid point. If you are not entirely ready, you handicap yourself. If you do this in jump-shooting, you will be defeated from the very beginning. Split seconds count.

The gun-carry should be close to port arms, ready for immediate action, thumb or forefinger on a safety catch. *Don't* slip that catch until flush! There is no need for it, since it can be done automatically at the first sound of wings while you are mounting the gun and beginning a swing that may be corrected, but is already roughly on target.

You haven't forgotten to wear shooting glasses? Plus a tight fitting visored cap that will shield glare and resist snatching briars? The glasses protect eyes from switching menaces and, if you can wear the yellow shades without discomfort they provide contrast. Some wear light gloves and some do not. Without them you will scratch hell out of hands and wrists, but that rarely kills a healthy human being.

All right, a bit more of the covert operation. Let's say that you've been there before, because—if you haven't—then you are going to miss a lot of main chances. Having checked the slant of sunlight and wind direction, there is a necessity to ponder season, ground cover and forage available. So-called "hot corners" are always tucked away in some niche of the brain that stores recollection. We'll never win them all, but we wouldn't want that.

I have a favorite apple tree that is kind to grouse. It is the best kind of apple tree, no bearer of classic fruit, only a maverick planted by some forgotten farmer. There is an ancient cellar hole, caved in, no more than a depression in the burgeoning brush.

Partridges harbor there, and they are difficult to approach, primarily due to one tiny avenue of hay-grown opening, and then the tree—gnarled and suckergrown, huddling at the edge of second-growth birch and maple, guarded on three sides.

It is difficult. There is no way to approach through the brush, for it is nearly an impenetrable screen, so one must come in from the miniature open side and then—of course—birds patter swiftly back into the jungle and go thundering off low and unseen. Now and then some foolish biddy towers, and a man can score. There are a lot of empty shells in that clearing.

There are more lucrative mother lodes, yet each requires study. You learn, after a while, that it is self-defeating to approach from any angle where heavy brush favors the bird and prevents a quick snap-shot at the very least. It is better to be right part of the time than never. Note that, if woodcock or grouse have been there before, they'll be there again if no other gunner has pushed them out just before your arrival, or the covert has not reverted to sterile pole timber.

As a hunter you will have been humbled in the past and, hopefully, you will have learned a little. You are aware of the fact that an early woodcock covert is likely to be barren after hard frost destroys ground cover, and then you must seek timberdoodle in thicker stuff. It is equally obvious that grouse change their feeding and loafing grounds, also depending on cover and forage.

It is often said that grouse and woodcock are found in the same coverts. This happens when seasonal requirements for the two birds intermesh, and it is usually an early or a late fall phenomenon. In the beginning, a 'doodle will be found on moist bottomlands, and pats may also frequent such an area. Then there is a hiatus in which the woodcock sticks to the lowlands and the grouse seeks height.

Briars scratch wrists, snatch caps off heads.

As fall winds boom across the backcountry and northern frosts drive migratory 'cock southward, there will be more occasions when you will find the heavenly twins sharing an environment—away up in high aspens, junipers, birch whips and clutching briars. It is a short and fleeting period, often the finest upland gunning period of the year.

Then, suddenly, woodcock are gone—obeying a built-in time clock that calls them southward. Grouse go to thickets, to sere swamp edges, to scattered conifers where it is warm in the crispy days of approaching winter and where there is a proliferation of shriveled berries and succulent buds. They will repair to sunny knolls and edges where the first thin sweeps of snow are soon burned away. They seek cover and sustenance, the keys to survival. That's where you'll find them.

None of us miss because we want to: We miss because we gamble on long odds. If there is a thick alder edge erecting an umbrella of greenleaves overhead, what's wrong with sending a flushing dog into the run while you stand outside? If a woodcock or grouse flushes into a hostile sky, there's a chance while you stand outside. If that bird goes low and twittering in the case of timberdoodle, or roaring through the stems with a clicking of wings where grouse are concerned, grin and bear it. There will be other days.

Count always a right way to go in, and a right way to come out, plus the tactical approach to bonanza corners that have produced in the past. Anything else is amateur, a worshipping at the shrine of luck that usually does not exist. The killers go in prepared, and they know what is *likely* to happen.

Having attained some skill in the rapid swinging of a shotgun, success boils down to understanding the quarry under differing weather and seasonal conditions, a knowledge of the ground and how it will probably influence flight-path. We do not dictate the rules: They are dictated to us.

No matter what the Constitution preaches, men are not created equal. There is never any norm where reflex action is called upon. Some of us are fast off the mark and some of us are slow to get cranked up. Men and women who do equally well with the guns of October may be ice-cold in the clutch, or steaming with the pressure-cooker of excitement. Either way, it's a good feeling.

I admit my own failings: I cry a lot and alibi upon missing a game bird. I take it hard, and then I get to laughing at myself. I still work every dodge, prospecting in all seasons, studying the topo maps, figure slant of sun and wind direction, try to learn every inch of a favored covert in order to outwit the grandest of American game birds.

Grouse and woodcock still cut me down to size. If they didn't, I'd rack my guns and retire to the steamy bogs of spectator sport.

Day's end. Time to hold an after-action critique with the dogs.

161

# SELECTING AND USING A TURKEY CALL

by BYRON W. DALRYMPLE

**SOME YEARS AGO** I sat with Mabry Anderson, a renowned turkey caller from Clarksdale, Mississippi, in deep woods behind the Mississippi river levee. I listened to him work on a tom in spring with a call made from the wing bone of a turkey he had shot years before. He held the hollow wing bone, about 6 inches long, cupped in his hands, and sucked on the small end, producing notes so perfectly imitating a love addled hen that when I closed my eyes I could imagine the bird standing there beside me.

The tom was reluctant. But step by step Mabry brought him in. It was a classic performance, done with a call that by today's standards would be considered extremely difficult. But it was one Mabry had fashioned himself, and it was a type not uncommon clear back to Colonial times. It was a matter of curious pride to him

brush, by heaving rocks into a canyon. Now we hoped to hide and call one to us as they talked back and forth trying to regroup. I didn't much like the inadvertent noise of that call.

As we eased into our position the box lid scraped again. The hunter took out his other call, a slate and striker type. Presently turkeys were talking around us. He pressed the striker against the slate surface and made a series of three scrapes. *Perk, perk, perk.* Not bad. A young tom replied, and they talked back and forth. The bird was coming in. Then on one stroke the striker slipped. It made a screaking sound not remotely like any turkey ever uttered. The hunter cussed under his breath and hitched around. The box lid scraped. The turkeys clammed up instantly, and we never heard or saw one of them afterward.

(Opposite) Full camouflage is mandatory if you want to give yourself every break. This hunter keeps hands working call low and steadies arm so movement is slight and no foul-ups occur.

(Right) This is the way a big gobbler looks when you do everything just right. A Rio Grande turkey in full strut moves in toward the *perk,perk,perk* of a lovesick hen.

to lure in one gobbler with a call made from another.

Anderson was, of course, extremely expert both in his knowledge of turkeys and his acumen with the call. Now consider another incident that is quite the opposite. I went hunting last year with a fellow who was doing his first turkey hunting. He was all fired up, had bought all the needed equipment to camouflage himself, and had even purchased two calls, both of which he carried.

This was in the fall. As we walked along, the big box-type call with hinged lid that he carried in his pocket let out a squawk intermittently when he ducked under a limb. The lid would move enough with his body movement to scrape the edge of the box, even though he carried it with a rubber band around it. We had scattered a group of young gobblers and hens that were in

The moral to be drawn from those two incidents is obvious. To be a successful turkey hunter one must know how to use a call expertly and efficiently, and of the numerous types of calls available nowadays, he should select one that is in line with his expertise or lack of it so that he *can* use it most easily and efficiently. Some kinds have advantages for beginners, and some require a certain kind of hunter personality to use them properly. Not all hunters will bother, for example, to become deft call operators. So, they need a call that is just about foolproof. Others want the best sound they can get and don't care how much practice is required to get it.

The reason the subject of calling is an important one for modern hunters is that nowhere in the realm of the shooting sports has a specialized endeavor been grow-

Box type with hinged lid. Lid secured by elastic cord. One lip makes more raucous tom sounds, the other mimics hen.

(Above) Photo shows bevel of lid and also of lip of box. This side is for hen sounds. When gripped by bottom, handle pointed away, and shaken, box will "gobble."

(Left) Hunter using box-type call. A spring gobbler — easiest turkey to call because these young toms are inexperienced — comes in close.

ing so swiftly as turkey hunting. This is because turkey flocks have been doing likewise. Not more than three decades ago the wild turkey was bemoaned in many places as a lost cause. It was, some wildlife experts said, surely headed for extinction. Bumbling efforts at restocking were patently unsuccessful. But at long last biologists learned the tricks for successful reestablishment of the wild turkey.

Indeed, wild turkeys not only came back in numbers on their original ranges where a few still hung on; they were also reestablished in huntable numbers in practically all of the range from which they had long ago disappeared. In Michigan, for example, where the last known wild gobbler was killed in 1914, there have been turkey hunts for some years now. That's not all. Turkeys are currently established in huntable numbers in numerous states where historically they never were present. There is turkey hunting literally from border to border and coast to coast.

This means that thousands of hunters totally new to the sport are getting into it every season. Many of them hunt in places where there are no experienced turkey hunters to act as mentors. The turkey is a "new" game bird in state after state. Selecting a call and knowing what to do with it is an important consideration each season for a myriad of newcomers to this sport. The wild turkey is a tough enough proposition without adding the hurdle of possibly scaring off birds by attempting to use a call you can't operate well, or of filling the air with sounds turkeys don't want to hear.

An inordinate amount of nonsense has been written about the difficulties of turkey calling. Among the solid instructions, there is invariably too much of a welter for the beginner to absorb and put into practice. What sounds do turkeys make that you as a caller need to copy? That is the most important place to start. I know callers who can mimic every sound turkeys make. It's an accomplishment. But *you* don't need to be able to do that in order to put a bird in the roasting pan. You shouldn't even begin by trying to imitate a lot of turkey talk. Far better is to get down pat just a single or a couple of their sounds so perfectly that you won't mess things up at the crucial moment.

The technique of calling is based upon the fact that turkeys are gregarious, flocking birds, and that they are also rather vocal. Further, around the year they pursue a varying kind of caste system. During the fall season the old, mature gobblers—long-bearded birds—will be by themselves, usually in small groups of three or four to possibly 10 or 12. Throughout the fall hens will also flock together. Often, where turkeys are plentiful, flocks of hens will be much larger.

Young gobblers—birds of the year or "spring" gobblers—also form their own groups. Some of the more timid or late-hatched ones, however, continue to hang around with groups of hens. You have to look sharp to see their brief beards, which may show only as

In some states rifles are used. More distant shots can be taken, for in this type of terrain turkeys can be seen at longer distances. It's no special advantage to have your hands free to keep gun mounted and ready.

a minor parting of feathers at the top of the breast. I've often seen young gobblers in groups of 12. They stay away from the old toms. If feeding conditions remain good during fall and winter, these groupings will remain constant. Occasionally lack of feed, or a specific abundance, will cause them to forego the caste system.

The groups have strong ties. As they feed along and become separated, they'll call back and forth. If something disturbs them and they scatter, by running or flying, they do likewise, even more urgently. The voices of the hens, the young gobblers, and the mature toms each have a different timbre. But the get-together or where-are-you call, the "lost" call as it is usually termed, is, except for voice quality, the same: *chalk, chalk, chalk.* It is usually quite loud, anxious and questing.

Too much has been made of the necessity to imitate

individual turkey voices. Each turkey sounds a bit different from every other. Don't worry about it. Do try, when you hear a turkey and call to it in the fall, to make a sound as close to what it is uttering as you can. An old gobbler, or a young one, or a hen, wondering where its group mates are, is expecting the same voice quality.

In autumn toms gobble very little. But they may gobble readily when they hear a sharp noise, or, for example, an owl hoot. They'll do this at any time of year. An owl hoot call is available, in fact, precisely for locating gobblers so that a stalk can be made to within proper calling range or even waylaying range. It is a good addition to one's general equipment. Turkeys make two sounds all year that callers should be aware of and never imitate. One is the *quit–quit–quit,* uttered sharply but not very loud. A turkey making it is highly disturbed and about to run or flush. The other is an explosive *putt!* When a gobbler utters that sound he's

loud, raucous *yowk, yowk, yowk* as well as gobbling. Some callers ease along a ridge when no gobbling has been heard and give a yelp with their call now and then. This often gets a rise from a gobbler that has so far been silent. He may gobble, or he may yelp back with that coarse *yowk.* Regardless, the caller now should stay right where he is and continue.

Hens in the spring mating season call plaintively. The sound is a close imitation of the "lost" call, but not so loud, nor with anxiety, but with soft seductiveness—*perk-perk-perk*—gently coaxing, not yelling "Hey—where are you?" as in the fall get-together version. After breeding, the hens of course begin nesting, and finally the baby turkeys are following their mother, while the gobblers, after the mating, have gone back into their groups again.

During the summer, with poults following hens, one of the most important sounds is uttered—so far as a

Two mature gobblers, heads thrust forward, both gobbling at once. They've been incessantly fighting during spring mating season and have torn up their tail feathers.

long gone, scared and suspicious, and on his way.

Turkeys *cluck,* hens give out a long-drawn *whine* sometimes in spring, and also an extra-subdued, long and stuttering *c-r-r-r-r.* Callers who become expert can use these sounds to great advantage especially with seductive insistence in spring, and on suspicious or hesitant toms. To begin, however, it's better to practice them at home but forget them afield.

During early spring the turkey flocks begin to break up. Toms now become loners, fighting with their winter buddies and vying with them for hens. Individual hens are in a breeding mood soon, and they too cease consorting in flocks, although a gobbler may corral several at a time. The gobbler now gobbles to show off and let hens—and other gobblers who may be feisty—know where he is.

A gobbler may also sound off intermittently with a

hunter is concerned. The young turkeys, their voices high, are incessantly anxious to keep in touch with their mother. They call: *kee, kee, kee*—over and over, whenever they are separated or even a bit unsure. They continue this on into fall.

I have a friend who has demonstrated repeatedly that the best notes to use in fall are those of the young. He foregoes all other sounds, and claims regardless of age or sex that the *kee, kee, kee* will fetch scattered or separated birds. This applies not just to flushed birds badly disturbed. When that occurs, they'll be quiet a few minutes and then begin calling to each other. But groups feeding in cover also drift apart. Single strayed birds can be called thus.

Carried one step farther, this repeated *kee* sound is a young turkey's version of the questing "lost" call, *chalk,* and that note is a variation of the softer *perk,* or

(Left and below) The diaphragm call that fits in the roof of caller's mouth. Made of plastic with latex diaphragm. It leaves both hands free.

Small canister type call with latex stretched across top.

Compact slate and striker. The two parts fit together to form a small box for easy carrying.

The hollow cedar box with cedar striker that is scraped across lip by slit (striker not shown), has long been popular.

Modern simulation by manufacturer of the wingbone call.

167

*turk* as some phonetically spell it, used by submissive hens in spring. Thus the tyro turkey hunter should concentrate on these sounds, and shy from all others. He can develop the whole turkey repertoire later, but if he never learns to make or never uses any other sounds, he can be assured, spring or fall, of success—or a chance at it anyway—with just these.

The type of call he selects to execute the sounds should be carefully pondered. I've mentioned the "Turkey Hooter," which imitates the hoot of a great horned owl. This is a specialized call that simply helps locate gobblers, which commonly respond to this particular noise as well as to any sharp sound. It doesn't

actually *call* a turkey. In general there are two categories of calls: Those that are operated by mouth and those consisting of some type of sounding board or resonator box plus a striker or scraper.

Mouth operated calls presently marketed are of two types. One type is the so-called "yelper." These produce only the yelps or "perks" and "chalks" described before. They are blown into or sucked on—like the old turkey wingbone. One very small call to be activated by exhaled breath is a small cannister with latex across the top. Yelper calls are compact and easy to carry, and not especially difficult to operate. They require the use of at least one hand. Some homemade yelpers have been

Hens stay together, usually in flocks larger than the males, during fall and winter and split up only to nest in the spring. Learning the mating call they make, and the "lost" call of the young — these are the main sounds you need.

trumped up out of soda straws, and a few old hands even produce a reasonable imitation by blowing across a leaf held between the thumbs.

An extremely popular mouth-operated call is the diaphragm. In modern version it is a half-circle of plastic that holds a stretched insert of latex. Originals of these now mass produced calls were conceived and hand-crafted years ago by dedicated turkey hunters in Alabama and other Deep South states. They passed the idea by word of mouth and made a few for friends. These were made from a horseshoe shaped piece of thin lead covered by adhesive tape and utilized for the diaphragm a section of thin rubber cut from a condom.

The diaphragm call is placed in the roof of the mouth. By silently forming the syllables *chirp, chirp, chirp* with lips and tongue the sounds of lost turkeys or the mating call are easily uttered. The *whine* of a hen can be done, too, by an expert manipulator, and also the *clucks* and the stuttering *c-r-r-r*. The advantage of this roof-of-mouth call is that both hands are left free. There's nothing to hold or operate by hand.

In dense cover, especially across the South, where a gobbler often isn't seen until the last second when it steps into shotgun range, use of this call allows one to

The western mountain turkey is the Merriam's, a large bird with bone white tail edging and rump. Often these turkeys, in mountain terrain, can be seen at a distance so that plans can be made to stalk or waylay or get in proper calling position.

The "turkey hooter" call, made by Olt. It imitates the hoot of great horned owl. Gobblers will often gobble at this sound, at any time of year and especially so in spring. It doesn't call them — just locates them. It's a valuable item of gear.

have the gun up and ready, pointed, both hands in place. It is the least cumbersome of all turkey calls. However, in much turkey hunting—in hilly areas in the West, where turkeys can be seen distantly and even where rifles are used—having the hands free is not as important. One disadvantage of this call is that many persons have difficulty perfecting the sounds with it. They get the hang eventually, but I'm not sure it is a rank tyro's best choice. Wait a bit. Try it after you get going.

The most abundant call designs made in infinite variety since time immemorial are of two general types. One employs a narrow hollow cedar box with a protruding lip on one side. This lip is chalked. A cedar striker is scraped across it to produce sounds. The other is a

Turkeys follow a caste system. In fall the old gobblers — long beards like these — group together, and so do hens and young toms.

piece of slate, generally affixed to a small cedar box to form a sounding chamber. The little flat box fits in the palm of one hand. Its slate is struck—or scraped— usually with a wooden peg with a handle. The end of the peg is roughened, and often chalked. Some operators draw the peg in a circle on the slate.

The sounds are produced by friction of striker and slate. Palm pressure and angle of holding the box changes the timbre of the sounds. Lost and mating calls, the *kee*, and all other sounds—except the gobble—can be formed by entrepreneurs with these calls. Designs of

homemade calls of this popular type are endless. No old-timer ever *bought* one! I once saw one fashioned with a half-coconut shell as a top for the striker, to form a sound reflecting chamber. A great many experienced turkey hunters are partial to slate and striker calls. These of course require use of both hands. They are compact, easily carried and used. The one problem for newcomers is that until you've had much practice, slip-ups are common. Results may be erratic and errors numerous—you hold the striker a bit wrong and make sounds no turkey ever did.

This is the way you hope things are going to look after you've done everything just right. Gobbler is suddenly alerted and starts to run. Head shot with shotgun and No. 4 or No. 6 highbase shell will successfully conclude this hunt.

(Right) Author with mature Rio Grande gobbler. If you work call properly you can get results both fall and spring. Many states have both seasons and allow hunters a bird each season.

The big box-type calls, sometimes called "gobble boxes," have become exceedingly popular over recent years. Basically this call is a cedar box 8 inches or more in length and 2 to 2½ inches wide. It has a lid hinged at one end by a pin of some sort with a small spring beneath it. Most boxes have a crisscross arrangement of rubber bands or elastic cord to keep a gentle pressure on the lid. The bottom of the lid is convex and beveled. The lips on either side of the box also are slightly convex in the long dimension, and one is a bit thicker than the other. The thin lip produces hen sounds, the thick one makes a slightly harsher sound to imitate a tom. When the lid, which has a handle, is drawn across a chalked lip—sometimes the convex lid surface also is chalked—the sounds are formed and amplified by the resonance of the box.

These big boxes can produce every sound a turkey makes. The lost and mating cries are easily done with surprisingly modest practice. the *whines* and stuttering *c-r-r-r-r* sounds, *clucks,* even the *quit* and *putt*—both no-nos—can be formed. With the rubber band or elastic harness in place, the box can be gripped in the palm, lid handle turned away, call tilted slightly downward, and shaken—and it gobbles. The lid, swinging swiftly across both lips and back, makes the sound, and very well, too.

There are other calls. One is a big bellows type that is shaken. A kind of foolproof box-type made several years ago by Olt is cranked. This assures that the lid scrapes exactly the same way every time. The operator simply turns the crank. An old-settler type turkey hunter I showed it to snorted and called it an "idiot box." Maybe so, but a beginner could do worse.

In my opinion, box calls are, in general, the best choices for hunters new to turkey calling. They do it all, and they form the basic syllables with less chance of error after only moderate practice. I have a rather extensive collection of turkey calls. I believe dedicated hunters should try several, especially the slate and striker types in varying designs, and the diaphragm. But a box, though a bit awkward, is a sensible place to start.

There are two cautions. Don't get carried away and try to make every sound the turkeys do. Learn the two basic sounds—lost and mating—and be satisfied to stay with them until you've mastered them and actually called in a few turkeys. Second, keep the darned box quiet while you're walking. Don't let it "talk" by itself in your pocket. A swatch of absorbent cotton placed under the lid and over both lips, with an extra rubber band slipped over the call to keep the lid snug, will do the trick.

# When Hunters Become Goose Decoys

by **RUSSELL TINSLEY**

**THESE GEESE WEREN'T FOOLED.** High overhead in a bright and incredibly clear sky, they crossed in a ragged v-formation. Sprawled among the sea of white, we dared not twitch a muscle, hoping the wary birds somehow could be persuaded to double back for a second look. Guide Clifton Tyler coaxed with his goose call. But it was no go.

Clifton rolled over and propped himself up on one elbow. "Those old snows are spooky," he said with a grin. "No telling how many white spreads they've looked at over the years."

Probably plenty, because hunting geese on the rice-growing prairies in southeastern Texas has changed little through the years. Come each fall it is business as usual, draping pieces of white rag or plastic on the rice stubble to simulate a bunch of feeding geese. Hunters garbed in white hide among the spread and actually become decoys themselves.

Hidden somewhere among the strewn-about plastic squares were my three companions: Winston Burnham, Leroy Gebert and A.W. McLaughlin. They never had hunted geese before, and I knew they were in for an education. We'd driven from our homes in central Texas the prior afternoon to the town of Columbus, northwest of Houston, where Clifton lives and operates his goose-guiding business. I've been hunting geese in this part of the country for the better part of 20 years, so it was nothing new. But seeing big geese gliding down, wings locked, toward the decoys still gives me a thrill.

Before daylight we made about a 30-minute drive to south of Eagle Lake, self-proclaimed as the "Goose Capital of the World." Parking along a backcountry road, each of us shouldered a big bag stuffed with plastic and hiked into the adjacent field. Then the fun began. Everyone pitched in and assembled the spread, more than 300 pieces of plastic. Then as shotguns were loaded with No. 4 Magnums, the newcomers got the familiar lecture.

A sight like this isn't uncommon on the rice prairies of Texas.

 (Opposite) This goose tried to land among the white decoy spread.

"When geese are coming, keep down and hide your faces," Clifton instructed. "If you just gotta look, peek from your parka hood out from under a cap. Don't shoot until I give the word. We want to be sure they are in range."

The eastern horizon was turning orange when the first vanguard of geese rose off a nearby holding pond. Then others came up, and others. The semi-dark sky was alive with moving, jabbering blobs. Clifton commenced talking back with his call.

It didn't take long.

A squadron of four turned our way. "Get down," Clifton hissed before resuming his conversation with the loquacious geese. Their voices grew louder as they drew closer. The suspense of waiting impatiently had my nerves raw.

"Now!"

Shapes came from the spread and shotguns warwhooped. One goose cartwheeled toward the ground.

The others flapped their wings frantically as they tried to change direction and gain altitude. Another fell.

"Only two?" Clifton asked. "Man, we should have gotten all four."

These were juvenile whitefront geese, locally called specklebellies. Of all the species that winter in the rice country, this goose is the most gullible. "Pete" Gebert and "Mac" McLaughlin were happy as they examined their first geese ever.

The goose season in Texas usually is quite liberal, running about 75 days from late October into January. Bag limit for years has been five geese per day, but only one can be a dark goose, a specklebelly or Canadian. The others have to be snows or blues, which are a color phase of snow geese.

Until late morning we enjoyed sporadic shooting. A bright sky didn't help as most geese stayed high as they crossed overhead. We eventually ended up with 11, which was about all the birds we wanted to tote, along with the sacks of plastic, back to the vehicles.

As we drove back to Columbus, Clifton and I relived some old memories. I had watched him grow up, guiding hunters for his dad, Marvin Tyler, who still has a goose-hunting business at the postage-stamp community of Altair, about halfway between Columbus and Eagle Lake.

We'd been fortunate in that we had found geese reasonably close. Sometimes Clifton and his clients have to drive more than 60 miles to find a concentration. A changing agricultural pattern has far-flung the birds.

Used to be, when rice was harvested, the stubble was left for the geese. Rice is hard on the land, and the land must be rested a year or two between plantings. But now, once the rice is gathered, some stubble is immediately ploughed under and the field sowed with soybeans, a legume which returns vital nitrogen to the soil. When the stubble is gone, the birds move in their search for food.

"I've got to scout 'em about every day," Clifton explained. "Find a holding pond where they are roosting and locate where the geese are feeding, put your spread on the flyway and the chances are good there will be some action."

Last season was one of the worse in recent history. Many factors were involved. The geese were scattered, the weather unseasonably nasty. But the primary culprit was the lack of teenage snow and blue geese. The spring hatch had been sub-par.

As Clifton had said earlier, the old birds are super-wild. It is the juvenile geese that can be hoodwinked by the white decoy spread. Get the attention of a lone young goose flying by, and the odds are good it will double-time toward the spread, looking for company.

Who the ingenious person was who first thought of the idea of spreading white rags to attract geese, no one knows. But generations of hunters are deeply indebted to him. The system keeps producing year after year.

In this hunting the white-garbed hunter becomes a decoy.

Clifton Tyler in conversation with geese.

When I first started coming to the rice country, white rags were used exclusively, either old sheets torn into chunks or baby diapers. The problem with rags is they must be laundered regularly. A rice field is often muddy.

Then someone discovered white plastic. The first time I saw it used was on a hunt with Mike Beard, who guides for Marvin Tyler. Mike carried a huge bundle of small sharpened sticks into the field. After the sticks were stuck into the gound, a piece of plastic was draped over each one.

"Putting the plastic on sticks gives the spread more lifelike movement," Mike told me. "I like the plastic, it's lighter, but when a pretty stout wind is blowing, then I go back to the rags. Too much movement, I'm convinced, is as bad as too little. On a foggy damp morning I especially like plastic; rags get soggy, and the spread seems dead."

While most guides prefer the rice stubble, it isn't absolutely necessary. The stick-plastic technique can be used in a ploughed field. One of the best hunts I have ever experienced came later that same season when I returned for another hunt with Mike. He was guiding four hunters from Waco and invited me to tag along.

It was the first time I'd ever hunted a ploughed field. Mike had brought plenty of plastic, and we improvised one gigantic spread. Geese are attracted to numbers. They like open spaces and feel secure in mass gatherings. If given a choice, they normally bunch near the middle of a field, far from steep levees and banks which loom as potential ambush spots. For this reason, the

The bigger a white spread the better it seems to attract. (Inset) A piece of plastic on a stick moves with the breeze to make a white spread seem alive.

(Above) Retriever brings in another to add to the collection.

(Right) Mike Beard shows proof that his white plastic technique produces.

The end of a successful hunt near Eagle Lake, Texas.

A juvenile whitefront goose like this is easiest to fool.

decoy spread is located a lung-taxing walk from the nearest road, and size or mass is more important than shape or detail when putting out a white spread.

Before we got the spread finished, a fog came rolling in, gaining intensity by the minute. Shades of London. By legal shooting time, 30 minutes before sunrise, we were completely socked in. Visibility was a few dozen yards at best.

We could hear geese somewhere up there as they left the roost. Mike went to work on his call. Shortly he reached and grabbed my arm. "Listen," he instructed in a low whisper.

A lone goose was circling above in the fog, and it was honking steadily. Mike honked back. "A speck," he muttered between calls.

All of a sudden the goose was right over us, a dark shape in the fog, its head twisted as it eye-balled the spread. Mike told me to take it, and I did. The other hunters didn't have a chance. I doubt if any of them even had seen the decoying bird.

Mike's golden retriever raced after the dead goose. Light grudgingly was penetrating the fog, which if anything was getting thicker. Prospects appeared dim.

Things were quiet now. I couldn't hear any geese.

"Hell, looks like we've had it," I complained to Mike.

"Be patient," he said. "Geese don't like to move early in a ground fog. Most of the geese still are on the holding pond. It'll be late before they take to the air. With fog like this, hunting usually is feast or famine; we'll either kill a bunch of geese or very few."

Mike picked up the goose the retriever had dropped beside him. "But one thing for sure, we won't get shut out."

It was nearing 8 o'clock when we heard a chorus of geese heading out for breakfast. Mike began calling again. He got results in a hurry. Suddenly the sky above us was alive with birds, shadowy silhouettes drifting through the fog, big flocks of them.

"M'gawd, shoot, shoot!" Mike hollered.

I already had my shotgun up. The 12-gauge with Magnum loads jolted my shoulder as I sent a goose pinwheeling. Other birds rained from the sky. There was so much shooting, so steady, that the muzzle blasts seemed to merge into one gigantic, continuous roar. Hunters and hunted had gone wild.

In 30 minutes it was over. Could you believe, the five of us had our aggregrate limit of 25 geese. Mike was so busy retrieving downed birds that he didn't have time to get in on the action. It was the kind of a hunt you judge all others by, fabulous shooting.

Mike said the elevated plastic squares made the difference and I, for one, find it difficult to argue with success.

A typical good buck antelope with foot-long horns. The horns grow somewhat bigger, but those bigger males are hard to find.

# Last of the Plains Big Game

## by ERWIN A. BAUER

**ALMOST EVERYONE** who ever hunts the American antelope or pronghorn, *Antilocapra americana,* is greatly impressed with the remarkable animal. John James Audubon was no exception, and during his trip on the Missouri River in 1843, he saw the species for the first time. Perhaps his description of the antelope has never been equalled by other writers since that memorable occasion.

"Hurra," the painter-naturalist enthused, "for the prairies and the swift antelope. They fleet by the hunter like flashes or meteors. They pass along, up or down hills, or along the level plains with the same apparent ease, while so rapidly their legs perform their graceful movements . . . that like the spokes of a fast-turning wheel we can hardly see them, but instead observe a gauzy, film-like appearance."

But then as now, the antelope was more than just fleet afoot. At the beginning of the 19th century it was the most abundant large animal in North America. Because it was such a huge impressive beast, and far more visible, the bison was most often mentioned in the reports and diaries of the first travelers across the Great Plains. The bison was also more important, especially

to the Plains Indians. But Ernest Thompson Seton, writer and illustrator, estimated the antelope population to be about 40 million in 1800—in other words far greater than the number of buffaloes.

In 1972, between 250,000 and 300,000 antelope survived in 15 western states and southwestern Canada, making it the third most abundant big game animal, after the whitetail and mule deer. Over half of the present population exists in just two states, Montana and Wyoming. However there was a period just after World War I when the future of the pronghorn was in grave doubt. By 1920 a mere 15,000 remained in scattered small bands and only a serious conservation effort was responsible for the present more favorable status.

Originally the species ranged across the entire 2 million square miles of open prairie lands from western Minnesota and Iowa to Washington and Oregon, and from Alberta to Mexico. Before fences and highways crisscrossed the landscape, antelope were much more migratory than today. At times the animals gathered in such vast herds that the rolling terrain seemed to undulate beneath a cloud of dust as they wandered about. More than one overland country traveler thought that the foothills ahead were shimmering in the noonday heat until at closer range the movement was identified as a vast herd of pronghorns. Then—almost mysteriously—the plains were empty of both bison and antelope.

A number of factors caused the sudden, disastrous decline. Disease introduced by domestic sheep exacted a heavy toll, but most of it was a matter of over-gunning. After the bison became too scarce to be hunted for profit, the host of western market hunters turned to pronghorns. In Denver, then a frontier community, the hog-dressed carcasses of antelope sold for only a dollar a dozen. In many mining and railroad construction camps, antelope meat was the only kind ever served—and since it was so available, only the tenderloin parts were used.

During the same era, ranches began to stretch barbed wire all over the West, and they regarded the antelope in their pastures only as competition for their cattle. For a long while antelope were about as welcome to ranch-men as wolves and coyotes. In addition, the animal had a natural curiosity and lack of wariness which made it very vulnerable, even to the comparatively short-range rifles of the 1800s. No wonder the pronghorn became an endangered species.

Fortunately American sportsmen and conservationists began to realize that saving the pronghorn was a moral obligation. After World War I, numerous state laws protecting the species were passed. But since most of these laws had either no teeth, or provided no penalties or funds for law enforcement, steps had to be taken at the federal level. These steps included the establishment of three refuges: the 1½ million-acre Charles Sheldon Range in high plateau country along the Oregon-Nevada border, the Hart Mountain Refuge in Oregon, and the National Game Range in Montana which was also meant as a sanctuary for bison.

But far more important than the refuges were the scientific studies begun by wildlife biologists to learn the life habits of the antelope. Everywhere this research

(Left and opposite) Herds of antelope in full flight. When running at full speed, it is often difficult to separate the bucks from the rest for a good shot.

revealed that the species in no way competed with livestock and could in fact get along with cattle. Not only were they browsers rather than grazers, depending to a large extent on sagebrush (which is of no use to cattle), but antelope ate a good many other plants which were either injurious or deadly to domestic animals. Some notable examples are prickly pear (which are eaten spines and all with no ill effects), loco weed, larkspurs, rubberwood, cockleburs, soapweed, needle and thread grass. In some areas antelope were found to *thrive* on native range plants which ranchers considered a menace. When these unexpected findings became known, persecution by landowners virtually ended. And better still, it was then possible to restock—reestablish—animals on large tracts of the former natural range from which they had been eliminated.

Today the antelope provides the only plains shooting for big game left on this continent. Only hunting the barren ground caribou on the open northern tundra compares with it; except that the caribou in no way matches the pronghorn as a game species. No longer is the antelope a curious creature easy to gun down; as a result of its close brush with oblivion, the animal has become extremely shy and wary. When hunted by "fair chase"—*without* motor vehicles, walkie-talkies or similar mechanical devices—the antelope is a great challenge and that is doubly true if the hunter is seeking a trophy head and will settle for nothing less.

Consider the animal itself. No relation whatsoever to any of the Old World antelopes, it is the sole member of the family *Antilocapridae,* is unique to western North America and has no counterpart anywhere else on earth. It is also our only big game animal with branched horns (members of the deer family have antlers, not horns), hence the common and certainly more appropriate name of pronghorn. The species is even more unusual in being our only hollow-horned ruminant; it sheds its horn sheaths early every winter. In other words, the black outer horns drop off annually and then larger horns begin to grow on the bony cores in

springtime. But its distinctive category and striking appearance aside, the antelope is among the fastest of all animals on four feet.

A mature antelope's speed is so great that there is no need at all to exaggerate, but any rifleman who has just missed a series of running shots is likely to view it as only a blur on the landscape. That is why speeds of 60 and even 70mph have been claimed. However the actual honest maximum is somewhat less. Antelope have *been* timed at near 50mph, covering typical plains country in seemingly effortless bounds, but this is not common.

Many other of the world's big game animals noted for their swiftness can maintain their top speeds only for short sprints. The cheetah is an excellent example of this. But the pronghorn has been known to maintain almost 50mph for a mile or so—and to average 30mph over 7 miles. At times whole herds seem to run just for the fun of it. When driving in the West, it isn't unusual (when in good antelope country) to have the animals speed parallel to a car for no apparent reason.

Still, and strange as it may seem, pronghorns depend more on extraordinary eyesight than on fleetness afoot for their protection. It has been compared to human vision through 8x or even 12x glasses and perhaps with reason. With such vision as that, it may not even be necessary to run to keep hunters at a safe distance. A common defense tactic is to stay within sight of a hunter, but still be out of sensible shooting range.

The first step in planning an antelope hunt is to secure a permit. Nowadays in all of the antelope states, these are awarded to applicants by public drawing. Usually it is necessary to state the particular area you want to hunt, which means consulting other hunters, landowners, guides or outfitters, and most likely the state fish and game department beforehand. Once you have a permit, it isn't too hard to find good areas to hunt, either on private or federally owned lands.

Most hunting is done by car—pickup truck or 4-wheel-drive Jeep—with the hunters trying to drive within shooting range of the animals. This can turn into a wild rat race which works well enough for the first few hours of opening day, and if legal is a good enough way to collect a supply of delicious meat. But it isn't exactly the most challenging sport. Far more satisfying is to locate a good trophy and then to stalk it alone and on foot. Another fascinating, productive strategy is to play the waiting game. It works as follows:

If possible, try to locate a herd of antelope—or at least the trophy you are seeking—at dusk. Chances are that they will bed down somewhere in that vicinity, but you cannot always bank on it. Then next morning well before dawn, be in the field somewhere nearby, hopefully on a ridge or other high area of ground from which you can scan all around. Wait there quietly and completely motionless. If the antelope *have* bedded close by, you might spot them before they spot you just as day

breaks. After that it is a matter of stalking into shooting range. If you are lucky, the animals may begin feeding in your direction, and all you must do then is avoid buck fever.

Against the green landscapes of spring and summertime, the handsome white and cinnamon antelope is easy enough to spot, even across great distances. But once lush summer dries up into the tan and brown grasses of autumn, it becomes another matter. Then the pronghorn is much harder to distinguish from its environment with which it blends very well.

Most often and especially when standing (rather than bedded down) it is the white rump or cream-colored belly which betrays the antelope. Both males and females are brown along the backs, but black collars and muzzles identify males as surely as do the longer black horns. The older bucks grow, the larger the area of black.

It is easy to tell when an antelope is alarmed, aroused, or uneasy about something—and hunters should know all these symptoms. Particularly when frightened, the animal will leap away, either before or just after "flashing"—erecting—the shiny white hairs on the rump. Almost certainly this is also a warning, in lieu of a vocal alarm, to other animals of the herd. It is very common for antelope rumps to quickly flash from one to another—in fact to every one in the herd like falling dominoes—whenever a human comes into view. A moment later all may be running and soon out of sight. After the first barrage of the first day of the season, it may be difficult to spot an antelope which is not already disappearing over the horizon in highest gear.

Perhaps the best advice to any antelope hunter is to get out in the field well before opening day and to thoroughly reconnoiter the hunting area. Know which areas the animals are "using." Know also the locations of all draws, gullies or depressions which may be useful in making an unseen approach toward a target. This advice is especially important if you are hunting in a new or unfamiliar area.

On the first close inspection, many sportsmen are astounded at the pronghorn's small size. A male stands only 3 feet or so at the shoulder and seldom weighs more than 100 to 115 pounds, even when full grown. Does average smaller than that. Under ideal conditions in the wild, or where the annual hunting "harvest" isn't too great, an antelope might reach 9 or 10 years. But according to all life history studies made to date, average longevity is much less than that.

Of course the best trophy heads come from the oldest males and to make the Boone and Crockett Records of North American Big Game, it must be a fairly ancient animal. A very good head is any one which measures 14 or 15 inches along the length of each horn. Lengths of 16 inches each will probably qualify the shooter for the record books. The longest pronghorn horns of which

As often as not, a hunter may see no more of a good buck than this. Incidentally that is a near record class head.

there is a substantiated record measured 20 inches on one side and 20⅛ inches on the other.

Although the most animals occur, and odds for a successful hunt are best, in Wyoming and Montana, Arizona bucks (according to Boone and Crockett listings) tend to average significantly larger horns. Wyoming heads fare better than Montana heads in the records.

Most of the best antelope country is fairly flat, gently rolling at the most, and not too irregular—therefore well suited to a swift animal equipped with telescopic vision. In addition, it was already pointed out that an antelope doesn't offer much area to shoot at—and that the range between gunner and game is normally long. This means that the ideal antelope rifle is one of high velocity and high trajectory—a cartridge which makes up as much as possible for a shooter's error in estimating the range. Failure to correctly judge distance is among the most common causes of missing shots at antelope.

A pronghorn hunter should also use a bullet which expands quickly and easily. Compared to other kinds of North American big game, the species is frail and a bullet which does not open on impact may pass right through, allowing the animal to run far before collapsing. But no matter what the rifle and caliber, hunters should avoid the temptation of running (or even standing) shots at extreme ranges. Instead the emphasis should be on stalking as close as possible and then of making the first shot the only one necessary.

A telescopic sight is more important for hunting antelope than any other North American big game, except possibly for sheep. Scopes of 4x or 6x are excellent. So are the many new variables now on the market. The rifle-scope combination should be carefully sighted in to hit dead center at 300 yards. In the case of the flat trajectory calibers that gives the shooter some margin for error in judging the range. Anyway, few shots will be much less than 300 yards and shots beyond 400 yards should not be attempted without a firm rest and at a standing target.

In much of the early literature on antelope hunting, written in the golden days when the animals roamed more widely on our plains, there are frequent references to a curious and deadly technique used by both market and sports hunters. A white handkerchief or streamer was knotted to a stick, held up and allowed to flutter in the breeze where antelope could easily see it. Curiosity, according to all accounts, got the best of the animals and they strolled into easy gun range to investigate.

Well, that stunt might have produced a generation or so ago, but it doesn't work anymore. Today's pronghorn is as sophisticated—or at least almost as sophisticated—as an old whitetail buck in an eastern woodland. Nowadays you work harder and shoot well at longer ranges to score.

And that is a lucky thing for a great game animal.

# by CHARLES NANSEN

BY DAYBREAK OF November 23, McDowell "Mac" Decker was sitting in a tree stand on the point of high wooded ridge. The time, he noted, was 7:20 AM. It was opening day of Ohio's brief deer season and by law (at that time) he couldn't shoot until 9:00. Still, he figured it was better to be waiting quietly than to be moving around.

It was. Only 10 minutes later the whitetail buck of any hunter's lifetime came walking warily along the trail that passed only 25 yards south of the blind. If Mac felt liquid in the knees, he can hardly be blamed. And he suffered assorted agonies while trying to remain silent as the animal continued past him, unalarmed. That deer had a really magnificent head.

"Should I break the law and shoot now," Mac recalls asking himself, "or wait?" Conscience raised a warning finger, and in another moment the matter settled itself. The deer dissolved into the bush.

Now time passed in slow motion. A drizzle set in and quickly obliterated the light snow that had fallen during the night. A shot rang out from far away and over toward the Ohio River. "Somebody else is jumping the gun," Mac muttered, half aloud. He noted the time—8:15.

The soft drizzle stopped, but in a few minutes it began again and turned into rain. Water trickled down the back of Mac's neck. He shivered. He had second thoughts about passing up the shot. He also considered getting out of the tree and following the deer trail. Maybe he could catch up to the deer and retrieve a lost opportunity. But something kept him in the blind, shivering and suffering. Eventually the hand on his wrist watch indicated only a few minutes until 9. *But it might as well be the 5 o'clock closing hour,* Mac thought, *because many of us Ohio deer hunters do not even see a deer, and I'll never again get a chance like the one I passed up.*

The rain increased. Mac tried to retreat deeper into his woolen jacket and that's when he caught a movement on the ground out of the corner of one eye. Turning his head cautiously he saw the buck coming his way again! The deer walked slowly, pawed at the wet earth with one hoof, and looked in all directions except up. Now, Mac had to begin fighting an acute case of buck fever because the deer bedded down less than 50 yards away, facing its own backtrail and away from the blind.

This deer returned to use a runway where the hunter saw him before opening day.

# JUMP THE GUN

Mac could hardly believe it. But he managed to calm his nerves and raise his 12-gauge pump gun and steady it across a tree limb. Then he squeezed off a shot. The deer bounced from its bed and went crashing away. For a moment, Mac was too weak to do anything but sit and mourn. He knew he'd missed his easy shot, but he was afraid to climb down and prove it. Finally he got going. Just beyond the deer bed the ground was splattered with blood. Following the red trail, Mac found the deer 100 yards or so away. It had run into the ground and was dead.

For some reason, Mac checked his watch again. It was 9:08.

With the season less than 10 minutes old, Mac Decker just might have made Ohio's first legal kill. He might also have made the best, because later the whitetail rack scored better than 161 points, which is

(Above) Spot a buck like this just before opening day and odds are good he'll remain close by until the shooting starts.

(Left) Drive the back roads well before opening day and watch for the white flags of deer.

just enough to make the Boone and Crockett record book.

Dumb luck? Not so. The kill was actually the climax of a hunt that had begun many weeks before that damp, late-November day. It began when Mac started driving the back roads and hiking across country in several southeastern Ohio counties on the lookout for a place to hunt when opening day finally rolled around. He put plenty of mileage on his station wagon and made more than his share of footprints on the landscape. But he saw deer. Luckily, Ohio has an early grouse season (it opens October 1) and Mac could combine grouse hunting with deer prospecting. By mid-November he had decided where he was going to be on opening day.

It was late in October when Mac first spotted the buck and a much smaller forkhorn. One evening he saw both bound across a fire trail and up onto a hardwood ridge in the Wayne National Forest. After that he began to drive all the back roads and fire lanes in that area just at dusk. As a result he saw the buck twice again—and very nearly in the same spot as the first occasion. So he decided to build his blind near the main deer trail along the crest of the hardwood ridge.

Of course there was a great deal of luck involved as there always is in hunting. Free-running dogs, for example, might have spooked the buck into another part of the forest. Or it might have spotted Mac that first time it passed the blind on opening day. But the point is, Mac had stacked as many factors as possible in his favor. First he located his deer. Then he put himself in the best possible position to bag it.

It seems to me there's a moral in this for any eastern deer hunter: Jump the gun—go hunting *before* opening day. Get out in the woods and look around. Look for deer exactly as if you were carrying a gun. And look for deer sign as well. Knowing the region you plan to hunt, and the whereabouts of deer, may be more important

Walk in the woods to get familiar with the land, but also watch for the trails these bucks use.

than any other single factor in collecting one. This is true anywhere that whitetail deer range.

Whitetails live fairly predictable lives, and we know a good deal about them—their food and travel habits, the habitat they prefer. But after the bombardment of opening day, nothing about whitetails is predictable until winter.

A check of the game departments of eastern states reveals that more than half of all deer bagged are bagged on opening day and the figure even runs as high as 80 percent. That also includes 80 percent of the best trophy deer. The really big bucks that survive usually manage to make it through the whole hunting period. Even the best woodsmen in the East have a tough time finding and killing deer toward the tag end of the season.

One of the best hunting trips in my memory was one that I went on several years ago with Frank Parsons and Lew Speaker to Michigan's upper peninsula. The hunting pressure is heavy there, even though the upper peninsula is a fairly remote hunk of wilderness. In recent years—and especially since construction of the Mackinac Bridge—the woods sometimes seem as full of redcoats as of whitetail deer. But on this occasion Frank had an idea.

"I'll schedule my vacation to begin a week before open season," he said, "and I'll go up there and do some scouting. You come up as usual the day before opening."

Arriving in camp was pure pleasure for Lew and me. The tents were already set up beside a pool of Stutz Creek, enough firewood to last the trip had been cut, and a fragrant snowshoe rabbit stew was simmering on a back burner. Frank even thrust a bourbon-and-branch-water into our hands. But best of all, he had news about the deer.

"A whole herd," he said, "is spending middays around a balsam swamp hardly a mile from here. I see them on the edges and along the creek every morning and evening. Tomorrow morning we should be on stand around the swamp, and if that doesn't work very soon, we'll drive it before other hunters discover the secret."

The whole thing proved to be a case of perfect planning. During a season when hunter success on the upper peninsula was only about 30 percent, we got three deer on opening day.

Before daybreak we took stands beside trails on three sides of the balsam bog. Not long afterward, a sleek spike buck almost ran over the top of Lew before discovering his mistake. By then it was too late and Frank and I helped Lew drag the venison out of the woods. That done, and with considerable shooting in the distance all around us, Lew made like a hound dog by circulating back and forth through the swamp while Frank and I waited on stands near the fringes. Whitetails began squirting out and we collected two.

Of course, it is necessary to scout intelligently. An inexperienced hunter, for instance, might walk through a woods that is full of deer sign and never see it. Probably game trails are the easiest to spot. Places where bucks have rubbed antlers against saplings are fairly obvious. But old beds, scratchings for acorns or beechnuts under leaf debris, and browse lines in the trees and brush are not so easy to identify. An abundance of squirrels and songbirds can indicate the presence of deer.

However, sign isn't always good evidence. It might show that deer *were* there rather than *are* there. So it is necessary to interpret the age of any deer sign you find.

Perhaps the best bet for the man with limited experience is to go by car and look for animals instead of sign. Cruise the back roads slowly and stop to study or glass every area where there is a good vista. But it's absolutely essential to do most of this at the very first and last light of day. Except during rainy, turbulent, or

Reconnaissance more than anything else results in trophy whitetails such as this one.

unsettled weather (as before a storm front) whitetails are not likely to be where they can be seen at midday. At least not in open hunting country.

Usually an even better way to locate deer is to drive in deer country at night, perhaps with a spotlight where one is legal. I suppose some game wardens and other law enforcement men may take a dim view of this procedure because they already have trouble enough with jacklighting deer poachers. But one way around that is to discuss it with your local game warden and tell him you would like to do some scouting at night. Tell him exactly where and when. And never, never carry a spotlight and firearms in the car at the same time.

In many states, it is actually possible to be hunting while you are scouting; all you need is a special archery tag for bowhunting season and a bow and arrows.

The very fundamentals of bowhunting are those of effective scouting. A really good archer does more sitting and watching than anything else. It is a technique that does not unduly disturb the deer, but one which is nearly perfect for observing where they are staying, where they feed and bed. And there is the added advantage of being able to take a shot if it should happen along. A deer narrowly missed by an arrow is seldom as badly spooked as he would be by the crack of gunfire in the distance.

One hunter says he had spotted his deer a full 2 years before he got a shot at it. And the place where it fell was only about 450 yards from where he first saw it, at dawn, in an abandoned apple orchard.

The best example of preseason deer scouting I've ever heard of concerns Hugh Cox, of Alton, Ohio. For him 2 years of scouting also paid off in a big way. Off and on all during this period, Hugh had had glimpses of an extraordinary buck in the Hocking County hills. And he took up bowhunting so that he would have a chance to bag it—if such a short-range shot ever came

along. Among other things, Hugh had patience, and he took no chances on alarming the animal out of the country. He played a stealthy waiting game. Toward the end of the second autumn of scouting, he figured he knew the deer's habits well enough, so he built a good blind near a trail that the deer frequently used evenings to feed in a cornfield. But since the regular shotgun season was still a few days away, Hugh decided that he would wait one weekend in the blind with his bow and arrows.

If you've guessed that the deer came as planned toward the blind, you're right. But it was at dusk, with daylight quickly evaporating, and Hugh could only hear twigs snapping closer and closer until the animal stood in flank-high horseweeds only 35 yards away. He drew an arrow and let it fly toward the target.

In the same split second the deer bounded away at top speed.

As is so often the case, Hugh thought he'd missed the target, or at least missed a vital area. Still he searched up and down the stream bank until well after pitch dark. He was just about to give up when he tripped and nearly fell over a large tree branch—only the branch proved to be one antler of his deer. He dressed the animal, but it was close to midnight before he reached a farmhouse on foot and borrowed a tractor to drag the carcass out of the woods.

Next morning the deer's head was measured by a taxidermist and scored more than 200 points. That rated it fifth among the best deer ever killed in Ohio by gun *or* bow—and first for bowhunting alone. A newspaper account of the hunt described Hugh Cox as "the lucky hunter."

Lucky? Of course he was, but he knew exactly where to be when luck came along to tap him on the shoulder. He'd found that rendezvous by going hunting before opening day.

# Ptarmigan:

## by THOMAS J. WALKER

"PTARMIGAN! PTARMIGAN on the river!" My partner's yell carried clearly across the frozen tundra.

Waving a reply, I started down the ridge toward the river, my snowshoes hissing softly through the soft snow. Our hunt had begun at first light, 9 AM on that December day, and it had taken 2 hours of searching to find the first birds. I hurried toward my partner, hoping he'd found a large covey for, until he called, we'd seen nothing but tracks and sign.

The area we were hunting was ideal ptarmigan habitat: low rolling hills covered with willow thickets and bisected by a large river. The ground and frozen river was blanketed with 2 feet of snow which made for ideal hunting conditions. Snowshoeing was easy for much of the brush was covered but enough was sticking through the snow to serve as food and cover for the birds. Ptarmigan tracks and trails were in nearly every thicket, and my partner found the first birds in the willows along the river.

A few minutes after he'd called, I slowly moved up behind my partner. He was intently watching something ahead, and as I came close, he pointed with mit- tened hand toward a nearby willow thicket. I could see tracks around the brush but no birds.

"There they are," he whispered, "six ptarmigan." Looking intently in the direction indicated, I saw nothing at first, then a slight movement caught my eye. In the brush, 60 yards away, the birds were busily feeding. They fed while walking, moving from branch to branch, nipping buds and willow twigs as they went. In the dull light without direct sun to cast shadows, the birds' camouflage was almost perfect. A stationary bird would have been nearly impossible to see. Except for their black eyes and beaks, they looked snow white.

"Here's what we'll do," my partner whispered. "I'll walk directly towards them and flush 'em. Because of the bank they'll fly outward toward the river. When I start forward you move out wide to my right and stay even with me. When they flush, you take the ones over the river, and I'll quit shooting just before they clear the brush."

We each stripped off our mittens and donned shooting gloves before starting forward. With loaded guns we carefully approached the birds. When we were within 40 yards of the ptarmigan, they stopped feeding and two began a soft, nervous clucking. At 20 yards the birds

# Mystery Birds of Winter

A willow ptarmigan, with well-cropped willow bushes nearby, preparing to flush from the hunter.

more beautiful game bird anywhere than the one I held in my hand.

"Let's get on. Daylight won't last long in this overcast," my partner said, breaking the reverie. "The birds are waiting." Upriver we each got one more bird and missed a few easy shots before the settling darkness forced us to call it quits.

That hunt wasn't a successful ptarmigan hunt by *numbers* as some Alaskan bird hunts can be, just four birds for 5 hours of hunting, but I can clearly remember, as if it were yesterday, my first ptarmigan hunt 12 years ago. A lot of hunts for all kinds of game have since taken place, but none can dim the memory of that first ptarmigan hunt. I've been on hunts that have produced 10 times as many birds per hunter, but one thing still hasn't changed, each winter-white ptarmigan is as beautiful as the first.

There's nothing quite like a long snowshoe hike on a cold, clear day, in search of white birds—"snow grouse," as the Indians of the lower Yukon call them. In some parts of Alaska, snow is on the ground for 8 months of the year, and a ptarmigan hunt is a refreshing way to beat "cabin fever." Ptarmigan can be hunted from August through April in most of Alaska and as late as May 15 in the southeastern panhandle.

Actually the only time the season is closed is during the spring nesting period and the summer brood-rearing months. This 9-month season—coupled with a generous bag limit of 20 birds per day—offers bird hunters the incentive to hunt ptarmigan in three distinct seasons —summer, fall, and winter. Because ptarmigan change colors as the seasons progress, it's almost like hunting three different birds. In August, ptarmigan are brown or gray and blend well with summer greenery; in fall as the tundra turns gold and red, the birds become mottled colored and begin turning white. By winter when the blanket of snow covers much of Alaska, ptarmigan have completed their moult and are all white. For many Alaskans—this writer included—it is the winter and early spring hunts on snowpack that are most enjoyable.

Three types of ptarmigan live in Alaska, the willow, rock, and whitetail. The largest, the willow, which weighs up to 1½ pounds, is also Alaska's state bird. Next in size is the rock ptarmigan which tips the scales at about 1-pound, and the smallest is the ¾-pound whitetail. Rock and willow ptarmigan are found in many countries of the Northern Hemisphere but whitetails are a uniquely North American bird found in Alaska, Canada and down into the mountains of the western U.S. as far south as New Mexico.

All three varieties turn white in winter, but actually only the whitetail is all-white, for both willow and rock

flushed—as predicted—toward the river. My partner got in one shot and dropped a single before the birds cleared the brush and were over the river. I swung on the lead bird, missed the first shot, recovered and dropped it with my second shot. The missed shot gave the rest of the covey a chance to get out of range. However they didn't go far, and soon set their wings, gliding into some willows 200 yards away.

"Like having a ringside seat watching you shoot," my partner laughed while bending to pick up his bird. "Hope we got lots of shells."

His barb was lost on me for I was busily searching for my downed bird. Finally I found the bird in the hole it'd made falling into the soft snow. It was the first willow ptarmigan I'd ever shot, and it was as beautiful as any I'd ever seen. I guessed it weighed about a pound and was all-white except for the black outer tail feathers. The plumage was soft and clean, and even the feet right down to the toes were feathered. The feathered feet explained the snowshoe-like, three-toed, oval tracks the birds left.

"Beautiful aren't they," my partner asked, walking up, his bird already stuffed in his game vest. I nodded silently in agreement, for up until then, I hadn't seen a ptarmigan have black tail feathers year around. Rock ptarmigan can be distinguished from willows by a black loral stripe that runs from the beak to a point slightly behind the eye on males. Females of willow and rock ptarmigan in winter plumage are hard to tell apart —except that each species has a distinctive call that can be used for field identification. Without the loral stripe, only a trained ornithologist could tell the two apart.

Each of the three species has distinct habitat requirements and seldom do the species intermingle. Willow ptarmigan are found in tundra lowlands and on brushy hills throughout most of Alaska. Rock ptarmigan prefer more open rocky terrain, while whitetails are found in the highest, most rugged alpine areas. Occasionally rock ptarmigan can be found in the same area as willows, especially in winter when food sources are more limited and, at times, whitetails can be found near rock ptarmigan. Generally speaking though, the species tend to segregate.

Winter hunting means snow and cold (down to −60 degrees Fahrenheit) and most Alaskan ptarmigan hunters either hunt when cloud cover brings the temperatures up, or they wait until March and April when the days are longer and the sun keeps daytime temperatures above zero. The majority of hunters seem to wait until the pleasant days of late winter before going afield after ptarmigan—and indeed such hunts are pure tonic when coming after a long, dark winter. But for those hardy enough to hunt in mid-winter, the rewards can sometimes be incomparable.

One mid-winter's day not too many years ago, I was living in a cabin in the bush on the north side of the Alaska Range, 45 air miles from the nearest road. The

Willow ptarmigan turn all white except for the black tail feathers which remain the same color year-round.

Cross-country skis will also carry a hunter to game in ptarmigan country.

early days of winter had been exceedingly cold, down into the −40-degree Fahrenheit range, and bird hunting had been out of the question. Shortly before Christmas, the thermometer rose to a balmy −10 despite clear skies. The sun didn't shine on that canyon-bottom cabin at all for over 2 months, although it did caress the mountain tops around us. When the peaks turned crimson that day, I was well out from the cabin, snowshoeing on the trail upriver, and hadn't gone more than a mile when I ran into a big covey of willow ptarmigan.

I was moving slowly along when unexpectedly several ptarmigan flushed from close by. They took me completely by surprise, and the first birds were away and out of range before I could react. Quickly jacking a shell into my Model 12, I started after the birds, marking the thicket 100 yards away that they had settled in. Before I reached the first flock, a second flushed from the willows along the way. That time I was ready, knocking down two birds with three shots. At the crack of the first shot, several dozen other birds flushed from the willow flat and flew across the river, settling into the brush there just as my third shot folded a straggler. After retrieving and stuffing the two ptarmigan into my game bag, I hurried off after the main flock.

The wind was beginning to build and on the open river, the chill factor dropped the effective temperature

Hunter with ptarmigan. A winter ptarmigan hunter needs good snowshoes, sunglasses, and extra cold weather gear just in case temperatures should plummet, as is possible in the mountains or arctic areas.

Seldom are ptarmigan found in timber, mostly they are tundra and brush game, but this hunter caught the birds migrating across country.

to well below the thermometer-measured −10. I was thankful for the heavy parka even though it hindered my movements. I'd marked the spot where the ptarmigan had landed, and upon entering the brush, I found tracks leading back into the dense thicket. Picking a track, I followed it for a short distance and flushed four birds. The Model 12 came up swiftly and felt good as I swung on the leader. At the shot, *two* birds fell—a lucky double, although I have, at times, been known to tell it had been *planned* that way. My second shot was a clean miss. Again the shooting spooked the covey, but this time birds went in all directions.

After retrieving the two ptarmigan, I started after the closest bunch but had gone just a few yards, when a single exploded from close by. Sighting hurriedly, I blew a hole in the arctic sky some 1½ feet behind the swift flyer. My second shot was closer but still behind.

My third shot folded him, and he dropped with a thump into the soft snow 30 yards away. Ptarmigan have a habit of calling whenever a flock becomes fragmented, and birds were calling from all quarters. It was a simple matter to find the scattered birds and by 1 PM, a full bag limit and a cold wind combined to end the hunt.

Ptarmigan hunting can be like that at any time of the year, not just in winter. Flocks are sometimes large and once found easily hunted. Ptarmigan are not overly wary, and at times, especially in remote areas, are difficult to flush. Winter birds especially, are difficult to flush since they at times prefer to run from danger rather than fly. This trait appears to be an adaptation to the extremes of the north, since it takes less "fuel" to run than it does to fly from danger, and thus body reserves are saved for heat production. Too, ptarmigan are very dependent on their camouflage and seem to rely on it for protection. Birds are easily tracked in soft snow, but on crusted snow or ice, it's tough to follow them and their camouflage becomes a real asset.

Winter ptarmigan hunting can be an exasperating "boom or bust" affair. Ptarmigan are erratically cyclic and can vary in abundance from year to year. They are also migratory and can travel great distances in search of forage. In Canada, rock ptarmigan have been known to migrate over 500 or 600 miles. In Alaska, migrations of 250 to 300 miles are not uncommon. One winter an area can produce outstanding hunting, and the next there might not be a bird in the area due to fluctuations in snow cover. Only those areas that consistently have ptarmigan feed and cover sticking up through the snow produce predictable hunting. An old sourdough, when asked where to hunt ptarmigan, probably gave the best answer to that question, when he said: "Them white birds is wherever, and whenever ye find 'em."

in waterproof container, and plenty of high energy food.

All of these listed items are important and some are essential, but are overlooked by far too many hunters. A number of ptarmigan hunters use snowmobiles to travel into good bird country, but it is appalling the number who fail to take with them any snowshoes or skis, to get back out of the area if the machine should fail. Legion are those who've been stranded in the backcountry by a broken-down machine. In some cases, these mishaps have proven fatal. Sunglasses are another item overlooked by winter hunters. Not only do glasses protect the eyes from glare, they also make it easier to see the white birds.

Hat, parka, boots, and mittens are essentials of winter outdoor wear. Studies have shown that 60 percent or more of the body's heat can be lost through an uncovered head. Mittens worn over shooting gloves, or lightweight wool gloves, are the ideal way to handle

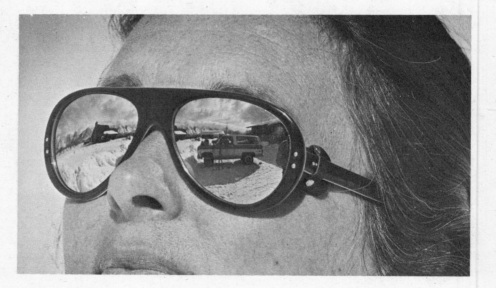

Sunglasses are a necessity for hunting — for finding birds — on bright days over snow cover.

Winter ptarmigan hunting—like all winter sports in Alaska—can turn into an unexpected struggle for survival. Arctic climates are characterized by severe weather and unpredictable fluctuations. If the hunter is unprepared to deal with the vagaries of Alaskan weather, he is asking for trouble. Storms can move in quickly and temperatures that were moderate when the hunt began can become sub-zero quickly.

A temperature of zero coupled with a 10mph wind has a chill factor equivalent of −21 degrees. A smart hunter, no matter how ideal the conditions are when the hunt begins, should go prepared to deal with more extreme conditions. Hypothermia, frostbite, and freezing are major hazards of winter outdoor excursions. Basic winter gear should include—but not be limited to—snowshoes or cross-country skis, sunglasses, warm hat, parka, winter boots, mittens with flexible glove liners, wool trousers or layers of cotton pants, matches

firearms in cold country. Mittens limit finger dexterity, but are essential in keeping hands warm, and if gloves are worn underneath them, it's a simple matter to strip off mittens and operate the firearm without risking frostbite. We won't go into the details of winter wear here, but layers of clothes seems to be the ideal way to go, rather than a single heavyweight parka. A rule of arctic hunting is to avoid sweating since the moisture can freeze when the activity of the person slows. Layering allows a hunter the chance to keep warm without overheating.

One area often overlooked by winter hunters is the intake of food and water while outdoors. High energy trail food—such as chocolate, mixed nuts and fruit—is an essential "pick-me-up" when hunting in cold weather. A good, hearty, hot breakfast before the hunt does more to keep a person warm outside than all the clothing piled on can do. "Stoking the inner stove" is an important element in staying warm. Dehydration is a common dilemma of winter hunters. Seldom do outdoorsmen take enough liquid to maintain themselves during a winter hunt. Experts say that 2 to 3 quarts of water per day per person is considered essential while hunting in winter. Few hunters heed this advice even though it has been demonstrated that the dangers of frostbite are believed to be much greater when a person becomes dehydrated.

Many ptarmigan hunters use .22 rifles when hunting winter birds. Because ptarmigan sometimes are unwilling to flush, a "stand" can be made and several birds picked off before a flock will rise. I've even heard of entire flocks being shot one bird after another without a single bird attempting to fly away. Most rimfire shooters aim for the head in an attempt to save meat. Twenty-two's are popular ptarmigan guns in some areas, especially in remote areas where subsistence hunters depend on game birds for food.

Most sport hunters prefer shotguns for wing shooting ptarmigan. It's true that the birds can be sluggish and difficult to flush at times, but in the air, they make excellent, sometimes difficult targets because of their erratic, jerky flight. Pumps, autoloaders, and double guns are all used on ptarmigan, but when in the midst of a large flock of ptarmigan, many double gun users have been heard to wish for a pump or auto. Shot sizes best suited for ptarmigan are 6's and 7½'s, although one bird hunter claims that 4's are ideal and waste little meat. Most hunters prefer the smaller shot sizes since ptarmigan are excellent table fare, and the meat should be as undamaged as possible.

Hunting ptarmigan on the spring snowpack when the days are long and the sun climbs high in the sky, is one of the finest outdoor experiences of all. A few years ago near Paxson, Alaska, a friend and I hunted ptarmigan during the last week of the season. Temperatures were in the low plus twenties, and the skies were clear. The snow was deep, over 4 feet of pack, but hard crusted and the snowshoeing was easy. The birds had been hunted all winter and were spooky and easily flushed. We ran into several large flocks, one of which probably numbered over 100 birds, and the shooting was great.

One afternoon on that spring hunt, we were snowshoeing up a small creek, walking on opposite sides of the open water, when we jumped a flock of willow ptarmigan. My partner saw them first and called out, pointing ahead to the birds that were coming out of the brush onto the creek ice. We watched as the birds single-filed down to the creek and drank their fill. We eased towards the birds and drew within 30 yards when one spotted us and alerted the rest with a danger call.

With wild wing beats, the flock rose, and we both swung on them, firing right and left as planned—my partner taking the birds to his right, and me the ones on the left. I hit one bird and an explosion of white feathers masked against the deep-blue arctic sky told me that it had been a solid hit. My friend shot three times, the zing of his shot dropping two birds.

As the day progressed we followed the flock higher and higher as they worked up a mountainside. By late that day we were on top of a low mountain, out of shells and with bulging game bags. To the southwest the sun had set and the mountain peaks around were glowing crimson. Off in the distance we could hear the ptarmigan calling back and forth across the frozen land. A fitting end to a day of hunting the white birds of winter.

A pair of snowshoes are as important as a firearm when hunting ptarmigan in Alaska.

# HUNTING WHITETAIL

If you're going to hunt in a crowded area, pre-season scouting becomes very important. You may even discover a buck like this.

# IN A CROWD

## by CHARLES J. FARMER

**A FRIEND OF MINE** once made the remark, after his unsuccessful deer hunting trip, "Every ridge, every point was punctuated with blaze orange. I couldn't even find a good spot to sit and wait," he added with disgust. "Sure, I heard a lot of shooting. But I got out of there in a hurry."

My friend was convinced that hunting in a crowd had little merit, and nothing I could say would change his mind. I have discovered since then that a good number of whitetail hunters feel the same way. They assume, and quite naturally so, that a barrage of nimrods will push all the game out of an area. Although this can happen with some species of game in certain areas, heavy hunting pressure in good deer habitat can benefit rather than hinder most hunters. Certain techniques however, should be employed in order to harness the effects that large numbers of hunters have on whitetail concentrations.

I have heard the same remarks in nearly every big game hunting situation from coast to coast. "Too many hunters—too much pressure." Those negative attitudes usually make me chuckle inside because they commonly arouse numerous true-life situations in my mind where other hunters rather than any special stalking skills on my part accounted for good shots at game.

My first bull elk in Wyoming came within 20 feet of where I was sitting because another hunter pushed the animal right to me. Buck antelope, spooked by road hunters, have presented me with easy shots as I waited at waterhole blinds. My best mule deer was driven to my position at the head of a canyon by two hunters who climbed through the middle of the canyon. And when it comes to whitetails, I credit nearly every kill to another hunter who pushed otherwise elusive bucks within good shooting range of my stand—whether rifle hunting or bowhunting.

Just last year while hunting U.S. Forest Service lands in southern Missouri, I had a small buck wander within 30 yards of my afternoon stand. Two friends and I had boated to the area surrounding an arm of Table Rock Lake. From the highway it was 15 miles as the crow flies to our camp. However, hunters utilizing vehicle access from the blacktop could drive into the area for only 5 miles before the rough 4WD drive petered out into a foot trail. While most of the hunters congregated in camps along the road, we had the water's edge to ourselves. And we used that position to our advantage.

The hunters would stalk the ridges and hollows in our direction and push deer toward us. We would assume the role of blockers from stands chosen because of their strategic locations—escape or feeding routes determined by the appearance of fresh sign.

The woods were full of hunters opening weekend, and the majority of them were hunting in our direction. Both my partners missed good opportunities opening morning and that afternoon I killed the small buck mentioned earlier. A heavy rain hit the area Sunday which dampened chances considerably. By Monday, a good portion of the weekend hunters had left, and the sightings of bucks and does diminished drastically that day. In fact we left camp with only one deer after 4 days of hunting. My friends returned to the same spot the following weekend, and each was successful in bagging a buck. They credited their success to heavy hunting pressure and the movement of deer in their direction.

I had the opportunity 2 years ago to hunt a small wildlife area that is open each year for 5 days to bowhunting for whitetail deer. Each season 200 permits are issued on a drawing basis, and the lucky hunters can sample an area otherwise closed to all forms of hunting. The area, however, is only about 3 miles long and 2 miles wide. On opening day, about 180 hunters (always some no-shows) took to the woods, and for one accustomed to the wide open spaces of Wyoming, the forward advance of camouflaged platoons is something to behold. Upon witnessing the throngs entering the forest I questioned my sanity and feared for my safety.

We all pretty well melded into the pre-dawn woods as silent, camouflaged archers will, and soon I had forgotten that 179 other deer hunters shared that patch of timber with me. The hunting turned out to be excellent even though my aim was far less than desired. The first morning 22 deer, mostly does and fawns, were counted from my stand. Although I was holding out for a buck, the excitement those animals provided made for a memorable hunt. I failed to bag a whitetail in 3 days of hunting but I have never had so many deer appearing before the bow, and if it were not for a pencil-size branch of a sapling oak, I might have had a nice buck.

I credited my numerous sightings and opportunities to the fact that I stayed in one spot—quiet and relatively camouflaged—and let other hunters, who were scattered throughout the woods, move deer. I discovered that some hunters will take a stand for an hour or two and then employ a stalking or stop-and-go method. Other hunters by their very acts of entering or leaving the woods were pushing deer, and the hunter who could keep a stand along a travel lane was likely to see a lot of action.

Since that hunt, I have had opportunities on numerous occasions to photograph deer on the wildlife area when I was the only person present. Naturally I thought the deer would be crawling all over me. I set up photo blinds, donned camo clothing, and used masking scents with the same care as in bowhunting. With only a few exceptions the deer stayed put and my opportunities for photos were few. Unless pressured, whitetails will often hold their ground in thick cover and travel only in pre-dawn and nighttime hours.

As is evident with many forms of duck hunting, it takes a good deal of pressure to keep the ducks flying. In large expanses of public forest the same holds true for deer. Hunters keep deer moving and in turn present opportunities for the still hunter.

There is no sure-fire formula for any kind of hunting, but when hunting in popular, heavy-pressure areas a man or woman can better his or her chances if a few tips are followed.

1. Pre-season scouting should be considered an integral part of the hunt even if scouting time is limited to the morning or afternoon preceding opening day. While natural deer movements in popular areas are altered after the shooting starts, the natural use areas of whitetails can be located in advance of the season.

Look for scrapes in the leaves, dirt or snow. These are areas, perhaps as large as a child's wading pool, which have been cleared by a buck's hooves and horns. Scrapes signal a male's dominance in a particular area, a warning to other bucks and a lure for does. Scrapes are formed at the beginning and during the peak of the rut. In some states hunting seasons are held after the rut, and bucks no longer use the scrapes. A hunter should then look for other signs.

Hoof depressions in leaves and dirt can be read for freshness as well as determining whether or not pellets are old or new. Antler rubs, appearing as skinned trunks of small trees, usually from a foot to 3 feet off the ground, can be old or new depending on the color of the skinned area and the bark. Old rubs may have been used to remove the velvet from a buck's horns. New rubs can be the result of a simulated fight with another buck or mid-rut frustration.

2. In the Midwest during the November deer seasons bucks are most often found on the ridges, where a good acorn crop can be located. Trails, feeding areas (cracked and chewed acorn sign), and escape routes

Best way to hunt in a crowd is to pick a spot—the best spot in the whole area—and wait patiently, alertly, there.

near the crests of ridges and the heads of hollows make excellent choices for deer stands.

During periods of extremely dry weather, stands near woodland ponds or streams in fairly dense cover can be good choices. In periods of average or above average moisture deer do not have to visit bodies of water but can obtain enough of it from leaves or depressions in rocks or earth.

Ordinarily a pressured buck is not concerned with eating or drinking. So think escape routes. Natural salt licks, smoothed out depressions with plenty of hoofprints, sometimes filled with water, make better stands in areas of low hunting pressure.

3. Taking advantage of the movements of other hunters means taking a stand before the majority of other hunters arrive and staying later in the afternoon than the others. A general rule to follow for whitetails in areas of heavy public use is that if you arrive after daybreak, you are too late, and if you get back to camp before dark, you left too soon.

By being on stand before dawn and during late afternoon hours, you are taking advantage of the natural movements of deer and the unnatural ones which are caused by human movement in the woods. If you arrive

after dawn or leave the stand before dark, chances are good you will spook a deer away from your position and quite possibly to another hunter.

Opening day, with lots of activity in the woods, I stay on my stand until noon, take a 3-hour lunch and rest break, and remain on stand until dark.

I feel a break is needed to revitalize body and spirit. Deer movement is naturally curtailed during midday, and hunter movement is commonly at a minimum.

4. Still hunting is not as easy as it sounds, and because of what other hunters have told me about their stand techniques, I'm convinced a good number of bucks are spooked by supposedly "invisible" hunters. Although specific methods are open to considerable debate and opinions can be as heated and varied as those of religion and politics, my views are the results of accumulated hours of personal research.

A successful stand hunter is a comfortable one, and what one wears, eats and sits on often makes the difference in sitting quietly enough to enable a deer to come within comfortable gun or bow range.

Dress more warmly than you think necessary and carry a small day pack on your shoulders. Extra clothing from the pack can be added or removed (as the day

Remember that where hunting pressure is heavy, deer are especially nervous and watchful. So blend yourself into the woods.

warms) and stowed in the pack, along with snacks, water, coffee, field dressing items and emergency gear. Even during early fall bow seasons, pre-dawn vigils can be cold and damp. A hunter not dressed warmly enough does a lot of squirming and finds a lot of excuses for getting up and walking around. The longer a hunter can sit absolutely still during prime morning hours, the better the chances of killing a deer. When still hunting special emphasis should be placed on warm footgear, cap and gloves.

Hunger also moves hunters off stands before prime time hours are over. Candy bars, trail snacks, jerky, hard candy and sandwiches increase endurance. Just remember to remove food from the pack and eat in slow motion. A canteen of water or pint thermos of coffee or hot chocolate has given me the extra staying power, both physical and mental, on several occasions, which resulted in chances at game.

Last fall, as I was climbing the last 100 yards up a steep hill to reach my stand, I passed a man and boy standing in the trail. The man commented on the boat cushion I had strapped on my lower back. "That will sure keep your butt from getting wet," he chided with a big grin on his face. "Not only that," I replied. "It's amazing how soft the ground can be when I sit on it, and it helps keep me warm too."

I have been using a boat cushion for warmth and comfort ever since I started hunting spring gobblers, some 10 years ago. Staying absolutely still on a turkey stand is vital for getting a glimpse of a tom, and the cushion is just another tool for making the job a bit easier. Placed near the base of a tree trunk, the cushion is responsible for making the virtue of patience more palatable.

I mask my human scent with some kind of natural ingredient available like pine needles, berries, apples or leaves. In case of a lack of natural masks, I carry commercially prepared scents appropriate to my particular area in my pack.

I am not one to jump for joy upon seeing the woods full of hunters. Solitude is a wonderful quality of any deer hunt and I appreciate it as much as other hunters. But as wildlife habitat continues to diminish and more and more hunters take to the woods, we learn to hunt effectively in a crowd. And although most of us do not like to admit it, there will be times when we thank the hordes. For as we sat silent and ready, the movers pushed deer into our laps.

# Rest In Peace Old Troop

## by GEORGE LAYCOCK

Troop, the first dog to be buried on the ridgetop in north Alabama.

**AS SURE AS LABOR DAY** comes to the hills of northern Alabama, folks assemble on a forested ridgetop 12 miles from Cherokee to honor the memories of the finest coonhounds they ever knew. Here they are surrounded by the final resting places of unforgettable dogs, buried in the world's first, and perhaps only, graveyard devoted entirely—or almost entirely—to bonafide coonhounds.

"It began with Troop," Key Underwood of Tuscumbia, Alabama, told me solemnly. There was a moment's pause during which I maintained respectful silence. After this instant of meditation, Underwood picked up his story. "I didn't get Troop until he was 11 years old, an age when most dogs are already too old to hunt much. But I had heard a lot about this dog and I wanted him."

Troop at the time had spent his life night-hunting through that wild section of northern Alabama known as the Freedom Hills. In the 1930s the hills harbored a breed of rugged individualists who divided their time between coon hunting and moonshining. It is said that many a revenuer made one-way trips into the Freedom Hills. Troop belonged to a moonshiner who for years managed to elude the Feds. But one night he found himself surrounded and had no viable choice but to lay down his arms and say, "Boys, I guess you got me. I'll come along peaceable." After due process he was carried off to the penitentiary, which, considering the charge and the times, was more honor than censure among his peers. But it did leave one serious problem—what to do with old Troop. The culprit's wife "pawned" Troop to a man over in Midway. "That's where Troop was when I heard about it," Underwood told me. "I knew right off I wanted that dog. I'd heard about him for a long time. Lot of people knew about him." Underwood drove down to bargain for the dog. "I paid $75 for him," Underwood added, "and in them times, and for a dog 11 years old, that was a lot of money. I took a chance."

When Underwood brought Troop home with him, his coon-hunting friends laughed. The hound was gaunt, his fur was rough, and he wobbled when he walked. But

(Left) Tree-climbing dogs are a source of pride to the owner.

in a matter of days Underwood's fine care and nourishing food had made a wonderful change in the dog's appearance. "He was a big dog," Underwood recalls, "not anything special in looks, but strong. I figure he was a cross between Redbone and Birdsong."

As Troop regained his strength, he seemed as eager to get back to coon hunting as Underwood was to take him into the woods. Troop and Underwood, along with his hunting buddies Raymond "Slim" Wheeler and Jimmy Driver, headed for the hills over near Cherokee. From the first, Troop was a pure joy to hunt with. Experience had taught him to know in advance what movements a coon would make.

"Lot of dogs," says Underwood, "can chase a coon up a tree, but that doesn't make them coon dogs. Troop wouldn't run anything except a coon. He just had more sense than any other dog I ever saw. Say it this way: He was just a special smart coon dog. Taught me a lot. And all by himself he could kill any coon he ever met. He would run right up to a coon like he was going to run over it. Then he would circle it and spar around watching it all the time, and when the coon tried to break away, Troop had him. He'd get the coon right behind the shoulders and, being a big dog, he would just give him a couple of shakes and lay him on the ground."

Those hunts with Troop continued until the dog was 15 years old. Right up to the last few weeks the old dog

This kind of enthusiasm may well mark a dog as deserving a final resting place in the Coon Dog Graveyard.

Repainted sign marks the entrance to perhaps the world's only graveyard for coonhounds.

(Above) Neat rows of markers indicate the graves of the most beloved coonhound's; those truly deserving of this honor.

(Left) Jim's collar, no longer needed, stays with its owner.

went strong. But Underwood knew the dog's time was coming. Finally Troop got so weak he could scarcely get up, and he would no longer eat. "Had him put to sleep," says Underwood quietly. We observed another moment of reverent silence.

The evening Troop died Slim and Jimmy were sitting up with Underwood, comforting him in his hour of sorrow. "Jimmy said we ought to take him back out to the campground and bury him there on the edge of the Freedom Hills where he always run," Underwood told me. This seemed a first-rate idea to all three men. The next morning, Underwood tenderly placed the body of the old hound in his car, and the little party headed out of town. They stopped long enough to pick up a cotton "pick sack" in which to wrap the dog for interment. They dug Troop's grave on the ridgetop beneath a giant white oak tree.

Later they were standing around, each wondering what he could say, when Jimmy suggested, "We ought to put up a stone for him."

"There had been an old house there," Underwood recalled, "and the rocks from the chimney was still there. We picked out a nice one about 2 feet high, a foot thick and 1½ feet wide, and I took a chisel and hammer, the only tools I had for the job, and carved his name on it." He then carved the date when he thought Troop had been born, and added the date of his death, 9-4-37. Underwood straightened from his task and studied the stone. Something special was needed to tell coon hunters what kind of dog lay beneath this marker. Underwood bent to the task again and near the top of the stone he chiseled a likeness of the boar coon's peculiar penis bone, the "toothpick," which serves as a symbol of the chase among coon hunters in the southern hills.

"At the time," Underwood told me, "we didn't have the slightest idea we would ever bury another dog out there. We'd just done this for Troop because it seemed the right thing to do."

While Underwood kept coonhounds, Mrs. Underwood had her own special pet, a little male rat terrier called "Trixie." The terrier didn't effect Underwood much one way or the other. He was just there, something of a misfit in a world of coonhounds. But some weeks after Troop was laid to rest, Trixie made a mistake. "He jumped in my car one night when I was going coon hunting," said Underwood, "and went along. That was a cold night, and he caught pneumonia from it and died."

"We'll take him out," said Mrs. Underwood, "and bury him beside Troop." Underwood did not give a second thought to the possibility that this might become an embarrassment in later years and, being basically a kind man, he agreed at once.

One burial makes a grave, two a graveyard, and the Underwood dogs had now become the pioneer occupants of a cemetery destined to grow. Next, one of

Underwood's friends decided to bury his finest coon dog on the ridge where Troop lay at rest.

Following that burial an idea began to take shape in Underwood's mind; he had founded a special cemetery for coon dogs. "I got a piece of wood," he explained, "and painted it white and made a sign saying 'Coon Dog Grave Yard,' and I nailed that up on a tree, and pretty soon the word spread."

An old photograph, lest we forget . . .

In time, others came seeking Key Underwood, explaining that their favorite coon dog had passed away, and asking if it would be permissible to honor the hound with space in the cemetery? From the beginning Underwood felt that there should be some rules for the cemetery. Troop had set the tone. This was to be a resting place for coon dog royalty.

The graveyard is a quiet place to relive exciting chases behind exceptional dogs.

Underwood had frequent pangs of guilt for having buried Trixie on this special hilltop. Once or twice he gently suggested disinterring the little dog and reburying Trixie in some less public spot. "He sure doesn't belong out on that hilltop," Underwood says, "but whenever I mention digging him up, the idea doesn't go over very big around here." Trixie remains the only non-coon dog buried there.

"We like to keep it for coon dogs that are really good ones," says Underwood. "Of course, the dog one man thinks isn't much good may be the finest hound in the world to another person. And you have to respect a man's opinion about his dog. They have to dig the right kind of grave and all," says Underwood, "2½ to 3 feet deep. We've got the cemetery laid off in burial plots of about this size." He extended his arms to show me the 2- by 4-foot proportions of a standard dog grave.

As word of the cemetery spread so did the number of burials there. When I talked with Underwood again recently, he said, "We got 111 graves there now. No, it's 112 because 2 days ago we had another funeral. They brought in a dog from Illinois, one that had been cremated."

Lulubelle. Ever remembered.

A moment of silence of observed.

That was the second burial of its type. The first interment of a cremated coonhound on this Alabama hilltop was in March of 1977. Underwood remembers it well. Old Red was said by some to be the best coon dog ever, to hunt the woods around Vicksburg, Mississippi. When he passed away, his owner wanted Old Red buried among his peers, and he contacted Underwood.

Old Red's ashes were transported from Vicksburg over into Alabama in a little polished mahogany box, escorted by three airplane loads of Vicksburg citizens determined to usher him to his final resting place in style. "They brought along the sheriff and the game wardens, and the preacher and everybody," says Underwood. "They held a regular service up there." The party of mourners then stayed for most of the day, swapping hunting stories and consuming the supplies they brought along.

Most of the hounds buried in the Coon Dog Grave Yard have their own headstones. Some are fancier than the field stone supplied for Troop. One hunter mounted

a weatherproof photograph of his dog on the monument. Another left behind his dog's collar draped over the edge of the stone.

The land used for the burial grounds has now been deeded over to the coon hunters by the pulpwood company that owned it. Underwood and his friends have installed rest rooms, picnic tables and a shelter where visitors can get in out of the weather. This is the site of the annual Labor Day celebration which draws visitors from all over Alabama and surrounding states to honor unforgettable coonhounds. Underwood estimates that the cemetery attracts 4,000 visitors a year. "They come from everywhere," he says.

On autumn nights the surrounding hills still echo the trail music of coonhounds. The best of them are destined to join Troop in his honored resting place. I asked Underwood if any of these dogs buried here, or any dog he ever knew before or since, was a better coon dog than Troop. "Not that I know of," he said, and we observed another moment of silence.

# How To Set Up A Comfortable Deer Camp

This party of hunters has pitched a two-tent camp (one for sleeping; one for cooking and living) high in the Colorado Rockies.

### by KEN S. BOURBON

MANY MONTANA SPORTSMEN will remember the opening of deer season around Fort Peck several years ago. A soft snow began to fall the afternoon before opening day and by morning about 8 inches covered the ground. But even that wasn't the end of it. The snow kept coming until more than a foot of it made serious deer hunting virtually impossible. Some hunters were lost and many, many others isolated in the Missouri Breaks area by drifts across remote trails and livestock roads.

Still I remember the event as nothing but high adventure and a pleasant experience. And it's all because the Sanderson brothers, Frank and Homer, and I had set up a comfortable camp the day before the deluge came.

We were as snug and warm as if we'd stayed at home. Our two-tent setup gave us plenty of room to play cards, to listen to the radio, to cook extravagant meals and to tell extravagant lies about other hunting trips. When the storm finally broke, we headed straight for Snow Creek, where Frank felt the deer would be yard-

ing up, and before the week was finished, three bucks were hanging up outside our cook tent. If anything, the trip ended too quickly.

"I wish we were just starting out," Homer commented, as we loaded the venison into a station wagon, "instead of going home."

Of all events on the sportsman's calendar, perhaps none exactly match the deer season. No doubt that's because deer hunting, no matter whether it's for mule deer, whitetails or blacktails, is such a wholesome and exciting sport. But for more reasons than we can list here, a certain number of deer hunts go sour. Unfortunately, they fail to materialize as the happy events which the hunters have anticipated for months. Nine times in 10 the reason is an inadequate camp.

A few years ago, Burt Heim and I spent a week hunting mulies in Idaho, and the weather couldn't have been worse. It rained or snowed for 6 straight days, and tramping through the soggy evergreen woods wasn't exactly a lark. But we had a dry and comfortable camp at day's end, and that made the difference. The first man to return each afternoon would build a fire. Then while a big dinner was cooking, someone would break out the bourbon. A hunter can stand plenty of bad weather during the day, as long as he can return to a scene like ours in the evening. The value of a comfortable camp just can't be overestimated.

But exactly what is an adequate deer camp?

Physically it can be a vast variety of structures—a tent, two tents, a trailer, an abandoned trapper's hut or cow camp, a cave or even an old school bus. The type of camp isn't too important as long as it provides shelter from the worst weather which can be expected in any given region. Generally speaking, deer hunting seasons come at a time of year when changeable, even foul weather can be expected. That's true in the southern United States, too.

A good deer camp should also be roomy. Some of the most addicted hunters, and I guess I'm one of them, can spend a week in the cramped quarters of one small tent used for both sleeping and cooking. But that isn't the ideal setup. It's much better to have a separate space (maybe two tents) for sleeping and living. The value of space is most important when the weather prevents hunting, as it did on our Montana trip. But more on this item later.

Finally, a deer camp must be well-located. It should be on well-drained ground, of course. Beyond that, the

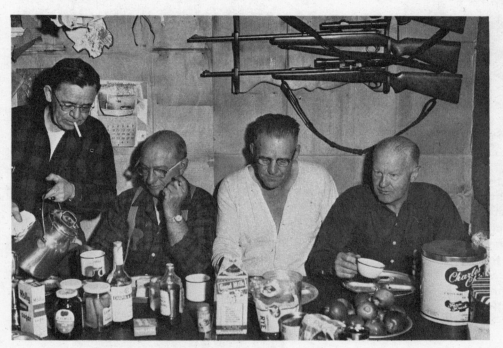

Hunters enjoy breakfast in an old, converted Montana cow camp. It's a comfortable place to plan the day.

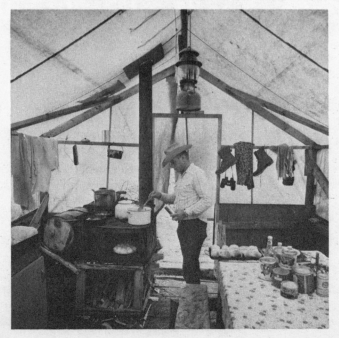

The camp cook bakes biscuits and makes vension stew while his buddies are in the field.

ideal situation is to be close to the game, to access roads and to water. Of course it isn't always possible to find all three, but the best compromise is the best bet. Being close to the game permits more time for hunting, and it's doubly important early in the morning when deer are most active. Being close to a water supply saves drudgery; the presence or lack of water can make or break a hunting trip.

Two of the best deer hunters I know are Handy Miner and Bill Garnett, and it's all because they take the camping phase of a hunt so seriously. When Bill and Handy take to the woods, as they do for at least 2 weeks each fall, they really live it up. As a result they can take any turn of the weather, short of a hurricane, in stride and in comfort.

"I can hunt harder all day," Bill will tell you, "if I

Sudden snowfall means cutting more firewood for camp cooking. Why not do this chore before the hunting begins?

know I can relax in comfort when it's over.''

Let's look at a typical Miner-Garnett camp. First, they use two tents. The sleeping tent is a G.I. surplus wall tent, which gives them room to stand up. It's heated by a coal- or woodburning, sheepherder-type stove, which is designed to fold into a flat sheet. This type of stove is manufactured by several companies, but it happens that Handy made this one himself because he's a do-it-yourself hobbyist as well as a sportsman. But he admits that a reliable kerosene stove is just as good.

Facilities are also provided in the sleeping tent to hang up damp clothes, socks and boots. Comfortable, dry boots have made the difference in many deer hunts—so, he is a wise hunter who makes provisions for a dry pair of footgear every morning. Usually brackets made by bending clothes hangers into shape are perfect for suspending boots upside down above the stove.

The Miner-Garnett ''living'' tent is really something to see, although actually it's quite simple. Besides a folding table and chairs, the pair also include two folding canvas lounge chairs which are great for post-mortem sessions in the evenings.

The cooking stove, which Handy also made, is a more complicated version of the sheepherder stove in that it can also be used for broiling. An oven which fits on the top prepares fresh bread, pies and meat roasts. Add to that a nesting set of dishes, utensils, pots and pans. But possibly the most convenient ''luxury'' in camp is a small power plant which provides electric power for both tents. This may be gilding the lily, because all sorts of white gas and battery-powered lights

A simple gun rack in the tent can conserve space and save accidents.

are available, but such a facility does make camp living more pleasant. Other good examples of Handy Miner's camp facilities include a portable gun rack (for safety as well as convenience), a boot jack, a washstand, and a small refrigerator, although the last often is not necessary.

In most deer camps there's a constant demand for firewood, so a saw is always essential. Most outdoorsmen use bow saws or two-man crosscut saws, but one of the greatest time-savers in any deer camp is a small power saw. It's as useful for cutting tent poles, removing deadfalls, for building meat racks and caches as it is for cutting firewood.

No camp can be completely comfortable without a comfortable bed, and today there's no reason not to have one. Some of today's best buys are sleeping bags, safari cots and air mattresses. But the bag especially should be a good, warm one; it's a mistake to get a very cheap bag. Use a ground cloth underneath it and then inflate your mattress only to about half or two-thirds of its capacity. Sleeping snugly is as easy as that.

Any sportsman who traveled west to hunt last fall couldn't have missed the vast number and variety of mobile camps along the major highways. This kind of camp seems to be creating a trend, maybe because new roads and more rugged vehicles keep opening up more backcountry. A typical camp nowadays is one made from a retired school or transit bus.

In most states the law limits the time a bus can be used as a public conveyance, and the result is that extremely good buys in used buses, still in good condition, are available on many used-car lots. If a small party of hunters is used to hunting together, they can obtain a bus and completely refit it for a small investment over a period of years. The idea is to remove most of the old seats, to install a simple kitchen and enough bunk-type beds to go around. With a bit of ingenuity and planning, it can be as comfortable as living in an expensive lodge. With an arrangement like this, the trip to the hunting grounds can be as much fun as the hunting. And of course it's a year-around, ready-made, instant camp

Be thankful if your deer camp is a log ranch building such as this one.

End of a great trip. Deer hunters load up their game and prepare to head home.

wherever you park it, even on summer fishing trips.

Long before the season is scheduled to open, the Sandersons begin to make a lengthy list. First, it includes such basics as an axe, a saw, tents, lamps, a shovel, stoves, a bucket and ropes. On the first available weekend they check over all material on the list. Repairs are made on the tent, the saw and axe sharpened, ropes replaced, lanterns cleaned, dishes and utensils washed. With this chore completed, there will be no leaky roofs or busted lamps to interfere with the important business of having fun in camp.

The next step is to prepare the menu, a department in which the budget is not spared. "You only go deer hunting once a year," Homer Sanderson explains, "and there's no good reason to skimp on food."

When the Sandersons finally leave for camp, the cooler contains several thick, aged steaks, a rib roast, a pork loin roast and a round of good cheese. Homer, who happens to be a farmer, always brings plenty of fresh eggs, fresh country sausage, his own maple syrup, preserves, wild honey and his own cornbread mix. The last isn't well-known outside the Sanderson circle of friends, but it should be.

Any Sanderson deer camp is also set up at least one day before the deer season opens. That permits them to do a thorough job. If the campsite needs trenching in case of rain, it gets trenched. If dead limbs are overhanging from the trees above, they're removed. A big supply of firewood is stacked and a dry latrine is built.

"That first day," Frank says, "we get all the chores out of the way so that nothing interferes with hunting."

Come to think about it, that's just about the entire secret of a happy hunting camp . . . anywhere in America.

## by ERWIN A. BAUER

# A GUN DOG

RECENTLY ONE OF America's best qualified waterfowl biologists made news when he suggested drastic changes in the nation's hunting regulations. "The law requires every hunter to buy a duck stamp for $5.00 before going afield," he said, "but it should also make him take along a good retriever."

Actually the statement makes good sense. Each fall one in every four ducks shot is merely crippled and lost. In other words the bird dies, but does not go into anybody's game bag and is wasted. The 25 percent is a result of scientific study, not just a guess, and it is far too high to tolerate in these days of dwindling wildlife populations. If all hunters used retrievers, the loss would be cut at least in half.

Fortunately more and more waterfowlers are using dogs to retrieve ducks and geese. A good many differ-

(Right) Completely alert as ducks pitch in to decoys, this Lab is ready for the call to retrieve.

ent breeds are being used for the purpose, but by far the most popular is the Labrador, and it's no wonder. Plenty of dog owners are certain to disagree — loudly — but I submit that the modern Lab is the best retriever of them all. Further than that, it is the best all-around dog that sportsmen have yet been able to develop.

One example does not prove a point, but let me tell you about Blackie anyway. Blackie is a big male Lab and the property of my longtime neighbor, wildlife biologist, Bill Hendershot. The dog is now 12 years old, the only native Ohio game he has not hunted is the whitetailed deer — and that simply because it is neither permitted nor practical. Bill obtained Blackie originally to retrieve waterfowl, at which I've never seen a better performer. As will any good Lab, Blackie would hit the water over and over, no matter how cold, and swim a mile if necessary to catch up with a cripple. It is absolute fact that one bitter morning the dog followed a wounded bluebill out across open Lake Erie until he was completely out of sight. We had to crank up an outboard boat to go find him. Blackie never knew when to quit.

But Blackie wasn't just a duck dog, and eventually Bill used him less for ducks than for upland game. It began early one fall when Bill was just exercising himself and the dog in a weed field on the edge of town. But immediately Blackie began making game, smelling pheasant and flushing them exactly as a well-trained springer spaniel is supposed to do. One bird, caught in a fence corner, didn't flush quickly enough, and this one Blackie caught and retrieved alive to Bill who released it unharmed. The dog didn't like that so well.

"Maybe we better give the pooch a chance to really

hunt ringnecks this year," Bill said over the back fence that evening.

A couple of decades ago pheasant hunting in Ohio was mighty good. The birds were abundant and well distributed. But the decline had begun, and after the big boom of opening day, the roosters were hard to find. Most of them retreated immediately to the heaviest cover on the landscape where they were safe from most hunters. In the dense borders of Lake Erie, for example, hunters alone (without dog power) couldn't flush them at all. And pointing dogs were next to useless because the gunners couldn't see the dogs in the tall cattails and marsh grass. Even if the dogs *could* be seen, the wily old roosters would simply run away from them. But Blackie turned the tables. Not inhibited by the need to point, he provided some of the greatest pheasant hunting I've ever enjoyed.

Believe me it wasn't easy, though. Bill would aim Blackie into the heavy cover where the cocks were concentrated, and the hunters would have to stay close behind. Once Blackie whiffed a bird, he would whine softly and then plunge in after it, forcing it to flush. Cover did not slow him down, and the bird had no chance to run away as it could from under the nose of a pointing dog. One day stands out particularly in my memory.

Frank Sayers was hunting with Bill and me, and we had located quite a concentration of birds in shoulder-high cattails right on the edge of a pond. About 20

Bringing home the mallard on a cold dawn is all in a dog-day's work.

# THAT DOES IT ALL . . .

flushed altogether and when the shooting was finished, five cocks were down. Two were not solidly hit at all and drifted down far away in the tall grass.

"We'll be lucky to retrieve any of the five in this jungle," I said to Frank.

But I'd spoken much too soon. Blackie easily found and brought back two birds which he plopped down close to us — stone dead. He had a little trouble finding a third which had fallen a little farther out — in fact out into the pond. But most remarkable was that during the next 15 minutes he found the tracks of both the other cripples, followed, caught and retrieved them, too.

"That dog," Frank conceded, "is worth his weight in pure platinum."

It was a remarkable incident, true enough. But hunters who have worked for a long time with Labs will realize that it wasn't all that unusual. When you have been around the breed for awhile, you take great performance for granted.

Here in Ohio our cottontail rabbit and ruffed grouse seasons continue for weeks after the ringneck season ends. That's how Bill happened to give Blackie a chance to hunt two other popular game species.

I couldn't possibly report that Blackie was comparable in any way to a good beagle on the rabbits. The breed just wasn't designed to run a bunny's track for long distances across a snowy landscape. But Blackie was the next best thing to a little hound. No thicket or blackberry bush was too dense to tackle, and if a rabbit

lurked inside, Blackie would flush it out. Then if our marksmanship was good, we could figure on hasenpfeffer for dinner. Just because the game was furred instead of feathered didn't make any difference to Blackie; he retrieved anything — fur coats included.

But on one occasion that backfired. Only minutes after Bill and I had parked the station wagon beside a farm woodlot at the beginning of a rabbit hunt, Blackie tackled a skunk which he easily killed and was completely sprayed in the process. What followed certainly must have been comical to watch because Blackie retrieved the animal, following us all for more than 10 acres trying to get us to accept the game. The dog was too well trained to drop it—and neither of us wanted him even close to us. Finally he dropped the skunk and appeared very ashamed.

Later we also hunted grouse and woodcock with Blackie. Although he wasn't as good as a pointing dog, he was the next best thing. He flushed birds we might have passed over if hunting alone and retrieved many which might have been lost.

I might as well mention also that Bill carried Blackie on plenty of coon hunts. The dog never really learned to yodel on a hot track as coonhounds do, but he enjoyed the game as much as any Plott or black-and-tan. Woe to the raccoon which Blackie caught on the ground before it could take refuge in a den tree.

It may be of interest that the Labrador didn't come from Labrador at all, but rather reached America from

A black Lab which works close to the gun is surely man's best friend in pheasant cover.

Newfoundland where it was developed, with an intermediate stop in England where it became very popular. Today there are two classes of Labs, black and so-called yellow (some of these are nearly white), but there are no structural or personality differences between the two of them.

A Lab's coat is close, short and dense, a combination which allows the breed to thrive in extreme cold and even to survive frequent dunkings in icy water. Beneath its coat the animal is compactly built, in reality as well as in appearance. One unique characteristic is its heavy "otter tail." Any Labrador of good breeding and given good conditioning has great stamina and strength both for hunting in the uplands and for swimming long distances.

The Lab's present popularity is mainly because of its excellence as a water dog. But there are other reasons, too. The Labrador is eager and willing to please. Most are friendly, even affectionate, and can become good family dogs; living indoors does not affect the dog's performance in the field. Generally most become keen and alert watchdogs, surely a bonus nowadays.

I have owned and trained several different species of hunting dogs. Except for a beagle which actually required no training at all to hunt game for the bag, the Lab was the easiest of all to prepare for hunting. Since a Lab of good hunting stock is a natural swimmer, retriever and hunter, it is only necessary to add discipline. This begins with obedience training—to come when called and to respond to other simple instructions. For waterfowling it is necessary to teach the dog to be steady to shot. And for upland gunning, the dog must be taught to hunt close and within shotgun range of the hunter. A number of good volumes about the care and training of Labs are on bookshelves today, and it is a good idea to read one or more of them.

Training a Lab can be a very pleasant and fascinating pastime during the off-season. Besides developing a valuable ally for hunting expeditions later on, the actual field training is also a great way for the trainer to keep in top physical shape.

As pointed out earlier, the most important step in training any retriever is the basic instruction in obedience. Without this background there is little use in

208

No matter what the cover, it's a rare Lab which will not instinctively find, flush and retrieve any game—furred or feathered.

proceeding further because an obstreperous or undisciplined dog cannot be tolerated in a boat, blind or grainfield. A Lab should be taught to lie down and to stay down quietly when he is commanded to do so. He must never become restless or a nuisance when confined inside the tight quarters of a waterfowl blind. It is also necessary that any Labrador respond instantly to the command "heel," which means that the dog closely follows in the footsteps of his master until permitted to do otherwise.

A good bit of duck shooting nowadays is jump shooting and sneaking up on ponds, and for this a trained Lab is indeed a valuable companion. But during the stalk, the dog must hunker down and follow just beside or behind the hunter. If out of control, the retriever will only flush the ducks before the hunter approaches within effective shooting range.

Of course there is an alternative to training a Lab in your spare time and that is to employ a professional trainer. Normally the results are very good, and the dog returns home well disciplined. But this can be very expensive, and it isn't very much fun for the owner,

who doesn't get a chance to really know his own dog. And most Lab owners understandably enjoy knowing their dogs.

No Labrador is any better than its physical condition. A poorly conditioned dog cannot swim the long distances that are sometimes necessary or crisscross a weed field all morning in high gear, no matter how good its breeding. You get top performance afield only from good condition, and this is a combination of plenty of exercise before the season opens and a proper diet at all times.

Correct feeding is especially important among such large breeds as the Lab. That is doubly true during the growing-up period. Although a Lab may weigh no more than a pound or two at birth, it will grow to 65 to 70 pounds and maybe even more during its first year. By comparison a human being needs 10 times that long for the same growth. Therefore, because Labs grow so rapidly, wise owners give plenty of attention to proper diet. A young Lab's diet should be fortified with calcium and phosphorous, vitamin D and proteins.

Many other sporting breeds, including individuals of

other retrieving breeds, must be taught or forced to retrieve. But I have never known a Lab, even a very small puppy, which didn't do so naturally. Labs are eager to retrieve, and any training must be on control. In other words the dog must be trained to retrieve only on the command "fetch"—and not to break out of a blind the instant a hunter fires at decoying or passing ducks. I have seen Labs so eager to reach a fallen duck that they charged right *through* the walls of a blind, rather than hit the water via a normal exit. I have also seen them willingly jump from very high elevations into the water to make a retrieve. Nothing is tempermental about the breed; you hit your target, and the dog will get it into your bag.

Many Labs learn to point—at least to flash-point game in the uplands. If they are further encouraged in this, many become excellent point dogs. Several years ago my friend Lon Parker raised a young female Lab, and during one of her first forays afield, Lon noticed that she would hesitate and stop whenever encountering a rabbit or a covey of quail. At these times, Lon would speak softly to the dog and encourage her not to flush or try to catch the game, which was her natural instinct. Eventually the young Lab steadied enough to compare with some fairly good pointers and setters I've seen.

Any hunting dog, well enough trained to be both an ally and a companion, is pure pleasure when the hunting season opens in the fall. Far more often than many sportsmen realize, the dog is the difference between a heavy game bag and a skunking. It's as uncomplicated as that. But of all the hunting breeds, none today matches the Labrador's immense versatility. At least that's the way I see it.

Lab brings back cackling goose to Idaho sportsman Lew Martindale.

A duck is down in near-freezing water too deep to wade. But send out a Labrador retriever to bring back your bird every time.

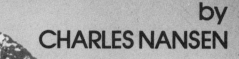

# CARIBOU
# COUNTRY

### by
### CHARLES NANSEN

Caribou country in central Alaska — perhaps the best caribou country on the face of the earth.

THE INDIANS OF THE Cassiar country of British Columbia have a saying that there are only two seasons — August and winter. Now August was finished, and on the first day of September snow began to fall. It fell softly at first on the lonely alpine landscape but quickly became a blinding blizzard.

Rusty Russell and I watched winter come in. We had climbed far into the high country to find mountain caribou. We'd climb for a while, then stop to rest and glass the barren slopes of Bowsprit Mountain, which fell away all around us. On the top of a narrow, rocky ridge we paused again, and this time Rusty focused on another ridge, one that seemed almost a world away in the growing snowstorm. Through my own glasses I barely picked out a small band of caribou, but in the next instant I could see nothing. Rusty's eyes, however, were better trained for this kind of scene.

"All bulls," he said, "and there might be one dandy in the bunch. But I think they're traveling, and that's bad. It could be a nightmare trying to catch up with them."

"Let's try anyway," I said, even though it didn't sound like a good idea. That dim ridge was a long way off.

There were two ways of approaching the animals; we could follow our ridge and make a wide circle around to them on the same level, or we could hurry back downhill and then climb the steep shale slope beneath them.

The second would be the shorter and probably the quicker way, but it would also be harder on legs and lungs that were already complaining. Still that's the way we went.

We needed only 15 or 20 minutes to reach a small noisy brook at the base of the mountain, but 2 hours later we were still laboring upward beneath the point where Rusty had last seen the caribou. Stopping frequently to rest, we climbed very slowly; more than an inch of snow made that rim of rocks extremely hazardous. We traveled the last 100 yards to the ridge inches at a time. Just under the crest I cleaned the snow and moisture from my scope, checked to see that the rifle barrel wasn't clogged, and then stood up full length to shoot.

But there was no target. As far as I could see there was nothing but white. Even the tracks of the bulls were blanketed with snow. For the third time in 4 days Rusty and I returned to camp in the dark, cold and wet and very tired. Each time we'd seen game—even trophy bulls—but hadn't scored.

The snowfall seemed an especially bad break, because all the caribou thereabout were moving out of the country—traveling to a rendezvous on the remote Spatzizi Plateau, far away across a range of mountains. These were Osborne caribou (*Rangifer osborni*) and the Spatzizi is a very common breeding ground. Every animal—male and female, young and old—within 50 miles or more gathers at this one place every Septem-ber, as they've probably been doing for centuries past. Now they were draining out of the region close to our camp; perhaps most had already gone. If we were to score at all, it would be on the odd bull late for his urgent engagement.

Four of us had traveled far to hunt grizzlies and caribou in this remote and primitive district of northern British Columbia. Homer Sayers, his bowhunting brother Frank, and I had flown from Columbus, Ohio, in Frank's 5-seat Cessna to meet John Moxley of Cleveland in Prince George, British Columbia. There we hired a vintage taxi for the 100-mile trip northward to Fort St. John where all roads end. The last lap was a 4-hour flight by Pacific Western float plane to Tuaton Lake, a place that few people have ever seen. Rusty Russell and his team of four guides, a wrangler and a cook were waiting for us. That was August 13, 3 days after the British Columbia big game season opened in that region.

John Moxley will always remember Wednesday, August 27. He was broiling ptarmigan over a willow campfire when he spotted a grizzly belly-deep in blueberries on a mountain ½-mile above camp. We watched the bear forage until it disappeared in the gathering dusk. At daybreak next morning John and his guide Dale Lefferson saddled horses before dawn and at first light were on the way up the slope. If the berries were plentiful enough, they figured the bear would still be nearby. If not, he might be 12 miles away.

But this time the breaks were in their favor. By midmorning John had a fine bicolored bruin completely skinned and the hide ready to carry to camp. But that was only the beginning. John and Dale had traveled less than ¼-mile back toward camp when they spotted another animal on another mountain across a deep, green valley. In the spotting scope it became a big bull caribou.

It was lying in a small depression between two peaks, protected from the wind but still able to watch all around it. Through the scope, John and Dale studied the terrain, looking for a good approach. When they found it, they doubled back, made an hour-long stalk and, at just under 200 yards, bagged the bull in his bed. It was a handsome 38-point, white-maned trophy, still partially in the velvet. John brought the liver to camp in time for supper. This had been one of those days when everything goes well. It was the last one like it for quite a while!

We saw caribou every day, hundreds of them, all heading northward, moving in groups of twos and threes and in large herds. Once Rusty and I crawled to the edge of a steep rock wall and looked down onto a circular basin scooped out by retreating icefields long ago. Even while we sat there a herd of 25 cows, calves and young bulls quietly slipped by, just beneath us, like gray ghosts in a single file. We could almost feel the urgency in the migration. Minutes after they'd passed, a wolverine hurried along the same trail. Maybe it was following them, maybe not. The caribou had passed without detecting us, but the wolverine spotted us immediately.

"Stink bear," Rusty whispered. "They're fairly plentiful here, but you'll live a long time before you see another one so close."

Later that day we located two bulls, stalked them across several steep rockslides and then passed them up because neither was in the trophy class.

Fortunately most of the snow lasted only overnight, and in the morning we fanned out from camp again. The color of the country had changed to bright red and rose and orange. John was after Stone sheep now, but the rest of us still had caribou in mind; by now we needed meat for camp use, not to mention a couple of trophy heads. Homer was the first to score.

With his guide Philip Louie he'd followed a rocky creek bed until it became too steep for the horses to negotiate. Climbing out of the creek, they angled slowly up a mountain, picking the easiest route between arctic birch, mossberries, and alpine spruce. At high altitudes the latter become gnarled and twisted, and hug the ground so closely that traveling through them becomes an ordeal. At intervals, as the men climbed, they dismounted to glass every foot of landscape they could see. It's the most effective way to hunt this lonely northern wilderness. Halfway up the mountain, Philip caught a movement with his naked eye and dropped easily from his horse to check with binoculars.

"Moose," he said a second later. "Bull."

"A good one?" Homer asked.

"Can't tell. Only see rump now."

"Let's have a closer look."

With horses tied head-to-tail and to the nearest spruce, Homer and Philip began a slow and tedious approach around the mountainside. The wind had been shifting all morning, but for the moment it was in their favor. They had covered 300 yards, maybe more, when Philip suddenly hit the ground. Homer hastily flattened out just behind him. At point-blank range—less than 100 yards ahead—a great bull caribou had walked out into the open from behind an evergreen clump. There it paused. Suspiciously it looked toward the hunters, looked away, looked back again, then turned downhill. Homer's heart pounded.

A wise caribou hunter saves himself plenty of footprints by using a spotting scope to carefully scan the landscape.

"Better shoot!" Philip whispered.

Homer flipped off the safety on his .280, jumped up and held well forward on the bull, which was now moving away at a brisk trot. The rifle cracked once— then again—but the big bull never missed a stride as it disappeared behind a low knoll.

"You got him," said Philip. And 200 yards away they found the animal dead. One shot had been too low in the neck, but the other had gone through the lungs.

The word that best sums up mountain caribou hunting is "unpredictable." Some bulls are unsophisticated; they stand and stare stupidly as a hunter walks or crawls toward them in full view. Even a shot may not drive all of them away. Many a hunter has bagged a bull from a herd and then watched while the others showed little or no concern.

On the other hand, some bulls are as nervous and elusive as a whitetail buck in the most heavily hunted country of Michigan or Pennsylvania. It was Frank Sayers' luck to encounter one of these the morning after Homer's bull had been converted to steaks, chops and 10-pound roasts.

Frank, his guide Charlie Abou, Rusty and I had left camp when daylight was still just a streak of lemon-colored light in the east. Our plan was to hunt slowly up a broad and soggy meadow drained by a tributary of the Stikine River. We'd do it in the early hours, because it's then that the biggest bulls are most likely to be circulating. By midmorning we could separate and hunt the higher country on opposite sides of the valley.

We spotted game as soon as it was light enough to see—first a cow with a yearling calf, next four young bulls traveling together. Then, a mile farther on, Charlie, who was leading the way, reined in his pony and slowly raised a hand.

Frank and I have hunted with many guides, from Costa Rica to Hudson Bay, but we've never known anyone with eyesight comparable to Charlie Abou's. Charlie is three-fourths Indian and one-fourth Chinese, and he has lived his lifetime deep in the Cassiars. He's shy and quiet, but he has near-radar vision. This time, in the dim light of early morning, he'd spotted a bull caribou that the rest of us couldn't see even with binoculars.

Charlie dismounted, tossed his reins to Rusty, and took Frank's spotting scope from its case. Then, in prone position, he placed the scope on the top of his black felt hat to take a closer look. (A wide-brimmed western hat makes an extremely handy rest for any scope. By shaping it to suit, it has all the flexibility of a tripod—a bulky item that the hat eliminates.) For several minutes Charlie focused and adjusted the scope. Finally he motioned Frank to take a look. For several minutes Frank just stared into the scope before he looked up and gave a low whistle.

"That one," he said, "I'd like to have."

The bull was grazing on a fairly gentle open slope backed by one much more steep and rugged. Below him was a dense willow jungle. It was a good spot for stalking by a rifleman, since the animal could be approached to within 200 yards from any side. But a bowhunter needed to be much closer. Fifty yards, Frank felt, was the absolute maximum for him. Actually he wanted to approach within 25 or 30. Fortunately the wind was blowing directly down the valley toward us. But we realized it might change several times before Frank could get within range.

In fact he had only one chance—to get above the caribou by climbing the mountain to our left. It would be painfully slow, and even dangerous, going along a steep outcropping of shale.

With luck the hunter will find a bull like this one in his scope. It is very early autumn and the caribou still has velvet on the antlers.

As Frank and Charlie pushed off up the mountain, Rusty and I found a comfortable place to watch the stalk through glasses. Perhaps no one before has ever had a better view of a contest between an archer and a giant bull caribou.

In the first hour Frank and Charlie covered only half the distance to the bull, and the roughest going was ahead. We saw them creep, crawl and fumble for handholds across a loose shale slide until it was almost too nerve-racking to watch. Once Frank lost his grip and made a lucky grab for his bow, which had started to fall away. Then, just as he was getting into a position above the bull, it looked up, startled, and trotted downhill, to disappear in the willows.

For a long time Frank and Charlie just sat motionless behind a pile of rocks, obviously waiting and wondering. If the caribou turned down the valley, I would certainly get a shot at it. If it turned up the valley, it would run dead-end into a steep, bare saddle between two peaks; by hurrying, Frank just might intercept it there. The bull turned up-valley, and we saw Frank and Charlie scrambling for altitude to reach the saddle first. The caribou didn't seem alarmed any more; probably it couldn't see or smell the hunters from below. It even stopped to graze as it meandered up the valley, then through a thicket of low rose-colored birch, and finally up the very slide on which Frank was waiting. But it was still far out of range.

Frank told us later it was an almost endless wait. He'd sweated plenty to reach his stand on the saddle, more than 1,000 feet above the valley, and now a raw wind was whistling all around him. It was like sitting in a cold wind tunnel, and he was quickly chilled to the bone. Another hour passed.

Once Frank chanced standing up to stretch and to look—and what he saw left him with a sick feeling in his stomach. The bull was standing broadside but far out of archery range, and was looking suspiciously right toward Frank. Then Frank's ticker skipped a beat when the bull started toward him again.

To within 100 yards it came, then 90, 80. Another pause; now it was only 70 yards away. Here the bull stopped. For a long time it tested the air and made false starts in different directions. Frank considered taking a long shot, but he knew that the odds were terribly stacked against him. There was the long distance, the wind and the buck fever. He'd almost decided to chance it when the bull suddenly turned and started toward him.

To 60 yards it walked, then 50. It was walking rapidly now. Forty yards, 30, and it stopped again. Frank knew this was his chance. The moment the animal looked away he rose, drew and plunked the broadhead amidships into the animal's body.

The startled, uncomprehending bull stood there while Frank nocked a second arrow, drew and missed completely. The caribou turned only slightly, and

Frank was able to send a third arrow high into its rump. Now the animal bolted down the loose and uncertain slope—half running, half stumbling, finally falling. When Frank reached the spot it was stone dead.

It was late afternoon before we could shake Frank's hand. He was still trembling when we joined him. Then Charlie gave a long speech—long for him anyway. "Frank make a good shot," he said. And that was all.

One of the many dividends of packtripping into the Cassiars is the fishing. Every evening trout would rise on Tuaton Lake, and if my timetable was right, rainbows would be spawning. The most likely place was at the lake's outlet. So next day we voted a change of pace and went fishing at the outlet.

On most casts we'd hook rainbows of from 15 to 19 inches, and they'd pinwheel all over the riffle before we could slide them out on the bank. Half an hour and half a dozen rainbows later I was downstream several hundred yards from the rest of the party. I'd just landed and released a 3-pound Dolly Varden when I heard something thumping in the willows nearby.

My first thought was of grizzlies, and in a cold sweat I began to look for the nearest exit. Then I saw a pair of giant caribou antlers moving through and above the willows, as if detached from the body. They were less than 50 feet away, and I was armed with nothing but a fly rod. Without even seeing the animal I half ran, half waded back to the streambank for my rifle, which fortunately was in my saddle scabbard.

What happened after that is vague, at best. I remember running and falling. Luckily the bull hadn't traveled very far from where I'd spotted him. By creeping on all fours I reached a patch of high ground beyond the animal, and there I waited. For a long time I could follow his movements by his rack alone. The body was still hidden by deep willows, now the bright yellow of autumn. This is how buck fever develops. When the bull finally did emerge into an opening, I was trembling much too much to risk an offhand shot; so I sat down. Using my arms and knees as a tripod, I held my .280 Remington on the caribou's shoulder, waited until he was clear of foliage, and squeezed. The animal fell in his tracks. I'd bagged a truly tremendous bull. In a minute or so John, Frank and Rusty were on the spot, their eyes bulging.

Like John Moxley's, this bull was still in the velvet, but it was loose and just beginning to fray off. The inside measurement between main beams was 56 inches, and no guide in the party could ever remember seeing a wider spread. Even in the newest *Records of North American Big Game* only one mountain caribou is recorded with a greater spread, and that is the top trophy of them all taken in 1923 in the same region. It measured 57⅜ inches. Actually, all but a few of the 39 heads listed in the *Records* came from the Cassiars.

Now I could enjoy Frank's steak, the grilled rainbows—and start looking for grizzlies tomorrow.

# THE BOWHUNTER'S

## by RUSSELL TINSLEY

**THE CONFRONTATION** led to a crucial decision. Looking back, I can understand what went wrong. But hindsight is cheap.

Actually, this hunter-met-buck situation was one of those freaky things. Here it was opening day of the Texas October bow season and I overslept and was tardy in arriving at the cattle ranch where I was to hunt. After the 45-minute drive from my home in Austin, dawn was coming rapidly to the quiet woods. It was a good ½-mile hike to my tree stand.

I knew better than to rush. This only would spook any deer within hearing distance. So with an arrow nocked and ready, I crept along. intently watching through a light fog.

Easing across a small flat covered with scattered low-slung bushes, I abruptly sensed I wasn't alone. Call it ESP or whatever, but every veteran hunter possibly has had the same kind of premonition at one time or another. Something inside tells you to stop and look.

As I slowly turned my head, I was astonished to see a deer not 35 yards away. The unsuspecting 8-point buck, head down, was no trophy, but when hunting with bow and arrow I am not too fussy. Opportunities are few and far between.

I stood motionless and quickly analyzed the scene. Periodically the relaxed buck would raise his head, briefly glance about, then go back to his business. His rump was toward me. I either could aim an arrow at that target or try for a better profile. If I'd been forced to make a split-second decision, the outcome probably would have been different. But unfortunately, the few moments gave me time to think, and sometimes when I think, I'm dangerous.

Despite what you might have heard, a sharp broadhead driven deep into a deer's rump is a fatal shot. This area has numerous blood vessels.

A few yards to my left was a brush clump. If I could ease over there, and skirt the bush, I'd then have a closer broadside shot at the preoccupied buck. When he lowered his head, I cautiously moved and as he raised up to look, I made like a statue.

Things went smoothly. I got to the bush all right, but then maybe I got careless. I don't know. Anyway, as I sidled around the thick-leafed cover, I suddenly heard the buck snort, and when I got to where I could see, he was trotting off, startled but not really alarmed.

I had disgustingly blown a golden chance. But it hadn't been the first time nor the last. In bowhunting, when the drama finally comes in sharp focus, everything hinges on that critical decision—precisely when to draw and release an arrow. You might call it bowhunting's moment of truth. One mistake here and the entire effort can be scuttled. In bowhunting there seldom is the luxury of a second chance.

The obvious limitations of the bow and arrow have a lot to do with it. The quarry must be close (most whitetailed deer are killed at a range of less than 25

Stalking this close to a buck isn't impossible, but it takes uncommon skill.

216

# BIGGEST CHALLENGE

yards). When the bow is raised and the arrow drawn, there is easily detected movement. A deer's nerves are as tight as a coil spring. At that close range not much is going to escape its scrutiny.

But that's not all. While packing a rifle, the hunter has a reasonable chance to kill about any deer he sees. It makes no difference whether the deer is staring at the hunter or looking away. A bullet can reach the animal before the deer has time to react. Yet with bow and arrow, the projectile, fletched with feathers or plastic

Hours of patient waiting in a tree stand paid off for the author.

vanes, travels much slower, not much more than 400 feet-per-second even with a faster compound bow. The deer can see it coming and move before the arrow arrives at its mark. This is why the bowhunter must ambush the deer when it is totally unaware the human poses a threat. An edgy deer, even one that hasn't detected the hunter, is much quicker to react than is one relaxed with its guard down. It isn't unusual for a nervous deer to "jump the string," as archers call it. Sound travels faster than the arrow, and the deer hears the audible "twang" of the released string and jumps away before the arrow arrives.

I've had it happen to me. A few seasons back I was hunting with a friend on his central Texas ranch. The man knew where deer habitually traveled so he parked me on a folding stool in a clump of oak brush and told me he would work around and attempt to drive some deer near my stand.

After maybe ½-hour or less, I heard a commotion and shortly two deer, a doe and a 6-point buck, came loping down the trail, pausing now and then to glance back over their shoulders. When the buck made one of his stops directly in front of my stand, I drew the arrow and aimed it just behind the deer's shoulder. The arrow flew true; it seemed like a sure thing. But at the last possible instant the animal jumped forward, and the arrow passed only an inch or two behind his rump. That buck was only 22 steps away.

One common mistake a beginning bowhunter makes is that he merely shoots at a deer rather than a specific point. The ideal impact of aim is right behind the shoulders, in the lung region. Any sharp broadhead put into this area normally results in a dead deer. The key word here is sharp; a broadhead's edges should shave hair. One of the best is a head that takes replaceable razor-blade edges for maximum sharpness. A broadhead kills by hemorrhage, and it must cut clean rather than simply push vital organs aside.

Most successful bowmen hunt from stands. The reason is rudimentary. Sitting quietly still, the hunter stands a much better chance of getting a deer close, an animal that doesn't know the human is there. It isn't impossible to stalk a crafty whitetail and approach within 30 yards or less without the deer suspecting anything—only improbable.

Two seasons back I made what I consider the perfect stalk. I was still hunting through the brush and oak timber when I noticed a doe in the distance. She was browsing on acorns and was completely at ease.

I tested the breeze. It was blowing toward me. Good.

It is imperative that the bowhunter has a broadhead that is razor sharp.

(Above) Successful stand hunting often is a matter of knowing where to put your stand, and the process of scouting and examining signs.

(Right) A portable tree stand puts the hunter above a deer's normal line of sight.

(Below) It is debatable how much scents really help, but they sure don't do any harm.

(Right) Where legal, a permanent tree stand gives the hunter more maneuverability.

(Below) When the deer turns its head, that is the time to make your play.

Also I'd earlier sprinkled myself liberally with cedar oil deer scent.

Positioning a large oak between me and the doe, I started toward her, watching each step, making sure I didn't step on anything that would create telltale noise. Once I reached the tree, I peeked around the trunk and noticed the deer, now within 100 yards, was still feeding placidly.

When the doe lowered her head to pick up acorns, I eased into the open and took a couple quick steps. As the head started up, I froze. My camouflage clothing, including a headnet and mesh gloves covering my hands, blended me into the background. The deer would glance about, satisfy herself that everything was okay, and would go down for more acorns. Only then would I gingerly move 3 or more feet.

A deer is more vulnerable when it is walking away from the hunter rather than toward him.

It was a test of willpower and nerves. Creep and stop, creep and stop. My heart was racing. Finally, after what seemed like eternity, I had slipped within 30 yards. Somehow the deer had failed to notice my presence. When she lowered her head again, I brought up the bow, drew the arrow, aimed and released in one continuous motion. There was only one thing wrong. The arrow sailed high, over the deer's back, and clattered through the underbrush—and that was that.

Most bowhunters I know prefer tree stands, putting them above the deer's normal line of sight. At a higher vantage human scent is more likely to be blown up and away rather than along the ground—another plus. Scent is the hunter's worst enemy. But there are some bowhunters who like ground-level stands, a ring of strategically placed brush perhaps with just enough opening to permit a shot.

A problem I have with stand hunting is my patience, or lack of it. After an hour or two my tolerance begins to wear thin. In this state of mind, I am more likely to make mistakes. Probably this is why I kill as few deer with a bow as I do.

The stand hunter must know what he is doing and have self-discipline. The temptation is to make your play prematurely. There is no perfect opportunity so the bowhunter should attempt to exploit the first reasonable chance he gets. But if he waits too long, his nervous system might go haywire, and he'll get a classic case of shakes called "buck fever." I have had it happen. It is part of the game.

Preparation is important. Once situated in his stand, the hunter should check to be sure he has ample maneuverability of his bow without striking anything that might alarm the deer. Last year a friend of mine had a 10-point buck come strolling almost beneath his tree stand. As he raised his bow, it hit and rattled a limb, and the buck didn't stand around to find what had made the noise. Yep, there often is a very thin line between success and failure.

The hunter also should be aware of the direction the wind is blowing at any time. I don't know how much commerical scents help, but I use them. If possible I like to place an uncapped jar of pure skunk musk a few yards downwind from my stand. The malodorous liquid might not completely mask human odor, but if a deer is near and the breeze capriciously shifts, the animal might be confused long enough for a quick shot.

A stand hunter also should stick it out as long as his patience allows. The more hours spent in the woods, the better are your odds of getting a deer within arrow range. It is that simple.

And if and when a deer does indeed come in range, timing becomes paramount. Wait until the animal's head is turned or is behind some obstruction such as a stump or bush. Should the deer be traveling, allow it to get slightly past, going away, before making your play. A deer approaching head-on is much more likely to radar in on any unnatural movement.

Unfortunately, many of the fine points which lead to eventual success are learned only through experience. The bowhunter must profit by his mistakes, and he probably will be guilty of many. But somewhere, sometime, all the pieces will come together. It is a very special time, for you no longer are just a bowhunter but a bowhunter who has gotten his deer. You now are among select company. This makes it all worthwhile.

BEN RODGERS LEE'S best hunting weight is 350 pounds. During the deer season he may shrink to 300 pounds. That's a lot of weight on the hoof for a 6-footer but Ben sneaks through brush like a fox and takes his portable tree stand up a tree like a squirrel toting a hickory nut.

Whenever I see Ben, he reminds me of the story about the fellow who was dancing with a barrel-like lady and wanted to pay her a compliment. He whispered in her ear, ''You sweat less than any fat lady I ever danced with.'' Trying to stay up with Ben in the woods causes me to sweat a lot.

I'm always happy to have a chance to hunt with Ben. Although only 34 years old, he's killed more than 340 whitetail bucks! Before you start counting on your fingers to see if that's legal, let me explain that much of Ben's hunting is done in Alabama where it's legal to take a buck a day in many counties for a season of 60 or more days—and that's not counting the bowhunting season and special hunts.

Ben got an early start. His father, James W., began taking him on deer drives when Ben was only 8 years old. His mother, Edna, is a deadly shot, and the family still gets together near Selma, Alabama, each season for two or three hunts.

Ben spends most of his time in the woods. He's best known as a turkey caller and makes his living by selling calls and related equipment from his plant in Coffeeville, Alabama. He's won the world champion turkey calling championship several times plus countless state contests. He's in constant demand at sportsmen's clubs and each spring works his way, hunting and teaching turkey talk, from Florida to Vermont.

Although he has a national reputation as a turkey hunter, few people know he's equally expert on whitetails. I spent a week hunting with him last season in central Alabama, studying his techniques. He bagged an 11-pointer which weighed 265 pounds on the hoof and a 7-pointer which weighed 237 pounds undressed. Those are real trophy deer for the South where deer don't normally grow nearly as large as the northern woodland subspecies.

Ben has an abundant supply of patience, desire to kill large deer and keen eyesight. He works hard without getting in a rush. It is common for him, especially during the bow season, to take a portable treestand up a

# The Bigger They Come

## by CHARLEY DICKEY

With light portable treestand, Ben Rodgers Lee eases along an Alabama Creek looking for deer and their signs.

Even in the open, whitetails tend to blend with their background.

tree before daylight and stay there until after dark. He takes two 1-gallon jugs. One is filled with water, and the other is empty for urinating in. He carries a ditty bag full of sandwiches and candy bars and is happy perched on a small platform all day. I quickly explained to Ben that I didn't want to kill a buck badly enough to do that. I can't even sit in a rocking chair for more than an hour without getting restless. Ben smiled and said nothing. He shoots more deer in an average season than I've killed all of my life. The tree time is never wasted. That's when Ben studies deer behavior and movements. Since he's nearly always after big bucks, he passes up shots at other bucks and doesn't bother with does, even when they're legal.

Of course, Ben doesn't just shinny up any old tree with all of his gear. He scouts an area and plots his tactics like a colonel planning a regimental attack. His favorite location for a treestand is near a scrape or a main runway leading to a fresh scrape. When a buck is in rut, he advertises it to the does, and perhaps as a territorial warning to other bucks, by pawing a rough circle in the ground about the diameter of a basketball or maybe as large as a washtub. Then he urinates in it,

deliberately spraying some of the urine on his hocks and rubbing them together. He may make more than one scrape but they are generally in the same area. The scrapes are usually made in small clearings or on old logging roads. There are nearly always branches overhanging the scrape, about 40 or so inches high. The buck chews on the branches and also hooks them.

A buck in rut roughly doubles the size of his range. He's on the prowl night and day for urgent does. But the buck frequently comes back to his scrapes to check them. There's a good reason for this. If a doe in heat locates the scrape, she'll urinate in it, spraying urine on her hocks and rubbing them together. The urine is her love note saying she's ready for action. When the buck returns, he gets a whiff and has no trouble tracking down the doe.

If a scrape is fresh, the buck will be back. Ben doesn't set up if tracks leading to and around a scrape are small or average-sized. When I pointed out to Ben that a large track didn't necessarily mean a big buck, Ben asked, "How many women do you know who wear a size 12 shoe?"

If Ben is hunting with a rifle, he puts his treestand up

(Right) Ben Lee and a big whitetail buck he took with a bow and arrow.

(Right) When he doesn't wear a face mask, Ben uses grease paint to camouflage his face. He uses three tubes, one each in black, brown and green.

(Below) Perched comfortably, and blending with background, Ben can sit patiently all day waiting for a big buck.

about 50 or more yards from a scrape or runway leading into it. The distance varies with the particular cover. It doesn't do the hunter any good for a deer to work a scrape if the hunter can't see him. When bowhunting, Ben tries to put his treestand within 10 or 20 yards of a runway or scrape. If possible, he does not want to draw on a buck more than 20 yards away.

A fresh scrape, with large tracks around it, is the best sign you can find. If you have the patience, sooner or later the buck will come back and check his scrape, usually freshening it. Ben once spent a total of 47 hours in a treestand waiting on a buck. His patience paid off in an 8-pointer which dressed out at 172 pounds.

In 1977, Ben killed 16 bucks with good body weight or large antlers or both. Twelve were taken with a rifle and four with a bow. He passed up 13 bucks in his sights that most hunters would have been proud to bag, plus countless forks and spikes. Although much of Alabama is overpopulated with deer, or about to be, and spikes need to be reduced, Ben goes after big or trophy deer. "If I know old Nathan is around, I don't care how long I have to hunt," Ben says. "The thrill I get is in outsmarting an old-timer on his home grounds. I'm glad to pass up the forks and spikes and leave them for hunters who don't get to go as often as I do."

Treestands are critical in much southern hunting, or any place where there is brushy ground cover or a dense understory. Visibility is restricted at ground level. Even getting in the forks of a tree 5 feet from the ground

Screwed-in L-bolts enable Ben to reach the first branches of an oak tree. That's all he needs to climb on up and attach seat. Note rope for pulling up bow or rifle.

greatly improves visibility. Of the 42 bucks he's killed with a bow, 40 were taken from treestands. Depending on cover conditions, Ben usually goes only 10 to 20 feet up a tree. At times, where bucks are hiding and sneaking in dense brush and weeds, Ben has climbed 40 feet up longleaf pines with his rifle.

Although he sometimes uses commercial treestands and climbers, his favorite rig is one he designed himself. It's light and portable. Ben stays out all day, and he may move several times. After choosing a spot to wait, he screws a couple of L-shaped bolts into a tree up high enough so that when he steps on two he can reach the first branches. From then on, he works up the branches until he finds a spot with good visibility. Then he mounts his seat and starts the long wait. He is careful, of course, not to screw the bolts into trees which might eventually make good timber.

Ben's second favorite place to hunt is where two or three deer trails feed together between a feeding area and bedding area. He is in his treestand at least 45 minutes before daylight. When conditions permit, he has scouted the area and knows there's at least one big buck around. If the deer are not under a lot of hunting pressure, they follow a fairly regular timetable before the rut. Of course, severe weather will throw them off schedule. Deer are restless just ahead of a cold front, Ben says. In severe cold, rain or snow, the deer may bed down in thick conifers. When the weather passes, that's a good time to go hunting. Deer will be active.

Bucks usually have a general area of 5 to 15 acres for bedding. Although they seldom sleep in the same bed, they return to the general area. It usually has two or three exits and entrances. Ben once located the bedding area of a huge 10-pointer. It was several acres of brushy cover with clumps of cedars that caused short visibility. Ben tried to stalk hunt the buck on 5 different days but the deer always sneaked out ahead of him. The buck drifted out on one runway once but he used another exit four times. Ben set up his treestand before daylight. At 9 AM, he had a buddy slowly drive the bedding area. The buck didn't run. He ambled along his favorite escape route. Ben nailed him from 40 yards.

Exceptional vision is a big asset to Ben. But he practices spotting deer any time he's in the woods, even when he's hunting turkeys. Many a time, driving major roads with him, I've had him pull off on the shoulder and point out a deer 400 or 500 yards away in the shadows at the edge of a field. Even when he pointed, I had trouble spotting the deer.

Ben's in the camouflage clothing business and practices what he preaches. On public lands he may wear color and in the states which require blaze orange he must wear it. But on private land, he wears a camouflage suit he designed with gloves and a face mask. Camouflage clothing is particularly important when bowhunting. He says, "Deer have trouble identifying a still object, such as a hunter. It's movement which they instantly pick up. Camouflage clothing helps break up movement.''

Sound is another factor which gives a hunter away. Ben prefers to hunt in tennis shoes and does until the weather drops below freezing. Then he shifts to L.L. Bean boots with leather tops and rubber soles.

Human scent instantly tells a deer that a hunter is present. When a buck gets a whiff of man, he's not in doubt. He knows that an enemy is near. Since much of Ben's hunting is in country dotted or soaked in pines, he uses turpentine as an odor masker. Even though he usually hunts from a tree, Ben puts turpentine on his boots and rubs a little on his clothing and bow or gun. He washes his tennis shoes and boots frequently to take away human scent. He washes his camouflage clothing in Pinesol, a deodorant with a basic pine smell. He hangs his clothes outside to dry so that they don't absorb house smells. Ben has tried skunk oil as a masker and says that without doubt it's the best cover-upper of human odor. However, he's given it up.

Somehow he always got skunk oil on his body and it created wife problems. Ben says at times his dog would run under the house when he came home from a hunt.

For most of his rifle hunting, he uses a Browning semi-automatic which holds five 30-06 cartridges, one in the chamber and four in the clip. He uses an 180-grain bullet since much of his shooting is in brush. He wants a bullet that will not be deflected easily by weeds and that will put a deer down and keep him down. Since he hunts only big or trophy deer, he needs the shocking power of a 30-06.

Sometimes a bullet goes all the way through. But that's not all bad, he says. If there's a tracking job there's more blood to follow. His rifle is mounted with a Leupold Vari-X III, 4-plex 3.5 x 10 variable. When stalk hunting, the scope is kept on the lowest power. When sitting in a tree, Ben usually keeps the scope at 5x. If the scope is used as binoculars, Ben switches to 10x.

Ben started bowhunting as a way of scouting ahead of

Ben took this beauty on the edge of a field from a treestand.

It's not easy to learn to shoot through branches "downhill" at a deer. Ben does a lot of target practice from trees.

the gun season. He says that the bowhunting has taught him more about deer behavior than anything else. Since he had to let them get close, preferably within 20 yards, he was compelled to watch. It also improved his patience. He usually shoots a Bear Alaskan compound bow at 52 pounds with aluminum shaft 1916 arrows and Bear inserts in a Broadhead. He quickly found out that there's a tendency to overshoot a deer from a treestand. He also discovered that punching holes in a ground target in the backyard is a lot easier than shooting from a tree stand. Despite the number of bucks he's bagged, Ben says the big bucks shake him up.

Before going up a tree with his bow, Ben paces off distances of 20, 30, 40 and 50 yards and puts in marker sticks, or breaks off weeds. This helps him when a deer is slowly working nearer. He doesn't have to guess at range. He knows!

Now Ben scouts ahead of the bowhunting season. For much of his scouting, he climbs a tree and has all of his equipment. He practices shooting from a tree ahead of the season.

Ben takes a lot of people hunting, many who have done little deer hunting. The most common mistakes are as follows: The hunter doesn't know his rifle or bow, its capabilities and limitations. He may be fair on the range but he's never shot through branches in an awkward position. He doesn't dress properly and is uncomfortable. This causes a lot of unnecessary moving. Ben is a layer man. Before dawn, he has on several layers of clothing. When the sun comes out, he begins peeling. As it gets cooler in the afternoon, he begins putting layers back on.

Perhaps the number one problem with the average hunter is that he doesn't know how to see a deer. He expects a calendar buck to stand on a cleared hill with the sun shining on his coat. The novice doesn't spend valuable time scouting and learning to see parts of deer and their signs. Also, too often the average hunter lacks patience. He moves around too much rather than sitting and waiting. After listening to Ben, I bought two 1-gallon jars and this season I'm going to see if I can sit up in a tree from before dawn until after dark.

# First Hunt for Trophy Pronghorn

## by STEVE SMITH

There they stood for a brief split second. I cranked a cartridge
into the Weatherby .240 magnum. Then they started to disappear.

**DAWN HAD NOT YET BROKEN** the darkness of the second day of the hunt. Our Jeep wagon slowly climbed the plateau. Today was going to be different. I could feel it inside, and I turned my eyes to the sage and hillsides. I strained to see through the predawn light, scoping every inch of terrain as it was uncovered. I was looking for some movement, a shadow, or that patch of white that would reveal an antelope.

As the Jeep followed the rocky road deeper into the sage, I thought about the animal I was after. The North American pronghorn is a very swift runner which, when spooked or threatened, has been clocked at 60mph. His tan and white camouflage hide makes him extremely hard to spot in the land of sage and cedar he calls home. Added to his coloring and great speed is the incredible eyesight of the animal. Antelope are said to have 8x vision. For these reasons alone, many people believe in running down their prey in trucks. These "sportsmen" might as well hunt in a pen. To me, the challenge of meeting a buck on his home ground was what I wished

for most of all. I had heard the stories of this elusive animal, and I was forming my own opinion of the "ghost of the prairie." As I scanned the sage I dreamed of what I hold to be the greatest thrill of the hunt—the stalk.

The sky was lighter now as we drove onward with growing anticipation of what was to come. I was glancing down at my watch, when my dad whispered to me, "There, on the hillside!" Not in my wildest dreams could I have pictured what was to happen next.

I would never have been here at all if I had not been plain lucky. I had drawn one of California's special antelope permits. All residents of the state who are at least 16 years old and have a valid California hunting license may apply. California has roughly 4,900 antelope which roam the extreme northeastern section of the state. To help control the population, the Department of Fish and Game holds an annual special hunt. The northeastern plains are divided into seven zones. Each zone, depending on the present population of

227

antelope, is awarded a limited number of permits. For this hunt, 375 permits were issued. To increase our chances of being drawn, my dad and I sent in separate applications. I was the lucky one who beat the 18-1 odds. Once drawn, a hunter may not apply again for 10 years. With this system the Department can both control the herd and keep the ''lucky'' hunters from being drawn again and again. Drawing a permit on my first year of eligibility was a great thrill for me, better than winning the Irish Sweepstakes.

My hunting career began early when my father enrolled me into a Hunter's Safety Course. I was 8 years old at the time. His enthusiasm about hunting rubbed off onto me or maybe I inherited it because 2 weeks later I was sitting at a dove stand ready to go. I vividly remember getting that first dove. I also remember my dad saying, ''If you're going to be a hunter, you clean what you shoot.''

From doves we went to ducks. The Merced Wildlife Refuge was my training ground. It seemed like endless miles of sloshing through the mud and rain, all for a couple of ducks. But I loved it. As I grew older, I was able to go off more on my own.

When I was 11, I made my first sneak on a flock of geese. It took me the better part of an hour to crawl the 100 yards that gave me the first possible chance for a shot. My inexperience had me lift my head too high, and the geese jumped; so did I. I was on my feet before they were 20 feet high and fired the first barrel of the Browning 20-gauge double barrel into the flock. To my amazement two birds dropped. So did my jaw. My final shot was in vain but that did nothing to destroy my satisfaction.

My twelfth year introduced me to big game. I bought my first deer tag and looked forward to my first deer hunt. Never during the first 4 years of deer hunting did I fire a single shot, but it thrilled me like no other form of hunting I had known. Now being drawn for a permit, I was determined to make things different. No silent hunts this time.

I wanted to know all about antelope. I went to the library and read every article I could lay my hands on. I began to form a picture of him. Writers told how elusive and wild they were, and I soon realized that a successful stalk would be more difficult than I first had thought. But then, that made it all the more exciting. First, however, I had to become comfortable with my gun. The 30-30 Winchester carbine I had been using for deer we felt would not shoot flat enough for the long shots I might have at antelope. With this in mind my dad said I could use his Weatherby .240 Magnum. I wanted to feel at home with it so I ran through box after box of shells. I shot at targets 100-450 yards away. Standing, sitting, prone, rapid fire, and reloading again. I wanted everything to feel natural. To have a shot at an antelope is probably a once in a lifetime opportunity. I wanted the memory to be something I would recall proudly.

Alturas, California, near the Nevada and Oregon borders, was the base of my area. It was a place I had never seen. Driving from our house in Merced, my dad and I wondered what the high desert of California would look like. Being in this part of the state would be a new experience for both of us. We also wondered about the antelope because neither of us had ever seen one in the wild.

Upon arriving in Alturas, we drove to our motel. Here we were introduced to Gus the owner who was also a part-time guide. We explained our situation to him, and he offered to get us started. Gus had trespass rights onto a number of ranches in the area, and he said he would be glad to take us to one. He explained that the antelope were usually found wandering in the sagebrush. However, in the heat of the afternoon, they will often seek the shade of trees. My dad and I had no idea what to look for until Gus pointed to some cedars. At first we couldn't see a thing. Then as if from nowhere, a tan and white animal stepped forward from the shadows. Then we spotted another. In all we saw three bucks that afternoon. We couldn't thank Gus enough. At last we knew what we were looking for, not from descriptions in a book, but from actual experience.

The following day the Department of Fish and Game had an orientation meeting for the hunters of this zone. The meeting is held the day before the 10-day season begins. At the 2-hour gathering we were told the habits, history, and other information about antelope. Most of it I already knew from my reading. We were told that the biggest herd in our zone roams on the 20-mile plateau which lies east of Alturas. We decided to try there first.

That same afternoon we scouted the area to find a draw where we would make a stand the next day. We drove through the sage and rocks searching for the white rump. After 6 miles of bouncing, we came around the hillside to a gully where we spooked four does from under the cedar trees. Their speed was awesome!

We walked up the near hill taking along a pair of binoculars and our 60x spotting scope. At the top we sat under a lone tree and surveyed the countryside. In front of us lay a flat which on the south side dropped off sharply into a great basin. We had been sitting under the tree for about 25 minutes when a buck and two does came around the hill below us and crossed the flat. At the orientation meeting we were told that the ears of an antelope were about 6 inches long. Judging the length of the horns is easier using this comparison. I was after a trophy head and wasn't about to shoot the first buck unless he qualified. This meant the prongs would have to be twice the size of the ears. We watched them leave and figured the buck to have about 15-inch prongs! If only he'd wait around until tomorrow!

About ½-mile away to the west ran a small ridge. Not long after the pronghorn left, another antelope stood on

The pronghorn is not abundant nowadays in California. But residents can apply to draw for a permit. The odds against drawing are 18-1.

the crest. We placed our spotting scope on it and stared in amazement. He was staring right back at us! He needed no scope. We hadn't waited 10 minutes more when we heard a noise behind us. Turning slowly we saw two bucks and a doe not 75 yards away! They had come up the backside of the hill. Here we had a great chance to look at them up close. In the 2 hours we were there we saw 13 bucks and 3 does. Not bad at all. This natural "draw" we hoped would work to our advantage tomorrow when the pronghorn were spooked by the other hunters. On opening day we would make our stand here. Walking over to the cliff we saw a great basin surrounded on three sides with hills. The hills formed draws which to us looked like naturals for antelope. We drove back to the motel hoping we were right and looking forward to the next day's hunt.

We rose in the dark the next morning, and the adrenalin had already started to flow. We reached our lone tree on the hill just as the light of the new-born day spread across the sage and cedar trees. We sat down and waited. And waited. Noon. No antelope. What was wrong? To the west the echoing *boom . . . boom . . . boom* of rifles filled the air. Maybe we had guessed wrong. We decided to hunt the rest of the plateau. If they wouldn't come to us, we'd find them.

Discouraged, we spent the entire afternoon riding through the sage and around the hills with no luck. Occasionally we spied a lone pronghorn running far off, but we hadn't come here to run down some animal. There had to be a better way to do it. At the end of the afternoon we called it quits and headed back to town.

On our way we came across a game warden and pulled over to talk with him. He told us that the hunters at the west end of the plateau were doing quite well. A large number of pronghorn had moved in there, and he suggested that we give that area a try. We thanked him for the help and drove on. Now it finally hit us! The 16 antelope that we had seen the day before were moving west! They had simply moved out of our area. It's not uncommon for antelope to move 10-20 miles in a day. Now with all the activity at that end, maybe the antelope would move back into ours. We guessed this would be exactly what they would do and decided to be waiting on the same hill the next day.

On this second morning of our hunt we were filled with confidence and anticipation. Our plan for the morning hunt would be to enter the field at first light. Reasoning that the antelope would be scattered in the area, we didn't want to pass any in the darkness. Arriving at the road that would lead us up to the plateau, we stopped the Jeep and waited for daybreak. Sitting in the darkness, Dad and I tried to list all the possible ways in which I might meet the pronghorn. Would today be different from the opening? What if we guessed wrong again? There was only one way to find out, and we began our journey up the plateau. My heart beat faster and faster, and when we rounded the next turn it seemed to stop altogether as I followed my father's pointing finger.

Quickly the Jeep came to a halt, and I jumped out to

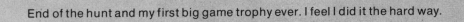
End of the hunt and my first big game trophy ever. I feel I did it the hard way.

'scope the two pronghorn on the hillside. The sight of the vehicle had momentarily frozen the antelope in place and at first glance, I couldn't distinguish whether one, both, or neither of the pronghorn were bucks. Taking no chances, I cranked the 100-grain cartridge into the Weatherby .240 Magnum. The two animals stood for an instant and then like ghosts, slipped around the hill and vanished. I had had only a split second to place the 9x scope on the two, but that was long enough to determine that one was a very nice buck. In fact he amazingly resembled one of the bucks we had seen on our scout 2 days earlier.

I walked toward the hill where I had last seen the two animals and climbed up. As I reached the crest, I realized that the pronghorn had played right into our hands. From my vantage point I could see just what they had seen. While hunting ducks in the San Joaquin Valley of California, I had often wondered what it was that compelled the duck to choose my pond over all the rest. Here on the plateau I was experiencing the same thing. Looking out ahead of me one hill met another, and together they formed a natural funnel which led into a great basin. Following this natural "escape" route the two would have to enter either the flats or basin where we waited yesterday. I returned to the Jeep and reported what I had seen. We drove on to our jump-off point about 1½ miles away.

With shaky fingers I filled my belt with cartridges. Then Dad and I with our 60x spotting scope, headed cautiously up the hill. It seemed an eternity walking up the hill, and my mind was spinning with fears of my getting "buck fever." At last we reached the lone cedar at the top. We glassed the countryside. Nothing. As we waited, I tried to figure where they could have gone. We had to have guessed right. The clues all lead to these flats, *unless* they had followed the draw all the way into the basin! I decided to go over to the dropoff and check. I headed toward the basin, and Dad waited at the top.

I walked on not knowing what awaited below and beyond. As I grew nearer I remembered what Dad had told me, "Make each sneak your best sneak." I instinctively hunched over and lined my path up with a tree. I edged closer to the tree and the dropoff into the valley. My heart sounded like a drummer at a parade.

At the base of the tree I sat down and searched the basin for signs of antelope. The plains were empty. Only the grass moved in the morning breeze. But they *had* to be down there. Still I could find no sign. Disappointed, and somewhat depressed, I checked the surrounding hills one more time. Suddenly a light patch stood out on a grassy hillside about 200 yards away. I blinked and there about 100 feet to the left of it in the base of a draw, lay another patch. I raised the rifle to my shoulder and peered through the 9x scope. There, chewing grass and looking over the whole basin, were the two pronghorn. These "ghosts of the prairie" had appeared just as quickly as they had disappeared 40

minutes earlier. From their vantage point they could see any sign of danger for miles around. Except mine. I had stumbled into the lone blind spot. Just as we had figured earlier, they had followed the draw until it opened in the basin. From here they could lie down to eat and rest in safety. But I had other plans.

I couldn't go back to Dad with my news. There was nothing for me to do but to begin my sneak alone. It was like something out of a fairy tale. Too good to be true. I was downwind, and for the time, unnoticed. Probably my greatest advantage was the sun. Since it was still quite early, the ledge below me was left in darkness. I wouldn't have to worry about the reflection of my rifle or having my body become silhouetted against the horizon. Under these conditions I would be invisible. The ledge below ran toward the antelope and the rocks would make ideal cover for my sneak. For the next 150 feet and 1 hour a metamorphosis would take place. I would become a 16-year-old snake. I carefully slid over the side and began my crawl. I moved a foot at a time following the countour of the land, never looking up. Time had no meaning or length. I wondered what Dad was doing.

Back at the tree, he had come to the conclusion that I was up to something. I must have run onto some antelope and begun making a sneak. No way was he going to miss this! As he drew nearer the ledge, he crouched down and scanned the basin floor. This way he could look forward without being seen. At last, 15 feet from the edge, he saw me. There in front of him, was his son inching over the rocks like a reptile. I was oblivious to him. My one concern was the buck in front of me. I edged forward, over, around, and almost through the rocks, praying with each passing foot that I wouldn't be seen.

Then without warning, the doe stood up! Had I been spotted? What was wrong? I leaned into the rocks and made myself a natural rest. Time was running out. This was the moment I had been waiting for. Then, just like the doe, the buck also stood. He was the buck of my dreams. His prongs were thick and high. From behind me a voice I never heard said, "Take him!" I raised the Weatherby .240 Magnum to my shoulder and took a deep breath. My heart stopped. The world had too until the crack of the rifle split the air and echoed through the bluffs.

The buck staggered 10 feet or so before he finally succumbed to the bullet and fell. "Great shot!" my dad yelled. With the sound of his voice, I realized that he had been there the whole time. He hadn't missed it.

We didn't say too much on the way down to the buck. We didn't have to. My real satisfaction was in the way I got him. A successful stalk.

My trophy weighed 115 pounds. The ebony horns were 14 inches long each. I could not imagine a greater thrill. I had done it the way it was supposed to be; and I was proud.

# MBOGO

Not a really big Cape buffalo, but this one is too close and could mean trouble.

# The Cape Buffalo

by ERWIN A. BAUER

AT FIRST THE TRAIL from the waterhole was as clearly marked as a busy state highway. The hoofprints of 100 buffalo were etched so deeply in the soft earth that a blind man could have followed them. But not for long. When the buffalo highway eventually reached high ground—and dense bush—the animals seemed to scatter.

Now narrow trails led in all directions, and some of them were nothing more than leafy tunnels through thornbush. Keith Cormack, Ed Frecker, Nderobo tracker Peeno and I selected one trail on which the dung was very fresh, and we followed it. Cormack held a finger to his lips to indicate we should travel in silence. I saw Ed double-check to see that he had a cartridge in the chamber of his .458.

Already a hot and muggy morning in the Ruhembe Valley of central Tanzania, it grew hotter and muggier as the minutes passed. Soon I was wringing-wet with

For another hour, and who knows how far, we followed the narrow trail. Suspense and tension built up. Now and then a slight breeze stirred and luckily it was always in our favor. Occasionally we had glimpses of black hide ahead of us—enough glimpses to know that there were three or four buffs and that they were big. Then all at once Peeno dropped to his knees and pointed straight ahead.

Not 25 yards away the ugly snout of a bull Cape buffalo was facing us.

Right away Ed Frecker also dropped to his knees and for an instant seemed to have trouble finding the target in his open iron sights. Finally he squeezed—and *blam!* In the same split second the buff wheeled about and was gone. We could hear him crashing through the bush.

"He's hit," Keith said.

For several minutes we simply stood and listened. The shot had spooked other buffalo and for awhile we

This splended Cape buffalo is an outstanding trophy. The heavy black horns exceed 5-foot spread.

sweat, and I had to keep changing my camera from one hand to the other to keep moisture from its innards. The bush all around us had the dank smell of buffalo as we pushed along in single file.

We'd covered maybe a mile when the column stopped and Keith pointed into the brush ahead. First there was only the sound of movement. Then I heard a snort and blowing noises. Finally I could see gleaming black hide through the dense screen of brush before us.

My pulse quickened. For a long time we stood motionless straining to see if the wide, curving horns of a bull were attached to the hide—but then it slowly evaporated into its background. Again we followed slowly. When we reached a large termite mound, Peeno climbed onto the top of it for a better view ahead, but it wasn't any use. We continued the tracking on foot, always trying to see ahead.

could hear them running all around, particularly to our right. Finally, it was quiet, and we walked ahead to the place where the target bull had been standing. Not far away was a pool of blood. Beyond it began a clear trail of foamy blood. "Lung shot," Cormack whispered.

Without another word we began trailing the wounded animal. In such dense bush—or in fact, anywhere—it is not a chore to be relished. I wished desperately I could trade my camera for a high-powered rifle.

We did not have too far to follow. But it was slow and cautious going. Perhaps ¼-mile beyond the first pool of blood, we came to a thicket where it was difficult to see as far as 10 yards ahead. Suddenly there was the buff again, facing us and trying to come after us. But the brute was already hurt badly, and a second shot put him down for keeps.

At last the pressure of the entire tense morning was

off. Ed had bagged a fine trophy. Even though I hadn't been actually hunting, I had to cope with a slight case of unsteady hands before I could shoot Ed's picture with the kill. It was a moment to be remembered.

In many ways it had been a typical hunt for one of the world's great game animals—at least, for an animal that is potentially among the most dangerous. The Cape buffalo is also the most abundant of the world's dangerous animals, and virtually no African safari ever organized has failed to include a buffalo hunt. Sometimes the hunt is easy, and the hunter simply rides out and selects his animal as if he were picking the bull from a herd of dairy cattle. But other times it isn't so easy. It may add up to days of trudging through nightmare bush with a final encounter that leaves the hunter limp. The one certain thing that can be said about buffalo hunting is that it is completely unpredictable.

The first European settlers in both East and South Africa found the veld—the plains and bush country—inhabited by huge herds of what they believed to be wild oxen, but which were Cape or southern, buffalo. It is estimated that their total number on the continent then exceeded 10 million. There was some attempt by early settlers to domesticate the buffs, but mostly it was a losing proposition. They shot and ate them instead.

An adult male buffalo is a most impressive, muscular beast which will weigh a ton. It is heavy of build and has a short, sinewy neck; large, flapping ears; a broad, naked muzzle and a thick-skinned body with coarse black hair. With age the hair becomes more sparse.

Both sexes have well-developed horns, but both the boss and the spread of horns are much larger on the male. Altogether it is a formidable and sullen, if not a downright evil-looking animal.

Buffs are very gregarious and often congregate in herds of several hundred. But two or more of the older, larger bulls may separate from the herd to live lonely bachelor lives. They are hardy and can survive in almost any kind of habitat from damp lowlands to high mountain meadows as long as water is available nearby. Buffs drink twice daily—perhaps nightly where hunting pressure is heavy—and sources of water are good places to find them. They like to loll and wallow in water as well as to drink it.

Early in the year cow buffalo drop single calves after a gestation period of about 10 months. The calves may reach 30 years of age, but average life expectancy is shorter than that. The buff's only natural enemies are lions, humans and disease. In many parts of Africa, lions become highly addicted to buffalo heifers and calves and will even take an occasional large bull. The tree-climbing lions of Lake Manyara National Park in Tanzania subsist largely on buffs and do not hesitate at all to tackle the biggest males. On one filming expedition there, I came across the carcass of a bull only recently killed by a pride of eight lions. Judging from the great size of the horns, it had been a huge, healthy, male animal.

Disease has often been a factor in buffalo popula-

Spend much time hunting in buffalo country of Africa and you're certain to meet elephants in the dense brush.

are harvestable surplus anyway. But when lands must be cleared for agriculture, *all* the buffs thereon must be eliminated. They are not compatible with fences and succulent crops.

Viewing the peaceful herds of buffs in Africa's national parks can be a disarming experience. There the animals graze placidly in the sun and usually seem to stare at passing Land Cruisers with utter lack of interest. But not always. Last year without any provocation and without any warning, a buff repeatedly rammed a carload of German tourists in Tsavo National Park until the animal could barely stagger away from the encounter. The car was ruined, its fenders ripped off, and the occupants badly shaken.

On another occasion, at Lake Manyara, a solitary bull made a chilling rush toward our Land Cruiser on a grassy flat, but veered away at the last moment. Two friends and professional hunters, Neil Millar (formerly of Tanzania Wildlife Safaris) and Brian Herne (formally of Uganda Wildlife Development) have had their Land Rovers unaccountably rammed by bulls in open hunting area. Herne's car was damaged to such an extent that it had to be traded for a new one.

Still, opinions differ widely as to whether buffs are very dangerous or not. A few professional hunters treat them lightly and (perhaps it's only bragadoccio) consider them no more dangerous than small antelope. But most have great respect for them. The late John Hunter, one of the best-known and most persistent of East African professionals, believed that only lions and leopards are more dangerous—and only because both cats are faster afoot and much smaller targets for a rifleman when charging.

The buffalo to fear is the wounded one. That point cannot be emphasized enough. If the first shot is well placed in a vital spot, it can be all over quickly. But often a wound seems to add to a buff's already tremendous vitality, and then a whole series of well-placed shots may not put the critter down permanently. That's when trouble develops.

Wounded buffs have often been credited with circling about and attempting to ambush the pursuer. Apparently this does happen, and it appeared that my first buff tried this tactic on me. The bull was hit too far back on the first shot for an instantly fatal hit, so we followed the blood trail for about 700 yards. At that point we had to cross a small bushy brook. As we reached the other side, some sixth sense caused us to look back. There stood the bull behind us: unsteady—but trying to get up momentum for a rush.

I have been on a number of buffalo hunts and do not share the belief that they are unexciting. On all but one there was plenty of action—if not from the quarry then from elephants which interdicted our stalking and other complications. Stalking buffs in heavy bush will always start the adrenaline flowing.

One buffalo hunt I will never forget was that one for

Speaking of trouble, this buff has one horn broken off and his eye on the opposite side has been torn from its socket. Maybe by a lion? But give this one a wide berth anyway.

tions. During the 1890s there was a disastrous outbreak of rinderpest among domestic animals in northeast Africa. Quickly it spread to the nearest buffalo, then swept southward all the way to the Cape of Good Hope. In East Africa the plague was so severe that only one buff (it was estimated at the time) of every 10,000 animals survived. But the survivors were tough and had developed resistance to rinderpest. By 1912 herds were figured to be back to normal again, and biologists believe that between 2 and 3 million buffalo exist today.

Human beings—though not big game trophy hunters—are the principal threat to the buff's survival in the future. Sportsmen crop only the biggest bulls, which

Cape buffalo taken in Tanzania several years ago. Recently, after a closure, hunting has opened again.

which I had a ringside seat atop a Land Rover. My son Bob, then only 15, was the hunter, and his guide was Brian Herne. The place was Uganda's beautiful, game-filled Semliki Valley.

We had spotted a herd of about 100 animals scattered over a wide area around a small mudhole. Although some of the buffs were lying down and a few were even wallowing in the mud, many appeared restless. After studying the animals for a long time through glasses, Brian spotted an unusually fine buff head on the side of the herd nearest to us. The herd was upwind, so Brian and Bob began the stalk while I climbed on top of the car to watch through binoculars.

It appeared to be an easy proposition—in the beginning. But things began to go wrong. While crouching low to take advantage of tall grass during the approach, the hunters did not see the bull move to a position on the far side of the herd. And when they finally stood up behind a tree trunk to look around, they found themselves almost completely surrounded by milling animals with the target bull all but hidden behind several cows. There was nothing to do but stand in place and wait—and hope they could climb the tree quickly enough if it became necessary.

Ten—15—20 minutes passed, and the herd seemed to relax. But the bull remained hidden. Waiting was tense enough for Brian, but how about the father watching his son surrounded by African buffalo. Suddenly something, perhaps a vagrant breeze, spooked a cow, and there followed a chain reaction. Suddenly the whole herd was on foot again and milling uncertainly. But that gave Bob the opening he needed.

For an instant the bull was out in the open, broadside. Too soon, a cow stepped in front of him; but only for a moment. When the bull strolled free again, Bob's sights were on the shoulder, and he squeezed.

At the shot, buffs exploded in all directions, but mostly in the direction of the Congo—the target bull included. A cloud of dust swirled around the hunters, and I lost them from view. Even from a distance I could hear the thunder of hoofs.

Bob's bull had been hit solidly, but not enough to anchor it on the spot. Instead, it ran off with the herd; and that was a bad turn, because the blood trail was all but obliterated by the other fleeing animals. Luckily, the bull was too sick to follow indefinitely at top speed, and so it turned off on its own path. Domenico, our Acholi tracker, saw it veer away. Two more shots by Bob in a dense thicket ended the hunt—and none too soon for an anxious parent.

It's necessary to actually see how much lead a buffalo can carry to believe it. Bob's first shot, which entered just behind one shoulder, caused terrible internal damage and would have dropped almost any other animal right on the spot. This one galloped away at full speed and for some distance as if not hit at all by a 300-grain bullet from a .375 Holland and Holland Magnum.

A head-on charge is a fearsome thing to see, and buff charges through the years have helped to fill both hospitals and graveyards. Most professional hunters agree that charging elephants and rhinos will be turned away by shots that do not kill them. But buffs keep coming on relentlessly, with head extended (not down, as occasionally stated) and zeroed in on the target. If the victim is knocked down or tossed, the buff invariably returns to gore and trample him.

Rhinos and elephants have good hearing and good scenting power, but lack good vision. Lions and leopards have good eyesight and excellent hearing but, at least for carnivores, only fair scenting ability. All of these senses are very keen in buffalo. The only weakness, probably is a lack of rapid acceleration. Some distance is required before a buff reaches top speed.

Rowland Ward, the London custodian of African big game records, divides African buffalo into three categories for scoring purposes: southern, or Cape, buffalo; Nile buffalo and dwarf buffalo. The first category covers all those from Kenya, Uganda and Tanzania southward through Zambia, Rhodesia and Mozambique, although few still remain south of the Zambezi River. Nile buffs cover the country of Chad and the eastern part of the Central African Republic eastward across southern Sudan to Ethiopia and southward along the Nile valley to Lake Kivu. The dwarf buffalo inhabits forest and marginal forest areas from Angola northward through the Congo, Gabon, Cameroons, Nigeria and Senegal.

The East African animals are the biggest in both body size and mass of horns. The largest bull of which there is record was bagged in northern Tanganyika (now Tanzania) in 1951 by Andy Holmberg, a well-known professional hunter, while he was on a postman's holiday. The overall spread of horns was 58 inches. The length along the front curve of one horn was 49 inches.

A female with a spread of 64 inches was collected in Tanganyika in 1946; but this must be considered a freak, because the breadth of palm, or boss, was only 7 inches. In other words, the cow had strange long, thin horns which were not typical of the species.

Because of their present abundance and widespread distribution, buffs could furnish good hunting for a longer time than other members of Africa's "big game." Rhinos are protected everywhere nowadays. Elephant hunting is finished, too. Leopards have greatly decreased in numbers, and lion aren't numerous anywhere any more except in national parks.

Where is the best place to bag a buffalo? Probably in Tanzania where the animals are often plentiful enough to constitute a nuisance and where control programs around farms and settlements are sometimes necessary. But there are also plenty of big bulls in Sudan, one of the few African countries where hunting is still permitted. In any case, Mbogo, the Cape buffalo, is by far the African hunter's best bet for the future.

# FLOAT FOR GAME

## by TOM HARDIN

**ON THE WALL OF MY DEN** and workshop is a yellowed old engraving called, "Chippewas Hunting on the Michigamme." It shows a pair of redskins drifting downstream in a birch-bark canoe covered with hides and reeds. Just below them is the quarry—a flock of geese. Although it represents a Michigan incident, the scene could have been the Muskingum or the Flambeau, the St. Lawrence or the Missouri, the Caloosanhatchee or the Quinault. They could have been hunting anything from canvasbacks to crocodiles, from muskrats to moose, because floating once was one of the Indian's deadliest methods of collecting calories for the tepee. Fact is, it's still one of the most deadly.

There is no more quiet way, no more stealthy way to travel through hunting country than to drift the rivers. With boat, canoe or rubber raft it's possible to cover a wider area than on foot—more quickly and in greater comfort. And the drier the season, the more advantages there are in taking to the water.

I remember one fall in Michigan when it was especially dry and when deer were especially nervous. Hunting pressure had been heavy, and the deer had retreated into the densest cover in the region—the swamp and deadfall areas along Big Indian River. We hunted diligently in there, found plenty of signs, but didn't even see a deer. Travel was too tedious and too noisy. In some places it was impossible. The season had only 2 days to run when someone suggested we take the river route through that evergreen jungle.

At daybreak two of us pushed off downstream in a canoe. By noon we'd collected a forkhorn buck and had seen several other deer—one standing in the water. Two other hunters made the float the next day, missed a deer, but bagged a black bear instead. Dozens of ducks were flushed on both trips. It was a lesson in hunting we've used many times since.

Although it's possible to float-hunt for virtually any

It is possible to hunt for a wide variety of game by floating rivers. Even bear hunting should not be overlooked.

type of game, squirrels are among the most accessible animals. Squirrel seasons in many states begin in late summer or early fall—at precisely the times the woods are most crisp and noisy. But find a waterway that passes through them, and you've found a system to consistently take a limit of squirrels.

Floating for squirrels has a charm all its own. It's a matter of drifting quietly and leisurely and of listening for the telltale sounds the critters make—barking, rustling the bright foilage along the stream or cutting on fall's new crop of nuts. This isn't always the best way for riflemen because neither a boat nor a canoe is the best foundation for pinpoint shooting at tiny jittery targets. A shotgun is by far the best bet.

One of the finest squirrel hunters I know makes steady use of an old canvas canoe, but he uses it more to reach the best woods than actually as a hunting vehicle. Before the season opens, he explores along his favorite rivers to survey the mast crop. When he finds sections full of nuts or squirrel sign he marks them well in his memory. After opening day he uses the canoe to drift to these places, one by one. Near each patch of timber, he climbs ashore, still-hunts for a while and then drifts to the next place.

Woodchucks are also susceptible to float-hunting because of certain habits of the animals. First, they like to build dens in the high earth-banks of many streams. Second, they like to spend autumn afternoons resting in

well camouflaged, much more carefully than for any other type of hunting. The simplest and most effective camouflage is always handy: Use available native materials and arrange them so the boat looks as much like a floating pile of debris as possible. When the boat is metal or has a shiny finish it's a wise waterfowler who covers the gunwales with discarded burlap bags. River-bank mud is also useful in hiding shiny spots.

All camouflage material should be lashed or fastened securely to the boat. Otherwise it can quickly work free in a high wind, when passing beneath brushy banks or when dragging the boat over deadfalls and shallow riffles. Extra oarlocks can be used for upright pieces, and to these other material can be fastened. A roll of Manila cord is fine to tie camouflage in place.

Occasionally it's possible to drift within easy scatter-gun range of ducks, but not always. It becomes more difficult toward the tag end of the season. When the stream is very winding, keep to the insides of bends

Wildly flushing waterfowl is a common, and exciting spectacle when floaters suddenly round a bend.

the sun near these same dens. They often provide an extra dividend for river squirrel hunters who find the most action early and late in the day. That leaves the middle of the day to concentrate on chucks.

The most obvious floating is for waterfowl, and it's certainly one of the most lively. Catch the ducks during the peaks of migrations or when their resting places on lakes and ponds have been frozen over (then they'll concentrate on rivers), and you have the ingredients for a trip with few dull moments.

The type of craft that's used isn't too important, but the more shallow its draft and the easier it is to guide with a single paddle, the better. Of course, it must be

and watch for ducks to flush from just below a bend—usually a patch of quiet water. If the stream is open, relatively straight and the ducks have been hunted hard, other tactics are necessary.

Several years ago conservation officers broke up a ring of market duck hunters in the Midwest. One method the lawbreakers used was to quietly drift the rivers and to potshoot ducks when they found them, in unbelievable numbers. Somewhat revised, their basic method of float-hunting can be employed by sportsmen—like this:

Drift the current as easily as possible until ducks are spotted far ahead. Field glasses are a big help in this. As

Consider a combination trip, as here for ducks, pheasants
and trout on the Missouri River.

soon as you see them, pull into the nearest bank. One
hunter should disembark and then make a wide and
cautious circle inland to reach a place below the ducks.
When he's had time to accomplish that, the other hunter
resumes the float downstream. If all goes well, the
ducks will be sandwiched in between and one hunter
will get shooting, either on the flush or as the birds pass
in full flight.

There's another possibility when three hunters are
involved that can be called "leapfrogging." This eliminates the use of two cars to pick up the boat at the end of
each float, and makes for a more pleasant hunt. While
the two hunters drift downstream, another drives to the
first bridge below to wait with the car. Perhaps he brews
a pot of coffee for all of them while he waits. When they
arrive, places are exchanged and another hunter takes
the car to the next bridge. It's premium hunting.

River waterfowlers should keep a couple of important facts in mind: Watch with an especially wary
eye just below riffles for ducks. It's hard to say why, but
often they do loiter there. Be alert when approaching
the lower ends of sand and mud bars; both ducks and
geese like these spots. In addition always have a patch-
ing kit for your boat or canoe, for float-hunting can
develop some sudden emergencies.

Float-hunting can be productive because cover is
usually more dense and more lush along waterways
than anywhere else. In highly developed lands, for instance, it's difficult to plow very near to the water's
edge, and thick vegetation results. Of course, this is
good wildlife cover—maybe the best in the whole region. While it's difficult to make a quiet approach from
the land side, a drifting sportsman can get close to any
game this cover contains—if he goes slowly enough.
That's important when stalking *any* kind of game.

Other good advice is to keep to the shadows as much
as possible. Any object drifting with a current is visible
for a longer distance in the sunlight—which also focuses

on any flaws in the camouflage.

Perhaps America' growing band of archers can best
benefit from floating, for of all hunters they depend the
most on a quiet approach for a killing shot. Last season
bad breaks kept a team of Ohio archers from drifting
into almost boxing glove range of a trophy buck. About
40 feet away, the aluminum canoe scraped against the
pebbles of a shallow riffle, and the deer bolted. In
addition to the experience, the hunters returned with a
pair of grouse. They stand a good chance to score on
deer this year.

Floating makes many extra bonuses possible for a
hunter. He can carry a camera, for example, and extra

A sheet of camouflage cloth or netting can help conceal a
hunter when drifting on waterfowl.

Ontario deer hunters have taken a good deer by quiet approach in a canoe.

clothing that would otherwise be a burden. A rainsuit or an extra shirt fits easily under a canoe seat. We've always made it a policy to have a good meal while floating, because a coffee pot, a roll of aluminum foil, charcoal and a few necessary ingredients don't weigh a thing if you don't have to carry them.

On various trips we've gathered watercress for a salad from the very stream we floated. We've picked paw-paws, hazelnuts and hard October apples for dessert. We've broiled grouse and doves over streamside willow fires. We've had hot soup on raw duck-hunting days and have sipped tea cooled in the current on squirrel-hunting trips; and we've had fresh fried fish, too.

In many sections of the land hunting and fishing seasons overlap. Certainly this is another break for the float-hunter. Fall runs of rainbows often coincide with gunning seasons, and the smallmouth bass in rivers are also most active when the leaves begin to fall. Muskies are on the prod, too. It's wonderful if you can combine hunting and fishing—and here's a perfect way to do it.

There are no limits to the possibilities of floating, really. I've drifted to within a paddle-length of moose on Manitoba rivers, and there's no reason why a canoe wouldn't be almost as valuable as a rifle during the bugling season. Drift a distance and stop to bugle, drift and bugle and so on. Moose naturally stay close to water, and a float-hunter could plan on always being within hearing of rutting bulls.

On the other hand, such small critters as frogs and turtles—even snipe and woodcock—could be hunted while traveling the rivers. Frogging is strictly an after-dark proposition and a sportsman needs a spotlight

rather than camouflage. Still, it's an exciting proposition. It's wise to check the legal weapons in your state, though, because in some places firearms are not permitted. This is a fertile field for archers to try, however.

What boat for float-hunting? In most cases, without a doubt, a canoe is the best bet. It's easy to maneuver, it's noiseless to paddle and on an average float it will cover a greater distance. But a canoe is always more fragile and not quite so comfortable as a larger rowboat—which means a canoe isn't the best for negotiating turbulent or dangerous water. Since it's more confining for its occupants, a canoe shouldn't be used for very lengthy trips in cold weather. Cold always becomes more unpleasant to a person cramped by being unable to move about just a little.

The chief advantage of the rowboat is its sturdy construction and its capacity. It's more difficult to guide than a canoe, though, and the flashing of oars is easily spotted far away. It's also noisy.

Many of the pioneer float-hunters have imitated the fishermen who float the wild rivers of the West—with inflatable rubber rafts or surplus army pontoons. Where the current is swift and steady these are suitable, but they're clumsy and difficult to paddle through stretches of dead or still water. They are durable and have the most shallow draft of all.

Recently, many collapsible boats have appeared on the market. These may work very well for floating, but they still need testing.

Float-hunting is an old, even a traditional, method to put game on the table. It's a way to score when normal methods fail. And it may be just the answer to your special hunting problem.

Natural brush and burlap is being used by these Midwest hunters to sneak on ducks.

241

# DOGGIN' DEER

### by GERALD R. HUNTER

Happy ending to a deer hunt with dogs. Field dressed small southern whitetails can be carried by a single hunter.

Sounding the hunting horn is a practice dating back centuries.

**WHEN I WAS GROWING UP** in Brooks County, there were no deer in south Georgia. Therefore, I was always excited when I heard that our local deer hunters were returning from a hunting trip to Nutall Rise, Florida. I would run down to the market where Audley Clanton, Morris Walker and other members of their club brought the carcasses to be dressed. While I listened to the stories of how their hounds had chased the deer into the river or lost the track of a big buck, I would pat the sleek coats of those wondrous 60- and 70-pound does or the occasional spike buck.

That was many years before the whitetail appeared in my part of south Georgia. However, the bug bit me at an early age, and I was determined to take part in the excitement of hunting with hounds. As soon as the adult hunters felt I was safe with a gun, I went whenever and wherever I could. During some 20 years, I learned enough about hunting deer with dogs to be elected, in 1953, as president of a deer hunting club (Middleton Lake Hunting Club). This was a position I held for more than 20 years before turning over the reins to younger blood. So, I feel qualified to write on this fascinating subject. (Middleton Lake, incidentally, is still in operation and is growing; it is one of the oldest, most active clubs in the Georgia Wildlife Federation.)

There are many important factors to consider when deer hunting with dogs. Organization, experience and planning certainly rank near the top.

It is almost impossible to successfully hunt deer with dogs unless you at least have a cadre of hunters who know what they're doing. This type of hunting can be more complicated than first appears. It can be done by one person or by hundreds if adequately organized.

I have hunted deer alone with one or two hounds; in such a case, you either get a jump shot, or you wait patiently until the race circles erratically and brings the deer back into range.

On the other hand, I have hunted with (and been chief deerskinner for) Gil Pirrung of Decatur County when more than 200 hunters were out on four "drifts" ahead of as many as eight packs of hounds. But the most successful hunting is done with a single pack of hounds and a group of 10 to 20 "standers." In any event, all members of the hunt, whether veteran or novice, must understand and comply with the rules of the game.

Typically, an area which is bounded by trails, firebreaks or woods roads is selected, and the huntmaster assigns the stands. These "stands" are not tree stands; they are merely locations at strategic spots. They may be numbered, but usually, they are merely assigned by name, such as the "black stump" stand or "turkey ridge" or the "sawgrass flat." Except among veteran hunters who have established full rapport, standers are not to move more than 50 yards off their specific stands for safety reasons. The huntmaster places the standers so they are in position a few minutes before the master of hounds releases the dogs.

When more than one or two hunters are afield with hounds, success depends on everyone understanding and complying with the rules of the game.

Most dogs hunt silently until they find a fresh track, which is signalled by a long bawl. Standers now prepare themselves for the chase they hope to come. When a dog jumps the deer, it signals with a short bawl that usually erupts into a sharp, hard chop, at which time other hounds in the pack, whether casting nearby or off at a distance, pick up the music and join in the race.

This is the time for the stander to face the music, remain motionless and keep his eyes peeled because there is no way to tell how far ahead of the dogs the deer may be. I have had dogs chopping wide open to within gun range before the deer broke cover. I have also killed and completely field dressed deer on drives before ever hearing the sound of the race. Most of the time the deer will run ¼-mile to ½-mile ahead of the pack.

When you see the deer, remain motionless. It doesn't even matter how you are clad if you stay perfectly still. Since the deer is moving, he can't resolve details and will reverse directions only if he sees a quick motion or gets a sharp scent of man. The harder the deer is pushed, the less likely he is to notice you. On the other hand, if the deer is far ahead of the dogs, he will stop frequently to scent the air, look back over his shoulder and spot you if you don't behave.

Always shoot the deer in the front half. Inexperienced hunters usually don't lead the animal enough, resulting in a hit too far to the rear. A front-end shot will more likely strike the vitals and drop the deer in his tracks or at least within a few yards. Even if the front-hit deer runs off for a distance, the dogs can usually follow it up quickly instead of spending all morning chasing a wounded deer.

In this type of hunting, it is important to immediately field dress and cool out your animal because the deer has been run by dogs and is heated up and full of adrenalin.

Huntmasters often give the standers special instructions on what to do if they kill a deer or even if they miss a deer. When you kill a deer, the dogs will show up at the site. If you are comfortable handling dogs, some

Woe be to the hunter who misses the shot. Failure is traditionally punished by having the shirttail cut off.

huntmasters like for you to try to catch the first (lead) dogs that show up, tie them up and wait for the huntmaster. This way the dogs can be started on a new drive. If you miss the deer, a huntmaster usually likes for you to wait beside its trail and try to catch the lead dogs. Of course, whether you are to catch them or let them pass will depend upon the terrain and whether there are other standers beyond you. If letting them pass would result in running the deer into a river or hopeless swamp where the dogs will be lost for hours, try to catch them by all means. Incidentally, deer hounds are usually docile. However, if a dog snaps at you or otherwise indicates hostility, use common sense.

When assigned to a stand, stay on it and do not leave for any reason until the huntmaster or a designee picks you up. If you are to return to camp or to another pickup spot alone, you should receive prior instructions. The only exceptions to the previous statement are the "cutoff" men who, when standers are too widely separated, may be permitted to run like wildfire to get ahead of a buck which otherwise might escape between standers. But, these people must be clearly designated before the hunt.

Guns used when hunting deer with dogs may be shotguns or rifles, provided that the management doesn't prohibit rifles, and provided that you know exactly what your shotgun will do. In my opinion, it is a crime against nature for someone to take a deer stand with a buckshot-loaded gun unless he knows how far its effective range is. At any rate, the gun should throw a lethal pattern at whatever range you shoot. Otherwise, unless you miss entirely, you are certain to cripple a noble animal that deserves better. Even if you eventually find a wounded deer, the hunt is likely to be held up for hours.

Deer dogs can be of any breed or mixture of breeds which will successfully run deer, and I've seen some unlikely combinations. But, most deer hunting is done with purebred hounds, chiefly Walker hounds and beagles, although you will see a lot of redbones, black-and-tans and some bluetickks.

For the sheer fun of it, I prefer Walker hounds because they make lovely music. Their drawback is that they are too fast; if a stander misses his buck, the Walkers will likely run the deer into a river, the next county or into the next state. I have hunted mostly with Walkers, and it was with such hounds that I experienced a unique situation. It was the only time I ever saw a pair of hounds *leading* the buck! It was while hunting with Dr. Homer Wells' "old Blue" and Dr. Ian Forbes' "Brucie," on Turkey Ridge in the Altamaha Swamp. This is what happened: The hounds took a shortcut around a knoll, and when they and the deer came out, the dogs were just ahead of the buck and so nearly in line that I could not shoot.

Probably the most effective deer hounds are beagles.

Cool humid mornings are the best time to hunt with hounds. A late start may result in a chase which lasts until nightfall.

They don't get the deer too excited. The deer can keep a slow lead, and split and circle without worrying about having his hamstrings cut by the little fellows. Such a race, while not as exhilarating, gives the standers a much better chance for a shot.

For those interested in using dogs to run deer but lack experience with this technique, there are a couple of other things to keep in mind. There isn't much use in putting your dog or dogs out unless you find fresh deer tracks. A few deer will make a heap of tracks, and deer don't range far, particularly in the early part of the season when food is plentiful. You don't have to start your dog on a specific track, although it's a good idea to start him off on a good, big, fresh track if you can.

The best deer hunting is on a cool, humid morning. The scent is more durable, and the dogs can smell better. A hot, dry afternoon is a poor choice.

Finally, it is still a good rule of thumb in most areas where hunting with dogs is allowed that "bucks run the ridges, does run the hollows." There are always exceptions, but exceptions are hard to fry, roast or broil.

Still-hunting for deer may be a far greater challenge than hunting them with dogs. But, there's nothing like facing a wide-open pack of howling Walker hounds that are threatening to push a deer out on you at any moment to raise your blood pressure and get your adrenalin flowing. If you can entirely ignore buck fever under such a situation, you're a cool-headed hunter or the thrill of the hunt has left you—in which case, you need to stay at home anyway.

## by ERWIN A. BAUER

A WANDERING WATERFOWLER might travel completely across America and never find more action than in western Kentucky in late November. I'm speaking now of the vast and soggy bottomlands where the Ohio River empties into the Mississippi, a region laced with murky oxbows and dense swamps. It is astride the main artery of the Mississippi Flyway, and ducks have been stopping there enroute southward long before there were hunters to intercept them.

Nowadays the west end of the Bluegrass State is also a major refueling point for Canada geese. I saw it first hand on a bitter day toward the tag end of the open season last fall. The specific place was the state-owned Ballard Waterfowl Area. It covers 6,000 acres near LaCenter, which is merely a crossroads on most road maps, and is due west of Paducah.

There had been a series of Indian-summer days with not much doing; a few odd birds in the bag and nothing more. But when Barton "Red" Bagley (who is a dean of goose hunters thereabouts), learned of the storm front racing across Missouri, he called me on the phone. "The honkers will be moving tomorrow," was all he needed to say to get me started.

Before daybreak the next morning we were crouched in a pit blind barely big enough for two. Even though a raw wind whistled around our heads and rain changed to sleet, it was warm in the beginning because we had to slog ¼-mile or so through the muck of a picked cornfield to reach the blind.

But gradually the cold began to penetrate heavy clothing and several pairs of socks inside hip boots. I shivered as I tried to look beyond a spread of decoys into the zero visibility beyond. The wind carried the voices of hunters from the nearest blind, and I saw the brief flicker of somebody lighting a cigarette. Then Red glanced at his watch.

Author crouches in pit blind and peers through screen of sagebrush in Idaho.

# This Year Become

"Just a few minutes until legal shooting time," he said.

Both war and goose hunting has been described as prolonged periods of great anxiety followed by sudden action. That wasn't the case this morning. There was no long wait. Even above the whine of the wind we soon heard the klaxon call of Canada geese coming from far away, and then it wasn't cold anymore.

Although we couldn't see them, we could tell that the birds were low and that they were winging our way. Still the odds of getting a shot were not great because at any minute they might pass over another of the blinds located in the area. Now the time passed in slow motion; perhaps because of the shifting current of wind we couldn't hear the geese at all. Buck fever. No—goose pimples. I flipped and reflipped the safety on my double.

Then suddenly a dozen big Canadas were right over the top of us and settling down. For an instant I simply couldn't react. Now the honkers spotted us and started to flare. That did it, and both Red and I were on our feet and firing. Birds fought to gain altitude and get out of there.

Exactly what followed in the next few seconds isn't clear and never was. But it makes no difference because four geese were down and Red was engaged in a foot-race to catch the fourth which was only winged. My partner won, but not easily, and it is a shame I do not have the victory over a muddy course on motion picture film. It would be hilarious.

"This has to be the shortest goose hunt of my life," I commented when things had settled down. Then we left the blind and trudged toward a potbellied stove at the area headquarters, where other happy hunters were gathering.

Last fall more American goose hunters enjoyed more happy experiences such as mine all across the country than they have in many years. And the reason is very

Canada geese seem slow on the wing, but that is deceptive.

# a Goose Hunter

Flock of six honkers passes close enough to decoys to give hunter in the blind a shot.

Usually the first flights come in before sunrise. The wise goose hunter is in his blind well before then.

basic—there are more Canada geese and hunting is better. This fall, goose hunters can expect even more improvement.

The future of all of our shooting sports, sadly, is not especially bright. Americans have not been the best conservationists; both shooting space and the quality of shooting are constantly diminishing. Duck hunting particularly is on a slow downgrade because the best wintering areas (and many good wetlands in between) are being drained or polluted or claimed for other nonsporting development. But by contrast, goose hunting in North America has one of the brightest futures of all kinds of hunting.

There are a number of reasons for this. First, Canada geese can be *managed* by wildlife biologists. The birds can be concentrated into fall and winter flocks—and then the annual harvest can be scientifically regulated so that both a high population and good shooting can be maintained, hopefully forever. More about that point later.

Another factor in the Canada goose's favor is that most of the species' traditional nesting grounds are so far north and in such remote places that they are not yet in any danger of exploitation. In addition, the honkers have been induced to nest in numbers of managed wildlife areas in the United States. In other words, few other sportsmen have it so good as goose hunters do today.

A good experienced caller can coax geese within good shooting range.

(Above) Sometimes a few goose decoys among the duck decoys will provide mixed bag gunning.

(Left) A sunset scene every serious goose hunter will recognize. Soon shooting will be finished for the day.

How does the American sportsman get in on the bonanza? It's simply a matter of going where the geese are. And there are many ways and places to do it.

Just for the record, the designated "Canada goose" includes several closely related subspecies which are alike in appearance but differ in size from the 3½-pound-average Richardson's goose through the cackler, the lesser Canada and the common Canada which runs about 8 or 9 pounds. The now rare greater Canadas are even bigger. All are distinctive from other geese by their black necks and white cheeks.

As soon as all the Canadas leave the northern nesting grounds, which are scattered irregularly across the roof of the continent from Alaska to Labrador, they follow ages-old flyways southward. Depending on many factors both known and unknown, the Canadas pause at places (which have been called "gathering grounds") along the way. These are probably "refueling spots," and how long they stay will depend on weather, on available food supply and on the physical ability of young birds to attempt a really long migration flight. The first gathering places (south of nesting areas), usually are tundra flats or sub-arctic grasslands, have long been traditional hunting spots of the northern Indians and Eskimos.

During the past decade or so, more and more sportsmen have been joining local hunters for the splendid hunting which exists here. Nowadays, for example, a number of excellent goose-hunting camps have been set up on the shores of James and Hudson flyways where vast numbers of geese collect in September and October to refuel before pushing on toward warmer altitudes. Most of these camps are either owned, operated or at least partially staffed by local Indians. They are many waterfowlers' best chance of getting the brand of shooting which greatgrandpa knew elsewhere.

On a map of northern Ontario, run your finger northwestward from James Bay along the shore of Hudson Bay near the Manitoba boundary. Below there at the mouth of the Winisk River is an abandoned (after World War II) R.C.A.F. air base near the Indian village of Winisk. What remains of the base now serves as headquarters for a typical hunting camp. Visiting sportsmen sleep in the old noncom barracks, eat meals in a deserted mess hall and are guided to the splendid goose hunting all around by Indian guides. Indian ladies dress the geese for taking home. The whole package is unique and well worth the money.

What does such a hunt cost? From Toronto or Windsor, the tab runs about $450 to $600 (all-expense except liquor, tips and ammo) for 5 days and 4 full days of shooting. The gunning is invariably good, but at certain times it's so great that it isn't necessary to spend much time in the blinds. Hunters also get blue and snow geese and ducks.

But probably 90 percent of all goose hunting will be

Hunter carries nesting series of portable decoys into the field. Heads must be affixed to the bodies.

Cardboard snow goose decoys can be set up in the field.

done after the migrating honkers have approached closer to their southern wintering areas or have actually arrived on them. Some of these are areas which the big birds have used year after year for centuries. Others are newly established by waterfowl managers in recent years. The gunning can be very good around both. Here's how it works.

The nucleus of a Canada-goose wintering or management area is a fairly large body of water which is by necessity a refuge (federal, state or private). No shooting is permitted right on the refuge water, so that the geese soon recognize it as an absolutely safe sanctuary. Sometimes the birds are artificially fed grain to hold them there. But shooting is permitted a safe distance beyond the water as the birds fly out once or twice daily to feed. Normally the flights are made early and late in the day. But winds, atmospheric conditions or very bad weather may cause them to fly at midday or even all day long. It is the hunter's strategy to be waiting in blinds where the geese are likely to feed.

Let's assume you are a beginner; you have never hunted geese, but want to try it for the first time this fall. First find out if there are any goose flocks nearby—or *which* goose flock is the handiest. If you do not already have knowledge of this, check with the state fish-and-game department, with the local game warden or perhaps with the outdoor editor or columnist in your local newspaper.

Once the geese are located, the hunting may be as easy as renting or leasing a blind from a landowner or guide who is in the goose-hunting business. In places like Mattamuskeet (North Carolina), Horshoe and Crab Orchard Lakes (Illinois), Chesapeake Bay and all along the Gulf Coast, blinds are available for rent by day, by the week or whole season in established good sites. Depending on just how consistently good, they rent for from $25 to $100 per day and that normally includes a good spread of decoys. It might also include a man who is pretty good at calling.

Even among the most experienced goose hunters, there are conflicting opinions on the value of calling. But most believe a good caller can produce results, but that a poor one is far worse than none. Neophytes at the game should keep this in mind.

Elsewhere on federal and state lands or public hunting areas, goose blinds can be obtained either free or for a nominal charge, the hunters being selected by lottery, by drawing, or on a first-come, first-serve basis. A good example of this type of excellent shooting facility is the Ballard Waterfowl Area where Red Bagley and I shared our shortest hunt and where hunter success is very high. About 1,000 birds are bagged each year at Ballard in a 30-day season.

But even in the absence of organized goose hunting, it is possible to free-lance geese and that may be the most fascinating way of all. And it begins, if possible, even before the season opens. How Lew Baker and I managed our hunting last fall is worth describing.

O'Shaughnessy Reservoir is a municipal water-supply reservoir in central Ohio. It's also a typical goose-holding lake in that it is a refuge. During the hunting season it may harbor 400 to 600 honkers. Last fall before opening day, Lew and I had followed the flocks from refuge to feeding areas by car, over backcountry roads, enough times so that we had a good idea of exactly which fields were being used. Then in darkness the evening before the opening, Lew and I dug pit blinds in a picked cornfield, spotted about 36 full-size papier-mâché decoys, plus a number of silhouettes, all around us.

The whole thing worked out far better than we might have hoped because in central Ohio there is plenty of

End of a great goose hunt on the northern prairies.

Hunter in Canada swings on goose which passes directly over his willow blind.

competition from other hunters. Still, we had a feeding flock come directly to our spread and bagged three of the birds. And the following morning we bagged a fourth.

Our strategy had been simple. When geese fly out of a sanctuary to feed and then find a good cornfield, they usually will keep coming back to that same place as long as ample grain remains, and they are not molested. In other words, they are creatures of habit until something happens to change the habit. Through binoculars and from a long distance, Lew and I had seen the Canadas feeding contentedly in one field the evening before opening day. If nothing disturbed them, we guessed correctly, the same flock would come back again in the morning.

Maybe the one best secret of the successful free-lance goose hunter is reconnaisance. Do plenty of scouting before you make a move. More than nine times in 10 it is a pure waste of time and energy to try to hunt the geese you have just then spotted in a field. Even

under the best of conditions, the big birds are not easy to sneak or to ambush and that is doubly true after the first couple of days of gunning.

The ideal situation is to scout thoroughly enough to detect a definite pattern in the flock's feeding habits. Watch for several days to be certain. Then locate yourself right on the flyway and build your blind. But dig it carefully. A telltale pile of fresh earth in the middle of an otherwise level grainfield can cause wary birds to flare out of range. So can movement on the part of the hunter as the birds approach.

Generally speaking, the more decoys, the better their drawing power. Goose decoys are heavy enough and bulky enough to be difficult to carry into the field in great quantity. But the extra effort pays dividends. Several years ago, a bag check of goose hunters was made in the Chesapeake Bay area and one important conclusion was that hunters with the most decoys also had by far the most shooting.

I have already mentioned a number of places where

Along coast of Hudson Bay in northern Manitoba, it's
possible to bag blue, snow and Canada geese at the same time.

geese are concentrated each fall, but these would comprise only a partial list. In Missouri the annual honker kill runs high into four figures around the Swan Lake NWR (National Wildlife Refuge), Squaw Creek Wildlife Refuge and the Fountain Grove State Wildlife Area. Last fall there was excellent gunning in Lucas and Ottawa counties around Ohio's Ottawa NWR and Magee Marsh. Buckeye sportsmen also bagged a few birds near Kildeer Plains, St. Marys Lake, Pymatuning Lake and at Mosquito Creek Reservoir.

Probably the best bet in Michigan is around the Seney NWR on the Upper Peninsula and Shiawassee NWR in Allegan County. Hovey Lake is the best bet in Indiana. Neenah and Horicon Marsh are the hot spots in Wisconsin and among the hottest in the Midwest.

Farther west, Canada goose flocks have been established at Red Lake, Agassiz and Tamarack NWR's in Minnesota; Crescent Lake in Nebraska; the Upper and Lower Souris NWR's in North Dakota; Lacreek, Sand Lake and Waubay NWR's in South Dakota. Still

farther west, Montana is a honker hunter's promised land, not only because birds are always abundant throughout the fall, but because hunting pressure is light. Some hot spots are Freezeout Lake northwest of Great Falls, the Missouri River bottoms around Canyon Ferry Lake and the Bowdoin NWR near Malta.

In the southeast, Canada goose hunting is excellent at Chickamauga Lake, Tennessee. About 35,000 honkers winter on South Carolina's Santee-Cooper lakes, and this flock furnishes good shooting on surrounding lands. Mattamuskeet Lake in North Carolina is still a major hunting area, despite heavy hunting pressure and although the shooting has fallen off in recent seasons. Probably many of the birds headed for Mattamuskeet have been short-stopped enroute at Chesapeake Bay.

Of course, there are many other places where Canadas pause each fall in smaller numbers—and it is only a matter of watching for them to arrive. In any case, the season promises to be a good one, so why not make the most of it?

# Looking for Bobwhite?

## by LARRY LAMINGTON

Portrait of old Bob. Look for this bird around old farms
where fencerows are grown up and stubble grows lush.

**"SHOW ME A LAZY** farmer, and I'll show you plenty of quail." That is the opinion of a veteran biologist of Ohio's Division of Wildlife whose business is quail.

"The finest bobwhite country I know," he continues, "is that where slipshod farming is practiced, where antiquated farm equipment is used, where weeds are not molested too much. Three times in four I can select the best quail lands in a township simply by looking at the farm buildings. When I find one in poor repair with equipment rusting all around it, I'm on the right track. The clincher comes if I can find the farmer resting on his front porch when it's a good enough day to be working in the fields. That place will have birds."

All this is unscientific deduction by a scientific man, but still it pretty well describes the habitat of a game bird many sportsmen consider the very finest. It is a fair claim too, for the bobwhite is the most abundant of native game birds, a strong flier which holds well before dogs, and hard to beat on the table. As with all other wild game, getting enough birds for the table is usually a matter of knowing their habits and where to find them.

Bobwhite, bobwhite quail, or partridge are members of a large group of gallinaceous birds. Literally, that means they scratch for a living—for seeds, grain, worms, and insects. Their range covers the eastern two-thirds of the United States. Except during nesting in springtime, they band together in coveys or bevies. These may be family groups or parts of several families. The later the time of year, the more they are composed of birds from many families because they are continually scattered by hunting and natural enemies. Always they reassemble, perhaps haphazardly, into covey groups.

led a "singing" count, and the number of calls is marked on the map. After several days of driving precisely the same route, a definite pattern is evident because calling is heard much more frequently in some places than in others.

The results do not guarantee that there will be more birds in the fall where there was more singing in spring, but it is a serviceable indication since a quail spends an entire lifetime in much less than a square mile, the area covered by each count. Nor does the count actually reveal how many birds are in the area, but from one season to another it is a good inventory of relative abundance.

The young birds are hatched in 3 weeks and almost immediately become independent. The young remain with the parents, but they are far more active and elusive than most young wildlife. Within 2 months, they grow to handsome, chestnut-colored birds weighing 8 or 9 ounces and measuring 9 to 10 inches overall. Their short, stubby wings are designed for sudden flushing

A big moment in bobwhite hunting anywhere is when a dog makes a good retrieve as here. A good quail dog will find birds a lone hunter would never see.

Quail flushes on edge of woodlot and zooms for cover. Will this hunter swing on the bird in time?

The coveys break up in April or May and the adults pair off. A canopied nest of grass, leaves, or other debris is built in light brush, sedge, or weeds along the edge of a woods or thicket, perhaps along a trail or farm roadway. In it the female will lay from six to 20 eggs.

During the nesting season an enterprising sportsman can lay plans for a successful hunting season later on, by borrowing a technique of the wildlife biologists. As early as May they can predict with some accuracy which places will have birds. With a county or township map, they drive the back roads beginning at daybreak. They stop at intervals of exactly 1-mile, pausing at each stop for exactly 4 minutes (during courtship each morning, a single male calls an average of every 4 minutes) to count every time a male calls "bobwhite." This is cal-

and short, fast flights rather than for long flights. They are not migratory.

In his native environment, the quail is wild and alert. He has to be to survive in a world of housecats and foxes, hawks and owls, terrapins and cotton rats which destroy nests wholesale. Weather, drought, and the elements also take a toll. Only a fraction of the autumn population survives to nest in spring. Biologists believe that this fraction, say one-fourth, survives almost no matter how heavy the hunting pressure. This would indicate that gunning is one of the lesser factors in bobwhite abundance.

A resourceful outdoorsman can save much time and effort by learning the quail's habitat. As with every living creature, they prefer certain types of country and definite types of food and cover. Bobwhites are always more plentiful where the country is broken enough to be farmed in smaller blocks, strips, or patches, rather than in large, unbroken fields. The reason is that quail need "edge"—the edge between crop fields, woods, thickets, fence rows.

Among other ingredients that make up bobwhite country is grain farming on a small scale mixed with plenty of permanent pastures. A hunter can also look for areas of land that are left fallow, for in these places a wide variety of weeds will quickly appear. Some of these act as magnets to coveys of quail.

In the northern part of the range, sportsmen should learn to identify wild plants like the several smartweeds, ragweed, foxtail, pokeweed, and hairy vetch. Quail are partial to all these. In the South, the crotons (wild members of the cotton family), sensitive or partridge peas, cow peas, and soy beans are telltale plants. The lespedeza, especially Korean lespedeza, provide good "grazing."

In sections of the South where longleaf pine is managed as a timber crop, sportsmen can figure on good quail shooting under unique circumstances. Controlled burning is practiced to encourage the growth of pine seedlings and to eliminate undesirable hardwood undergrowth. Partridge peas, bush clovers, wild beans, and assorted other wild legumes then spring up. All these are choice quail foods and during the second year following a burning there is fast quail shooting.

Some wild creatures, notably cottontails, can be definitely associated with certain soil types and with fertility or alkalinity of the soil. Bobwhites seem to be an exception. They prosper as much on poor land as on fertile countrysides. The amount of edge or suitable food is more important. The Missouri Conservation Commission made soil-nutrition studies on every native species of game, but found nothing of interest on quail.

Because of the generally rolling land and the colorful plants which cover it, bobwhite country is always picturesque. It is always a pleasure to hunt, in autumn in

After an early snowfall, bobwhite retreats to second growth thickets where he's well camouflaged, despite snow.

Hunting quail anywhere in their range may be the best way of all to spend a golden autumn day.

the North and as late as January in some southern states. It is the spot in which dogs are the most valuable allies. Depending on how hard they have been hunted, coveys of quail will either hold tight as a hunter alone passes nearby, or they will flush far out of range. A good dog will find and pin them down for a shot. A good dog is good conservation too—to retrieve dead and crippled birds.

Especially in areas where the birds are heavily hunted, it is almost essential for a hunter to get a shot on the first covey flush. Otherwise he is out of luck, for the birds will invariably aim for the heaviest cover available. It may be a dense pine plantation, a swamp, or a greenbrier jungle, but in any case, it will not be a place where good shooting is possible at single birds.

The best bet for a hunter without dogs is to walk along strips of edge stopping frequently for a few seconds.

Pausing will cause birds to flush that otherwise would hold fast. A gunner should also walk through all the patches of ragweed, lespedeza, vetch or the other favorite plants. No matter what the cover, though, quail hunting should be leisurely. To hurry is neither the most productive course nor the best way to enjoy one of America's most pleasant pastimes.

On many of the old quail preserves and plantation coverts of the South, the small-bore double-barrel guns are almost traditional. It is hard to beat a double-barreled 20-gauge, either side-by-side or over-and-under. Boring must be open. It will put quail in the bag, and it will be a pleasure to carry in the field and to shoot. Small shot sizes give more dense patterns and are most effective on quail.

The fact is, everything concerned with bobwhites, bobwhite country, and bobwhite hunting is a pleasure.

# Let the Doves Come in Range

*by* CHARLEY DICKEY

**IT'S EASY TO MISS** a diving dove at 15 yards. It's even easier at 40 yards. Mourning doves at 50 yards are for expert gunners, and there are not many who can consistently kill cleanly past 40 yards. The trick is to lure the dove to within a range of 40 yards or less where you can handle him. To do this, most hunters wear camouflage clothing, some build blinds, others use shadows and natural cover and more and more gunners are putting up a few decoys.

On the opening day of the dove season, about 80 percent of the birds are juveniles. They've never been shot at. They don't know what a man with a shotgun is doing in their favorite feeding field. It's surprising how quickly they get educated. By the second or third day, they're spooky. They're particularly spooky about movement. Whatever the abilities of dove eyes, they don't readily distinguish still objects. But apparently they connect movement with man—their sudden enemy.

Camouflage clothing is not so much designed to hide the hunter as to hide his movement. The irregular, blending and broken lines, make it more difficult to detect movement. Most hunters today wear camouflage clothing. It's the nearest thing to a uniform in the world of hunting. If they don't wear clothing of basic brown or green camouflage, they at least wear drab clothing which blends with the surroundings.

Every hunter has been caught in an open field when the doves suddenly zoom in. If the hunter remains

branches and put them in the ground or pile them on top of existing cover.

A common mistake of dove shooters is to mount their shotguns too soon. We've all done it. We see a dove 100 yards away flying towards us. So what happens? We stand up when the dove is 60 yards away and begin to wave our shotguns around. If the bird sees the movement, as he's very apt to be watching for, he will swerve out of range and we will not get a shot.

The correct way to handle the approach is to wait until the bird is within 40 yards, and as you quickly stand up you mount your gun at the same time and shoot. You don't balk, correct and waver. You swing past the dove quickly, pull the trigger and keep swinging. You may get your first shot off this way before the dove sees you and quickly begins to jink and change speeds. Remember, that your best chance to clobber a dove is to take him before he knows you're around. If you miss your first shot, you still have time for a second and possibly a third before he darts out of range.

The real problem is that most hunters have difficulty estimating range. I do, too, and I have learned that I don't have to depend totally on guessing. Once I choose a stand, or put up a blind, I pace off 40 yards and make a nearby stump or bush a marker. I make markers at about 40 yards in a circle like the numbers on a clock. I often carry orange strips of cloth and hang them on weeds and bushes. I then draw an imaginary line through the markers. Anything which flies inside the

Author and friend put out a few dove decoys along a fencerow in preparation for a small shoot. The decoys can be easily moved to another spot.

perfectly still, the birds may fly within range, or even right over him. It's when the hunter moves or raises his shotgun that the birds usually swerve and go into their aerobatics for which they are famous.

It's a typical situation to be caught in the open whether you're shooting a feeding field, a flight line, water hole or near a roost. The trick is not to move until your target dove, or the flock, is within 35 or 40 yards. Then you quickly mount your shotgun and shoot. The doves may instantly see your movement and react—but they can't get out of range before you fire one or two shots.

The better you are camouflaged and hidden by vegetation, the less chance the dove has of seeing you—until it's too late. Your best chance of bagging a bird is firing at him when he's flying a straight line, before he goes into his didoes. You hit him before he suspects there is a gunner below.

A sharp machete comes in handy for quickly making a small blind or building up the cover you're standing in. It only takes a minute to cut some tall weeds or

circle is within range, assuming it's not real high. Obviously a dove with an altitude of 100 yards is out of range no matter where he crosses. But any dove not over 25 yards high will be in range when he flies into my circle, especially when you figure that there is a lag time when he crosses the border until I stand up, mount my gun and shoot. Using this simple and handy range system, my mind doesn't have to worry about an incomer being in range. I am free to concentrate on the shooting.

There is a strange thing about dove shooting or any kind of wing shooting. The more you shoot with your conscious mind, correcting like you would with a rifle, the more apt you are to miss. There are too many complicated mechanical and mathematical problems for the mind to handle simultaneously if you operate using your conscious mind.

Think back about some of the best shots you have made. A dove slipped in before you knew he was in range. All of a sudden you looked up and there he was—getting away! You quickly mounted your shotgun and fired. The dove collapsed. After it was over, you could not remember taking the safety off or mounting the gun. You do not remember how you swung the gun. You may not even recall the sight picture when you pulled the trigger. Because you were shooting positively and in a hurry, you automatically followed through with your gun swing.

We shoot best when we let our unconscious or subconscious minds handle the operations. Let's take another example, the extreme opposite. We see a dove coming towards us ¼-mile away. We "know" he's coming to us. We have all of the time in the world. We begin to consciously calculate the dove's speed and angle and think about how we will lead the bird. The dove swerves a bit and speeds up. We have a new set of calculations. When the bird is 75 yards away, we raise our shotguns and begin wavering, the muzzle first in front of the bird and then behind. All of a sudden the bird is in range and we are operating on our conscious minds. We balk, correct, hesitate and then rush off three shots at nothing in particular.

We're much better off to relax our conscious minds and let our subconscious computer take over. We wait patiently until the dove crosses our 40-yard circle, then in one smooth, positive motion we stand and at the same time mount our gun. We start the muzzle from behind the dove, pull through and pass the bird, pull the trigger and follow through with the swing. The bird drops.

The reason most of us waste a lot of shells in a dove field is that we try to take shots beyond our ability and that of our shotgun. If we want our dove-shell ratios to improve, all we have to do is decide before we leave home that we won't take any shots over 40 yards. If you stick with that resolution for an afternoon, your ratio has already improved.

Use camouflage clothing, natural cover, built-up cover, blinds and shadows to hide your movements and

Dove decoys in a tree may command an approaching dove's attention away from the hunters.

allow the birds to come within 40 yards. The camouflage and cover give you a chance to get off the first shot before the dove knows you're around. Deliberately shoot instinctively by making no movement before the dove is within your 40-yard circle. Then shoot quickly and positively on subconscious control, even deliberately forcing your conscious mind to submerge. If you operate on the subconscious level, your computer knows how to handle the shots. It's your conscious mind that makes you balk, hesitate, rush and worry what the guy in the next blind is thinking. Will he laugh if I miss three times?

Mourning dove decoys are becoming more popular, especially for small shoots. I've never had much luck with them on large shoots where there are 20 to 40 gunners surrounding a large grain field. But with two or three gunners at a small grain field, on a flight line, near a water hole or close to a roost, the decoys sometimes help.

I often carry about 10 decoys on a small shoot, some slightly oversize and some nearly double the size of a mature dove. I put them up in bare limbs I can reach and try to silhouette them. At a water hole, I may put a few on a bare bank near the water.

The decoys are not put out with the idea that doves will actually try to land in and around them, as with waterfowl decoys. I've never had much luck with that, perhaps the main reason being that once the incomers are within 40 yards or less I begin shooting, or one of my partners does.

I put the doves out as distractors, to distract the doves' eyes away from me. If the real doves are focusing on the decoys, the birds are not as likely to see me.

The decoys may cause a single or small flock to

(Above) Some of the best shots a hunter ever makes are those which are sudden and unexpected.

(Below and right) A dog — any dog, mongrel or purebred — which can find and retrieve birds is a great plus on a dove hunt.

swerve in my direction and within range. Without the decoys, they might have flown by out of range. It's not always easy to tell how much good the decoys actually do. I only put about 10 or so out. If I have to move, as usually happens in an afternoon's shooting, I can carry the decoys and my other gear with me in one trip. I don't want so much gear that I have to make two trips when I move. The best shooting in the afternoon zones at water holes and roosts is the last hour of the day. I don't like to spend a lot of that time toting gear back and forth.

Doves, especially after they've been pounded, change flight lines and patterns. There will nearly always be one or two main directions from which they enter and leave a field, pond or roost on a given day. The shooter needs to stay light and portable so he can change stands or blinds.

I like to carry some sort of dove stool so that I can rest comfortably, especially when I go to a field early in the afternoon. Sometimes it can be a long wait between flights. I have never been able to shoot well sitting down, although some of my buddies can. I shoot much better standing up and well balanced on both feet.

When one is sitting, the physics of his body are such that he can swing his shotgun in a limited arc only. Standing erect, he can swivel on his ankles, knees and hips and swing in a much wider arc. This helps a great deal for the second and third shots.

One of the best shooting stools to come on the market lately is the Sportsman's Pal made in Newton, Georgia. It's a bucket with a swivel cushioned seat. It enables the shooter to swivel 360 degrees while seated. Since he stays low while swiveling, he is not as likely to be seen by incoming doves as with other stools where he has to get up to change sitting angles. The Sportsman's Pal has a storage area for shells and an insulated compartment for ice and refreshments. The styrofoam insulated area is a good place to store doves when you leave the shooting area to walk back to your vehicle. The stool has a handy rope for carrying and is an improvement over most shooting stools on the market.

If conditions allow, I like to hunt with someone who has a retrieving dog such as a Labrador or Golden. If the dog is a good one, I don't have to worry about finding dead or crippled birds. It's not only good conservation for someone in the party to have a retriever, but it improves your dove-shell ratio.

It's not necessary to have a retriever breed. As long as the dog has a good nose and will hunt and fetch dead and crippled birds, that's what matters. The cocker or springer spaniels, both flushing breeds, often make good retrievers in a dove field. I have frequently used English setters which were forced-broken to retrieve.

I would not hesitate to use a mongrel if he would do the job. No matter what the hunting conditions, when a dove falls he immediately blends in with the soil and vegetation. Even in a harvested peanut field, where the hogs have rooted out the vegetation, a dead dove melts into the dirt. Without a dog, one can spend a lot of time looking for lost birds.

It upsets me to lose two or three birds, or even one. It affects my shooting. When I don't have a dog, I try to mark a downed bird and immediately go to it. When I reach the spot where I think the bird hit, I make a marker, sometimes by putting out a white handkerchief.

If I knock down one bird from a flight, I try never to take my eyes from the spot and walk directly to it. If I'm lucky enough to have gotten a double, I had to swing to the second bird before the first hit the ground. I go to the second bird and if I do not immediately spot it, I put out a marker. Then I go back to my stand and take a bearing on where I think the first bird would hit. I walk to that spot and perhaps put a strip of orange cloth on a weed, or make some sort of mark. My first guess will nearly always be the best one.

When searching for a downed dove, I try not to wander but work in a definite pattern, such as a square search. It saves a lot of time and that can be important if the birds are coming in.

When dove hunting, I need all of the odds I can get. After all, it's the toughest wing shooting we have in America.

A dove goes into the author's game pocket. Camouflage garments are practically the uniforms of dove hunters today.

# BETTERING THE ODDS
# FOR BOWHUNTERS
### by CHARLES NANSEN

Moment of truth! You have crept close to a fine bull elk. Can you put the arrow where you have to?

**ONE GOLDEN DAY** last fall I had a ringside seat for a most perfect performance—a classic stalk of a splendid mule deer buck. It was also a lesson in how to hunt big game with a bow and arrow.

The performance and the lesson began at daybreak on the topmost rim of the Missouri Breaks in extreme northeastern Montana. From his 7-V Ranch near Brussett, Glen Childers had driven Nat Franklin and me in darkness to this edge of the awesome badlands which stretch almost 100 miles both east and west along the Missouri River. Nearly all of that unfriendly real estate is now included in the Charles M. Russell National Game Range. It is excellent mule deer country, probably as good as any in America.

"As soon as it's light enough," Childers had advised, "you should see plenty of deer feeding both on top of the rim and down in the breaks. Now you're on your own." A moment later the rancher-outfitter was on his way back to chores at the 7-V.

By the first lemon light of dawn Nat and I sat, backs against cold rimrock, and looked out across a vast expanse of wilderness. We carried binoculars and beside us were recurved hunting bows, each of about 60 pounds draw. Razor-sharp broadhead arrows were carried in a metal frame quiver clamped onto the bows. It was early October, and the archery season had not yet given away to the gun season.

As time passed in slow motion, I shivered and tried to retreat deeper into a soft woolen jacket. But eventually it became lighter, and we could distinguish trees and shadows from their strange, eroded backgrounds. The fieldglasses made it possible to peer into the gloom long before we could see with eyes alone.

Then—"That shadow moved," Nat whispered. "Just below us."

Looking downward to where Nat pointed, I watched as six deer cautiously strolled out into the open. All antlerless. A moment later four more were within our sight, also antlerless. Now, with the light improving rapidly, we spotted another small herd farther away. Then scanning far to the left, to the first grassy slope to be bathed in orange sunlight, I saw a single deer. This one had antlers, and in sharper focus they appeared huge.

"Big buck," I said softly.

For a long time, as the sun drenched more and more of the landscape, we never took our eyes off that buck. When I had first spotted it, the animal had been on a bench about 100 yards below us and maybe 350 yards or more to the west. Range is harder to estimate when the sun is very low and the shadows long. But while we watched, the muley climbed upward to a higher bench and then followed it westward, drifting away from us.

"Should we try that one," I asked, "before it gets out of sight?"

"One of us should," my partner answered, "but right now let's be patient and just watch."

I have been bowhunting for several years, but never as seriously or as often as many bowhunters do. Nat, on the other hand, has been intently at the game for a long time and has shot more than his share of big game the hard way. So I followed his suggestion.

Fifteen minutes passed, then 30, and the buck was nearly out of our sight when abruptly it turned back and evaporated into shadow. Minutes later it emerged and then bedded down at the base of a pine tree which curved out and upward from a pile of rocks. There it was almost entirely hidden—screened behind the tree's overhanging boughs. If we hadn't actually seen the deer lie down there, we would never have spotted the animal by scanning the slopes with glasses. Now we figured the buck to be only about 100 feet below our badlands rim and about 550 yards away.

"Heads you try him," Nat said, flipping a quarter. "Tails I go."

It came up tails. The lesson began. On hands and knees my partner crawled away behind me until he was certain the deer couldn't see him stand. Then he began the long circle around, hopefully to arrive above and behind the deer without being seen or heard. At the moment there was only a light wind and it blew upward from the bottom of the badlands toward the rim. That was good. If Nat could make it to a spot directly above the deer, he would have a short and (even for archers) easy shot. But getting so close is never easy.

Now time *really* passed in slow motion. I checked my watch an hour after Nat had begun his stalk and still he hadn't come into sight on top the rim to the west. If the deer moved at all, I couldn't see it.

A golden eagle soared over the Breaks and for a moment I turned away to enjoy the magnificent spectacle. But the instant I looked back, I caught a flick of motion. Nat was in sight and on his belly again crawling inches at a time toward the rimrock right over the deer. Suddenly I had buck fever. It was difficult to hold the glasses steady.

I wish I could report that my partner shot the buck in its bed, a feat which isn't easy for a rifleman, let alone for a bowhunter whose effective range is only a fraction

Only patience can describe the bowhunter who can spend a long time in this lofty predicament.

of that of a high-velocity bullet. But just as Nat reached the edge and started to rise, the deer sensed danger.

Quickly the animal was on its feet—looking everywhere but up. I saw the streak of the arrow, and the deer bounded full speed downhill into a deep draw and out of sight. Later Nat and I found it, stone dead, the arrow having passed through its lungs.

"The stalk was a masterpiece," I said as we field dressed the deer.

"You may wish it hadn't been," Nat grinned, "after we start dragging this animal out of here."

It was a chore, all right; a brutal back-breaking chore. But never before had I seen the basics of bowhunting—of successfully stalking and downing big game—illustrated so dramatically as they were there. These basics are knowing the game, knowing the country, patience, and practice to make perfect. Our early morning reconnaissance had spotted the buck before it spotted us. Knowledge of the species told us that the animal would probably bed down for the day before too much of the morning elapsed. Patience restrained Nat from making a hurried and therefore unsuccessful stalk.

And he had practiced enough in the weeks before to make good his shot when the opportunity was presented.

In all the outdoors, there is nothing that quite matches bowhunting for big game. The odds for success are not very high, but anyone who does decide to go hunting this difficult way can greatly improve the odds by concentration on the basics listed above. Let's consider those basics one by one.

To successfully hunt wildlife by any means it is necessary to know something about the target; the more the better. There is little point, for example, in seeking a bragging-size mule deer buck in deep valleys or river bottoms at a time of year (early fall, when most archers venture afield) when all the big antlers will be in the vicinity of timberline. Of course fawns, does, and maybe even very young males may be down in less lofty places, but the bucks live bachelor lives upstairs until the rut or deep snows (whichever occurs first) drive them down. The same is true of any bull elk big enough for trophy-room status.

Knowing the game also means knowing such vital

Hunt a lifetime and you may never even see, let alone bag a fine whitetail such as this with bow and arrow.

details as the fact that most big game animals seldom look up. They are constantly on the alert for danger all around them except, it seems, from above. Nat Franklin had that fact in mind when he approached his deer from above rather than from any other direction. And the fact that bull elk challenge rival males or establish territories by bugling (it's really more a fife-like whistle than a bugle) is well worth knowing because it can be used against them. Thus, an artificial call used to imitate a lovesick bull can make any bowhunter's task of getting closer to the game much easier.

Fred Bear of Grayling, Michigan, just may be archery's best known name. Chances are he has killed more game and more different kinds of big game than anyone else. He believes that patience is an archer's greatest virtue.

"Patience," Bear has often explained, "is a lot of things. In a bowhunter's case it is taking time to plan strategy carefully."

But patience is also playing the waiting game as much as possible. It's moving about as little as possible and thereby avoiding noise and movement which the keen senses of wildlife quickly detect.

In the case of deer (and in those states where it is legal), the best place to play a waiting game is in a tree. You pick your spot, say beside a busy trail or runway, and wait in an overhead ambush. That tactic is well known to eastern bowhunters after whitetails, but it works just as well with western muleys, although unaccountably it's a trick not widely used in the big sky country. Of course the edge of a rimrock or a canyon is as good an overhead vantage point as a treetop. It all depends on how well it's located. More on that later.

Obviously it is not always possible or necessary to play the waiting game. But what *is* necessary is to spot the game before it spots you, after which patience is again the greatest virtue, although in this case restraint may be a better word. Beginning right now you approach the target in absolute silence and with as little motion as possible. Stealth describes it. So does woodsmanship.

The Berger brothers of Denver, Colorado, Mason and Jack, are two of the most successful bowhunters I know. They get a deer and an elk apiece every year and occasionally even an antelope or a black bear. But they work hard at it, and they start long before the season opens. The two actually go out and hunt one another!

Here's how it works. On weekends they drive up into Rocky Mountain National Park, which isn't far away and which is fairly similar to the mountain country they hunt farther west. There they go into a woodland from opposite sides and try, at the same time, to sneak within bow range of each other and to avoid being seen. It may seem slightly looney, but does it make less sense than

Spend those hours in camp wisely, honing arrowheads, checking out all of your equipment.

spring training for baseball players or preseason camp for football players? Of course not. In addition, there are plenty of completely wild mule deer and elk in Rocky Mountain Park on which the Berger brothers can tune-up their stalking.

It may not seem impossible to walk any more quietly through a woods than you presently do, but try this during your spare time before opening day. Walk through the driest, brushiest (strewn with dry leaves if possible) woods you can find and make a conscious effort to be quiet. Carefully avoid brushing against low bushes and stepping on twigs. As much as possible, try to put your feet down only on solid or bare places. Keep doing it long enough and eventually it will become second nature.

My friend Karl Maslowski has another theory on how to be a better woodsman and to be more inconspicuous in any forest. Go bird watching, he advises, serious bird watching. Laugh at that suggestion too, if you like, but it is worth thinking about. To correctly identify the small birds in any woodland, it is necessary to proceed very quietly with both eyes and ears alert for brief glimpses of telltale plumage or for various bird songs. It is a great way to sharpen all the senses, the same senses that can first spot buckskin hiding among the trees.

Frank Sayers has been a close friend and hunting companion for many years, and he too has accounted for much big game by bow. Frank does not deny the importance of any of the other basics we have discussed, but he believes that another may be even more vital.

"There is no substitute," he insists, "for either knowing the country from having hunted there before or making a thorough reconnaissance beforehand."

Last fall Frank was another of the archers who hunted where Glen Childer's of 7-V Ranch borders the Missouri Breaks. Before he strung a bow, he and Childers spent a couple of days jeeping around the ranch and stopping to glass wherever there was a suitable viewpoint. In the process they inventoried lots of wide open spaces and saw plenty of deer. Of course they learned which areas deer were using.

One thing Frank noticed during his reconnaissance was that a good many deer were spending daytimes bedded in one particular draw. The draw was very well hidden and a casual hunter might never have found it at all. Mornings the deer would retreat back into this draw after feeding in the open, and evenings they would emerge again. Frank picked a spot on the rim, where the draw was the narrowest, to be waiting at daylight. Scarcely 30 minutes later he dropped an 8-point buck!

Let us assume that the bowhunting season on big game begins on a certain day. Assume also that you've saved 2 week's vacation time for a hunt, beginning that very day. But if you would heed Frank Sayer's advice, you would jump the gun and spend at least the first few days of your holiday in the field *before* the season opens and *before* other hunters appear on the scene. These days should be spent in thorough reconnaissance, in getting acquainted with the animals and where they live. There is no better way, for instance, to pick out the best tree for a stand, the one best place to wait at daybreak.

Glen Childers seconds the motion. Each fall Glen hosts a couple of dozen deer and elk hunters on his own ranch and on the adjacent Russell Game Range, and these men have almost 100-percent hunting success. The secret, he believes, is scouting the place thoroughly before the hunters ever arrive.

At the very best, bowhunting for big game is an uncertain proposition. The wise bowhunter stacks the odds as much as possible in his favor.

Tree stand in a southern hardwood forest. It's an uncomfortable perch, but you must stand motionless, quiet.

A summertime woodchuck from the edge of a hayfield is as good as chicken or rabbit on the table.

# Tune-up With Chucks

*by HAL HARRMON*

**EVERY YEAR ON** February 2—Candlemas Day—a good many winter-weary sportsmen wait for the groundhog to make an important weather prediction. They hope he will bring good news. If the animal, on emerging from his den, does not see his shadow, spring is just around the corner. If the shadow is visible, 6 more weeks of winter weather are in store.

But don't count on it. Except in the deepest South, few groundhogs will ever be seen above-ground in February, and zero temperatures are most likely to follow any promises of spring. Most sportsmen, however, are willing to forgive the species its faulty predictions, be-

The yellow-bellied marmot is the woodchuck's western cousin.

cause it is among the best sporting targets since the bull's-eye. The groundhog, or woodchuck, is even more than that. *He's a splendid year-round game animal.*

One dewy morning last summer, my son Bob, his buddy Jon Parsons and I witnessed a good example of it. We had obtained permission to hunt across a livestock farm in Ross County, southern Ohio. That is a rolling green region of open meadows and pasturelands punctuated with forested ridges and open woodlots. It is also the sort of terrain likely to become infested with chucks to a point where they may be a nuisance. For that reason, and because the landowner knew we were safe gun handlers and no threat to his cattle, we were very welcome to hunt. "We have more chucks around here," the farmer said firmly, "than we need."

We parked my station wagon in a woods about 200 yards from the cluster of farm buildings, slipped cartridges into a pair of scope-sighted .222 Remington Magnum varminters and climbed another 300 yards to the crest of a high grassy ridge. Careful not to silhouette ourselves against the sky, we crawled the last few feet. From a prone position, we scanned the meadows through binoculars. What we saw was a chuck hunter's dream come true. Bob whistled softly.

"All the pasture poodles in the county," Jon said, "must be right out there."

It seemed that way. On a low knoll directly ahead of us, one chuck sat by a mound of yellow earth from a den

he had dug beside a crumbling old log cabin. To the left two more busily scurried back and forth along a fencerow. Directly to my right a single chuck was grazing at the edge of a farm woodlot. We could see others, too, but all farther away. Unable to stand the prosperity very long, Bob couldn't wait to take a shot.

"The dark one by the cabin," he whispered, "looks like the biggest. I'll take that one."

The target chuck was about 125 yards away—easy range—and no wind was blowing to require sighting adjustment. Bob shifted his prone position slightly and squeezed, and the rifle cracked. The puff of earth seemed to be right behind the chuck. But the animal quickly raced for its den a few feet away and dropped into it unhurt. Bob couldn't believe what he saw.

"What's the matter?" I chided. I knew that the rifle and scope were perfectly sighted-in and that the lad is a very fine marksman.

"Too much in a hurry," he answered. "I'll get the next one for sure."

But it didn't happen that way. That single shot completely cleared the landscape of chucks. Although we waited for nearly 30 minutes without moving, not another groundhog showed its head.

"We'd better find another spot," I suggested.

We followed a meandering creek bed for ¼-mile or so, then circled to the opposite side of the meadows we had covered before. We kept out of sight all the way, but the chucks were still as spooky as ever. During 30

In Alaska, the woodchuck's closest relative is the pale-colored hoary marmot.

more minutes of glassing, only one young chuck looked out of a den. Satisfied that all was safe enough, it came all the way out 15 minutes later. Bob nailed that one neatly.

"You can call them varmints, if you like," Jon concluded, "but I call pasture poodles a 100-percent game species."

The varmint classification comes from certain qualities that do not endear woodchucks to farmers. Given the chance, a chuck will plunder gardens, and a colony of them can eat a sizable chunk out of a clover or alfalfa hayfield. Livestock, although this danger may be exaggerated, may stumble into burrow entrances and break legs. In addition mounds of excavated earth at burrow exits can damage modern mechanized farm machinery. It was in 1883, however, long before mechanized farming that rural landowners in the New Hampshire Legislature pronounced the woodchuck "destitute of any valuable qualities" and offered a 10¢ bounty for each dead one. The groundhog has been a varmint on the WANTED list ever since.

Wherever chucks exist in any numbers, farmers wage at least limited war on them. Sometimes it becomes all-out war. As a result woodchuck hunters are hardly ever refused permission to hunt, even on lands that are otherwise posted. In addition, the groundhog is a fairly important prey of such predators as coyotes, foxes, weasels and some larger hawks and owls. Despite all the pressure against him, the pasture poodle survives.

Much of a sportsman's success in hunting chucks, as in hunting any game animal, depends on his understanding of the game, its habits and its habitat. To begin, it is stocky, and one of our larger rodents, averaging, when fully grown, 4 or 5 pounds. Occasionally a chuck may

reach 10 pounds. An extremely large boar of 14 pounds has been weighed. The species breeds at the age of 1 year, and litters of four to six young are produced.

Unlike some close cousins among the rodents, groundhogs do not lay up stores for the winter. Instead they gorge on green vegetation all summer, feeding in the area around the entrances to their underground homes, to store up fat. As summer wanes, they become increasingly heavy and lethargic, until they finally turn in to hibernate through the winter.

A typical den, which a chuck digs for himself, will have at least two entrances and usually several. In a side chamber of his branching subterranean tunnel, the inhabitant builds a soft bed of grass. Groundhog burrows eventually provide havens for cottontails and skunks as well as for chucks. Foxes enlarge them to raise puppies in the spring.

Chucks greatly prefer certain types of soil or habitat, and it is a waste of time to search for them elsewhere. They need dry earth where the digging is easy—in open woodlands, in thickets, in and around open crop fields and clearings, often within the root masses of large trees or in rockpiles. They rarely wander too far from these burrows. The average home range or territory is less than 100 yards from the home den, and most chucks will spend a lifetime without ever leaving this area.

Occasionally chucks will be seen wandering far from dens early in the year, say in March or April. Invariably these are males enroute to mate with any number of females within walking distance, and after the trip they retreat to familiar home territory.

Mid-May is when most young are born throughout the central states. Farther south the time will be earlier; in the Great Lakes country, slightly later. At about 6 weeks, the young ones either leave the mother's den or are forced out to find their own lodging. They are the most vulnerable chucks of all—to predators and hunters alike.

Hunters who go afield before the young are self-sufficient (which is when hunting is best because vegetation has not yet grown up to obscure spotting) face a moral dilemma. To shoot a female is probably also to destroy a whole litter left untended in a den somewhere. On the other hand, the landowner may well want groundhogs of any age eliminated by any means.

Hunting in all seasons is by far the best during early morning and late in the afternoon, simply because most chucks are most active and feeding then. During midday they rest, either inside or just outside the den (the choice probably depending on sunlight and temperature), but in any case are almost impossible to spot. I have often seen chucks outdoors on cold or threatening days, but have never seen one out in the rain. On the other hand, they also avoid hot, bright sun.

Chucks have a habit of sitting upright and motionless for long periods at the mouths of their dens. The appearance is of a sentinel, alert to any danger threatening the entire chuck community—and maybe that is exactly the case. Let a hawk or fox or hunter appear and the animal whistles a loud, shrill warning just before disappearing under the turf.

The more heavily groundhogs are hunted, the shyer and more secretive they become. Thus a hunter may walk through an area where they are quite abundant without ever seeing one. The best way, therefore, to hunt an unfamiliar area may be to sit down at a vantage point somewhere and to search for sign rather than for the game itself. Fresh bare mounds of earth are telltale of course, although the den marked by an older mound may be abandoned. If it has been abandoned very long fresh green shoots will be growing up through the earth. Occasionally a worn trail through grass from a burrow to a favorite feeding area can be spotted. And feeding areas, which are usually roughly circular or oval in shape appear to be clipped or mown. Look for all these signs especially along fencerows, grassy or brushy knolls, embankments (but only well above high water lines) and railroad grades. Many farmers have built "living fences" of multiflora rose, and chucks particularly like to dig homes beneath their protective cover. Always check these out.

Pasture poodles tend to use the same areas and often the very same dens year after year. So if you locate a good denning area some summer day, look in the same spot again next summer, even if you have shot the previous inhabitants.

Pasture-poodle hunting has much to recommend it besides the animals' abundance and wide distribution. The season is long—extending through the summer, when other shooting opportunities are more limited—and there are no bag limits. Most states have no closed season, though shooters should be certain of the local regulations before going afield.

But hunting chucks is never better or more challenging than it is in autumn—when it furnishes the perfect warm-up for big game hunting.

A hunter can practice on an autumn groundhog hunt the very skills he will need for a later big game trip. First it's necessary to spot the game before it spots the hunter. A stalk to shorten the range may be necessary. And finally it requires a good killing shot at a small target. In fact a pasture-poodle hunt today may mean a bighorn ram or trophy elk tomorrow.

Ask permission from the landowner, park your car on a country lane, and then study the field borders for signs of chucks.

# Devil Bear

# of Hell's Hole

## by ERWIN A. BAUER

**NO BEAR HUNT** I ever made got off to a more dramatic start. The door of the cabin burst open to reveal the icicle-hung figure of Willis Butolph, a government lion hunter. "Damn bear like to get me froze to death," he growled, bits of ice and snow falling from his clothes as he made for the open fire.

Until this moment I had come to Don, Budge and Waldo Wilcox's ranch in northern Utah for a deer hunt. But as the story of the bear unfolded I soon found myself putting this plan aside.

"I've been hunting over on Mike Himmonas' ranch," the lion hunter told us. "As you know, he lost 300 lambs this summer to a bear, maybe a couple of bears. This morning a big one killed a heifer, and I found his track heading this way. But I lost it in the snow near your south fence.

"Now, I've got a hunch," Willis continued, "that the bear will come back to the kill tonight and bed down nearby during the storm. Anyway, first thing in the morning I'll find out. He's one hell of a big bear."

Nobody mentioned deer hunting after that.

Budge Wilcox remarked that bears had given him plenty of headaches during nearly half a century of ranching. He recalled an autumn 40 years ago when a huge bear had practically terrorized the region.

"He'd even invade a corral to kill a colt and drag it away," Budge said. "Regular bear traps couldn't hold him and poison didn't even make him sick."

The old rancher pitched another log on the fire and continued. "Eventually I had to ride into the Union Pacific shops in Salt Lake City where railroad blacksmiths made me a pair of traps with 30-inch jaws. It took

Hound bays furiously at bear as hunt comes to an end.

◄ (Opposite) Caught again, bear turns on hounds and mauls one.

two men with a jack to set them, but early the next spring we finally caught our killer.''

"What you needed," Willis commented, "was a pack of good dogs. Traps are a waste of time with some bears I've seen. Once I found where a big old black dragged two traps—chains, anchor logs and all—to his den in a Mokie house."

Mokies were 4-foot-tall cliff dwellers who lived in this part of Utah about 20 centuries ago. Cowpokes and prospectors still find their remains and cliff houses in remote places. Black bears and lions often use the cliff houses for their own dens.

"That bear chewed off his own feet—and the traps—right on the spot."

Hound-dog men seldom take kindly to trapping, and Willis Butolph was no exception. Cut from the same rough cloth as the almost legendary bear hunter, Ben Lilly, who had hunted nearby, Willis felt that even a cattle-killing bear deserved a better fate than a chunk of hardware on his feet. Chasing was the only "honorable" way.

Butolph is among the last of his leathery, walnut-necked breed. If he hasn't chased more bears than anyone else alive today in his 30 to 40 years of hunting, he'll certainly rank somewhere near the top. The last thing I remember when turning in that night was his colorful account of how he followed a bear for 5 days and nights with just one hound, living off the land as he went.

Daylight was still only a promise when everyone on the ranch was stirring. With a minimum of preliminaries we climbed aboard Don Wilcox's Jeep and were under way with the seven hounds harnessed in pairs and loping close behind.

"Got to work off the edge," Willis remarked, "before we put 'em on a hot track."

The dogs aren't the kind of hounds you see in calendar paintings. They were bred to trail lions or bears and to fight when necessary. Their ears were chewed to ribbons and all showed plenty of evidence of battle.

Willis led us directly to the kill. Although a blanket of snow now covered most of the carcass, we could see that the entrails were only recently eaten away. As Willis had hoped, the bear *had* returned during the night and gorged. That was an extra-good break. But best of all, the bear's tracks etched deep in the snow were almost steaming fresh. On all fours Willis squatted down to study them.

"They could be only a few minutes old," he said. "With luck we'll have that bugger up a tree before he gets halfway down to the canyon."

With that Willis unleashed the hounds. There was no hesitation, no casting about. One by one they gave tongue and vanished into the clouds. For several minutes we stood and listened to the savage symphony of the pack in full cry. Even on that cold and bitter morning it was enough to raise the hair on the back of your neck. It sounded as if the barking dogs were running right up the bear's back.

"Yes, sir," Willis smiled, as the music faded into the distance, "we'll be looking up a tree at that bear's behind before we know it."

But instead of a short, fast hunt, we started on a wild and woolly marathon which no one was prepared for and which none of us will ever forget.

At times it was a frantic footrace, and sometimes it seemed almost suicidal, clawing and clutching for fingerholds on canyon walls. And it didn't end until 2 days later.

For ¼-mile we followed the trail in snow which was wet and waist deep in the drifts. Just the same, Willis led at a half trot, hallooing all the way. Even when I couldn't hear the dogs, I could hear Willis. The rest of us plodded and stumbled after him until we reached the rim of the 10,000-foot-high Tavaputs flat. Here the land fell away suddenly, and we plunged down a steep slope and into a dense fog. We must have looked like ghosts disappearing and reappearing in a misty, silent movie.

Willis Butolph drops to hands and knees to check on freshness of bear tracks.

Then all at once the pack was running several trails at once. In one small clearing we presently found the tracks of three bears; one small, one medium size and one tremendous. The dogs were running all three.

"What do you do in a case like this?" I asked.

"You keep following Willis."

Butolph wasn't greatly upset by the dogs' behavior. He just uncovered his bald head, listened for a few minutes, then he poked around in the snow on hands and knees. Finally he stood up again.

"Nig's close to one of those bears," he said. "As near as I can tell, he's a-riding the critter right down the North Fork, and the others will join him."

You could safely say that Willis Butolph has one of the toughest jobs in the West and not just because he's a professional hunter. Rather it's because his territory includes some of the most remote and impenetrable portions of Utah, a state full of such badlands. Butolph hasn't even seen most of his territory and that's easy to explain because *nobody* has ever seen it except from the air. Much of the country is all but impassable to both men and horses.

Whenever a sheep or cattle killer turns up, Willis has to go after it in this unknown country pretty much as the lions and bears do, by feel and by instinct, in the blast-furnace heat of August or in a blizzard.

This rugged country is ideal for the survival of bears because when foraging for natural foods is poor, they can stay fat on spring lambs and heifers which are easy to bushwhack on the high plateau grasslands. Once ranchers get after them, they can practically dissolve into the deep corridors and canyons surrounding the Tavaputs plateau. And in addition, few big game animals are better able to cope with men and civilization than black bears. Whereas grizzlies were doomed wherever they came in contact with men and their livestock, it's practically impossible to ever kill a wily blackie without resorting to traps, poison bait or a pack of hounds. And only a few of the best hounds are equal to the task.

We kept descending, deeper and deeper into an awesome canyon. Eventually we even passed out of the snow belt.

"Where does this come out?" I asked Budge Wilcox when we stopped once for a breather.

"Hell's Hole. The bottom is about 2,000 feet below

Now the big bruin is well up in a tree and Butolph encourages his dogs after the long, hard chase.

where we started and dead-ends into Desolation Canyon, a dangerous part of the Green River."

I swallowed hard because I knew Desolation Canyon. I'd flown over it in a rescue plane the summer before and had seen its wild rapids and cataracts. More boatmen are drowned in that water than ever negotiate it—which meant we'd have to climb out the same way we came in.

Then a freak gust of wind brought the sound of several dogs far below.

"That biggest bear's headed for Hell's Hole," Willis said. "I'd bet my last penny on it. But the acoustics down here make it tough. Let's keep moving."

We separated, looking for ways down. Following Budge Wilcox, I presently found myself at a point from which there seemed no return. Behind us towered a slope too steep for anything but a goat to climb. A thin game trail vanished into near-vertical rock walls on either side of us. Even after we'd rested a bit, it still looked bad.

Finally Budge said, "Our only way is down."

Clutching even the smallest stems of brush and using the seat of my pants as a brake, I followed the old-timer feet first and inches at a time until we reached what appeared to be another dead end. That's when we heard the high chop-chop of a hound dog in a hurry, faint and very far away.

This time we sat for a long while as the afternoon ticked away, and we strained to hear the dog again. But the wind was all we heard. Now the canyon was falling under deep blue shadows and total darkness wouldn't be too far behind.

"We'll have to find a spot big enough and level enough to spend the night," Budge said.

It was slow, painful going but we found our spot about 200 yards below where a tiny spring-fed brook had undercut its bank to form a sort of cave. And here, with fresh lion sign all about, we spent a cold, cold night with dinner a candy bar apiece.

By midnight we gave up trying to sleep and huddled close to a fire of pine twigs.

"You ever been down here before?" I asked Budge.

"Not for a long, long time. When we first come to this country, I had an experience I'll never forget. Some say black bears aren't mean and won't attack, but on that first trip I found out different.

275

"I was exploring the canyon and I'd gone as far as I could on my pony—so I tied her and traveled on foot. It was a blistering hot day, and I dropped down into a deep wash, hoping to find a pool of water. That's when I practically stumbled over a mule-deer carcass with a bear standing right on top of it.

"The minute he saw me he growled and came head on. No hesitation, no sparring, no nothing. I was wearing a six-gun then, and in all the years I carried it, I never had more urgent need for it. I dropped the bear only a few feet away."

"That was close," I commented. "Did you always run into bears down here?"

"Not face to face like that. But I never saw half as much bear sign anywhere else."

Except for the gnawing hunger around daybreak, it wasn't too bad a night in the cave. At dawn a light snow began to fall, eventually changing to sleet and finally to a cold drizzle. When we heard nothing after an hour of listening, we decided to descend some more.

We side-hilled where deer had made a thin game trail and eventually reached a spine of rock which formed a sort of gate to the canyon. Hell's Hole seemed bottomless beneath the mist covering it. Far beyond we could just barely see the pale-orange cliffs of Desolation Canyon.

Budge and I sat wearily atop the spine, and that's when I heard, very faintly at first, but unmistakably the bawling of dogs far below. And as we strained to listen, the noise seemed to come closer and closer until it didn't seem far away at all. Then abruptly it faded, and I realized it was some strange phenomenon of canyon acoustics.

"Sounded as if they had something up a tree," I remarked as we clawed our way down the face of the rock. One misstep here would mean pitching headlong 500 feet into the bottom. We'd made about half the distance when I dislodged a rock, froze in place and listened to the avalanche I started. But in an instant it was quiet again, I heard Don calling from far below. Ten minutes later we joined him on the canyon floor.

Don was a sorry sight; wet to the skin and red-eyed but with wild excitement on his face.

"The dogs have a tremendous bear up a tree about ¼-mile down the creek. Waldo and Willis are with the dogs," he told us with a big grin.

"The dogs kept the bear treed all night," Don continued, "but we couldn't reach them in the dark. Then at first light the bear came down, and there was a hell of a fight. Toughy's dead. But the other dogs treed the bear again."

We ran the rest of the way. I remember passing a spot where about ½-acre was plowed up, and Don shouted that it was where Toughy was killed. My heart began to

After a long chase downhill into a deep canyon, the black bear confronts the dogs and drives them off.

Shot out of the tree, devil bear makes its way to a creek where dogs and hunter Butolph catch up with it.

pound and my lungs were on fire, but I kept running until I could hear hounds baying and Willis urging them to keep it up.

"Watch him, boy, watch him," he was hollering at Nig and pointing upward.

Even 40 feet above and largely hidden, I could see that the bear was tremendous—and slavering mad. I've seen my share of bruins before, but none ever looked as menacing as this one. Then he started edging downward.

"Watch the bugger!" Willis shouted.

"Give him plenty of room!" someone yelled.

Willis was moving about like a madman, trying to get a clear view of the bear for a shot.

"That bear's fixing to come down and fight again," he shouted above the din. "And I'm afraid he'll kill more dogs."

Nig never stopped barking for a second. The battle-scarred brindle kept trying to claw his way upward into the tree but kept falling back. Somehow Ranger managed to reach the first low branch before he lost his balance and fell back again. Still he kept trying.

Now the bear started backing straight down the tree, and the dogs really went crazy. Their barking echoed against the canyon walls until it sounded like a thousand dogs. I half looked around for a tree to climb.

"Better shoot, somebody!" Willis shouted.

Waldo had the only rifle but not much of a target; big as it was, the bear was only a vague moving shape in the dense evergreen and Waldo's shot with the .270 only nicked it in the front leg. The bear roared, bit savagely at the wound and then lost its grasp on the tree.

The bear plunged squarely among the dogs, and Willis and I had to scramble frantically to get out of the melee of black bear and dogs. What happened after that was pure bedlam.

The bear is so heavy we have a hard time dragging it out of the small creek.

The bear gave another terrible roar and charged into the middle of the hounds, whacking about with his good foreleg. I felt a cold chill when I saw the look in that bear's eyes.

I saw Waldo maneuvering for another shot that didn't come. And I heard Willis swear when the brute raked Nig across the neck with long claws and sent Buck sprawling across the turf. I thought the dog was dead for sure, but he bounced right back. Then the bear knocked another dog howling into the air like a basketball. One leg was split wide open.

That big bear seemed to face several directions at once.

"Stay clear, stay clear!" Willis hollered when the bear suddenly tried to break from the ring of dogs.

The bear grabbed Ranger, the skinny bluetick, and tried to bite through his skull. But tired and bloodied as they were, the other dogs came to the rescue. They kept punishing and biting the bear from all sides until Ranger squirmed free.

Left to right, Willis Butolph, Waldo and Budge Wilcox with the devil bear of Hell's Hole.

At end of hunt, all hounds are finally collected and leashed. It's a tired footsore bunch of dogs.

"Shoot the bugger!" Willis shouted more frantically than ever. "Or he'll kill all the dogs."

At this point the bear backed into the creek. Though he was formidable on the ground, he was positively deadly in the water. This was too much for Willis—with only a .22 pistol he waded in to help his dogs.

For a minute it looked bad for the old bear hunter. He misjudged the depth of the creek which now was running red and lost his footing. I saw him flounder and almost go down as the bear started for him. We jumped forward to help but he was quickly upright again and sputtering. The bear came on, clothed with dogs.

Somehow Willis steadied himself and fired three shots point blank at the bear's head. For several seconds the bear raged about, then suddenly collapsed.

While the dogs kept worrying the bear's carcass the rest of us slumped on the bank to unwind. I felt as weak as a day-old kitten, and you could have stirred my knees with a spoon.

Later we revived enough to drag the bear from the creek. It was a tremendous brown-phase black, easily the largest any of us had ever seen. We skinned it, removed the liver and then wearily began the long, steep climb up out of Hell's Hole.

We siwashed it again that night in another cave and broiled strips of bear liver over an open fire. It was actually a comfortable, almost pleasant night, and more agreeable than it had been for the last inhabitant—we found the ashes of an old campfire, bits of woolen cloth, a rusted-out tin can and a few assorted human bones.

"A cowpoke who got lost," Budge suggested.

"Or went bear hunting," Waldo said.

Willis was feeling especially good about the hunt. "We were lucky," he said. "Mighty lucky. I remember a chase on Deserter Creek, over west of here, when I started after an old bear with eight hounds and got back with two. Bear got three of them, and I'll never know what happened to the rest. I made enough footprints that time to stretch around the world.

"This time," he continued, "we only lost one——although Pat and Bess won't be worth a hoot for a long time."

There's no way to tell what our bear weighed, but it must have been at least 400 pounds. He wasn't fat as black bears usually are in the fall, but still his green hide squared out at almost 8½ feet, extraordinary for a black. But weight and hide dimensions are unreliable, and the only acceptable way of rating any bear is by skull measurements—the length plus the breadth in inches provides the "score."

Back at camp, after we'd boiled the skull, our bear scored $20^5/_{16}$ "green" (it would have to dry and shrink for at least 60 days before it could be scored officially), but even so it would land well up in the all-time records. No larger bear ever came out of Utah, so far as I can determine.

Getting ready for a deer hunt seemed anticlimatic now. Willis Butolph gave his pack a day to lick its wounds, then saddled up and pushed on again. I almost wished I were going with him.

# The Fascinating Fox

by KEN BOURBON

Red foxes are sly and seldom seen, but a hunter who knows where to look for them will spot plenty.

**A CERTAIN MIDWESTERN** red fox consistently made fools of four hunters and their dogs—among them me and my dogs. Almost any day we could strike his trail in about the same place. And every time he ran straight for the same steep hollow ½-mile away. There he abruptly disappeared.

We searched the hollow carefully for dens or other hiding places, because it was a rocky spot with a series of ledges beneath the hemlocks that grew on both sides. One old hemlock had fallen across the hollow forming a bridge. We found nothing, though, and the mystery deepened until one day we struck the fox after a fresh snow. His footprints told an interesting story.

The fox charged full tilt up the hollow and leaped high up on the fallen hemlock. He probably paused there to see if the dogs were pursuing as usual. Then he trotted off—all this remember, we found in footprints—while the pack milled around where the trail ended in the hollow below. It was certainly a dramatic exit.

From Aesop's Fables to Uncle Remus, the red fox has been known as one of the cleverest animals in the world. There's no fiction about it. Among American wild animals, foxes rank with wild turkeys and Canada geese as the most wary; some others like raccoons and whitetails are dim-witted by comparison. But foxes are controversial as well as clever. They may have extremely good or extremely bad reputations, depending on the viewpoint, but one thing is obvious to friends and detractors alike: Reynard is surely one of the land's finest game animals. Nowadays, in addition, he is more widely distributed than ever before.

To hunt any animal successfully is to understand it and its habits the year around. That is especially true of the red fox, which can be really abundant in a region but still be rarely seen by hunters or anyone else. Deer? Drive through any deer country at night, and you can spot them easily. Coons? They are a little harder to see; but consider the heavy road kill after any warm, moist night in autumn, and they are no match for a good pack of hounds. Neither automobiles, nor hunters, nor packs of dogs give red foxes very much trouble.

Hunters can locate many species of game by learning the food they prefer and then by concentrating where this food exists. With the fox it is not so easy. They eat everything, animal or vegetable. The truth is that the day the settlers began to clear land westward they began making a bigger, better, and happier home for Reynard. One writer said, "Every additional clearing, every orchard, puts more fat around his middle—but it doesn't make him soft in the head."

Red foxes are not creatures of the deep woods nor will they be plentiful in completely open farmlands or barren prairie. They like rolling, broken country best, land that is interrupted with gullies and fence rows. Orchards are especially attractive, perhaps because the sod there is undisturbed and is happy hunting ground for field mice. In other words, any field that has not been plowed recently is likely to be a better place for foxes to forage for mice, rabbits, and other small animals.

Hunting foxes? Check with a busy farmer doing chores around any farmyard. He'll know where and when foxes have been seen.

Wildlife biologists have uncovered some interesting vital statistics about foxes. An average male weighs 9 pounds, for example; a female, 8 pounds. In an average year on an average countryside, figures from New York biologists reveal that about 3.6 foxes may live on 1-square-mile. In certain areas it has run as high as seven per square mile, and in others less than one fox per 4 or 5 square miles.

Foxes are extremely mobile in the normal living environment, and the size of their home range depends on how much food it contains. Iowa biologists believe that an average home range will have a radius of about 2 miles, but experience in other states shows it may be as much as 5 miles. Most of the moving about takes place in late winter during the mating season. That is a restless time, and a general shifting of fox populations may occur then. For a period after mating, fox movements are confined to foraging near a home den. It picks up again in fall when family groups begin to disperse.

Foxes are loosely monogamous. They pair off, but on a 1-year rather than on a lifetime basis. A dog fox remains with a vixen from mid-January until fall when the five to nine kits are able to care for themselves. All the while the male forages to help feed the family. It is at this time, more than any other, that he is more vulnerable to hunters and hunting—the exception being during the mating season when some caution is forgotten.

It is easier to locate red foxes if the type of den country they prefer is known. The animals are not well adapted to digging and so must find a place where woodchuck dens, sawdust piles, large hollow logs, or slab piles are numerous. Generally, the more loose and sandy the soil in a region, the better, because such hollows must be enlarged to handle a fox family.

During the early spring "hunger moon" the reds are most likely to raid poultry houses—and there is a weakness hunters can exploit. It is only a matter of finding out which farmers in the community are having trouble and of casting the hounds in that vicinity.

At other times, as we have pointed out, foxes are inclined to travel far—over an area that may be 5 miles in diameter. This trait can also be exploited by hunters. They can divide, as nearly as possible, a land area into sections of 2 or 3 square miles, each somewhat smaller than a fox's maximum range. The next step is to work the dogs completely around the perimeter, rather than to work through in a haphazard manner. If a fox has circulated at all, the dogs are bound to strike the trail. The same thing can be accomplished when snow covers the ground by driving slowly around the area and watching for fresh tracks. Since reds move primarily at night, the best time to pick up a hot trail is at daybreak.

Simply to strike a fox trail, though, is no assurance

Foxes often lurk in heavy brush on the fringes of croplands. Look for them there.

that there will be a fox tail trophy, for even with the finest hounds on earth the odds are still against seeing the quarry, let alone bagging him. Foxes do keep to well-defined courses, sometimes to old familiar runways, but they do not follow them blindly. Except to cross wide open spaces, a fox runs cautiously ahead of dogs. He runs only fast enough, in fact, to keep plenty of space between them and him, and not to outdistance them. A persistent hunter can even follow a fox (in the snow) on foot until he eventually gets in range for a long shot.

The average fox will cross a ridge only where there is a saddle or a dense patch of cover. Watch places like those. He will never run on a ridge, but will run just under it, especially on the shady side if both sides have the same amount of cover. He will follow natural drainages, too, along deep gullies and small creeks, frequently crossing and recrossing them if they are shallow enough. This is a difficult tactic for experienced dogs to unravel, and virtually impossible for young or mediocre hounds.

I have never seen it happen, but I've heard old fox hunters insist that red will follow paved roads for long distances where the traffic permits. The odor of exhausts and petroleum products covers the animal's trail, they believe. One old veteran told me it was merely the fox's answer to vitamin fortified dog food.

Perhaps the greatest undoing of the red fox is his curiosity. He will come to investigate strange sounds—sounds unlike any heard in the wild or even from a barnyard. That makes him a sucker—sometimes—for some of the so-called predator calls on the market nowadays. They are designed to imitate a rabbit in distress, but most of them are poor and piercing imitations. Still they work often enough to make an investment in one worthwhile.

Fox calling works best in mid-winter and a reasonable theory is offered for it. At that time, many old standbys of a fox diet are hibernating out of reach; many mice, chipmunks, and woodchucks are underground—so a fox's flanks are thin. That is the time to call him to dinner.

On warm days especially, reds will lie out in open hayfields to doze in the sun. Usually they will be on knolls or small rises, the better to keep an eye on the landscape all around. This is good for the man with binoculars and a varmint rifle, because the patch of bright orange fur makes a conspicuous target. In all fox hunting, incidentally, watch for telltale flashes of orange.

One thing is certain: There are few less rewarding sports, as far as collecting pelts is concerned, than fox hunting. But there is no more fascinating game—anywhere.

HUNTING DUCKS AND GEESE has been a rite of autumn in America ever since the Pilgrims waded ashore at Plymouth Rock. Even though the continental waterfowl population has been drastically reduced while guns for waterfowling have been greatly improved, the techniques of the sport have changed little during the past 3 centuries. Duck or goose hunting is still among the best ways of all to spend the cool days of fall.

There are two basic ways to hunt waterfowl, although there are many variations to each. Either you play the waiting game or you go afield looking for the birds in a manner similar to upland hunting. The latter method is often called jump shooting.

The waiting game is by far the most traditional. It's a matter of hunting from a fixed blind located on a marsh, swamp or grainfield. A spread of decoys placed around the blind, sometimes abetted by a duck or goose call, is figured to attract waterfowl within shotgun range of hunters in the blind.

Taking into consideration that more than 30 different species of ducks and geese range the four major flyways of North America (Atlantic, Mississippi, Central, Pacific) and that each of these species frequents a different environment and has vastly different habits (some species prefer prairie potholes, some stay on saltwater marshes, others are found on southern bayous, etc.), it is difficult to describe all blind hunting in great detail here. But success does depend on certain considerations no matter whether you're hunting for brant along the Atlantic seaboard or shooting mallards on a Montana slough.

First consider the location. It must be an area where waterfowl feed or rest, or frequently cross in flight. If you do not already know such locations, you will have to do a good deal of reconnoitering to discover them.

# Super Secrets of a Wildfowler

by ERWIN A. BAUER

Mixed bag of teal and mallards make a jump-shooting expedition worthwhile.

Hunter Lew Martindale and Labrador wait beside pond for incoming ducks.

Sunrise and a hunter retrieves the first duck of the day. It's a magic time.

The next step is to build a blind nearby. Of course, there are instances when no blind is necessary at all—when the hunter can simply hide in tall cattails or behind standing pin oaks in a flooded woods. But it is always necessary to be completely hidden from the remarkable vision of the birds and usually this means building a blind.

All sorts of materials, from burlap sacking and 2x4s to Spanish moss and shovels, have been used to construct blinds. But what is most important is for a blind to blend into its setting or its background. In other words, the exterior should be of natural materials (marsh grass, cornstalks, foliage) or of such materials as weathered canvas and camouflage cloth which resemble the real thing. A typical blind on a freshwater marsh may be built of wooden framing and covered on the outside with woven cattails or marsh grasses. It may also be a small boat staked out and camouflaged with natural materials. Another type of blind is a pit dug deep enough in the middle of a grainfield (in which waterfowl are known to feed) to hide a couple of hunters.

When locating blinds, keep in mind such factors as tides, fluctuating water levels and property lines. Low tide may leave a blind high and dry for hours and high tide may inundate it. You cannot build a blind on private property without permission to do so. And keep in mind that a good many of the most productive wetlands may be leased or owned outright by other sportsmen.

Even the best blind, alone, will not always provide much shooting. A spread of decoys is often necessary—and, as a rule, the more of them the better.

Old-time waterfowlers used handmade wooden or cork dekes which often were works of art. But today's counterfeits run mostly to plastic, are less expensive and extremely lifelike.

However, not all duck and goose hunters agree on what makes a good decoy. Some insist on colorful replicas, while others believe that just dull-colored (no brightness or glitter) blocks of fairly good silhouette are all that is necessary to capture a passing bird's attention. They point to the fact that geese are often fooled by simple silhouettes of honkers sawed out of plywood sheets—and also to the white rags and baby diapers and cardboard rectangles which are used for snow geese along the Texas and Louisiana Gulf coasts. But perhaps it is safest to use the most natural decoys you can afford. Light weight is also important since it is always necessary to transport your dekes out to the shooting sites and back again. But a common mistake of beginners is not to use heavy enough anchors and sturdy natural-colored (never white) anchor line or staging. Fall is a windy, gusty time on the water, and improperly secured blocks are easily blown away.

Placement of decoys about the blind is important. Keep in mind that when waterfowl decide to alight, they descend into the wind, and the stool should be arranged

Plump mallard is reward for hunting along irrigation ditch in western ranch country.

Never neglect hunting even the smallest waterways and drainage ditches in late fall.

so that hunters will have the best possible shots at the approaching birds. If it is a good set-up, and the birds have not yet been subjected to heavy gunning pressure, they may try to settle directly among the dekes. Later in the season they may circle warily several times before coming down, and even then may land outside the blocks if at all. Quite often it is necessary to change the location of decoys during a day's shooting, especially if the wind changes direction.

There are a good many excellent duck and goose calls on the market, and with experience a hunter can produce sounds almost indistinguishable from those of wildfowl. A skillful caller can persuade wary birds to come in closer—at least close enough to be shot. But the concensus among the best waterfowlers is that no calling at all is vastly preferable to poor calling.

The hunting seasons in all states are normally scheduled to coincide with the maximum numbers of waterfowl—in other words to take advantage of the peaks in migration in any given state from northern nesting areas to southern wintering areas. But all ducks and geese do not migrate en masse at the same time.

Very often the more decoys a hunter uses, the better the shooting.

(Right) Dog fetches mallard dropped in a small pothole on northern plains.

There are really many migration flights, since some species depart earlier than others, and old birds leave before the young ones. Weather patterns and the moon also have some effect on when ducks arrive in a region. He is a wise duck hunter, then, who tries to schedule his hunting days to take advantage of the most ducks.

There are a number of ways to do this. Both federal and state waterfowl biologists (both usually with head-quarters in the state capital) can accurately predict where and when waterfowl arrive, and they willingly pass on the information. Local ornithologists and bird-watchers also have this data.

More and more during recent seasons, the most serious duck hunters have taken to bird watching. Because of special species seasons now being held, it is necessary to be able to identify waterfowl quickly and accurately in flight, often in dim light. For example, there was the series of early seasons when only teal could be taken. Elsewhere the bag has been limited to only one or two of a species per day. The best way any sportsman can become adept at this is to spend spare time in the field, especially around wetlands, learning to identify all birds.

If hunting from a blind over decoys is the most traditional way of waterfowlers, jump shooting is at times the most exciting and productive way. It also requires a good bit more physical effort. The first step is to locate the birds: on marshes, in flooded woods, on rivers, wherever they happen to be.

The next step is to approach unseen into good shotgun range. Then, when the birds flush, you shoot. It is similar to gunning for grouse or cottontails except that for these, stealth is not nearly so important.

Jump shooting is seldom possible on large open bodies of water because there is no covered way to approach. But it is made to order for potholes and farm ponds, for marshes where cattails grow tall and rank, and for meandering streams. To take birds on the ponds or potholes, you make your approach on foot. On streams, the best way to go is via canoe or a light, shallowdraft, cartop boat.

One, two or occasionally three hunters can play the game. With more than one, it may be possible to walk from opposite directions and to sandwich the birds between hunters so that no matter which way the ducks flush, somebody is certain to get a good shot. The best strategy is to reconnoiter the waters from afar with a spotting scope or binoculars and then to carefully plan the approach.

Hunter heading out to blind for day of shooting. He would have been better off going before daylight.

It's pretty hard to match float-tripping a river for ducks. One technique is to camouflage a canoe with brush and vegetation so that it resembles as much as possible a floating pile of flotsam. With that done, you drift downstream with the current, using a paddle as little as possible and keeping close to the inside bank around the bends. Be ready for ducks to flush out ahead, in good range and often enough to keep the trip exciting.

It is possible to get almost as many opinions on guns and loads for waterfowling as there are waterfowlers. This is understandable because the character of the sport differs greatly, as already pointed out, from one region to another. But nationwide the most popular guns for use in blinds are full-choked 12-gauge pumps or autoloaders. If these are not already three-shell capacity guns, they must be plugged to hold only three to comply with federal regulations. A recent survey of state game-management officials and waterfowl biologists across the country revealed almost unanimous agreement that nothing smaller than 12-gauge should be used for waterfowl. They pointed out that ducks and geese can carry plenty of lead, are tenacious of life, and far too many are only crippled and lost. One reason for this is the abominable habit of sky-busting—taking shots at targets beyond sensible range. Another is failure to own a good retriever. For jump shooting, the guns most preferred are those often favored for large upland birds—for instance, a 12-gauge double with 26-inch improved and modified barrels. Short barrels facilitate a fast swing, and one bore should be open enough for fast, short-range shooting.

Because much waterfowling is done in weather which is very cold, wet, or windy—or all three—clothing is extremely important. A wise duck hunter would never go afield without waterproof outer wear and except in the deep south, without woolen or synthetic quilted undergarments.

Of course, warmer clothing is required for the more sedentary hunting from a fixed blind than for jump shooting. A jump shooter's best bet is to wear moderately light clothing in layers, and then to strip or add as the temperature and physical exertion demand. Most waterfowlers will also have need for waders or, in sufficiently shallow waters, hipboots. Waders obviously give more protection, but are heavier and make walking more difficult for long distances. Handwarmers in the pockets can be extremely valuable when handling wet decoys.

When traveling over open water by boat, or when floating on rivers, it's best to wear a life preserver or some other reliable flotation device. It's never possible to swim very far in heavy clothing or with waders in case of emergency.

It has been stated—correctly—that the best investment a duck or goose hunter can make is a good retriever (say, a Labrador, Chesapeake or golden). Besides saving birds which might fall far out of the hunter's reach, a dog can also save plenty of footsteps and slogging through freezing muck. Training and exercising the dog can make waterfowling much more fascinating by turning it into a year-around sport.

The end of a successful duck hunt. Duck or goose hunting is still among the best ways of all to spend the cool days of fall.